The
Structure of
Experience

Gordon Nagel

The Structure of Experience
Kant's System of Principles

The University of Chicago Press

Chicago and London

The University of Chicago Press, Chicago 60637
The University of Chicago Press, Ltd., London

Library of Congress Cataloging in Publication Data

Nagel, Gordon.
   The structure of experience.

   Bibliography: p.
   Includes index.
   1. Kant, Immanuel, 1724–1804. Kritik der reinen
Vernunft.   2. Knowledge, Theory of.   3. Causation.
4. Reason.   I. Title.
B2779.N33 1983   121   82-24814
ISBN 0-226-56766-4

Gordon Nagel is associate professor of
philosophy at the University of Toronto.

Contents

Preface

The *Critique of Pure Reason* is Kant's account of experience—not in the broad sense that includes action, emotion, and aesthetic response, but only the aspect of experience that involves knowledge. Kant does not deal with the production of knowledge epistemologically, that is, as though it presented us mainly with problems of justifying what we believe or claim to know. His theory is explanatory rather than justificatory. The problem as he sees it is to discover the essential elements and processes of cognition.

After an introductory first chapter, and a second chapter that offers an unorthodox reading of Kant's doctrines of space and geometry, this book follows the text of the Analytic of Principles, to which it may be read as a commentary by those interested in Kant. I have tried, however, not to presuppose a background in Kant studies, in order that it might be read by anyone interested in perception, cognition, or the philosophy of mind.

I am particularly indebted to Jonathan Bennett. His books and articles were nearly always the point from which I began, though I usually ended up taking issue with him. The other books I found most helpful are by Graham Bird, Felix Grayeff, Norman Kemp Smith, Arthur Melnick, Peter Strawson, and Robert Paul Wolff. A number of people read earlier drafts and made comments. I want to thank Ronnie de Sousa, Ed MacKinnon, Rolf Meerbote, Calvin Normore, David Savan, Jack Stevenson, and all the others who helped. Two who deserve special thanks are Ian Hacking, who supervised my doctoral research at Cambridge from 1970 to 1973, and my wife, Katherine. She alone discussed and criticized everything throughout the whole long and wonderful ordeal of making sense of the *Critique*.

1

Language, Phenomenalism, and Transcendental Idealism

1. The Basic Problem

Transcendental idealism involves two complementary doctrines. One doctrine concerns the objects of experience, or appearances. According to Kant, everything that we can know in the world corresponds to our thought because in order to encounter it we must employ certain rules, and these rules impose some formal or structural features on all objects of experience. He says, "The order and regularity of the appearances, which we entitle *nature,* we ourselves introduce" (A 125).* Kant thinks that his study of the conditions for the possibility of experience is also a discovery of significant features of the empirical realm that are determined a priori. The other doctrine of transcendental idealism concerns things-in-themselves. Unless there is an aspect of reality that is independent of experience, everything that exists is subject to the structure-imposing rules that make experience possible. Since these rules create a causally deterministic order of nature, freedom (and with it morality) would be impossible. But Kant claims that there are things-in-themselves, unknown to us, exempt from causal determinism, and even outside space and time, and that these things-in-themselves are the objects of moral considerations.[1] Transcendental idealism maintains that there are two orders of reality: the empirical order that we know, and partially create, in our experience, and the moral order that remains unknown.

Transcendental idealism is the basic problem confronting any reader of the *Critique of Pure Reason*. Its main doctrines, or the details that follow from them, occur on nearly every page.

The basic problem can take many forms. One may wonder how, if at all, Kant differs from Berkeley in respect of the things we know. More specifically, one may wonder about the contrast between Berkeley's empiricist associationism and Kant's a priori principles that he purports to derive from his twelve categories. Are they both phenomenalists who

*All passages quoted in the body of the text from Kant's *Critique of Pure Reason* will be accompanied by references employing the usual convention of A and B to indicate the pagination of the first and second editions respectively. The translation will be Kemp Smith's unless otherwise noted. All other references will be given in the notes at the end of this book.

differ only in respect of the proposed methods by which knowledge is to be constructed? From Mach's *The Analysis of Sensations* and from Carnap's *Aufbau*,[2] we have a fairly clear understanding of the possibilities open to the empiricist construction of knowledge. We have nothing comparable in respect of Kant's construction because his critics generally reject his apriorism and the elaborate architectonic of the twelve categories with its three- and fourfold divisions. Can sense be made of the architectonic? Or must we reject it and find the only significant departure from Berkeley in Kant's posit of things-in-themselves? Can one take a defensible stand somewhere between outright rejection and complete acceptance of Kant's system of categories when Kant says the following?

> *As regards this second edition* . . . in the propositions themselves and their proofs, and also in the form and completeness of the [architectonic] plan, I have found nothing to alter. This is due partly to the long examination to which I have subjected them, before offering them to the public, partly to the nature of the subject-matter with which we are dealing. For pure speculative reason has a structure wherein everything is an *organ,* the whole being for the sake of every part, and every part for the sake of all the others, so that even the smallest imperfection, be it a fault (error) or a deficiency, must inevitably betray itself in use. This system will, as I hope, maintain, throughout the future, this unchangeableness (B xxxvii–xxxviii).

The basic epistemic doctrine of transcendental idealism, that the empirical world is appearance structured by the mind's own principles of operation, at once suggests a phenomenalism, but Kant counters that suggestion with such claims of unchanging completeness. How much can be chalked up to Kant's psychological makeup (perhaps to a compulsive desire to have everything sort neatly)?[3] How much of it is merely the (bad, mistaken) faculty psychology of the Enlightenment?[4] If we take Kant's psychology the one way or the other to dismiss his claims to completeness, how much remains acceptable? Is what remains enough to warrant positing things-in-themselves? These are just some of the problems raised by transcendental idealism.

What interests me is whether it is possible to take Kant seriously in all he says: to show his differences with Berkeley, to defend his system of categories, to indicate how his theory of experience does provide for his ethical theory, and, in general, to explain, and argue for, transcendental idealism. I think it is possible, and I try to do it.

2. Methods of Dealing with the Problem

A critic has two tasks. One task is the scholarly work of interpretation and exegesis. The other task is somehow to engage directly in the topic matter and problems of the original work. The balance between these may be struck in any number of ways. One may downplay the scholarship to play up the direct confrontation with the topics and problems. This is often Bennett's way with Kant; for he is not much concerned to seek out Kant's intentions, and he often employs remarks from the *Critique* as springboards to his own philosophical discussions.[5] Paton's approach is just the reverse. He interprets and explains without offering much insight or argument of his own into the topics that Kant deals with.[6]

However one strikes the balance, there is, I think, a relationship between the two tasks that should not be ignored. One will get more out of the *Critique* if one tries on one's own to solve some of Kant's problems; but care must be exercised in the identification of the problems. If they are misidentified, one's own thoughts will misdirect the interpretation rather than enhance it. Parts of the text will seem obscure, puzzling, or irrelevant—as indeed they will be, since, by hypothesis, the critic and Kant have different problems. I believe this happens often, and that it is the chief reason the *Critique* has a reputation for being seriously flawed.[7] It is supposed that Kant's general concerns are epistemological in the tradition of Descartes, that the Transcendental Deduction addresses some problem about the ownership of mental states, and that the Second Analogy is Kant's reply to Hume; on these suppositions much that Kant says is found wanting.[8] So it may be, but it is also possible that what reads as difficult and inconsistent epistemology can be found to be consistent on a different reading, that the notorious tangle of the Deduction can be unraveled on a different supposition of what Kant's problem is, and that the Second Analogy looks better if not viewed in terms of Hume's doubts about the causal principle. There are thus two possibilities: either that critical thought about his topic matter and the problems reveals faults in Kant's discussion, or that the emergence of faults on a given interpretation shows that Kant's topics and problems have been misidentified. It need not be cleanly or entirely one way or the other, since presumably one could be sure one knows what he is talking about and sure also that what he says is wrong; but in general whatever serves to draw critical objections could serve instead as evidence of misinterpretation.

The existence of the two possibilities always raises doubts for me when I find what seem to be mistakes or inconsistencies in the *Critique*. I am then unsure whether I do understand and do find faults, or whether I fail to understand and the faults I seem to find are simply in the Kant of my interpretation, but not (necessarily) in the original. I try to give Kant the benefit of all such doubts, and this seems to pay off. What slowly develops is a reading of the *Critique* that fits well with the entire text.

To fit Kant to the main traditions in modern philosophy, other critics set aside major aspects of his work, usually the architectonic. Kemp Smith establishes Vaihinger's patchwork theory as a methodological principle by which any passage can be set aside on the ground that it expresses some earlier point of view, rather than the final, critical position.[9] There are more recent efforts to depsychologize the *Critique*.[10] Strawson describes transcendental idealism as an obstacle "to a sympathetic understanding of the *Critique*";[11] and he does not mean that it is an obstacle to be overcome. It is rather something he proposes to set aside at the beginning of his discussion. These measures attest to the difficulty of interpreting Kant in accordance with the topics and problems of modern philosophy. So interpreted, Kant is indeed a sometimes brilliant, if curiously reluctant, contributor to familiar philosophical discussions.

3. Language-Models and Phenomenalism

One of the problems of explaining Kant's transcendental idealism has simply to do with the unfamiliarity of his technical vocabulary. To describe Kant's system one must provide some explanation of the interpretation given to such terms as the following: intuitions (pure and empirical), concepts, appearances, phenomena, noumena, apprehension, perception, and so on. For some terms, such as concept, apprehension, and perception, our knowledge of the normal, nontechnical meaning may be more hindrance than help.

Another problem is to explain how Kant's transcendental idealism differs from Berkeley's idealism. There must be differences, at least in Kant's mind, because he claims to refute Berkelian idealism.[12] Others, notably Turbayne,[13] are not persuaded.

The whole first paragraph of the *Critique* strongly suggests that Kant is some sort of phenomenalist. Here is the second half of the paragraph.

> Objects are *given* to us by means of sensibility, and it alone yields us *intuitions;* they are *thought* through the understanding, and from the understanding arise *concepts.* But all thought must, directly or indirectly, by way of definite criteria, relate ultimately to intuitions, and therefore, with us, to sensibility, because in no other way can an object be given to us (A 19 = B 33).[14]

Kant continues his insistence on the relation of all thought to intuition throughout the *Critique*. The suggestion of phenomenalism is also conveyed by his description of the objects of knowledge as appearances, and by the near synonymy he seems to maintain between appearances and phenomena.

Kemp Smith and Prichard take up these suggestions and others, and their interpretations have an enduring influence on Kant criticism in English. Bird argues against Prichard in the first chapter of *Kant's Theory of Knowledge,* but in *Kant's Analytic* and *Kant's Dialectic* Bennett returns to a thoroughly phenomenalist reading of the *Critique.*[15]

I think one must deal with the two problems together. If one thinks of intuitions as sense-data, of appearances as constructs out of sense-data, and if one takes Kant's repeated contention that all thought must *relate* to intuition as the claim that it must *reduce* to intuition, then much of the *Critique* must be read as an expression of some version of phenomenalism. Much, but not all, of the *Critique* can be read in this way. The reading leaves out passages Bird uses in his arguments against Prichard,[16] and it fails to make sense of Kant's explicit objections to Berkeley. What is needed is an interpretation of Kant's terminology that fits all his uses of it.

A critic can, of course, make his job much easier by simply asserting that Kant uses his terminology inconsistently, and that he exaggerates his differences with Berkeley. However, both of the assertions are negative existentials (there is no consistent interpretation of the terminology; there is no significant difference between Kant and Berkeley) and, as such, they cannot be warranted by one's failure to find the interpretation or the difference.[17]

To provide an initial solution to the problem of terminology, I will use language as a model of Kant's transcendental idealism (most fully in section 7). For example, I will compare intuitions with words, appearances and phenomena with two different sorts of meanings of words, and the connections between intuitions, on one hand, and appearances and phenomena, on the other, with the connections between words and their meanings. I will also compare the roles of cognitive processes such as apprehension, perception, and reasoning as they occur in language and as Kant describes them in transcendental idealism.

The primarily expository purpose of using language as a model of Kant's system accomplishes a secondary aim as well. Phenomenalists also use language as a model of their system, and the differences in the ways language is regarded in the construction of the two models will illustrate the differences between Kant and the phenomenalists.

I will begin by describing the way that phenomenalists use language as a model. They distinguish between two sorts of factual statement. There are statements about how things are in the world. For example, "There is an apple on the tree near the beach." There are other statements that describe only the content of one's immediate sensory awareness. For example, "I see a red round patch in a green color-field; I hear a rhythmical roaring sound; and I smell/taste a fresh saltiness." According to phenomenalists, subjective statements of the second sort are epistemically prior to objective statements of the first sort because any knowledge of how things are in the world must be based on, and reducible to, what is given in sense experience. Phenomenalists further claim that the very meaning of an objective statement is no more than what can be said in the subjective statements that would tend to confirm or disconfirm the objective statement. Thus, to say that there is an apple on the tree near the beach can mean no more than that one would have (in the appropriate circumstances) the sorts of immediate sensory content described in the example of a subjective judgment.

Two points deserve special attention. First, there is a wide range of possible sense experience relevant to the truth of an objective statement such as "There is an apple on the tree near the beach." Second, we do make objective statements. Phenomenalists connect the two matters in their accounts. An objective statement, even though it could be cashed out into some set of subjective statements, serves a purpose. It provides a sort of abbreviation for the very large and loosely defined cluster of immediate sensory experiences that are relevant to its truth. Even though, in principle, objective statements are eliminable by analysis into subjective statements, in practice objective statements are justified by the economy they effect.[18]

Phenomenalism succeeds in a number of ways. It presents a vivid contrast between the singularity of each object and the great variety of sensation it can produce. It provides an explanation of the relationship between the objective and subjective aspects of experience. Phenomenalism continues, but also improves upon, the empiricist tradition in philosophy. It continues the tradition by claiming the epistemic priority of sense experience, and also by treating objects as equivalent to, rather than inferred from, sensory contents; but the linguistic formulation of this equivalence strikes me as an improvement over the mentalistic formulation by the earlier empiricists. When Berkeley describes objects as mere collections of ideas, his thesis sounds needlessly paradoxical. He invites the following sort of objection: the claimed equivalence does not hold because material bodies are continuous in their existence, while the sensory ideas to which they are supposedly equivalent are fleeting and fragmentary. By putting the equivalence in linguistic terms, phenomenalists make it a relationship between statements of one sort and statements of another. No readily apparent disparities between the relata remain to provoke the sort of objection Berkeley invites. Phenomenalism also seems to provide a plausible reply to the skeptic.

4. Some Objections to Phenomenalism

Despite its attractiveness as a philosophical theory, and despite the precedents in criticism for including Kant as one of its proponents, both phenomenalism and the phenomenalist reading of the *Critique* should be resisted.

The first clue to why they should be resisted is supplied by the language-model they use to explain their theory. The relationship of objective statements to subjective statements is said to be the dependence of the former on the latter. However, when we describe our sensory experiences, we do so in a language learned and used primarily in application to objective situations. That is, we acquire the language in objective contexts shared by the transmitters and learners of language, and only then can we extend its use to the description of our inner states. But phenomenalism suggests that conceptualization is primarily on the level of what seems to be the case, and only derivatively, for practical reasons of economy and communication, on the level of what is actually the case. As well as the acquisition of language, the determination of meaning is also the reverse of what is described in the phenomenalists' language-model. Meaning rests ultimately on the public conventions of its use, not on the reference of terms to inner states.[19]

The phenomenalist may be untroubled by the objection that subjective and objective discourse are in fact related in a way that is just the reverse of the way that he relates them to explain his theory. He may reply that his talk of objective and subjective statements is merely expository of his theory, and that it is not at all intended to account for the actual order in which we learn objective and subjective uses of language.

Of course we often do explain things in metaphorical ways. We use analogies whose explanatory value is unquestioned despite the fact that the analogy cannot be pressed very far. However, in this case the analogy should be pushed as far as possible. It would be an inadequate defense of phenomenalism to reply that the talk of two languages, one subjective, the other objective, is meant only to convey the basic notion of the theory. The reason that that defense is inadequate is that facts about language have an intrinsic relation to the theory. This is not a case like the planetary model of the atom, with electrons as the planets around a nucleic sun; nor is it like explanations of electricity in terms of the flow of water through pipes. In those cases there is just metaphorical comparison between distinct phenomena. The relations between subjective and objective uses of language are not similarly distinct from the things described by the theory of phenomenalism. On the contrary, they are among the things to be accounted for by any philosophical theory of the relation of mind to nature. If the subjective and objective do not relate in language as phenomenalism claims they relate in general, then language is an important counterexample to phenomenalist theory because, at least in one case, the objective is not based on, and reducible to, the subjective.

The fundamental tenet of phenomenalism is that the objective reduces to, and hence is no more than, what is given in sense. In the passage from the first page of the *Critique,* quoted in section 3, Kant does insist on the relation of all thought to intuition, but he elsewhere complains that Berkeley degrades bodies to mere seemings.[20] If to be a phenomenalist is to think that how (or what) things are can, in the end, amount to nothing more than some aggregate of what seems to be, Kant is not a phenomenalist. He argues for the *relation* of all thought to the given, but he argues against the *reduction* of objects of thought to the given. The interpretation of Kant as a phenomenalist takes account of the former, but it neglects the latter.

5. Berkeley and Nonreductive Relation

In the phenomenalist construction of knowledge, one begins with what is given in sense. In the first stage of the construction in Carnap's *Aufbau,* physical objects are defined as complexes formed from elementary experiences. This is just a modern, and more formal, version of Berkeley's doctrine that objects are collections of ideas. The next stage constructs (very behavioristically) the minds of others from their physical appearance. The final stage constructs social phenomena from collective mental states. The constructive relations are such that they can be analytically reversed. The social can be analytically reduced to the mental, the mental to the physical, and the physical to elementary experiences. In the final analysis, nothing exists but simple sensations. Everything more complex is formed from them. Reductionism is thus a central doctrine of phenomenalism (or a dogma of empiricism, as Quine describes it in his classic paper).[21]

The most likely candidate for the fundamental relation in Kant's system is *representation.* To find a significant difference between Kant and Berkeley, we would do well to consider that representation in language is not a reductive relationship. Words, whether sounds or written letters, represent meanings, thoughts, or ideas; but the latter are not reducible to the former. Statements represent empirical situations, but empirical situations are not mere collections of statements. So we do not need to follow the phenomenalists in taking the two sorts of statement, of how things are and of how they seem to be, as the analogues in the language-model of the objective and the subjective, respectively. We could instead construct a different model by taking the sensible signs of language (sounds or marks) as the analogues of the subjective, since they are what is sensorily given, and the meanings of those signs as the analogues of the objective, since they are represented by the given. This proposal accords with what Kant says in that first paragraph, and it also makes sense of his objections to Berkeley. What he says is that all thought must relate ultimately to intuitions because in no other way can an object be given to us. The corresponding claim in terms of the proposed language-model would be the following: all meaning must relate ultimately to the sensible signs of language because meaning cannot be conveyed except through some physical means such as sounds, marks, or gestures. We are to think of meanings, whatever is represented by the physical signs of a language, as the analogues of physical objects, which Kant describes both as appearances and as representations; but because we need not, and probably should not, think of the relation of meanings to the words that convey them as one of analytic reducibility, we can avoid the reductionist dogma of empiricism. We thereby block the attribution to Kant of a Berkelian phenomenalism.

Although Berkeley ends up a phenomenalist, at one point in his writings he uses the sort of relation that I am proposing here as an interpretation of Kant's notion of representation. Berkeley's considered view is that objects are, and must be, just collections of ideas because they are represented by ideas. In general, Berkeley thinks that representation requires sameness of kind such that if objects are to be represented by ideas, then objects must be ideas. That is what Berkeley generally thinks; but there is an exception to this in *An Essay Towards a New Theory of Vision.* Berkeley there employs a representation relation that obtains between things that are not of the same kind, and hence not reducible one to the other, though they are related.

Throughout the remainder of this section, I will describe Berkeley's comments on representation as a nonreductive relation. I accept some of his comments and reject or qualify others to develop material that will then be used to interpret Kant.

Berkeley says that no one will suppose that written letters are of the same species as spoken letters. Written letters are one sort of thing and speech sounds are another, yet the written can represent the spoken because part-for-part comparisons can be made between them. I quote Berkeley's example.

> Visible figures represent tangible figures much after the same manner that written words do sounds. Now, in this respect words are not arbitrary, it not being indifferent what written word stands for any sound: but it is requisite that each word contain in it so many distinct characters as there are variations in the sound it stands for. Thus the single letter *a* is proper to mark one simple uniform sound; and the word *adultery* is accommodated to represent the sound annexed to it, in the formation thereof there being eight different collisions or modifications of air by the organs of speech, each of which produces a difference of sound, it was fit the word representing it should consist of as many distinct

characters, thereby to mark each particular difference or part of the whole sound.[22]

Having described this relation of the written to the spoken as obtaining, not in virtue of sameness of kind but in virtue of a simple isomorphism, Berkeley goes on to describe the visible as merely the sign of what may be touched. He says,

> the proper objects of vision constitute an universal language of the Author of Nature, whereby we are instructed how to regulate our actions in order to attain those things that are necessary to the preservation of our bodies, as also to avoid whatever might be hurtful or destructive of them.[23]

At this one point in his writings, Berkeley recognizes that one thing of one kind can represent another thing of a different kind provided the two have some structural features in common. In this case he thinks that having the same number of parts is sufficient. Elsewhere he retreats from this insight and goes back to the assertion that representation requires sameness, not of structure or form, but of kind. For example, in the *Principles* he insists that an idea can be like nothing but an idea; and he means this as an argument against the claim that ideas can represent an external reality distinct from the mind and its states.[24] For the argument to work, representation must be thought to require resemblance in kind; otherwise the sort of relation he himself describes between written and spoken words might prove sufficient to ground representation even between things that are not of the same species.

Berkeley is inconsistent not only in what he thinks is required for one thing to represent another. He is also inconsistent in his account of the relation between vision and touch. Sometimes objects of sight are treated as mere signs signifying what may be touched, and, in turn, the objects of touch are treated as signs signifying an external reality of things needful or hurtful. This is the case in the essay on vision, where Berkeley employs the analogy to written words that signify spoken words that in turn signify an external reality. Elsewhere, Berkeley denies that the chain of representational connection carries through to an external reality. In the *Principles,* he remarks that "the proper objects of sight neither exist without the mind, nor are they images of external things." He then goes on to say that the contrary was supposed true of tangible objects in the essay on vision, but not, he says, because "it was necessary for the notion therein laid down; but because it was beside my purpose to examine and refute it in a discourse concerning *vision*".[25] His considered view then is that none of the senses, not even touch, represents things external to the mind.

Berkeley cannot have it both ways—at least not without more argument. In the essay on vision, despite his disclaimer, he does seem to need the ultimate representation of reality to establish the notion therein laid down. In the analogy he uses, the eight letters represent the spoken word which in turn represents a certain extralinguistic activity. This is meant to model vision representing touch which in turn represents external things needful or hurtful. The model breaks down if there is nothing that spoken words represent in their turn. Written language is not a mere transcription of sounds. It is rather an alternative way of doing what spoken language does. It is a way of communicating information, requests, warnings, promises, and so on. The production of a written language does not involve merely finding a notation for speech sounds. It involves finding a visible way of doing what is otherwise done with sound.

In his discussion of how writing represents speech, Berkeley oversimplifies things in saying that a letter marks one simple, uniform sound. Even in the systems of phonetic representation used by linguists, each written symbol marks a whole range of sounds. In devising his notation the linguist does not try to reproduce the sound-structure of the language. Rather he devises a notation for the patterns of *significant variation* in sound. He decides whether different sounds belong to different types, or are merely variants of the same type, by finding whether there are contexts in which the substitution of the one sound for the other makes a difference in meaning. Even in natural languages, writing represents only significant variations in sound, while ignoring variations that lack significance. I will cite two examples. In English we aspirate the *p* in *pin,* but not in *spin.* In general, we aspirate *p,* or not, only according to ease of pronunciation. We have only the one letter for the two sounds, and it is difficult for us to hear any difference between them. In certain dialects of India it does make a difference of meaning. They need two letters, and they can readily hear the difference. The second example involves heard differences we ignore sometimes and attend to others. Some pronounce *tomato* with long *a,* others with short; but we keep the same spelling for both because both are talking about the same thing. By contrast, there is the very same difference in sound between *pat* and *pate,* but we employ difference in spelling to preserve the difference between the referents of the two spoken words.[26]

Berkeley's general contention is right enough. The written serves to represent the spoken because it is structurally similar to it. However, what counts as the structure of either the written or the spoken cannot be determined just by looking at samples of writing or by listening to samples of speech. One must also take into account the meaning of what is written or said. With all the differences in typeface and handwriting, there is no end to the ways in which letters are formed, and there is no requirement of common shape to the letter-tokens of a single type. With all the differences among voices, there is even more variation among tokens of the same speech sounds. None of this troubles the reader or listener very much, since it is not the letter-by-letter or sound-by-sound structure that matters. What matters is the meaning of what is written or said, and all that the reader or listener requires is enough overall structure to indicate one meaning rather than another.

Berkeley uses the analogy to writing and speech to show how he thinks the objects of vision and touch, though different in kind, can nonetheless be correlated with one another. With very little pressing, the analogy creates a serious challenge either to his account of how the senses relate to each other or to his reductionism. Since the production of a written language is not made just by connecting letters to sounds, but by relating both to what they mean, the model requires reference to referents that are not reducible to the signs that signify them. No one supposes that adultery itself is made up of eight simple, uniform parts. The analogue, taken seriously, threatens Berkeley's reductionism by arguing for the need to carry the chain of representation through to extralinguistic (external) reality. To preserve the analogy one would have to posit external objects signified by the immediate objects of sense. If one abandons the analogy, there is no account of the relation of one sensory modality to another.

Berkeley does offer an example to dispute the need to refer to external objects in order to correlate different senses. His example is of a visible and a tangible square. The square that we see corresponds to the square that we feel just as the written word corresponds to the spoken. The correspondence consists in a matching number and arrangement of parts. Berkeley intends the example to show that the two senses relate to one another directly by virtue of a simple isomorphism.[27]

The example of the two squares is like a case in which two sentences in two different languages just happen to have the same syntactic order. We would be much mistaken if from two such sentences we concluded that translation between the two languages requires only word-for-word substitutions. We would be as much mistaken if from Berkeley's example of the two squares we concluded that the sensations of vision correspond generally one for one with the sensations of touch. In proof of this consider the look and feel of any random collection of things: a printed fabric and a plain one, a warm surface and a cool one, and so on. If we expand the consideration to include all the senses, we find that aromas, textures, colors, tastes, and sounds do not in general map directly onto one another. Sometimes there is direct correspondence, but that is more rare than typical.

The more general issue the example raises is whether the correlation of the senses with each other is possible without recourse to external objects. The answer must be no. Except for a few odd cases, each sensory modality has its own field of operation. Each monitors an aspect of reality that has little overlap with the aspects that the other modalities monitor.[28] Imagine the difficulties that would confront a translator working with one language in which only the sounds of things could be described, and with another language limited to the description of smells. The difficulties are no less if we pick any other pair of sensory modalities—even Berkeley's favored two, vision and touch. Between touch and vision there are a few overlaps, but they are very few unless we deliberately seek them out. In the normal operation of our sense of touch, we do not feel all around the edge of a thing to determine its shape since vision so reliably informs us of that at a glance. Most of what we feel has to do with textures, weights, degrees of hardness or resistance, and temperatures, and these lack regular correlates in vision. In general then, the integration of information from the various senses must be accomplished in reference to external objects, rather than directly from one sensory modality to another.

6. The Relative Priority of Subjective and Objective

The obvious question raised by the conclusion of the last section is how we are in any position to make reference to external objects before we have accomplished the coordination of the senses. One might think that before there can be acquaintance with objects there must first be some basis for this acquaintance established at the sensory level, and that this basis will minimally consist *first* in some organization of the content within each sensory modality and *then* in some correlation among the modalities.[29] Berkeley certainly thinks so because his approach is always to begin with the simple ideas of sense. For him that is the proper starting point in any account of our knowledge of things. So to say, as I do, that the senses are correlated with each other by virtue of their common relations to external objects would seem to Berkeley, and to most empiricists, a mistake about the order in which the questions of knowledge must be posed and answered.

If the acquisition of language is used as an indicator of cognitive development in general, the Berkelian ordering of epistemological questions is not the only one possible. We need not think that the mastering of complexity begins inevitably with the most elementary and then advances step by step toward greater complexity. Another possible approach is as follows: one may instead begin with generality that is initially ill-defined and then gradually introduce greater definition. I think that this is what actually happens in the acquisition of vocabulary. A first stock of a few words serves to describe and request everything. Some item of vocabulary at first serves to describe anything that flies; another indicates something amiss; a third demands food, and so on. Bit by bit, the classes of things are broken down into more and more specific subclasses, as the early omnipurpose words give way to increasingly well-defined terms. Progressions of this sort, from an initially ill-defined generality to an eventual specificity, are the reverse of the progressions adopted by empiricists.

The empiricist thinks of the mind as a blank slate on which elementary sensory experiences are entered as dots. Then the dots pertaining to each sensory modality are joined together as clusters. Then clusters from several of the sensory modalities are joined together in groups. Then reification of sensory content joins the groups together as objects. Then objects are connected up by empirical generalizations.

The empiricist construction, with phenomenalism as a principal variant, may seem to be the only philosophically proper way to tackle the problems of knowledge: begin with what is supposed to be incontestably given and advance step by step in the construction of more complex objects of knowledge. Of course, the objective of the proponents of the empiricist construction is not to account *genetically* for the acquisition of knowledge. They take their task to be the *analysis* of knowledge claims by the production of justifications that in their view must be grounded in something that requires no justification itself; and since they take Descartes and Hume to show that doubts can be raised about everything other than the immediate content of the senses, they take elementary sensory experiences as the natural and proper first terms in any account of knowledge.[30]

I am not convinced that genesis and analysis sort so neatly. If our claims to know are simply right or wrong, defensible or indefensible, then perhaps one may properly ask which they are, and demand their justification. But suppose that the questions of knowledge are matters of degree, and that what we claim to know is more or less well-defined. It is then important not just to accept or dismiss a knowledge-claim, but to understand it in its context. The context could be either historical or personal. I imagine the claims of early scientists such as Kepler and Darwin contain enough inaccuracies that they cannot be accepted as true, but I would hesitate to say that they knew nothing about the stars or the origin of species, or to say that what they knew consisted in a few true propositions among a number of false ones. I would rather suppose that they were on the right track, but that they oversimplified some things and failed to draw a few distinctions—leaving their claims right enough if taken in one way, but wrong if taken in others. Equally, one may be reluctant to say whether a child knows something or not. If knowledge is taken to be true justified belief, and justification is taken to be the sort of evidence one could advance for one's beliefs, then little children know nothing. They cannot argue for what they say. But if knowledge is taken to be the variable amount of veridical content in what they say, even little children know a lot, though it may well be lacking in specificity and detail.

The doubts that Hume and Descartes raise question the justification of any belief that goes beyond the immediate content of the senses. This does not show that epistemic priority must be given to the first-person singular and his states of consciousness.[31] One also has unproblematic access to one's own dreams, fantasies, and speculations, but the mere fact of unproblematic access does not convert these into the foundations of empirical knowledge. Nor is it unproblematically answerable which of our inner states are sense-data and which dreams and imaginings. My point is that there is nothing inherently right and sacrosanct about beginning an account of knowledge with the self and its states of consciousness.

The acquisition of vocabulary suggests an alternative approach. Suppose that one again starts with a blank slate, but that the entries are not made as dots representing sensory particulars. Suppose instead that the early entries take the form of lines roughly marking broad distinctions. Perhaps smiles and distress cries mark the first rough sorting of things into, to use Berkeley's words, "those things that are necessary to the preservation of our bodies," and "whatever may be hurtful or destructive of them." Further distinctions and finer sortings require that more and sharper lines be drawn.

Nor is it essential to suppose that the slate is initially blank. Whether the mind is initially empty or possessed of certain innate ideas ought to remain an open question. If the analysis of knowledge is supposed to have a bearing on its genesis, then facts about its genesis ought to have a bearing on the determination of whether the analysis is accurate and true to the facts. We should look to the empirical evidence to see whether newborns show signs of knowing unlearned things.[32] If, on the other hand, we chose to regard analytic and genetic accounts as having no such connection, and if we think of the analysis of knowledge as an a priori enterprise that does not stand subject to empirical findings, we should at least judge any proposed analysis in comparison to the results of alternative analytic enterprises. Since some alternatives might well include the positing of certain innate capacities to make distinctions, the blank-slate approach cannot be considered right in advance of the comparison of one alternative to another.

I am fairly sure that, in respect of the genesis of knowledge, distinctions that are *not* among the first to be drawn are those between how things are and how they appear to be, between the properties of the object and the sensory qualities to which the object gives rise, or between reality and appearance. Those distinctions arise after years of acquaintance with all sorts of objects. I am also fairly sure that the distinction between the look of an object and its feel, or between its smell and its taste, or in respect of any other pairing of sensory modalities, is also a late development. If so, it is by no means evident that the proper ordering of epistemological questions precludes any reference to external objects in the explanation of how we correlate the content of one of our senses with the content of another. The problem of split-particulars is to explain how the objects proper to one sensory modality are brought into relation with the objects proper to the other senses. An alternative approach to cognitive development lets us pose a different, and more tractable, problem of explaining how we split up a previously undifferentiated experience between its subjective and objective aspects, and how we then go on to further subdivide the subjective aspect of experience as the contents of five distinct senses. The one explanation presupposes that knowledge begins with sensory particulars. The alternative presupposes that knowledge, in its earliest forms, is an undifferentiated amalgam of subjectivity and objectivity.

I have yet to consider arguments favoring one approach over the other. In general we should prefer an account that minimizes presupposition; and this, at least, commends the empiricist approach for attempting to construct everything that is known from a simple and purportedly indubitable base. If the alternative is to provide an account of knowledge by assuming *without argument* that certain ideas are innate, we should prefer the empiricists' more demanding approach. But the alternative need not be, and in Kant's case it is not, just the unargued assumption of innate ideas. Provided that any postulation of innate ideas is well supported, there should be no objection to an account that credits the mind with certain initial capacities instead of attempting to show that everything is acquired from a sensory base.

At this point we cannot assess Kant's account of knowledge, but we can judge the accounts that form the empiricist tradition. They leave unresolved the problem of other minds, the problem of induction, the problem of split-particulars, the problem of causality, and the problems associated with Descartes' doubts—whether we are merely dreaming, whether an external world exists, whether we are deceived by an evil genius. These problems are the perennial topics of epistemology. They arise from the assumption that accounts of knowledge should begin with first-person states of consciousness. They do not, despite several centuries of philosophical effort, initiate a program of research that yields decisive results.

Kant is implicitly thought to share enough of the assumptions that give rise to the problems of epistemology to make it worth looking for his answers to the problems. Kant protests against philosophy as "a battleground quite peculiarly suited for those who desire to exercise themselves in mock combats, and in which no participant has ever yet succeeded in gaining even so much as an inch of territory, not at least in such a manner as to secure him of its permanent possession" (B xv). This is not the battle cry of someone about to join in the same old mock combat. Berkeley is obviously in the middle of the epistemological fray, but Kant avails himself of none of the easy means by which he could indicate that he is tackling the traditional problems of knowledge. To attempt to read Kant into the epistemological tradition, or to conflate his position with Berkeley's, is to overlook the glaring lack of evidence that Kant has a problem of other minds, or of induction, or of split-particulars, etc. One cannot plausibly suppose that Kant is unaware of these problems. It must be that these are not problems for him, and that can only be because he is working with different assumptions, and taking a different approach to the problems of knowledge.

7. The Elements of Kant's System

To describe Kant's approach and the problems (quite different from the standard ones of other minds, induction, and so on) that he deals with, I will now develop the language-model to explain the main elements of his system.

Central to Kant's approach is the notion of representation that Berkeley makes brief use of in his theory of vision, but elsewhere abandons in favor of representation that depends on likeness of kind, such that what an idea of sense represents must itself be just an idea or a complex of ideas. For Kant there is no restriction of representation to things of the same kind. Things represented stand to the sensory ideas that represent them in somewhat the same fashion that written words stand to spoken words, or in ways in which words of either sort stand to the things we talk about.

Neither in the transcription of speech nor in the linguistic description of things does the sign/signified relationship depend on the sign and the signified being things of the same kind. What it does depend on is some affinity between the pattern structure of the signs and the structural features of the things signified. This structural affinity need not be the rigid isomorphism that Berkeley thinks obtains between written letters and speech sounds. It can instead be a looser connection—perhaps family resemblance, or whatever—and it need not obtain at the lowest level of generality. Once we depart from Berkeley's simple and elementary isomorphisms, we are afforded the possibility of many more complex structural relationships obtaining at various levels of generality.

Some of the connections within language, or between language and the world, are suggestive of the connections Kant makes among the terms of his theory.

At the lowest level, a language involves physical signs through which all meaning is conveyed. These signs may be gestures or sounds or the marks of writing or whatever, but they alone are the means by which linguistic expression is possible. The physical signs of a language are the analogues of intuitions in Kant's system. Just as all representation in language relates ultimately to physical signs, all representation in experience in general relates ultimately to intuitions.

There is a further comparison to be made at the lowest levels in language and experience. Signs have both a form and a content. The content consists in the sensory qualities of the elements taken individually, the form in the relation of those elements. For example, the spoken words *cat* and *tack* have the same three sounds as content, but different forms because the sounds are differently arranged. A written sentence has an entirely different content from the same sentence read aloud, but they have closely corresponding forms. Kantian intuitions involve a similar distinction between form and content. Sensations provide their content. Space and time provide their form. For example, we have the same visual sensations whether we view an object directly or in a mirror, or whether we view a film projected normally or run backwards through the projector. Even though the sensory content remains constant in each pair of cases, the form changes. With the first pair the change is spatial, with the second pair it is temporal. These cases also point out that what is given in sense is never merely a set of sensations. What is given is always sensation in some spatiotemporal pattern. Analogously, linguistic input is never just speech sounds or visible letters, but sounds or letters in some particular order.

Before going on to other features of language that can be used to model Kant's system, I want to remark on the difference it makes if one considers the given to involve the form/content distinction. Empiricists in general, but Berkeley in particular, concentrate on the sensory content of the given almost to the exclusion of its form. For Berkeley, space must be constructed from sensations, especially of the motion of one's body, or from distance-indicating qualities of sensations such as the fuzziness or clarity of visual sensations.[33] The empiricist doctrine of the origin of ideas cannot be equated with Kant's contention that all thought must relate ultimately to intuitions. First, because Kant's notion of relation does not admit of reduction; and, now, because intuitions have a dual nature in virtue of the form/content distinction. Intuitions are more than simple ideas of sense. With Kant and the empiricists we have something like an early version of the difference between Gestalt and introspectionist theories of perception, with Kant and the Gestalt theorists taking the given as structurally complex, and the empiricists and introspectionists regarding it as consisting in sensory simples.[34] By considering the form as well as the content of the given, Kant is able to set up the nonreductionist relations of representation between the given and the objects we perceive on the basis of what is given in sense.

Language has also a second level that consists in the meanings of the first-level physical signs. While I do not propose, and could not give, a full account of the relation between linguistic signs and their meanings, I will develop a few points of comparison between meanings and the terms that correspond to them in Kant's system. The first comparisons will indicate the difference between appearances and phenomena. Further comparisons will concern attention, perception, reason, and the correction of error.

The physical signs of language have two sorts of meaning that may be contrasted as being, on the one hand, immediate or undetermined, and, on the other, as worked-out or determinate. The latter is given in dictionaries, or it is arrived at when we reflect on what someone has said and are content that we do understand what was said. The former is what we get on first hearing. For example, suppose someone says there are allegories on the banks of the Nile. When we hear the word *allegories* we may spontaneously understand it to mean a certain sort of narrative. That is what the speaker at first appears to be talking about; but it is not really what he means, as the phrase that follows it makes clear. What he really means is *alligators*. Most often utterances are not malappropriate, so the meaning that we spontaneously represent to ourselves on first hearing is identical with the meaning we would rest content with on reflection. However, haste, incorrect pronunciation, faults in diction and bad telephone connections supply some examples of apparent meaning that are not sustained on reflection. As well, reflection may supply meanings that are not apparent until we ponder the choice of a particular word, work out the probable completion of a partially overheard remark, or draw an inference. So there is a large overlap between the two sorts of meanings, but there are some departures on either side.

Appearances and phenomena have the same large overlap. For the most part, things in the world (phenomena) are as they immediately appear to be. Some appearances such as mirages, misperceptions, hallucinations, illusions, dreams, and tricks of the lighting are not also phenomena. Phenomena may be supplied for the most by the spontaneity of perception; but they can instead by supplied by extrapolation from appearance, by inference, or by the correction of appearance. Because most of the objects represented in sense are veridical, the two terms could often be used interchangeably. When Kant seems to use them selectively, it is usually to make a point of emphasis.

Since Kant's primary concerns in the *Critique* are the conditions of experience, he more often speaks of *appearances*. That is, since he is working out the way in which we come to know objects, he uses the term that connotes our first acquaintance with them. They first appear to us by virtue of being represented in sense; and so long as Kant is concerned with how they appear, with the conditions governing the representation of objects, he describes them as appearances.[35]

Kant's only extensive use of the term *phenomena* is to contrast two sorts of rational reflection: empirical thought, which confines itself to objects that can be known on the basis of experience; and thought that goes beyond the restrictive conditions of knowledge. Empirical thought deals with phenomena; they are properly called phenomena, rather than appearances, because in this context the emphasis is on rational reflection. Thought that transcends knowledge concerns itself with noumena.[36]

The second levels of language and of experience (as Kant describes it) are also comparable in respect of the normal focus of attention. Although the signs of a language (intuitions, in Kant's description of experience) provide the basis for the representation of meanings (appearances), we normally attend, not to that which represents, but to that which is represented. We mainly attend to what a speaker is saying, and we give only peripheral attention to the sounds he employs to say it. The derisive comment that someone likes the sound of his own voice insinuates an improper inwardness of his concerns. He should care more about what it is he is saying, less about how it is said, and least about who gets to do all the talking. The wisdom of the reproach is its recognition that what matters is meaning. What matters is what is said. The listener, too, who starts listening to the sound of the voice instead of attending to meaning can easily get lost. Of course there are warranted exceptions. Exceptionally pleasant voices, fine penmanship, and poetic fusions of sign and signified are all cases in which the signs themselves draw and deserve a larger than usual share of our attention. Appearances, like the meanings of utterances, also command attention; and of the intuitions that represent them we have, in normal circumstances, scant awareness. Again there are exceptions—when the sheer look or sound or feel or taste or smell of something diverts part of our attention from the object itself to the state of our own sensibility.

Although pleasure and absentmindedness are commonly causes of shifts in attention from its usual focus on the second level, there is also a different mechanism. On occasions when representation fails, we are forced back to the first level to figure out what it is that is represented. For example, we must sometimes stop reading while we puzzle out an initially indecipherable bit of handwriting. In experience, too, we sometimes cannot recognize at a glance what it is that we are looking at, and we need to pause to think out what it is; or we cannot think what a certain noise is, and we are not satisfied until we determine what is making it. It is significant that in our puzzlement we refer to an item on the first level such as a squiggle or an unclearly enunciated word or a strange sound, and that in our resolution of the puzzle we settle happily on a second-level object such as a meaning or the thing making the sound. The significance is simply that consciousness of, and attention to, second-level objects is the norm from which departures, except those mentioned in the preceding paragraph (the descents into sensory pleasure) are annoyances. The mind seeks meaning, and for the most part attends to the second level.

The breakdowns of representation with the things that give us pause lead into further comparisons to be made between signs and their meanings, on the one hand, and intuitions and appearances, on the other.

One can compare the way that the spontaneity of normal representation, both in language and in experience in general, is replaced in difficult cases by a deliberative process. The flow of representation must be impeded in some way. We must be stopped short. Otherwise we at once apprehend what is meant or what object we are confronted with. If we *must,* we can usually *figure out* what is meant, what it is we are looking at, or what is making the noise; but, ordinarily, there is no need to engage ourselves in any deliberative process of working out what is meant, seen, or heard.

Kant describes the faculty of understanding as spontaneous in the production of concepts,[37] and he says that it is in concepts that the material given in sensibility is united.[38] There is ordinarily no process of reason or deliberation required to arrive at an object on the second level. Things fall smoothly into place with meanings mapping easily onto the sounds of speech or with objects conforming readily to our sensory input. Only when the inputs are insufficient or unclear, or the mappings are difficult, do we have to think. Otherwise we simply understand. For Kant the business of representation is normally carried on by the faculty of understanding, which is spontaneous in its operations. It is only in cases of difficulty that the faculty of reason is called in to resolve matters.

In his assignment of representation to understanding, which he characterizes as a faculty quite distinct from reason, Kant removes perception from the province of reason—to which Descartes and the empiricists consign it. They consider perception to be a kind of inference from inner states of mind to nonmental objects in the world. Because they think of it in this way, they have all the difficulties of justifying the inference from the one to the other—the litany of traditional epistemological problems. Specific difficulties cannot be resolved within the framework of their approach by reference to general empirical knowledge. On their conception of the processes involved, it would beg the question to explain our knowledge of the representational significance of a particular inner state by referring, in the explanation, to general knowledge acquired through the senses. They think that all such knowledge requires similar justification.

Kant, by contrast, does not regard perception in terms of inference from the mental to the nonmental.

Nor should he. If the language-model can be maintained on this point, the representations of the second level by the first are rarely the results of rational workings-out. We do puzzle out the indecipherable bit of hand-writing, or figure out what the unheard word must have been, and these indeed are inferences, operations of reason; but they are operations based on a wealth of information arrived at, not by reason at all, but by simply understanding. If we cannot understand anything at all that a speaker says, we cannot begin the attempt to figure out what he is saying because we lack the basis for the sorts of inference that could carry us over the trouble spot by allowing us to work out the one puzzling part of something that, for the most part, is understood. If the analogy to language holds here, we can make inferences from certain of our sensory states to the objects that those states represent only by bringing to bear the general knowledge we have obtained noninferentially.

Of course, it remains to be explained how we do obtain the bulk of our knowledge, and how it is that the understanding functions; but it is an important first step to see that the explanation of knowledge will not take the form of a general justification of inference from the inner to the outer.[39] There have been no decisive (or moderately satisfactory?) answers to the problems of epistemology because we have asked the wrong questions. We have wondered how reason does the job, when we should have asked how the understanding works.

There is a further point to be made about the respective roles of reason and understanding. Often what begins its life as a concept of reason may in time become a concept of the understanding. For example, suppose that we have hitherto attached only one meaning to a certain word, and that we then encounter that word in a context in which the assigned meaning does not seem to fit. We may think up another meaning that would be more appropriate. Perhaps on some later occasion when we meet with the word again, we will again pause, but then recall the alter-native we thought of; eventually the apprehension of either meaning, of whichever is more appropriate to the context, will become as spontaneous and automatic as our usual understanding of other words. One may sim-ilarly enhance one's perceptual skills and learn in time to perceive at once things that formerly had to be thought about. A *resident's-spleen* is a spleen that is so slightly enlarged a medical student or intern could not feel it, though a resident could just manage to feel it, and a specialist would find it easily. It is not that the sense of touch grows more acute, but that the brain learns to read the signals of the senses. (In the next chapter, I describe converse ways in which reason can acquire concepts from understanding.)

While there is much more that could be said to develop the language-model in respect of the first and second levels of language and the first and second levels in the description Kant gives of experience, I propose to go on to what might be described either as a third level or else as lying just beyond language or experience.

8. Interpretation and Things-in-Themselves

The second level in language consists in meanings that are closely related to first-level items. Particular propositions are expressed in particular groups or strings of words. But meaning is not confined to the second level with its close relations to the first. We may talk also of what a certain author means or thinks without intending to restrict ourselves to a discussion of what he says in so many words. Such talk is interpretation. It goes beyond what the words and strings of words mean to encompass the entire work. The analogue in Kant's system to the object of an interpretation is the (notorious) thing-in-itself.

There are problems associated with things-in-themselves. With Kant's insistence on the limitation of knowledge to things as they appear to us, one wonders how he can legitimately talk at all about things that he says cannot be known. A further complication is that the unknown things-in-themselves are said to constitute the realms of morality and faith. There are also problems with the terminology Kant uses. One wonders how, if at all, things-in-themselves differ from noumena or from the transcendental object $= x$. Even if one grants the legitimacy of Kant's references to things-in-themselves, some means must still be found to integrate them into the rest of his ontology.

If we extend the language-model beyond the second level, we can find solutions to these problems. As readers, critics, friends, or psychoanalysts, we often attempt interpretation. Just by reading or listening we understand, one after another, the things written or said; with newspapers, detective stories, and idle conversations, such understanding is enough, and often all that is possible. With more serious written works, or in conversations of more involvement, we may look for a meaning that is not apparent. We then take up on a passage here, a remark there, and from these we try to construct the thoughts that underlie the thoughts expressed on the page, or the abiding thoughts and attitudes of those we converse with. In the construction of an interpretation of discourse, we seek an object that is not merely the sum of the meanings on the second level, although second-level meanings do supply the raw material of the construction. In the process of interpretation we emphasize and discount, we draw out implications, we note things said that might not have been said and things not said that might have been. In one way and another, we restructure the material of the second level to fashion a new thing in our minds. This new thing is what we *think* the author is after in his work, or what we *think* our acquaintance really feels, believes, or values.

All that we *know,* strictly speaking, is limited to what is actually expressed. The best evidence that someone thinks such-and-such is his saying it in so many words. As soon as we go on to ask ourselves, "Does he really think that?", we attempt an interpretative conjecture. We are not questioning that in some sense he thinks it. What we wonder is whether, and perhaps how, the thought belongs to his abiding or dispositional framework of ideas. Of course, he may just have been insincere, joking, ironical, or drunk; but even the determination that one of those conditions did obtain would not resolve the matter. Think of the importance that Freud attaches to slips of the tongue. Jokes may be just jokes, or the sorts of jokes one tells may be telling. There is, of course, no end to the amount of empirical evidence that could, practical considerations aside, be gathered about another person (and many of our questions can be taken as questions about phenomena) but the very wealth of possible evidence deprives us of determinateness and certainty in our attempts to interpret. It always remains possible to point to a piece of evidence that an interpretation neglects, or to discount one it relies on, or to assemble the evidence in alternative ways.

Many of the things we perceive are like the newspaper or detective story in so far as it would be out of place to seek an interpretation of them. Other objects, especially people,[40] have such complexity that it would often seem perverse to stop at what is apparent. Just as we try to piece together the passages of a serious novel or essay, we try to piece together the things a person says and does. We know that he said this and did that. What we wonder is why he said it or did it. What does he really think? What does he value? By what principles does he try to act? The answers to such questions would characterize the self-in-itself; but, although we do come up with answers, we do not obtain knowledge of things-in-themselves.

Interpretations have two sorts of criteria to satisfy: they must be grounded in what is known, but they must also be comprehensive and explanatory. There is tension between these criteria. To be an appropriate subject of interpretation a thing must present us with much detail and with intimations that there is more than meets the eye. If an interpretation were to take up every point of detail, and give each point equal weight, it would be admirably grounded in fact, but utterly useless—the thing itself already confronts us with all its detail. There must be culling and selection, and extrapolation beyond the facts; but if there is, then there is also bound to be indeterminacy. The culls and selections could be made in other ways, and we could take off from the facts in other directions. A good interpretation persuades us that full account is taken of its subject, but it also makes the subject intelligible to us as a whole. Bad interpretations are badly grounded or they shed little light.

I am unsure whether to describe interpretation as a third level of language or as lying just beyond language. From one point of view the former seems preferable because what concerns us when we interpret forms a third term in a progression of representations. Words are the vehicles that express second-level entities such as propositions; and propositions, in turn, express third-level entities such as philosophical systems, theories, and religious doctrines. Yet these third-level entities are in several ways extralinguistic. They are tied to no particular language. We talk of making discoveries concerning them and of struggling to find words to express them, as though they existed independently of being thought or described. They also have a nonlinear structure unlike strings of words and sentences.

Kant has no such hesitation in placing things-in-themselves beyond experience, but this is because he restricts experience to empirical knowledge.[41] We ordinarily construe experience more broadly to include daydreams, pleasures, emotions, decisions, and anything whatever that happens to us or that we do. Things-in-themselves would be among the chief objects of experience in the broad sense, but Kant has a serious purpose in restricting experience to exclude them. The *Critique of Pure Reason* is a study of what we know and of how we come to know it; and, as its title suggests, it limits the epistemic pretensions of reason. To lump things-in-themselves in with other objects of experience might be to blur the line between what we actually know and what, despite our confidence in our own interpretations, we cannot know. References in the *Critique* to things-in-themselves are usually sobering reminders that we know things only as they appear to us, never as they are in themselves.[42] This is not to make mystery-entities of things-in-themselves, nor to stop us thinking about them. It is to draw very clearly the line at which knowledge stops.

The importance of drawing the line is twofold. On the side of knowledge and experience (in Kant's restrictive sense), we can expect to find rules and principles that provide determinateness. On the side beyond there are criteria that make some interpretative constructions more reasonable and others less so, but there is not the bipolarity of truth and falsity.

Kant puts space and time in with the rules and principles of experience. One of the few things that we do know about things-in-themselves is that they are not in time and space. I will deal with the apparent contradiction of knowing something about the unknown in a moment. First I want to use the language-model to explain how things-in-themselves lie beyond space and time. I will take Descartes' philosophy as the example within the model of an object of interpretation. This object is not identical with all the words that Descartes ever wrote or said about philosophy. Nor is it identical with the second-level correlates of those words. His various books were written one after another, and, within each book, the words and sentences are also in sequence. The order of composition and expression is often incidental. We can imagine all sorts of rearrangement that would have no significance—these two paragraphs reversed, that argument put in a different Meditation, and so on. In reading Descartes' works, we, too, must take up the material just as he had to lay it down, one thing at a time; but, even at the beginning stages of interpretation we appreciate that the ideas form a complex whole with all sorts of nonlinear connections and relations. If we transferred it all to a blackboard, we would not simply list in order all the things he says. We would set out some things as main headings to collect under themselves supporting points, and we would draw arrows here and there to illustrate relations of implication. The words that express the philosophy must be written and read in a linear ordering; but the ideas expressed are not linear in themselves, only as they appear to us. So, likewise, we cannot encounter another person all at once. We experience one thing after another; but even at the beginning of an acquaintance, we appreciate that the order of appearance is not also the order of the self-in-itself. No one can express the whole of his thought except bit by bit over time, and as the occasion warrants, and in this place or that; but it does not follow that he in himself is so strung out and scattered.[43]

The paradox of knowing that unknown things-in-themselves are not in space and time dissolves with recognition that space and time belong to experience and that things-in-themselves do not. It is not that we enjoy a partial glimpse of the mysteries. It is rather as though someone said that syntactical orderings apply to words and sentences, but not to the philosophical systems they may be used to express. So too, all the sayings and doings, all the episodes of a life, occur perforce at particular times and in particular places. Dates and places fall away when consideration turns to the person himself.

On this account of things-in-themselves it is easy to see why they are essential for morality. Where we do not deem it appropriate to construct an object beyond appearances, we also suspend moral judgment. Conversely, we make moral judgments only when we are prepared to take what is evident as a sign of what is not itself evident. For instance, if we take a bit of behavior not to reflect on the agent's nature as a person, we suppress, or attempt to suppress, any irritation we may feel if the behavior *is* unpleasant to us; but, on the other hand, even if a bit of behavior *is not* intrinsically unpleasant, but we take it as a sign of ill will, disdain, or nastiness, we then think that resentment is not only appropriate, but justified. From a moral point of view, at least from Kant's moral point of view, the primary application of value terms is to the self-in-itself, and only derivatively to the conduct of the individual, and to the conduct, not in respect of its utility, its production of pleasure or pain, but to the conduct as a sign indicating the maxims by which the individual wills to act.[44]

Even in his writings on ethics, Kant does not provide much detail on how appearances signify things-in-themselves. Instead, his ethical writings direct us to consider the sorts of action that are right and wrong as determined by their relation to the moral law. As a moral agent, as advised by Kant, one's deliberations are not to be directed at the assessment of character, whether one's own or the character of others, for there is no way of knowing what lies beyond experience. Moral deliberation does not aim at knowledge at all. It aims instead at determining which rules of conduct are in accordance with moral law, and which are opposed to it. The purpose of this determination is not that it serves as a preliminary to the evaluation of persons and their conduct. Rather, in making the determinations, reason decides what ought, or ought not, to be willed.

9. Noumena, Things-in-Themselves, and the Transcendental Object = x

Kant seems to use the terms *noumena* and *things-in-themselves* as nearly interchangeable synonyms, but I think that there may be the following slight difference in the sense of the two terms. The thing-in-itself is opposed to the appearance (that is, to the object as it appears to us) in contrasts that draw attention to what we do not know and what we do. We know appearances, not things-in-themselves; and we know them only as they appear, not as they are in themselves. Noumena on the other hand are fashioned by the mind in its attempts to interpret appearances. Their natural terms of contrast are phenomena, which are also the products of reason. When reason goes beyond what can be determinately checked back against appearances it produces noumena. When reason confines itself to its empirical employments, it then produces phenomena.[45]

All that I perceive of a person pertains to him as an appearance. I may add to my knowledge of his empirical character by drawing certain inferences from what I know, or by correcting and modifying what appears to me. For instance, I may allow for the fact that only certain aspects of his nature will come to the fore in his dealings with me, and that these aspects may be exaggerated. With these corrections made, and certain inferences drawn from what is apparent, I know him not just as he appears to me, but as a phenomenon. If I go on to interpret his empirical character, I take everything I know, not as complete in itself, but as the sensible indication of his intelligible character, which includes all that pertains to him as he is in himself. The self I then think him to be is the noumenal self, the self as an object of my thought. In an interpretation, we are indeed trying to characterize the self-in-itself; but in recognition of the indeterminacy of interpretation, we should qualify our description as a description of the person *as we think him to be,* as an object of our intellect, and hence, as a noumenon.

Both things-in-themselves and noumena are transcendental objects in the straightforward sense that they lie beyond anything we could possibly experience. When Kant talks in the Deduction of the transcendental object = x,[46] the point is very different from the sort of point he makes when he talks about things-in-themselves or noumena. The variable, the algebraic *x,* in mathematics symbolizes a value yet to be determined. The transcendental object = x likewise symbolizes what we have yet to come to know in detail as an object of knowledge.

Experience does provide us with determinate knowledge of objects (albeit, only as they appear to us), and it does so by adding bit by bit to what we know of them. This progressive determination of the characteristics of objects in the course of experience should not be thought akin to the incremental growth of knowledge described by the empiricists. For Kant, it is not as though we acquire bits of sensory data that we associate until the collected bits have enough complexity to be regarded as objects in their own right. It is rather more like a problem in algebra where we are given a variable and we must work out its value. We start with the object itself from our first encounter with it, when we have no detailed characterization of it. As experience progresses, we learn more and more about it. But the *it*—the thing itself—confronts us from the outset. The empiricist describes us as starting with the heterogeneity of sensory particulars that are gradually unified. Kant describes us as starting with the unity of the object, its determinate character as yet unknown, to which subsequent experience brings detail and specificity.

There are two reasons that the object = x should be described as transcendental. *First,* it lies beyond experience as the point towards which the empirical advance is made. From our first encounter with it, the object confronts us as something to get to know; but getting to know it is not a finite process that is completed at a certain point. There is always more to know. As experience continues there are details to be added, questions to be answered and finer distinctions to be drawn.[47] Because of this ongoing possibility of further determination, the value of x is never fully resolved; and the object = x always transcends experience. The *second* reason for calling the object = x transcendental pertains to the essential role it plays in experience. Kant uses *transcendental* as an adjective to indicate those things that are required for the acquisition of knowledge. Thus, for example, the transcendental employment of the categories is their employment in experience as essential parts of cognitive processes. The contrast here is to the adjective *transcendent* which indicates an illegitimate extension beyond experience.[48] Kant considers the notions of causality and purpose to be used transcendently, rather that transcendentally, in the proofs for the existence of God because the proofs take notions that have a legitimate use within experience, but they attempt to employ them to acquire knowledge of an object that lies beyond all experience. This is not what happens with the transcendental object = x. Although knowledge of it cannot come *to completion* in the course of experience, the object is an object of experience. Kant thinks it is essential to the acquisition of knowledge that we begin with the notion of the object, even though that notion is initially without empirical or determinate content. It does have a priori content in virtue of the description the categories give of any possible object of experience. The transcendental object = x serves as a focal point toward which we advance. It thus secures the unity of empirical information. If unity was not presupposed, and posited in the object at the outset, we could not bring it in later on, except as an arbitrary unification of all the heterogeneous material given in the senses.

We are back to one of the main points of contrast between Kant and Berkeley. According to Berkeley's phenomenalism, we begin with sensory simples and the unification of experience takes place later on and at higher levels of complexity. By contrast, according to Kant's transcendental idealism, experience has two origins: in its sensory inputs, but also in the concepts of the understanding.[49] Unity is constantly imposed by concepts on the sensory inputs, and the sensory inputs constantly add to the determinateness and detail of concepts.

We are also back to another point of contrast in their differing conceptions of what is required for representation. Starting with sensory simples, and working in only one direction (toward complexity) Berkeley treats representation as requiring sameness of kind between sign and signified. Since Kant's account involves two sources of knowledge, and two directions (both the application of concepts to the given and the taking up of sensory material to give greater definition to concepts) his notion of representation does not involve sameness of kind. In fact it is required to join together things of radically different kinds.

2

Kant's Theory of Spatial Forms

10. The Purpose of This Chapter

Kant turns his attention to space again and again in his earliest works, in the Inaugural Dissertation, in the first *Critique,* in the *Prolegomena,* and in the *Metaphysical Foundations of Natural Science.* There is no one problem, topic, or focus common to all the discussions in these various works. Where there is a common topic from one discussion to another, there may or may not be consistency in the views he expresses. Even if we confine our attention to what Kant says about space in the *Critique,* we will find suggestions of both sorts of diversity—of topic and of view.[1]

The purpose of this chapter is not to consider all the things that Kant has to say about space. Nor does it attempt to do justice to the extensive secondary literature.

My concern throughout this book is with Kant's general theory of experience. As I understand it, Kant's theory of experience is the basis of all his other theories—of science, of mathematics, of religion, ethics, aesthetics, and education—so far as I understand them. Kant's theory of experience plays a somewhat different foundational role in the case of each of the offshoot theories, but to each it is in some way fundamental. Science takes its topic matter from the empirical content of experience. Mathematics relies on, and explores, some of the formal aspects of experience. Because religion and ethics transcend experience, the theory of experience defines boundaries beyond which they may operate and sets conditions to which they are subject. Kant's theories of aesthetics and education rely on discoveries that he makes about the nature of the mind in the course of his investigation of experience.[2]

The purpose of this chapter is set by my general concern. Space and spatial considerations enter into experience in a variety of ways and at a variety of levels. At its lowest level, in sensibility, experience involves space in two distinct ways: as the patterns in which sensations—especially visual sensations—are apprehended; and, as pure patterns or forms considered apart from all sensation. At higher levels of experience, other aspects of spatiality enter in as the shapes of objects, as locations, as features of motion. Space also carries over into the offshoot theories of science and mathematics, where the concerns are with the geometry of empirical space or with geometry as a formal study. One cannot consider experience without considering space, and that sets out for me what I have to do in this chapter. Kant sometimes, and critics often, look ahead to the offshoot theories and discuss space in relation to geometries applied and pure. While I do try to bear in mind the foundational role in the philosophies of science and mathematics that Kant intends for his remarks on space in the general theory of experience, I discuss for the most part spatial matters that are too primitive to have much bearing on issues of geometry.

Space enters into the earliest and most elementary aspects of experience—primarily, I think, as a basic feature of both concept-formation and object-recognition. It may provide the first connections between sensing and reasoning. What I call Kant's theory of spatial forms is concerned with spatiality only so far as it can be considered in isolation from matter and causality, and only as it can be considered to precede, and help to make possible, the development of knowledge. It is a theory of what might be thought of as innate spatial ideas. Such issues as the displacement of Euclidean geometry or the interrelations of physical and geometrical laws lie a very long way down the road because they presuppose, respectively, millenia of mathematical thought and a wealth of empirical information. Even the correlation of one's immediate perceptual space (the space of here, there, right, and left) with the public space (the space of objective location) is too complex a matter to be dealt with by the theory. I leave treatment of it to the discussion of Kant's Third Analogy in chapter seven, where I contend that the correlation depends on dynamical considerations to differentiate between apparent motions caused by the motions of the perceiver and apparent motions caused by movement in the objects of perceptions. The theory of spatial forms treats only simple matters; but, of course, what one says about the simple matters must be consistent with what will have to be said later on about the more complex ones, so some initial regard must be given to the development of spatiality throughout experience.

In this chapter I leave behind the language-model that was used to introduce the basic elements of transcendental idealism. In its place, the theory of spatial forms will be used to provide examples of intuitions, concepts, and the more perspicuous relations of representation. The theory of spatial forms is almost a working model of experience. It lacks a mechanism for making the distinction between subjectivity and objectivity, which is the reason that resolution of apparent motion must wait for the introduction of dynamics. However, there are several reasons for beginning with a theory that almost works, instead of going directly to Kant's entire theory of experience.

First, Kant's own method is to argue in this fashion. He constructs his entire system stage by stage. Each stage in turn is shown to be necessary but insufficient to account for experience. Additional stages are then brought in to remedy the insufficiencies of the preceding ones, until finally the system is complete. Kant calls this method "transcendental argument." Additions are justified by showing that they are required as conditions for the possibility of experience. Transcendental argument is contrasted with metaphysical argument, which we now call philosophical analysis. By starting with an incomplete theory in this chapter, I can follow Kant's own method of constructive argument in later chapters.[3]

Second, the later chapters deal mainly with the Analytic of Principles, in which Kant emphasizes time and almost neglects space. Critics are puzzled by this imbalance in the treatment of time and space in the Analytic of Principles. The insufficiency of spatial considerations to provide a subjective/objective distinction explains why Kant resorts to temporal considerations to establish the representation of appearances.[4]

Third, because the theory of spatial forms involves no distinction between objective and subjective, it is an epistemologically neutral starting place. Its objects may be supposed to exist only in the mind until reasons are given later for considering them to be material bodies. This initial agnosticism satisfies an important consideration for any theory of experience: it should show how we come to know objects in the world. Even though the theory of spatial forms is incomplete, it provides a good working *sketch* of transcendental idealism, and it makes evident what more is needed. The sketch also gives us a stark contrast between transcendental idealism and epistemologies that follow in the tradition of Descartes and Hume. They, too, begin from a position of epistemological neutrality; but their implicit models of the mind, as evident from the sorts of justification they seek, differ utterly from Kant's.

Although my general concerns dictate that I restrict myself in this chapter to the most elementary aspects of spatiality, there are viable alternatives in other contexts. Vuillemin, in "The Kantian Theory of Space in the Light of Groups of Transformations,"[5] considers the mathematical aspects of what Kant has to say about space. He thus begins at the top end of experience, with its highest, most critical and reflective developments. He nonetheless does try to indicate how Kant's remarks about space at that level of experience tie back to his remarks concerning the spatiality of lower levels. Whether one begins at the bottom or the top, one must, as Vuillemin does, pay some attention to the entire system from which the selected remarks are taken. Otherwise, I think *especially* if one begins at the top, it is easy to misconstrue what Kant says. The top end is particularly risky, as I argue in the next section, because nineteenth and twentieth century developments in geometry and changes in the meanings of philosophical terms together make Kant's descriptions of geometry very liable to misinterpretation. Anglo-American critics standardly begin at the top end, treat it all as a matter of geometry, claim that Kant is committed to Euclid, and then go on to discuss non-Euclidean geometries and their connections with physics. That this approach does not yield a plausible theory is then taken as proof that Kant lacks one.[6] I think that they mistakenly project on Kant current ways of thinking about space, and miss what he says.

11. Visual Geometry

The section title is taken from a paper by Hopkins,[7] in which discussion of Kant's ideas about space comes down to a discussion of whether the space of visualization, imagination, and perception is Euclidean (as Kant is said to think) or non-Euclidean. The paper draws on, and provides an excellent summary of, some of the major sources of the Anglo-American interpretation of Kant on space. Because it draws on these sources and yet concerns itself with spatiality at a fairly low level of experience, Hopkins's paper may seem to counterinstance my contention that they standardly begin at the top end. Not so. The focus of the discussion in Hopkins's paper is indeed toward the bottom end; but this focus is the culmination of a critical tradition that finds fault earlier with everything higher up. By the time of Hopkins's paper, the tradition takes for granted that Kant's commitment to Euclid makes everything he has to say about the geometry of empirical space and the foundations of pure geometry just wrong. This leaves them with the question of whether Kant was right about anything having to do with space. Fault having been found with everything higher up, Hopkins is left wondering if something of Kant's purported Euclidean commitment might be salvaged in respect of what he terms visual space. As it turns out, even the salvage fails. At least Hopkins argues that it does, and he argues well.

I do not, however, accept the conclusion that what Kant has to say about space is wrong from top to bottom. I think that the tradition that arrives at that conclusion is wrongheaded from the outset. It is not wrong to take seriously the recent—the post-Kantian—developments in mathematics and physics, but it is wrong to make these and non-Kantian uses of certain key philosophical terms the basis for their attempt to interpret Kant on space.

Because Kant says that geometry is synthetic a priori, he is easily put in opposition to contemporary explanations of geometry. Without further analysis, that claim alone draws the following criticisms. To be synthetic, geometry must describe objects; and to be a priori, its descriptions must be necessarily true. Nineteenth century mathematics provides a variety of formal systems that can be given interpretations as geometries. Each system is consistent or formally true, that is, true so long as it remains pure or uninterpreted. Because physics has a number of systems to select from, the questions of which is the best choice and of how it should be interpreted are to be answered empirically. The modern consensus is that it should be a non-Euclidean geometry with lines interpreted as paths taken by light. These developments explain the objection that Einstein makes to Kant's claim that geometry is synthetic a priori. Hopkins quotes Einstein as saying, "As far as the laws of mathematics refer to reality they are not certain; as far as they are certain they do not refer to reality."[8] Thus the modern view, represented by Einstein, is that geometry is either synthetic or a priori; but that it cannot be both together because that would be tantamount to its being both interpreted and uninterpreted— both pure and applied.

Other critical objections are directed, not at the *claim* Kant makes, but at his *defense* of it. Kant says that we have pure intuitions of such nonempirical objects as imaginary lines and figures, and that our geometrical reasoning rests on considering these pure objects—pure, because they are not given through the senses; rather they originate in the mind itself. He also says that our senses just give matter or content to the forms accessible to us in pure intuition, with the result that the pure objects we can study a priori are also the forms that empirically perceived objects take. Consequently, whatever can be discovered in geometrical reasoning a priori can be carried over to relationships in empirical space. At least this is how Kant is thought to reason in defense of his claim that geometry is synthetic a priori.

Some critics object to the first part of the defense by pointing out that modern geometrical thought in mathematics has freed itself from reliance on constructed figures. It can all now be done in an abstract notation— a formal symbolism—that in no way limits the geometrician to what can be pictured.

There are some supporters, tentative or outright, who accept part of Kant's defense by granting that what we can picture or construct may be Euclidean. This is the last remnant of the Kantian position. Some critics are willing to grant it, but Hopkins argues that even this is too much. He cites Bennett, Strawson, and Frege as, more or less, willing to concede the Euclidean character of *visual* geometry (if not of empirical or objective geometry). Hopkins argues against what he takes to be this very weak version of the Kantian position. Even it claims too much. He points out that the scale of visualization is too small to reveal discrepancies between Euclidean figures and non-Euclidean figures of a modest degree of curvature. Only when we advance to objects on a much larger scale can we tell which sort of figure we are dealing with. We could, of course, say that even though non-Euclidean geometry wins out at the scale of astrophysical distances, Euclidean geometry holds for the small scale objects of vision or visualization. But this, in light of the equal applicability of both non-Euclidean and Euclidean geometries to small-scale objects, would seem a feeble effort to salvage something of the Kantian position.

In this brief survey of the criticisms that are standardly leveled at Kant, the discussion begins with him but very quickly turns to Euclid and to modern mathematics and physics.

Euclid's system of geometry contrasts with non-Euclidean systems in two ways. First, the laws are different. In Euclid's system only one parallel to a given line can be drawn through a point external to the line. In some non-Euclidean geometries more than one parallel can be drawn; and in others there are no parallels at all. The second contrast is in the method of proof. In Euclid's system, rules of inference are implicit, and proofs involve the construction of figures. In modern axiomatizations of geometry, rules of inference are stated explicitly, and the construction of drawings plays no part in the proofs.

Since the laws and theorems of Euclidean geometry can be expressed in a modern axiomatic way, we can distinguish two senses of Euclidean geometry. There is Euclidean geometry as the one-parallel system. As well there is Euclidean geometry as a constructive or intuitive method of proof. The two senses are related because the development of alternative geometries, with different laws of the parallel, depended largely on freeing proofs from reliance on diagrammatic constructions. Once proofs became expressible in symbolic notations in accordance with formal rules, it was possible to create alternative geometries and to establish their consistency.

Since there are two senses of Euclidean geometry, Kant's purported commitment to Euclid can be taken in either of the two ways. He can be taken to be committed to the Euclidean character of space, that is, to the description of space given by Euclid's laws. Or he can be taken to be committed to the Euclidean type of proof in mathematics. Kant's critics standardly take it both ways, and they say he is mistaken about the one because he is mistaken about the other. He thinks that space is Euclidean because he thinks that the laws of space derive from what we can intuit or construct; and he adopts the theory of pure intuition to explain how we have, and why we have, synthetic a priori knowledge of the (Euclidean) character of space. Whichever way the connection is considered, the consensus seems to be that modern physics proves Kant wrong about the laws of space, and that modern mathematics proves him wrong about the methods of proof.

The combined thrust of the two modern developments leaves little of what is supposed to be the Kantian position intact. All that remains is to ask whether there might not be something salvaged in respect of visual geometry. Until Hopkins's paper argued to the contrary, one could wonder whether little diagrams might perhaps be Euclidean.

What one may now wonder—now that the critical dismissal is complete—is whether Kant was originally caught within the circle of beaters. If he was, the hunt is over. If not, the critics have just flailed the bushes. There are several reasons to be cautious about claiming the trophy just yet.

First, there is the matter of Kant's purported commitment to Euclid, on which the standard objections are utterly dependent. Hopkins begins his paper by saying, "Kant thought Euclid's geometry true of everything spatially intuitable. This implied that only Euclid's geometry—Euclidean figures or a Euclidean space—could be seen, imagined, or visualized."[9] This attribution is crucial to Hopkins's entire enterprise, but he offers no textual references to support it. Other critics are equally lax on this point.[10]

It would be pedantic to demand textual support if the point were obvious, but it is not. Kant only mentions Euclid a couple of times in passing. Some of Kant's examples are Euclidean, but others seem deliberately not to be. Here are two passages from Vuillemin:

> The examples of the proofs Kant uses to legitimize T_1 [Geometry proceeds synthetically, that is, by sensible intuition] are of two kinds. Some use the fifth Euclidean postulate, but they are only to be found in the Transcendental Methodology, which is considered to be the oldest section of the *Critique,* thereby letting us think that through inadvertence alone did Kant abandon this example, which would imply that geometrical intuition is, for him, Euclidean. The other examples carefully avoid appeal to the fifth postulate. They are: "In a triangle, two sides together are greater than the third"; "Two straight lines could not enclose a space"; and "Three straight lines make possible a figure."
>
> These examples, therefore, leave open the question of knowing which geometry is implied by the Kantian exposition. But do they show the intuitive nature of geometry? Is not demonstration reduced to a simple logical sequence by reduction to axioms?[11]

As the concluding questions suggest, Kant's examples may not do the job for which he intends them. There is a puzzle that I cannot resolve earlier in the passage. I wonder why we should want to think that it was through *inadvertence* that Kant abandoned his Euclidean example if his other examples *carefully avoid* appeal to the fifth postulate. However, I quote the passage for the doubts it raises about Kant's purported commitment to Euclid. The second passage, taken out of context, does not fully make sense, but it, too, raises doubts.

> Since Kant has isolated the latter in the second edition, it must be noted that he had a sense of the Riemannian distinction between the relations

of extension or of region, and the metrical relations, and, furthermore, that he probably envisaged the possibility of geometries other than Euclid's, even if only to eliminate them in the end as Lambert had done.[12]

I do not take these passages to show that Kant was *not* committed to Euclid, but only to show that there is a serious (I think unresolvable) question about whether he was.

Vuillemin has a very considerable advantage over Kant in respect of the mathematical knowledge each possesses. Which is reasonable enough. Vuillemin has an additional two centuries of highly productive work to draw on. The overall impression I take from Vuillemin's discussion is that, taken mathematically, Kant's remarks on space are interesting, but ambiguous, unsatisfactory, exploratory, tentative—in short, just what one would expect of early thought by an able thinker in an intellectual discipline about to take off in unprecedented development, but at the moment still uncertain and only beginning to find its way.

In view of the unsettled state in late eighteenth century geometrical thought, the absence of explicit textual commitment on Kant's part to Euclid, and the changes of example and the ambiguities noted by Vuillemin, I do not think that the critics are entitled to a bald and unsupported attribution to Kant of a commitment to Euclid.

A *second* reason to question the critical dismissal of Kant's remarks about space has to do with the critics' heavy emphasis on mathematics. Here there is some textual basis for the discussion. Kant does pose the following as a fundamental question to be answered by the *Critique:* "How is pure mathematics possible?" But it is one thing to recognize an objective Kant sets for his theory, and quite another to take the objective as achieved by mathematicians in the next two centuries, and then to look back at Kant in terms of their achievement. It is conceivable that Kant recognized the possibility of developments and changes in mathematics. If so, perhaps the question he posed was not about some body of fixed mathematical doctrines (including Euclid's), but about the ongoing enterprise of mathematics. If so, we should look to Kant's general account of the mind for those aspects of thought he could regard as giving rise to mathematical enquiry. Perhaps Kant had reason to change examples to "carefully avoid appeal to the fifth postulate." He would have such reason if his concern were more with the processes than the products of mathematical thought. He would then want his account to cover whatever mathematics might discover, and not want it to be wedded to the products of a particular time. The effect of beginning with the displacement of Euclidean geometry and then proceeding to the critical dismissal of Kant is to foreclose prematurely on more sympathetic interpretations—interpretations that could grant happily many failures to anticipate the particular subsequent developments of mathematics, but which might nontheless find something valuable in the general account of our mathematical knowledge.

However much mathematics may have changed in the past two centuries, it is doubtful that the spatial aspects of sensing and perception have changed at all. If mathematical thought is in some way grounded in the formal aspects of lower-level cognitive processes, then an adequate account of the grounding of eighteenth century mathematical thought should admit of extension to accommodate later mathematical thought, since it is presumably the same base giving rise to both.

Even if one supposes that the offshoot theory of mathematics is too rigid to accommodate change, it does not follow that the base theory—Kant's general theory of experience—is itself defective. It might be that the trouble, if there is any, starts only with the attempt to use the base in a particular way in the offshoot.

I repeat that it is risky to start at the top end.

A *third* reason for caution has to do with pure intuition and the method of proof. Consider the two questions that conclude the first quote from Vuillemin above. The first question asks of Kant's examples, "But do they show the intuitive nature of geometry?"; and the second asks, "Is not demonstration reduced to a simple logical sequence by reduction to axioms?" Taken together the two questions represent the standard contrast between Kant's method of proof (which somehow involves intuition) and modern axiomatic methods.

Axiomatization of proofs in symbolic notation is a post-Kantian development in geometry; but nondiagrammatic representations of individual proofs would be well known to him as analytic geometry, which allows geometrical representation in algebraic terms. Whatever Kant's method of proof amounts to, two points must be noted: he thinks that it applies equally to arithmetic and geometry;[13] and he does not think that geometry must be done diagrammatically.

In an early paper on the feasibility of using mathematical reasoning in ethics,[14] Kant contrasts the relationship between mathematical proofs and the symbols in which they are expressed, on the one hand, with the relationship between ethical arguments and their words, on the other. A moral argument proceeds by abstract analytic inferences that have no direct, part-for-part relation to the words that express the connections of ideas. Thus, for example, I infer from the fact that someone was justly punished that he did wrong knowingly. No amount of inspection of the words "he was justly punished" will reveal their connection to the words "he did wrong knowingly." The inference is abstract because it is from meaning to meaning, not from word to word. This contrasts with mathematical proof, which does depend directly on its notation. For example, from $x(y + z) = 0$, I infer $xy + xz = 0$. Here the connection is not just from thought to thought as in ethics, but direct and perspicuous between the two sets of symbols. It is this role of symbols in mathematics that Kant refers to in his theory of pure intuition.[15]

I will come back to mathematics and notation later in this chapter. My point in calling attention to it now is to show that the identification of Kant's notions of proof with diagrammatic construction oversimplifies his thought on the matter. It also creates a false opposition with modern notions of proof.[16]

12. Two Models of the Mind

While it is impossible to attribute a single philosophical position to all Kant's critics, there is an approach to unanimity in their tacit acceptance of a two-element model of the mind. One element is reason. The other is sense experience. There are many indicators of acceptance of this model, for example, the divisions between the mathematical and the empirical, the pure and the applied, the certain and the real, the analytic and the synthetic. The employment of any of these pairs of terms as dichotomies usually indicates that the user thinks of the mind as comprising a capacity *to infer* and a capacity *to sense*. Other indications of the two-element model will be described in the course of the discussion.

Kant, by contrast, employs a three-element model of the mind. To *reason* and *sensibility,* Kant adds *understanding* as a third faculty that mediates between the other two. The addition of a third faculty makes it impossible to correlate directly the terms Kant uses with their modern cognates. For example, Kant describes geometrical knowledge as synthetic a priori. In modern philosophy, synthetic is used as a synonym for empirical, and both are opposed to the a priori.[17] The synonymy and opposition are not precise enough to make Kant's description flatly contradictory on a modern reading, but they are near enough to invite Einstein's sort of rejoinder. Kant's use of the terms, however, is quite different. There is no neat pairing of half the terms with sense and of the other half with reason. The a priori aspects of experience may have their source in any of the three faculties. That is why there is pure intuition, pure concepts of the understanding, and pure reason. Moreover, any of the three faculties may be employed empirically.

The *origin* of the two-element model could be attributed to Hume's dichotomy between matters of fact and relations of ideas. The *development* of the model depends on a shift in the emphasis of modern thought from mental activity to language, or alternatively, from psychologism (as it is disparagingly called) to logic.

The philosophies of Kant's time and earlier abound in references to mental faculties. Reflection on the diversity of mental activity supports many distinctions such as reason, sense, imagination, conscience, memory, wit, and, of course, reflection itself. Psychologism attempts to describe the workings of these various faculties, and it has an unpromising record.

Modern thought is partly a rejection of psychologism and all its empty promises, but more it is a response to the new insights that logic provides. The *processes* of the mind are complex and hidden from us. The *products* of the mind may be equally complex, but they are directly accessible. They admit of an illuminating dichotomy between a formal, logical, or syntactical aspect and a material, empirical, or observational aspect. This dichotomy is the foundation of the two-element model. One element of the mind can be associated with forms, the other with content. The element associated with forms is thought to be responsible for, and revealed in, logic and mathematics. The element associated with content is thought simply to be sensation, and it is thought to be the source of all empirical aspects of experience.

In the propositions of logic and mathematics, form occurs without content. These occurrences of form are thought to be paradigmatic products of mental activity. They say nothing about the world, but they show how the mind works. What they show is that it works by inference from one judgment or proposition to another.

However, the separation of the formal and the material gives rise to a troublesome asymmetry. Form can be isolated from its content; but the content—what is given in sense—cannot occur apart from form. Even the simplest descriptive statement has a syntactic structure. Even a one-word description reflects a system of categorization. Thus, while it is comparatively easy to isolate form and, for example, set out patterns of valid and invalid argument, it is bafflingly difficult to say anything whatever about what is given in sense. Various efforts are made to indicate the given. Some philosophers posit atomic propositions, others opt for sense-data. Neither of these measures isolates the material aspect of thought in the way that the formal aspect can be isolated in logic, that is, in a way that then makes it possible to go on to informative descriptions of it.

Yet the given cannot be simply ignored since it is what transforms the abstract and analytic into the empirically meaningful. Most of the problems of modern epistemology relate specifically to empirical judgment, and they do so because the forms of judgment are comparatively unproblematic (except as problems that can be met in logic); but to solve problems in logic is not to solve problems that arise when the forms of judgment are given content.

One expedient that is widely adopted is to try to relate philosophy directly to mathematics and natural science by taking them as showing how the two elements interrelate. In the application of mathematics to natural phenomena, the two-element model has an analogue of the combined operations of the two aspects of the mind in the production of empirical knowledge. Mathematics is construed as being capable of fashioning a variety of formal systems without any reliance on the empirical. The mathematical constructions are then given interpretations that transform them from formal systems to empirical theories that are supported or challenged, modified or rejected, according to our sensory observations. The classic account of this understanding of the interrelation of mathematics and natural science is given by Ernest Nagel in *The Structure of Science*.[18] What is thought to obtain in respect of mathematics and science is thought also to obtain, though perhaps in a somewhat less structured way, in respect of the two elements of the mind. Reason and the a priori explore the realm of the possible; but it is left to sense-experience to determine which possibilities are actual.

The analogy between mathematics and science, on the one hand, and the two elements of the model, on the other, produces another shift of emphasis, in addition to the shift from the processes to the products of the mind. This is the shift away from the lowest levels—the most primitive aspects—of experience. In science there is nothing that corresponds to a primitive given. We instead find just low-level observations that are already, to some extent, shaped by theory. So the given is no longer much discussed.[19] Instead, most discussions in contemporary philosophy deal only with what is already in the form of a judgment or proposition. As a result, the break with psychologism is complete since all relations of thought under active consideration are between elements that can be expressed in sentential forms. Philosophical logic, construed broadly, thus displaces the study of mental activity in modern philosophy.

A number of problems result from the tacit acceptance of the two-element model. What remains especially problematic is any extension of thought beyond what can be taken on the model to be immediately given in sense. Ampliative inferences, inductions and predictions, do work; but there is no reason for their success that can be given by the model. It always remains an open possibility that whatever is next given in sense experience will not at all conform to the empirical interpretations of the formal patterns that have so far found application in experience.

As Einstein says, the formal is the sole realm of certainty, and what is certain has no essential relation to reality; and if this were all that needed to be said, it would not matter in the least. We could surely accept something just short, or even well short, of certainty in our empirical thought (after all, Kant asks us to accept in principle uncertainty in respect of our interpretations of things-in-themselves) but the fact of the matter is that we cannot assign even a small, but comforting, degree of plausibility to any empirical judgment *taken in itself*. The model explains why this is so. According to the model, the formal is entirely the product of our own thought, with no intrinsic relation to reality; and the real is given only in sense-experience. We can assign conditional probabilities to empirical judgments *in their relation to other judgments,* but we cannot detach probabilities and assign them to individual judgments.[20] That is, we can—so far as we agree on a logic of confirmation—formally analyze the extent to which the truth or falsity of certain judgments bears on the truth or falsity of other judgments; but we cannot analyze the truth, falsity, or degree of probability of judgments individually. We can, of course, just say that we perceive things to be, or not to be, as they are described in a judgment; but to say that is not to explain how it is that we perceive what is, or is not, the case.

Working with the two-element model, we cannot give explanations of empirical truth comparable to the explanations logic provides of formal truth. We cannot because whatever admits of analysis—whatever has complexity of structure and rules—falls, according to the two-element model, on the other side of the dichotomy, away from the given. As a result, the two-element model itself gives rise to the problems of empirical knowledge, since nowhere within it can the primitive epistemic tie between thought and reality be represented as a formal, rule-governed relationship. The problems of induction, of objectivity in science, of the relation of theory to observation, together with all the basic problems of epistemology (our knowledge of the external world, whether our senses deceive, etc.) are all problems that arise from the two-element model.

One indicator that the two-element model is being tacitly adopted is the framing of questions in accordance with Hume's dichotomy between matters of fact and relations of ideas. The model is in play whenever anything logically possible could be given in sense, and when whatever is given in sense determines empirical truth or falsity. According to Hume, one idea of sense does not imply any other, so anything—anything within the bounds of logical possibility, that is—could follow whatever sense-experiences we have had to date.[21] Questions need not be addressed to the future. Whenever imaginary situations of the sort that Shoemaker, for example, uses in "Time Without Change,"[22] are taken as test cases in which to try philosophical doctrines, the two-element model provides the implicit framework of the discussion. Philosophy is then regarded as analyzing ideas that must hold good in any conceivable situation. This presupposes, as do most skeptical arguments,[23] that the concern of philosophy is entirely with relations of ideas, not matters of fact. Philosophy is thought to be wholly analytic and a priori; yet, so far as it attempts to deal with epistemological problems, it is trying in vain to establish empirical knowledge. The skeptic is sure to win because the given is assumed to be constrained only by logical possibility, which means it supplies no constraints of its own. Yet the given is also thought to determine which relations of ideas are empirically valid. If anything whatsoever could be given in sense, any of the relations of ideas that are not self-contradictory could obtain empirically, or fail to obtain. If any relation could fail to be borne out, no amount of analysis can produce anything except logical truths, and every effort to defend an empirical judgment philosophically is sure to fail.

The epistemology of the two-element model tries to show how knowledge of reality derives from sense-experience. That it is an attempted *derivation* for which justification is sought indicates that the operative paradigm of mental activity is the truth-functional relation of inference. Since the model takes the given to consist in simple ideas of sense, impressions, or sensations, the attempted derivation is impossible. It is hopeless to try to solve the problems of empirical knowledge within the terms of the two-element model. Because simple ideas of sense lack truth-values, they are totally unsuitable as premises for inferences of any truth-functional sort, whether inductive or deductive.

There are other difficulties with the model. Hume thinks that our concepts of objects are the products of repeated and habit-forming experiences of conjunctions of qualities.[24] We form the concept of bread, for example, from sensory impressions of color, texture, taste, and smell. This is no doubt partly true, but it cannot be the basic truth because it leaves unexplained why we ever experience *those* sensations *as conjoined*.[25] We do not experience objects in isolation from other objects. Nor do we experience all the sensory qualities of a thing in every encounter with it. Since sensory qualities of things overlap, intermingle, and seldom (if ever) are experienced as an entire set, we require an explanation of how it is that we manage to sort out which qualities go with which in the composition of an object. The usual answer from empiricists is that we solve such problems over time, by association and by trial and error. The answer avoids the deep difficulty, which is not to account for how we end up at the right place. The difficulty is to explain how we ever get started. We can easily appreciate how conditioning adds another association to ideas that are already fairly well sorted out. One can explain how trial and error could correct the odd fault in a network of ideas. But these measures do not meet the need for an explanation of the origins of objective thought, which, though drawn from individual and very different courses of sensation, converges nonetheless on a common body of knowledge—instead of remaining as varied and individual as our habits and chance associations.

Inference is ruled out as the initiator of whatever processes lead to knowledge of the world through sense-experience, since inference requires truth-values and sensations lack them. Where we already have some theories (however crude), some concepts (however faulty) and make observations (however unscientific), there is a basis for talk of induction, hypothesis, and testing—or, if we prefer, talk of conjecture and refutation.[26] Such talk does not address the fundamental matters of cognition. It begins too far on in the story to explain how the story starts.

Kant is able to begin at the beginning because he uses an entirely different model of the mind. Sensibility and reason differ in the three-element model from their nominal counterparts in the two-element model, and understanding has no counterpart. Because Kant distinguishes between the form and the content of intuitions, the given is analyzable in his system. I will discuss the details of the analysis in chapter four. Suffice it to say here that the mere fact of analyzability of intuitions makes them significantly different from the simple ideas of sense in the two-element model. Reason has the same characteristic mode of function in both systems, but the introduction of the third element, understanding, greatly reduces the role of reason. By dividing the activities of cognition between understanding and reason, Kant is able to do what is impossible in the terms of the two-element model. He has understanding bridge the gap between the given and the truth-functional entities—judgments or propositions—required by reason.

The device that links the three elements is the nonreductive relation of representation. Intuitions have certain structural features in virtue of their form, and others in virtue of their content. These features do not render them truth-functional—intuitions are not atomic propositions or sense-data statements—so reason cannot take them as the premises of its inferences. However, understanding can take them as the bases of its representations. Because they have structural features, intuitions can be related to concepts of objects, which also have structural features. Once that relation is established by understanding, the mind is dealing with concepts, objects, and judgments of perception. These perceptual judgments are the materials that reason needs for its operations.

The two keys to Kant's system are the complexities of intuition and the mapping functions of the representations of understanding; for these are what make possible Kant's departure from the two-element model. They also enable him to avoid the problems that inevitably confront accounts in which the given is unanalyzable and the connection between inner and outer, subjective and objective, is imagined to be some species of inference that requires a justification.

Kant's system has its problems, but they are utterly unlike the standard problems of knowledge. Kant's problems are intrinsic to the approach his model dictates. He must explain how the given is structured, how the features of intuitions that pertain to their form connect with the features that pertain to their content, how both sets of features combine to provide an adequate basis for the representation of appearances. He must explain the role of the categories—the pure concepts of the understanding—in the conceptualization of appearance. Finally, he must show how reason in its empirical employment corrects and extends perceptual information. All of these, in all their detail, are Kant's problems.

If the text of the *Critique* is studied piecemeal, it will nonetheless need to be put in some context. The dominant context in contemporary philosophy is that provided by the two-element model. Thus, if what he says about space is taken apart from the rest of what he says, his claims for the aprioricity of geometry will be related to reason in the two-element model—instead of being related, as they should be, to the formal aspects of intuition, to the uses the understanding can make of these aspects, and to the constraints these uses put on reason. His account of the role of the category of cause and effect in the conceptualization of appearance will be put in the alien context of Hume's skeptical doubts. His contention that there cannot be time without change will not be taken in terms of the significance it has within his system. Instead it will be tried in connection with the sort of imaginary situation that makes sense only as a piece of methodological apparatus of the other model of the mind.[27]

13. A Spatial Version of Kant's Model

Patterns of sensation no more have truth-values than do individual sensations. However, patterns do have structural features that set up relations of representation. The relation between a person and his portrait is quite different from the relation of a premise to a conclusion, but it is quite like the relation of intuition to concept that Kant takes to be the basic and characteristic product of the faculty of understanding.

From one moment to the next our sensory experience of any moving object changes. Sensory experience can also be changed just by movements of our bodies or our eyes. Although these changes may be in the sensations we receive, they need not be. The changes that are more significant are those respecting form—position in the visual field, relative size, angular distance, orientation with respect to other objects, and so on. Changes in such respects are unlike the changes to which Hume draws attention—the flux of sensations that admit of no implications from one to another, so that what next is given in sense bears no necessary connection to what has presently or previously been given. Rather the purely formal changes (of pattern, arrangement, or whatever) do have connections—perhaps not necessary connections, but regular ones. Regularity is just the sort of midground between the necessities of reason and the sheer contingencies of sense that Hume's stark dichotomies can make no provision for.

Of course, not all the changes in the spatial forms in which sensations occur are regular, but many are. Consider, for example the simple movement of a simple object. Imagine a penny held before you and rotated so the orientation goes from edge-on to perpendicular. The apparent shape of the penny will range continuously through ovals of less and less elongation. At the beginning its apparent shape is a curved band. At the end, when it is perpendicular, its apparent shape is a round disk. The two apparent shapes, though very different, are linked by an infinite range or continuum of intermediate shapes. Now as Hume rightly observes, we cannot infer the next apparent shape from the one currently given in sense—the rotation could stop, or speed up, or change direction—but, on the other hand, there is regularity, rather than merely haphazard variety, in the sequence of sensory images. Next consider a small ring just the size and shape of a penny. Edge-on it is indistinguishable from a penny, but the least movement reveals that it is a cylinder. Finally, consider cylinders of various ratios of height to diameter. As its height is less in proportion to its diameter, we can, for a longer portion of its arc of rotation, see right through a cylinder. That is, we could look right through a wide flat ring at most angles of view, whereas, we could see through a narrow tube only when it was near to being end-on.

These experiments of imagination provide useful examples of what Kant means by *pure* intuitions. We are not having visual *sensations* when we visualize these objects. We are considering merely the visual *forms* that cylindrical and round objects present when they move in certain ways.

The experiments are also useful in indicating the characteristic activity of the understanding. A single static image could be of any of variously shaped objects at some appropriate orientation—as the penny and ring have the same apparent shape when edge-on, and so produce the same image. However, the sequences of images they generate differ at all other points. The understanding can map from one shape in a sequence to the next because there is near isomorphism between ovals that differ only very slightly in elongation. The mapping from next to next among the members of the sequence ties together the whole range of different shapes in a smooth continuum. Understanding, together with imagination, can fashion many such continua as the spatial concepts of different sorts of objects. Understanding can also map the images given in sense onto the various continua. Again it maps by virtue of near isomorphisms.

To see the twofold function of the understanding, we need to distinguish between the pure images of the experiment in visualization and the patterns in which visual sensations occur. The pure images supply the basis for the spatial concepts of the understanding, but it is the understanding that actually fashions the concepts by connecting up the pure images. The patterns in visual sensation are seldom wholly random. They consist rather in segments of sensory experience within each of which there is just the same sort of regularity of change one finds in the continua. These segments of regularity in visual experience correspond to the time we spend looking at a certain object, before we break away to look at another. We need only look long enough at any one thing to obtain from it a unique series of images. We may have to crane our necks or tilt the object to tell whether it has a hole in it or not—whether it is a ring or a penny, a tube or a rod. Once the segment of visual experience is long enough to reveal that, it maps onto only one concept of shape. The *first* function of the understanding is to generate concepts on the basis of pure intuitions or visualizations. Its *second* function is to unite the images of empirical intuition by bringing them under concepts; and, it is not just that the images within a short coherent segment are united—rather various segments are joined together as different views of the same object. To fulfill both of its functions, understanding works in the same way. It maps from form to form.

My use of *first* and *second* in the last paragraph is not meant merely to sort out separate points. It is intended also to order them. The capacity to generate images in pure sensibility and then to base concepts on them is presupposed by the capacity to connect together empirical intuitions by bringing them under concepts.

Hume agrees that there is an ordering, but he thinks that it is the reverse of the order I give. For Hume the sensory experiences come first, and conceptualization follows. In order to tie experiences together at the level of sensation, without presupposing the possession of concepts, Hume posits, as part of his doctrine of fictions, a kind of blurring together of similar sensory experiences given from one moment to the next. Because the changes are so slight, we suppose that there is no change at all. Identity is thus introduced on the supposition of invariance; what changes there are are slight enough to be overlooked, and to permit us to think there is sameness where, if we were to be strict and thoughtful about it, we would have to admit there is difference.[28]

Perhaps there is some plausibility to the notion that adjacent sensory states may be enough alike that the mind can slip from one to the next without really registering the difference, and so be led, as Hume suggests, to posit a fictional identity in respect of short segments of experience within which there is no true identity, but only a constant variation. Whatever plausibility the doctrine of fictions may seem to have vanishes on critical consideration. Penelhum contends that change is an essential part of many of our concepts of objects; so, for an object to preserve its identity, it is by no means necessary that it remain invariant.[29] Hume's explanation supposes us to be imperceptive of slight change, or, if perceptive of it, to be nonetheless disposed to slur over it; but we do combine very different sensory images in the concept of an object. For example, both the curved band and the round disk belong to the recognitional concept of a penny. On Hume's account, all images that depart only slightly from the curved band would be lumped together, as would all the oval images that are almost round. The result of imposing invariance on a uniform continuum of shapes by ignoring small differences would be the same as the result of treating neighboring shades of the rainbow's continuum as being the same color. The continuum of shapes would be broken up into discrete groupings about a number of paradigms: bands, ellipses, ovals, egg-shapes, and rounds, each a catchall for its portion of the continuum. Hume would then have to invoke the association of ideas to explain how these disconnected groupings of images get reconnected in the concept of a penny. Not only is the account too cumbersome now to retain its initial plausibility, but the supposition of the mind's indifference to small changes remains to frustrate attempts that must be made to account for our ability to detect very minute, but significant, changes. Here, I suppose, trial and error can be invoked as the mechanism that restores the differentiations that were earlier removed by the fictional imposition of invariance.[30]

The true test of a theory is not whether its parts sound simple and plausible piece by piece, but whether it retains its simplicity and plausibility as a systematic whole. In advance of any theory, we know a great deal about experience. We should hold to what we know—not dogmatically and rigidly—as that against which any theory of experience must be measured. If we find ourselves forced step by step into a paradoxical reconception of what we thought we knew, we should back off to consider the whole theoretical enterprise. If we do this in Hume's case, we see that the doctrine that all ideas have their origin in the senses commits the entire system to a certain approach. Considered in isolation, the doctrine may be as plausible as any, and methodologically more attractive than most, since it promises to do everything without resorting to innate ideas. Once one accepts the doctrine it is easy to arrive at skeptical conclusions and a paradoxical reappraisal of what we thought we knew about experience and the world. The promise to do without innate ideas must now be weighed against what the theory actually manages to do; and this accomplishment must be judged, not in terms of the theoretical reconception of experience, but in terms of any reasonable pretheoretical expectation.[31] Finally, we must weigh the methodological attractiveness of the simplicity effected by setting aside innate ideas against the inelegance of the ad hoc measures (like the doctrine of fictions) required to derive all ideas from the senses.

Kant does not describe our spatial ideas as *innate*, but his description of them as *a priori* amounts practically to the same thing. Consider the following paragraph from the Aesthetic:

> Space is nothing but the form of all appearances of outer sense. It is the subjective condition of sensibility, under which alone outer intuition is possible for us. Since, then, the receptivity of the subject, its capacity to be affected by objects, must necessarily precede all intuitions of these objects, it can readily be understood how the form of all appearances can be given prior to all actual perceptions, and so exist in the mind *a priori,* and how, as a pure intuition, in which all objects must be determined, it can contain, prior to all experience, principles which determine the relations of these objects (A 26 = B 42).

In the next section, I will discuss Kant's defense of these claims as the only possible explanation of our possession of geometrical knowledge. I will conclude this section with some examples of "how the form of all appearances can be given prior to all actual perceptions." The purpose of the following examples is to show that the synthetic a priori is an ordinary part of our experience.

Suppose we want to construct a machine with two parallel shafts to be gear-driven in the same direction. We know straight off that we cannot simply put a gear on the end of each shaft, and then have the two gears mesh. If we did this, the shafts would turn in opposite directions. We must insert an idler-gear between them. We also may want one shaft to turn twice as fast as the other. To accomplish this, we will make its gear have half the number of cogs on the other gear.

How we know these things is not by the sort of inference we make in ethics. These are visual matters, not verbal matters; but the vision involved is not an actual perception, it is an exercise in imagination. Here are some diagrams that represent our thoughts.

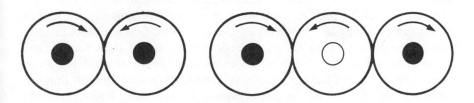

The three elements of Kant's model are sensibility, understanding, and reason. Each plays a part in the example. First, sensibility pictures the object. Then understanding explores the possibilities and patterns of its motion—as in the earlier examples involving the penny. Then reason draws inferences from the discoveries of understanding. The employment of all three faculties is pure or a priori because the object of thought is constructed by the mind itself, not given in sense.

The connection between pure and empirical is direct so long as it is confined to form. Sensory experience alone can provide us with many sorts of information about gear-driven systems: which materials are best for the construction, whether lubricants are required, and so on. These are matters to be determined a posteriori. However, no *sensory* experience is needed to know about the relative directions of rotation and the relative speeds. These are determined a priori.

Many similar examples could be given—the sorts of things that fill the pages in elementary school science books with pulleys and levers and inclined planes. Engineering blueprints and diagrams offer more complex examples, such as electrical circuits, machine designs, and beam and girder constructions. With all of these there is an empirical element that must be left to observation to determine, but there is also a formal element. A rough guide to the division between the two elements is as follows: the empirical aspects pertain to the characteristics of the materials or physical substances involved; the formal aspects all have to do with space and time.[32]

Recollection of the earlier examples involving the penny and the various cylinders should remind us that the a priori determination of the relation of appearances is not confined to the construction of apparatus. Shapes, positions, and motions all play an important part in perception and in the organization of perceptual information. We know without having actually to construct them that a row of five gears will have the first, third, and fifth all turn one way, while the second and fourth both turn the opposite way. We also know that if we walked a block from home, turned right for a block, then left for one block, and left again for another, we would be two blocks from home in the direction we had first taken. To know this, as to know about the gears, it is in no way necessary to draw on sensory experience. All we need to do is map the instructions for the walk onto an imaginary shape like a square question mark. Of course, blocks may not be of uniform length and intersections may not be right-angled; but these possibilities do not defeat the example or promote observation to replace the a priori determination of relations. We would find out that the blocks were not even or the intersections not square by finding out that things did not work out as envisaged.

There are several noteworthy features of our knowledge of formal relations. Single examples support general conclusions. The route from pure intuition in sensibility to the inference that reason draws from the understanding's exploration of the intuition is secure because of the absence of empirical considerations. There is no need to imagine different pairs of gears locked together and turning in opposite directions, until finally we have amassed enough cases to be confident in drawing the conclusion that they all exhibit reverse rotations. One pair will do. Since we are ignoring empirical differentia to concentrate just on form, one pair is any pair. One wiring diagram shows the form common to a million radios. The particular, the intuited example, because it is pure, is also general. Our knowledge of formal relations is also noteworthy for its distribution across all levels and aspects of thought—from the child's simple turning of a puzzle piece to make it fit, to the design of complex electronic circuits; from pictures in picture books to schematic diagrams of DNA; from the immediacy of visual images to abstract verbal descriptions.

14. Geometry and Transcendental Exposition

In the paragraph from A 26 = B 42 quoted in the last section, Kant claims that space is the form of all appearances of outer sense, the subjective condition of sensibility, and that it contains the principles of the relations of objects. Kant proposes these claims as conclusions to be drawn from our possession of geometrical knowledge. At the beginning of the section in which the paragraph occurs, he explains his method of argument: "I understand by a transcendental exposition the explanation of a concept, as a principle from which the possibility of other a priori synthetic knowledge can be understood. For this purpose it is required (1) that such knowledge does really flow from the given concept, (2) that this knowledge is possible only on the assumption of a given mode of explaining the concept" (B 40). Kant then goes on to claim that geometry provides synthetic knowledge a priori. This claim is intended as the transcendental justification for the paragraph.

In short, Kant thinks that geometry provides synthetic knowledge a priori, and that the only possible explanation of this is given (in part) in the paragraph.

Kant's essay of 1763, "Enquiry Concerning the Clarity of the Principles of Natural Theology and Ethics,"[33] contrasts the methods of mathematics and philosophy. Admittedly the essay is an early work, and Kant's understanding of philosophical method has yet to undergo the nearly two decades of development that culminate in the *Critique,* but the *Enquiry* is nonetheless important. Kant characterizes philosophy as basically analytic and mathematics as basically synthetic. His explanation of the contrast is as follows: in philosophy the concepts are given, but they are "confused or insufficiently determined";[34] in mathematics the concepts are constructed by the mathematician. The philosopher is not free to create his own topic matter. He must deal with truth, beauty, goodness, God, responsibility, or whatever he takes as his object of enquiry. His method of enquiry (or so Kant thought in 1763, and so think many philosophers today) consists in the *analysis* of these concepts; he is not the inventor of the things he studies. The mathematician constructs the objects he studies. His method is the method of *synthesis,* because he creates his topic matter by putting it together.

In modern philosophy the analytic/synthetic distinction is primarily adjectival upon bearers of truth-values. Sentences or propositions are analytic if their truth turns on *formal* considerations (of semantics or syntax). They are synthetic if their truth-values depend, in some vague way, on *informal* support from sensory observation. The modern distinction is a result of the turn toward language. It is also nearly the reverse of Kant's distinction. For Kant, the analytic/synthetic distinction has its primary meaning in the verbs from which it derives, and these verbs describe two sorts of intellectual activity, not two sorts of sentence. So far as the formal/informal contrast pairs at all with Kant's analytic/synthetic distinction, formal pairs with synthetic and informal with analytic.

Analysis—even as it is practiced by modern philosophers—is never decisive and clear-cut.

> The signs used in the philosophical way of thinking are never anything other than words, which can neither show, in their composition, the parts of the concept out of which the whole idea, indicated by the word, consists; nor can they show in their combinations the relations of philosophical thoughts. Thus, in all reflection, in this kind of knowledge, one must have the matter itself before one's eyes and one is obliged to conceive the matter abstractly, without being able to avail oneself of that important facility: namely handling the individual symbols themselves, instead of the universal concepts of things. . . . Here neither figures nor visible signs can express either the thoughts or their relations; nor can the transposition of symbols, according to rules, be substituted for abstract observation, so that the representation of the matters themselves is exchanged, in this procedure, for the clearer and easier representation of signs. Rather must the universal be considered in abstraction.[35]

Synthesis—as exemplified in mathematical method in any age—has all the advantages of clarity, rule, and representation of its relations and inferences *in concreto.*

In terms of Kant's analytic/synthetic distinction formalism goes with synthesis, not with analysis. We must now reexamine his contention that geometry gives us synthetic knowledge a priori in the light of the changes in terminology.

The modern critics read him as saying that geometry is formally true because it is a priori, and empirically informative because it is synthetic. The *Enquiry* suggests a very different reading. Geometry is synthetic because it involves the construction of its objects in its notation. It is a priori because the constructions build on pure intuitions. The word *knowledge* is not now redundant as it is on the modern reading. Kant's claim is that these formal constructions, based on pure intuitions, provide us with knowledge. The claim is significant because not all pure constructions do provide knowledge—games, for instance, are created just by the arbitrary specification of their rules and procedures, but they tell us nothing about the world. Kant thinks that geometry does tell us about the world. He thinks that the reason it does is that it employs the same processes of synthesis that we use in the empirical construction of the world from our sensory experiences.

Kant is not in utter opposition to modern philosophy after all. The common ground is a presumption that the mind supplies the form of experience and the senses supply the content. One major difference is in the characterization of the form supplied by the mind. Modern philosophers look to language and logic for examples or models of the forms. Kant looks, initially, to mathematics.

In my criticisms of the two-element model I have contended that the linguistic characterization of form is inadequate to deal with the lower-level processes of cognition. I have also contended that the two elements are too disparate—one lacking truth-values, the other requiring them—to combine in their contributions to experience.

No such problems beset Kant's three-element model. Our capacities to visualize, to discern patterns, to modify patterns according to rules, and so on, could, if posited as innate capacities, work in all sorts of ways with the material given in sensory experience. Nor would initial reliance on spatial skills produce, later on in the theory, problems comparable to the ones that the two-element model generates. It is open to Kant both to maintain that geometry and empirical constructions share certain processes in common and yet to maintain also that other, nongeometrical, processes are involved elsewhere in the empirical construction. The three-element model does not force all relations into just one species determined by a single paradigm—like the connection between premises and conclusion, which is paradigmatic throughout the two-element model.

The developments of mathematical thought in the past two hundred years do raise a question about Kant's contentions. The line between mathematical constructions and games is no longer—if it ever was—clear. This is one of the strong points of the standard criticisms of Kant. Mathematical construction is far richer and more varied now than in Kant's time. Not all the inventions of modern mathematics find application in the world. The question is what this does to Kant's position, and the answer is (perhaps surprisingly) not much. If Kant were arguing that *everything* we construct on the basis of pure intuitions applies *automatically* in sensory experience, he would clearly be proved wrong by the recent history of mathematics. His argument is in fact quite different. He contends that, because mathematics is based on pure constructions and yet provides us with knowledge of reality, reality must be shaped for us by some of the same thought processes that go into mathematical construction. That is the whole point of his transcendental method: to discover something of the nature of our experiential thought by arguing to the best explanation for certain evident features of our knowledge. He takes it as evident that mathematics provides knowledge. He argues that this can be explained if, and only if, our minds structure objects mathematically in the course of coming to know them. The argument goes not from some evident features of our minds to the automatic applicability of mathematics, but from the evident applicability of mathematics to inferences about certain features of our minds.

Kant's first condition on the transcendental justification of a concept is that it be actually explanatory. This raises two matters. First, do we actually have something in need of explanation. Second, does Kant's proposed explanation suffice? With respect to the first, the answer must be an unqualified yes. Our calculations today provide an unprecedented wealth of predictions and ampliative inferences. In practical and technological matters we take for granted the competence of our calculations to determine, in advance, the results of the things we do and design. The second matter is much more difficult. Kant's proposal is not very definite. He does not single out the specific capacities and spatial skills he thinks must underlie, and explain, our geometrical knowledge a priori. About all he says is that there must be some such capacities affecting (and effecting) our empirical constructions. He is so vague on what he means that we are left with the undefined notion that the cognitive processes responsible for mathematics are responsible also for the processing of empirical data, with the result that whatever data the senses supply are bound to conform to the forms that we lay out and explore on the basis of pure intuition.

It is only Kant's second condition on transcendental exposition that saves his position from benign truism. Kant requires a transcendental explanation to be the only one possible. I think that that condition is too strong. We cannot know that the inferred explanans is the only one possible.[36] Some condition is indeed required to rule out ad hoc explanations; but it may be possible to frame a condition that manages this without having to purport finality. In place of Kant's condition "(2) that this knowledge is possible only on the assumption of a given mode of explaining the concept,"[37] we might say that the assumption is warranted if it supplies the most reasonable explanation we can find. Reasonableness provides a good heading for whatever features we may decide are valuable in explanations.[38] By expressing the condition in terms of what we can find, we retain the strictness of the condition while making provision for improvement.

One obvious improvement would be in the specificity of the assumption. Kant does not tell us, except in very general terms, what it is that he infers about the concepts of space from our possession of geometrical knowledge. He describes space as a form of all outer[39] appearances, containing relations determined a priori by geometry. From this he infers that space is a condition of our sensibility. But Kant does not, in any detail, examine what we know a priori, what requires empirical determination, and how a priori and empirical determinants combine to set spatial relations. Does Kant think that it is the introduction of metrical considerations that marks the transition from a priori to empirical? He does not say. Is the Kantian a priori equivalent to modern projective geometry? I cannot say. All that Kant is concerned to claim is that the explanation for the successes of mathematics lies in the principles that the mind uses both to do mathematics and to construct appearances from empirical intuitions.

I am confident that there is an opportunity for research into the innate spatial capacities of the mind. The research could follow Kant's own procedure of transcendental exposition by making inferences from knowledge that is apparently a priori to the assumption of structures in the mind that would explain why appearances necessarily conform to certain patterns. Or the research could be more direct, as it is in contemporary psychology.[40]

The generality of Kant's account leaves much room for more work, but it by no means makes the account worthlessly vague. It stands in sharp contrast to Hume's account, and it shows Hume's whole approach to be wrong. If Hume were right, all ideas would have their origin in the senses, all knowledge drawn from direct observation would admit of no more than chance extension to matters unobserved, and the only explanation that could be given for the success of mathematics and science over the past few centuries would be that we have somehow formed habits and expectations that seem (for the moment anyway) to be in keeping with nature. Kant is right to think that this will not do.[41]

Kant's account is also preferable to the standard modern account of geometry which relies on the separation of pure from applied. It is preferable because it is more general in a good sense of generality. That is, Kant's account is at a high enough level to provide a unifying perspective. Although he does not specify them in detail, Kant does point to the conditions responsible for all aspects of spatiality in our thought and experience. He supplies a framework within which what is right in the modern account can be fitted. We can also see what is wrong.

It is right that geometries can be reduced to logical sequences by reduction to axioms, but it is wrong to oppose such reductions to Kant's notion of intuitive proof. It is also wrong to suppose that axiomatic reduction avoids reliance on intuition. If anything, it increases our reliance. Kant explains why: "Since mathematical signs are sensuous epistemological tools, it is possible to know that no concept has been neglected and that each single comparison has occurred, according to easy rules, etc.—it is possible to know this with the same confidence with which one is assured of what one sees with one's eyes."[42]

Logical sequences do involve reason and inference, but they also involve understanding and sensibility. The mathematical signs are sensuous epistemological tools; but they are pure intuitions because what matters about them is their form, not the sensations they may arouse. Because they are pure, they are both particular and general.[43] A proof is a concrete object that can be checked out point for point. Every transposition of the symbols can be gone over and compared with precise rules. Yet the proof is not just a certain set of ink or chalk marks. It is also an exhibition of the connections and relations that obtain among any objects within which the same forms can be discerned. The rules of any formal system are representations of the functions of the understanding. They set the patterns of permissable manipulations of the symbols in the object-language. Every inference is secure because it is so directly grounded in intuition and explicit rules.

Kant's framework provides a distribution of experience across various levels of complexity. We have yet to see in any detail how he connects up the various levels, but even the little we now have, together with his notion of transcendental exposition, is enough to correct a widespread mistake. The mistake is to regard the employment of spatial concepts in experience as being directly revealed by the employment of mathematics in science. When critics point to the possibility of setting out pure geometries in uninterpreted systems of axioms, they mean to be objecting to Kant's methods of intuitive proof. The objection not only fails to take into account the generality of Kant's remarks about intuition, and his explicit extensions of those remarks to the sorts of symbolic structure used even in axiom systems,[44] it also fails to consider the different levels of experience. It is indeed true that geometries can be set out in axiom systems, but it does not follow that the geometrical thoughts and the spatial skills of the ordinary man rest on a similar logical foundation. Of course, it could be the case that they do—that work in the foundations of geometry actually does uncover the basis of all our spatial concepts—but it would be a gross misapplication of transcendental exposition to assume straight off that the fact of the axiomatization of geometry supports inference to a directly corresponding pattern in ordinary thought. Similarly, mathematical forms and empirical observations may both be expressed sententially in physics; but it does not follow that form and content in experience can be directly modeled on analytic and synthetic sentences (in the contemporary sense of the analytic/synthetic distinction). Nor does it follow that the primary connections in experience are truth-functional or made by reason.[45]

The conflation of experience to the math-science model is a mistake. It is a mistake as well to address the problems of knowledge as problems requiring the justification of inferences—to the existence of the external world, to the unobserved, and so on. These are mistakes because the resulting accounts do not work, and the problems cannot be solved. The two-element model and the epistemological approach may have some merits in respect of advanced thought; but the picture they paint of our ordinary experience is so colored with skeptical doubt and so lacking in perspective that it requires us to set aside almost everything we commonly believe that we know about experience. A powerfully explanatory theory that works well can force us to reconsider our beliefs, and adopt new ones. The two-element model and the epistemological approach do no such thing. They do force us into one set of beliefs whenever we do philosophy in that manner; but when we stop philosophizing, we take up unchanged the beliefs we had.

Kant's distribution of experience across various levels creates an alternative. Rudimentary visual skills, whether empirical or pure, admit of development. We can go from the manipulation of physical objects to the visualization of such manipulations. We can go from visualization to diagram, from diagrams to more abstract schemata, and from abstract schemata to symbols. These progressions in complexity and abstraction are all reversable and transposable. The verbal is more complex and advanced than the visual, but we can go back and forth from one to the other. Visual information can make certain areas of discourse accessible to us. What we are then able to learn discursively can enhance what we are able to learn by visual inspection, and knowledge gained in one mode of experience can be carried over into others. I take it that this is the point of combining lectures with laboratory work. (Incidentally, with respect to the example, there may be as much to be learned about the nature of experience from reflections on education as from reflection on the findings of modern mathematics and physics.)[46] There are countless examples of the multilayered interplay of the various aspects of experience. We discuss a project, do calculations and draw up plans, build according to our plans, and, at the end, see completed on the site what we saw initially only in our mind's eye. Parts of the enterprise are verbal, parts visual. Some of the parts are pure or a priori, others are empirical. There is some knowing how, and some knowing that. The various aspects of experience are combined in various ways, and we need a theory to account for this complexity.

The theory must have the sort of generality we find in Kant's account. He gives enough divisions and distinctions to approximate the complexities of experience—unlike the two-element model, which collapses everything into two categories. Kant's notion of the understanding as a faculty that maps from one set of structures to another suggests ways in which the combinations and connections of elements could be explained.

Kant does deliver on the promise of his approach, but the delivery does not come as a detailed working out of the theory of spatial forms. We could, and we would have to, turn to different authors, and even to different disciplines, for work that would add detail to the theory that Kant develops as little more than a sketch of the spatial aspects of experience.[47] Kant chooses time instead of space as the basic form of intuition to be set out in detail. The spatial is not just proposed and then dropped, and Kant does require as much of the spatial as he sketches; but Kant discovers that temporal forms are more basic to experience.

The contrast, as more and less basic, between time and space can be indicated by a simple model. Think of the sensations that occur at any moment as marks on a flat disk. At each moment the content of the sensory manifold changes with the temporal succession of sensations. It is as though the disks were added one by one to a string, and so brought into serial relation. Spatial relations, as they are directly evident in sensibility, obtain only between sensations that occur at the same time (marks on the same disk); but temporal relations obtain between any two sensations, since they are either on the same disk and simultaneous, or on different disks and one succeeds the other. In order to transform the spatial relations to a corresponding comprehensiveness, some means must be found to align the disks—as it were, to rotate the disks in various ways so that the positions on any one disk would be related to the positions on any other. For example, suppose one were to stand upright to look at something and then to bend over and look at it through his legs, as little children do. The sensations in these two visual displays would have virtually the same internal spatial relations, but from one to the other they are left/right reversed and inverted. The two disks are the same, and, to construct a common space, all one need do is rotate one disk a half turn. Of course, there are many more complicated ways in which successively apprehended spatial relations interrelate; but even in this simple case there is a problem that cannot be resolved by purely spatial considerations. We do not know which disk to turn until we have some means of determining which disk-to-disk changes are due to movements in objects (and so should be left as they are), and which are due to the perceiver's own motions (and so require correction).

In compensation for the fragmentary and local character of spatial relations in sensibility, we do possess pure spatial intuition and geometrical thought, and these alone are sufficient to account for much of what is involved in the coordination of spatial relations given in sensibility at different times; but pure intuition and geometry are not enough to resolve the problem of whether the motion is in us or in the object. This is not a trivial and isolated problem. It is an example of perhaps the most fundamental problem confronting any attempt to explain experience. Unless we can sort out the subjective elements in intuition from the objective, we cannot maintain a nonreductive theory of reality.

The theory of spatial forms could not be developed to do the job because—quibbles about non-Euclidean geometry apart—there is no significant distinction to be drawn between subjective and objective spatiality. Basically, all the spatial relations and concepts involved in intuition, imagination, and geometrical thought are involved also in the empirical order. What differences there may be between visual geometry and the geometry of empirical space are nowhere near as deep and complex as the differences between subjective and objective temporality. Consider that in its spatial characteristics I may visualize an object much as it actually is, but that the temporal aspects of my experience of an object may be quite unlike any corresponding temporal aspects in the object itself. Subjective time lacks duration. Objective time abounds in it. To account for these and other temporal differences, one must seek the best available explanation of our knowledge of things in time. It is this demand for transcendental exposition that generates Kant's detailed theory of the structure of experience.

3

Architectonic and Schematism

15. Transition to the System of Principles

The system of principles is Kant's theory of experience. It is what Kant refers to when he proclaims his discovery of a science of metaphysics.[1] System is central to Kant's conception of a science. Without it, philosophers can do nothing more than argue; and their arguments will not provide the conclusiveness that sets science apart from other enterprises of the intellect. Of course, Descartes has one system, and Hume another; and yet Kant regards neither of them as having put metaphysics on "the secure path of a science" (B xix). To be scientific, a system must do more than merely order and integrate some complex of elements into a plausible theoretical whole. It must ward off alternatives, and win, not just the day, but the ongoing adherence of intellectual laborers in a common field of enquiry. Not even this is enough, because every school of philosophy has its followers, and some schools hold the field for a long time. The system must preempt opposition and overthrow, except by systems that make genuine advances beyond it, rather than just starting over again at the beginning. Only if a system gives this promise of yielding enduring results can it be counted as scientific.[2]

To understand Kant's system, we must understand what he thinks he has discovered. Whether his discovery actually merits his claims for it is a question apart. Even if Kant's system is just another system, it is nonetheless the context in which he places his principles; to understand them, we must take account of the general strategy that Kant uses to develop his system. We must appreciate his reasons for his approach, even if those reasons are not as decisive as he supposes. Any question of assessment must be set aside until we properly understand the object we mean to assess. If that contention sounds too obvious to deserve to be made explicit, consider how routinely, and with how little prior effort to understand it, the architectonic is assessed unfavorably and dismissed. Yet, the architectonic is Kant's system of twelve categories together with the principles he derives from them. It provides the order and arrangement of his discussion. It backs his claim to have discovered a science of metaphysics. It provides the context in which he places his principles because the architectonic is Kant's system. If we set aside the architectonic, we set it all aside.[3]

Before I launch into a discussion of the categorial system and the system of principles derived from the categories, I will say what I take the whole theory to be about. It is a theory of experience, and experience is, for Kant, closely connected with empirical knowledge;[4] but Kant's theory is neither an epistemology nor a cognitive psychology, though it does have important implications for both.

Epistemology is concerned with the philosophical justification of knowledge. I contend that the concern about justification is not, from an atheoretical or pretheoretical point of view, reasonable with respect to empirical knowledge in general. We are reasonably and rightly concerned about the justification of particular aspects of empirical knowledge and particular knowledge claims, but we have to be talked into being concerned about the justification of empirical knowledge in general. The epistemologist does not raise doubts by giving an incontrovertible, neutral description of empirical knowledge from which we come to realize that it stands in need of justification. His description puts us in a solipsistic predicament and then asks us to extricate ourselves using only the devices of the model he proposes for experience. Kant refuses the initial position of solipsism, and he proposes a quite different model. Kant does describe knowledge neutrally—as neutrally as one can—in terms of its objectivity and unity and expressibility in judgment;[5] and he then asks how we come to have it. The fact is that knowledge is unitary, objective, and expressible in judgment. Kant attempts the transcendental exposition of experience as the best explanation of the fact. Even the search for the best explanation does not move Kant to think of us as ever occupying a position of solipsism. Nor should he be so moved since one of his conditions on the adoption of a concept as an explanans is "that such knowledge does really flow from the given concept" (B 40). All that flows from solipsism is doubt, so Kant never sets up for himself the conditions within which epistemological concerns operate. His attempt is rather to propose mechanisms that would generate unitary, objective, and judgmentally expressible knowledge.

Cognitive psychology also constructs models to account for knowledge, and the mode of argument is not unlike Kant's. Facts requiring an explanation are advanced first, and then a model is constructed to provide an explanation. Through Piaget, Kant is something of a spiritual forefather of cognitive psychology;[6] but his enterprise differs in two interrelated ways from theirs—in abstractness and generality. Kant is concerned to explain the very possibility of any experience that yields knowledge. Cognitive psychologists are concerned to explain what we actually know. Kant starts from an absolutely minimal characterization of knowledge;

cognitive psychologists from as much data as possible. They need the data because they want specificity in their models. That is, they want their models to deal with the particularities of mind—the exact stages of development, and the detailed workings of perceptual apparatus.[7] Kant wants his model to be comprehensive and synoptic, not just of our actual cognitive processes, but of any processes that would satisfy the minimal characterization. If both approaches are successful, they are complementary despite their differences—Kant supplies a unifying general theory; and cognitive psychology supplies both specificity and, with specificity, a link to the physiological basis of cognition. Kant's explanations of the conditions for the possibility of experience are much too abstract to be correlated directly with physiology.[8]

Any construction of an explanans from a given explanandum must face the difficulties of possible alternatives. Every new thriller gives a new explanation for a violent death. However, the detective in each case satisfies us that his alone is the correct way to explain *this* violent death. We are satisfied when there is direct factual support for each point of his explanation, and so many facts that his explanation alone will fit. With its recourse to experimental data, cognitive psychology can supply itself with a similar constraint on the construction of its models. By contrast, Kant's minimal characterization of the things to be explained deprives him of the sort of detail that rules out alternatives by supplying more facts than can be fitted to any explanation other than the one proposed. Kant's approach requires a quite different constraint. In order to address any possible experience, he must eschew reliance on the facts of our actual knowledge, to content himself with a description of anything we could consider knowledge; and this requires that he find a different sort of constraint to rule out alternative explanations.

The architectonic gives Kant what he needs. In place of an expansion of the facts to be explained, the table of categories gives him an outline of the form the explanans must take. We know that knowledge is expressible in judgments, and that feature provides us with a clue to the discovery of the pure concepts of the understanding.[9] Kant adapts the clue to his purposes by first drawing up a table of judgments and then isolating the concepts required for each sort of judgment. By itself, this is far from enough to constrain the explanation. It does not ensure that all and only the concepts required to make judgments have been discovered, nor does it properly order them. I do not mean that, as Kant presents them in the Metaphysical Deduction, the table of categories and the table of judgments are not properly ordered. They are. What I mean is that the analysis of judgments by itself would not reveal just those twelve forms in just that order under those four headings. If all one is doing is analyzing the forms judgments can, and must, take, the activity of analysis is itself unconstrained, and it is quite arbitrary to arrange the results of the analysis in one way rather than another. To this extent I agree with critics who observe that the Metaphysical Deduction does not prove that there are precisely these forms to be found by analytic reflection on judgment.[10] However, my method requires me to try to find Kant's reason to be so pleased with his table of categories. The explanation of experience is unconstrained. So is the analysis of the forms of judgment. So too is the abstraction of categories from the forms of judgment. Each by itself is unconstrained; but, when they are taken together, each partially constrains the other. Because the analysis must produce a set of categories that can be used in the explanation, it is not wholly arbitrary how the forms of judgment should be analyzed and arranged. Equally, because the explanation must be of an experience that produces knowledge that can be expressed in judgments, it is constrained to credit the subject of any possible experience with the possession of concepts required to make judgments.

From the fact that it is quite arbitrary how one thing be done, and equally arbitrary how another be done, it does not follow that the doing of the two together will also be arbitrary; and even if the combined activity does remain to some extent arbitrary, it does not follow that the extent of its arbitrariness will be proportional to the arbitrariness of the component activities.

Though I agree with critics who find the Metaphysical Deduction unsatisfactory in and of itself, I disagree with their extension of the fault they find in the Metaphysical Deduction to the subsequent occurrences of the architectonic in the Analytic of Principles. It is as though they see the faults of the former compounded—or at least perpetuated—in the latter. The fault, such as it is, with the Metaphysical Deduction is only that it does not itself give sufficient reason to draw up from an analysis of the forms of judgment the particular categorial framework it presents. The fault of insufficiency can often be mended by more, and I see this happening in this case. When we first encounter it, the architectonic looks to be just made up; but when we reencounter it we can find the reason it was made up as it was. We cannot seriously suppose that Kant first thought up the Metaphysical Deduction with no notion of what he would later do with its table of categories; and that he then was forced to contrive the system of principles along lines arbitrarily laid down. Yet this, since they do not take account of the mutual constraints of explanation on analysis, and vice versa, is what critics who reject the architectonic ask us to suppose.

Kant's views on analysis, as reflected in the *Critique,* seem to be basically unchanged from the essay of 1763, in which he contrasts mathematical and philosophical method. Much of the Dialectic is direct criticism of attempts to provide informative analyses of the self, nature, and God. Yet Kant uses analysis himself—not just in the Metaphysical Deduction, but in sections of the Aesthetic, and from time to time throughout the Transcendental Deduction and the Analytic of Principles. The difference between his earlier and later views, and the difference between what he criticizes and what he himself does, is not to be found in respect of the character of philosophical analysis; both differences pertain to the absence or presence, respectively, of accompanying arguments of a nonanalytic sort. It is not analysis per se that Kant criticizes in the Dialectic, but the attempt to use analysis on its own. When Kant uses analysis himself it is always in the service of explanations. When Kant explains he always relies on analysis to draw out details of both explanans and explanandum. Kant expresses the contrast between analysis and explanation as a contrast between the metaphysical and the transcendental. Thus the Metaphysical Expositions of space and time are predominantly analytic, as is the Metaphysical Deduction. The Transcendental Deduction is predominantly explanatory, as are the Transcendental Expositions of space and time in the Aesthetic. To construct his system of principles, Kant fully integrates the two sorts of argument.

The integration takes place on two levels. First, in the general structure of the system, with both metaphysical and transcendental considerations combining to determine the architectonic. Second, in the detailed argument for each principle. For example, the principle of the First Analogy is drawn from the category of substance and attribute. To defend the principle, Kant relies partly on an analysis of the concepts of substance and attribute (that substance persists while attributes change, that substance is the subject of which attributes are predicated, and so on). His defense of the principle relies also on showing that the concepts so analyzed provide an essential part of the explanation of knowledge and experience.

It is quite mistaken to suppose, as Bennett does,[11] that Kant's philosophical method in the *Critique* consists merely in analysis; and that the paradox of analysis[12]—how it is that analysis can make significant revelations when it relies on connections of meaning—can be met by a distinction between the obviously analytic and the unobviously analytic. That distinction neither works nor reflects Kant's method. To whatever extent analyticities are unobvious, the analysis is doubtful; and it is not enough to maintain that a series of obvious connections might nonetheless add up to something unobvious and revelatory.[13] We lack any guarantee that the meaning-connections of language are sufficiently precise, and consistent enough, to carry us from meaning to meaning in the way Bennett proposes. Nor does his proposal explain why Kant thinks that metaphysics without transcendental argument inevitably leads to the positions he criticizes throughout the Dialectic.

In "A Plea for Excuses," Austin discusses ways in which attention to language can be philosophically profitable. Here is one of the reasons he gives for attending to the sorts of things we say and to the sorts of situation in which we say them.

> Our common stock of words embodies all the distinctions men have found worth drawing, and the connections they have found worth marking, in the lifetimes of many generations: these surely are likely to be more numerous, more sound, since they have stood up to the long test of the survival of the fittest, and more subtle, at least in all ordinary and reasonably practical matters, than any that you or I are likely to think up in our arm-chairs of an afternoon—the most favoured alternative method.[14]

Austin has in mind a much finer-textured method, one involving lots of example sentences and nice choices of words; but much the same reason could be given in support of Kant's uses of analysis. Austin, however, disagrees for two reasons.

> It is plainly preferable to investigate a field where ordinary language is rich and subtle, as it is in the pressingly practical matter of Excuses, but certainly is not in the matter, say, of Time. At the same time we should prefer a field which is not too much trodden into bogs or tracks by traditional philosophy, for in that case even "ordinary" language will often have become infected with the jargon of extinct theories, and our own prejudices too, as the upholders or imbibers of theoretical views, will be too readily, and often insensibly, engaged.[15]

Time is one of the principal objects of analysis for Kant, as we shall see in the next section and throughout the development of his system. Many of Kant's categories belong to fields much trodden by traditional philosophy. So Austin would think that on both counts Kant's metaphysical expositions are not preferable to his own, which he thinks have a more suitable topic matter and a clearer field.

Austin is wrong on both counts. Language is far richer in temporality than in excuses. Time pervades language in the tense of every verb and in a huge list of the most ordinary words: now, when, old, sometimes, before, until, once, then, never, morning, noon, night, early, late, and so on. The common stock of temporal words really is a common stock—common to all persons on all occasions. The stock of excuses has mostly been blurted out in guilt and shame, infected by improbable contrivance, colored by self-pity and self-deception, in response often to the highly artificial and frightening circumstances of the courtroom. It is not the best that men have done to mark distinctions over many generations. It is the worst. It is what comes out when we are caught, accused, scolded—and scarce know what to say, or know too well and try to lie or brazen it out.

Even mild excuses for mild offenses are contrivances to cover up rather than reveal. Not that we cannot learn from a study of excuses. We can, especially from Austin.[16] The question is whether there is more to be learned by a study of excuses or a study of time. There is certainly more to be learned from the latter about the structure of experience.

Kant also analyzes his categories, and many of them are marks left on the language by traditional philosophy. Austin suggests that these will engage our theoretical prejudices "too readily, and often insensibly." I think we can exercise critical care in the analysis of words used mostly by philosophers. It is generally easy to do so; we have texts to refer to. Austin reveals his own antitheoretical prejudice in the phrase "the jargon of extinct theories"; and the prejudice is made explicit when he goes on to commend excuses as a topic we can pursue, "without remembering what Kant thought, and so progress by degrees even to discussing deliberation without for once remembering Aristotle or self-control without Plato."[17] Why should we not remember them? Or better still, study them with care? Their theories may be wrong, but they put great thought into the drawing of distinctions and the marking of connections. Austin's excuses are a weedpatch in contrast to their cultivars. Their theories may be wrong, but they are important.[18]

Philosophical terms like 'reality', 'negation', 'substance', 'cause', 'existence', and 'necessity' lend themselves as well as any words to analysis. The categories with philosophically unfamiliar titles turn out to have equally analyzable meanings. For example, the category of limitation is the concept of degree which figures in a broad range of adverbial modifications. Limitation is the concept involved in many scales of comparison such as degrees of warmth, softness, or hardness, or shades of color from light to dark. When Kant analyzes the category involved in such comparisons, or when he analyzes time or any of the more familiar categories (e.g., substance, cause, necessity), he does not rest his case on subtle shades of meaning-difference or verbal niceties. He instead looks just for plain, well-marked features.

Austin says "It is plainly preferable to investigate a field where ordinary language is rich and subtle"; but the word *plainly* adorns a doubtful assertion. Language may be subtle in its excuses; but, in contrast to the linguistic wealth associated with time, substance, causality, etc., the language of excuses is pretty poor. (Words like 'plainly', 'clearly', 'surely', and 'obviously' usually preface remarks that we sense are in need of strengthening. Where a matter really is plain, clear, sure, or obvious, we feel no urge to say so.)

Kant has no need of example sentences in his metaphysical analyses of time and the categories because he stays with what is ordinary and straightforward. Nor does the metaphysical side of his argument ever stand alone and unchecked. Analysis is always conducted in conjunction with explanation. The transcendental side of the account provides assurance that we have not been led astray by puns, ambiguities, chance connections of meaning—things that make unsupported analysis uncertain.

16. The Schematism: Categories, Time, and Sensibility

The Schematism introduces the Analytic of Principles as the solution to a problem about concept-application. Kant poses the problem of applying the pure concepts of the understanding—the categories—by contrasting them to other, less problematic concepts. We can think back to the theory of spatial forms to find examples of concepts that are applicable because they are rules for the production of images that are like the images of sensible intuition. The application of the categories is not so easy. No simple isomorphisms obtain to connect, say, the category of causality with the things given in sense. There is a problem of explaining how, if not by images and isomorphisms, the categories relate to intuitions and appearances. Kant outlines in the Schematism the course taken by his solution throughout the Analytic of Principles. The outline shows how he takes time, rather than space, as the link between the pure concepts of the understanding and the things given in sense.

Kant's account of *un*problematic concept-application could be just passed over here as having been treated adequately in chapter two. However, it is worth pointing out how much Kant offers his readers—even in what amounts to an aside. The unproblematically applicable concepts are mentioned only to put the problem of the categories in contrast; and yet Kant, in his brief mention of them, manages to correct a widespread mistake about the role of images in thought.

The mistake is to suppose that concepts are images. Other philosophers recognize that the doctrine that concepts are images is inherently difficult. How can the concept of a triangle, if an image, be adequate to all the triangles we meet with in sense? Berkeley considers this question; but he gives the wrong answer when he concludes that, because no image can be adequate to all the varieties of triangles, we can really have no concept at all of a triangle-in-general.[19] The notion that general concepts are blurred copies of the particulars that are grouped under them is also unsatisfactory. Any image sufficiently blurred to encompass the diversity among its particulars will be too blurry to differentiate them from other things.[20] Wittgenstein raises another difficulty about the image-theory of concepts. If images are invoked to explain recognition and classification, they seem just to recreate the problems they set out to solve; for we can think of the images as replaced by a set of sample objects, but we would then have the problem of knowing which sample was which. Wittgenstein is right to conclude that concepts as images do not explain the matter except by creating something as much, and in just the same way, in need of explanation.[21] But it does not follow that images play no part at all in recognition and classification. What follows is that we need a mechanism to combine mental images as much as we need a mechanism for grouping diverse particulars in classes. As rules for generating images, the schemata of spatial concepts are just such mechanisms. They are generalized procedures for unifying diversity, and whatever problems there are with schemata are bound to be different from, and not mere recreations of, the problems with images.

Kant starts with Berkeley's observation.

No image could ever be adequate to the concept of a triangle in general. It would never attain to that universality of the concept which renders it valid of all triangles, whether right-angled, obtuse-angled, or acute-angled; it would always be limited to a part of this sphere. The schema of the triangle can exist nowhere but in thought. It is a rule of synthesis of the imagination, in respect to pure figures in space (A 141 = B 180).

We can think of the schema of a triangle as consisting simply in three lines of variable length—like telescoping rods—with each line joined at its ends to the ends of the others. Like the pure intuitions of chapter two, this device can be manipulated and explored in imagination, with all the various shapes it can generate being mapped together by the understanding. The device fits any triangle, and only triangles. It overcomes the inadequacy of a single-image concept without acquiring the inadequacy of a blurred-image concept.

Kant thinks that something like the schemata of pure concepts must be involved in ordinary empirical concepts—at least, or so his example suggests, in empirical concepts where figure or shape plays a major part in object recognition.

The concept "dog" signifies a rule according to which my imagination can delineate the figure of a four-footed animal in a general manner, without limitation to any single determinate figure such as experience, or any possible image that I can represent *in concreto,* actually presents. This schematism of our understanding, in its application to appearances and their mere form, is an art concealed in the depths of the human soul, whose real modes of activity nature is hardly likely ever to allow us to discover, and to have open to our gaze (A 141 = B 180–81).

I can find no simple device for the schema of the concept of a dog that is comparable to the telescoping lines used to express the schema of a triangle. Maybe the closest we can come to representations of the schemata "concealed in the depths of the human soul" are the artless drawings a child makes after it has gained some control of a pencil and before it begins to imitate the representationalist drawings most adults make. About age three or four a child produces a sort of stylized ideograph which would be more naturally described as a schematic presentation of the key components of recognition than as simply a clumsy effort at realistic depiction. For example, a drawing of a table standardly includes a closed figure for the top and a few short lines appended to suggest legs. It may be noteworthy that, while such drawings do preserve important spatial relations such as top and bottom, the presentation is not of what can be seen from the child's head-height—or from any other possible perspective, since it combines both top and side view. What is quite marked is the abrupt change in drawing-style when the child first starts to attempt the sorts of drawings found in picture books. There is then a clumsiness of line quite unlike the earlier easy and unselfconscious work.[22]

What Kant's choice of example suggests, his comment makes explicit in the phrase "application to appearances *and their mere form*" (my italics). Schemata pertain to the spatial aspect of shape or figure in a concept.

Even without more detail, and even with his admission that he cannot go into the matter beyond a certain point, Kant does a lot in just one paragraph to correct the doctrine of concepts as images. His theory of schematism avoids the over- and under specificity of images, without giving up images altogether. Perhaps more could be added to Kant's notion of concepts as rules for the production of images by incorporating Wittgenstein's notion of family resemblance, which, though deployed originally to combat essentialism in verbal definition, might be redeployed to account for families of spatial images such a dog-shapes.[23] Kant does deserve credit for the doctrine of concepts as rules, and the modern restriction of that doctrine to language should be reconsidered.[24]

Kant is content to conclude the short aside about (relatively) unproblematic concept-application with the following remark:

> This much only we can assert: the *image* is a product of the empirical faculty of productive imagination; the *schema* of sensible concepts, such as of figures in space, is a product and, as it were, a monogram, of pure a priori imagination, through which, and in accordance with which, images themselves first become possible. These images can be connected with the concept only be means of the schema that they indicate. In themselves they are never completely congruent with the concept (A 141–42 = B 181).[25]

I will conclude my remarks on the aside by pointing out that Kant includes it only to create a contrast to the problem of applying the categories. He is not setting out a model of application in general, to which, with a bit of fiddling, he hopes to make category-application conform.

When he first states the problem of the schematism of the categories, he says,

> But pure concepts of the understanding being quite heterogeneous from empirical intuitions, and indeed from all sensible intuitions, can never be met with in any intuition. For no one will say that a category, such as that of causality, can be intuited through sense and is itself contained in appearance. How, then, is the *subsumption* of intuitions under pure concepts, the *application* of a category to appearances, possible? (A 137–38 = B 176–77).

Then, when he has ended the aside, he turns again to the problem of the categories and says,

> By contrast, the schema of a *pure* concept of understanding can never be brought into any image whatsoever. On the contrary . . ." (A 142 = B 181).[26]

We shall see presently what the schema of a category is. What it is *not* is anything in any way involving images. The theory of spatial forms, and the doctrine of schematic images in respect of the mere form of appearances, have run their course, and a new and different approach must now be taken.[27]

It should not be thought that the problem of the application of the categories to intuitions and appearances is a problem that can be confined to a dozen abstract and remote concepts—such that should they prove inapplicable, or should the problem be unresolvable, we could then just set aside the schematism of the categories and carry on. A great many of our concepts have applications in experience that cannot be explained in terms of schematic images and spatial forms. Many such concepts are indeed acquired in the course of experience; but Kant thinks that, so far as they contain categorial aspects or elements, they cannot be explained as mere derivations from sensory inputs. The categories are not just remote abstractions we can do without or leave unexplained. As conditions for the possibility of experience, the categories are presupposed by any account of the experiential acquisition of concepts. With both the spatial and the empirical explanation ruled out for many concepts, the solution to the problem of the schematism must be found.

Kant looks, naturally enough, to time to provide the answer. The problem arises because of the differences between the categories, on the one hand, and intuitions and appearances, on the other. Kant says,

> Obviously there must be some third thing, which is homogeneous on the one hand with the category, and on the other hand with the appearance, and which thus makes the application of the former to the latter possible. This mediating representation must be pure, that is, void

of all empirical content, and yet at the same time, while it must in one respect be *intellectual,* it must in another be *sensible.* Such a representation is the *transcendental schema* (A 138 = B 177).

This third thing that mediates between categories and things that are given in sense Kant identifies in the next paragraph as time.

How the mediation works, and why time is the third thing, and what a transcendental schema is, are all questions I will take up in the next section. I think that I must first try to disarm some objections that have flourished in the recent critical literature. A number of commentators find nothing good to say about the problem of the Schematism or the solution Kant proposes. Wolff says, "The artificiality of both the problem and the solution is evident upon reflection."[28] Bennett says, "Warnock and I disagree about the scope, and about the disreputability, of Kant's 'problem'. We agree, however, that Kant does not solve whatever problem he has. His solution of the hopelessly confused 'problem' about *category*-application is as follows."[29] Wilkerson says, "He solves this fatuous problem by re-interpreting all the categories in temporal terms."[30]

I recognize that not everyone finds in the Schematism a genuine problem and the outline of its solution, and I shall try to say why they do not. In general, they fail to come to terms with the level of Kant's concerns, and they fail to read the Schematism with care. The first failure leads them to construe the problem and solution too narrowly. The second leads to the confusion and frustration evident in the tone of their comments.

One must first appreciate the role of the categories in experience to appreciate the problem about their application. The categories are not just a dozen abstract words together with their cognates. The problem is not a problem about how we use words like 'reality', 'negation', 'cause' and 'possibility'. Remember that Kant's clue to the discovery of the categories is his analysis of the forms of judgment in the Metaphysical Deduction, and that he thinks of the categories as indispensable conditions for the possibility of experience. We must, then, think of the problem as arising on a very fundamental level. Someone who never learned those particular words (or synonyms or cognates of them) could still have experience. However, one could not have experience without also having the capacity to make judgments. We must think of the categories, not as identical with the words we may use to refer to them, but as the general cognitive capacities to which those words refer. We must remember too that the categories are a priori because they are the capacities which precede experience and make it possible. Thus, for example, to think that the application-problem about the category of causality is a problem about how we learn to apply the word 'cause' is to be wrong on two counts: it is not a problem about words, and it is not a problem about learning. It is a problem about us, and a very deep problem. Causality pervades experience. It is implicit in many of our expectations, expressed in many of our judgments. The problem which should be evident to anyone who has read Hume is to explain the origin of this pervasive aspect of experience. One may think that Hume himself answers the problem; but it should be evident that Kant does not think so. Having contended that the origin of the causal aspect of experience is to be found in our capacities to have any experience at all, Kant should (and he does) have the problem of explaining how that capacity is engaged and brought to bear on the input of the senses. This, with respect to the category of causality, and *mutatis mutandis* for the other categories, is Kant's problem of the Schematism. What do these very general, and very fundamental capacities consist in? And how do they work?

If one starts off on the wrong track by mislocating the level of the concerns that give rise to the problem, there will be little hope of making sense of the proposed solution. Here is Bennett's summary of what he takes to be Kant's solution, followed by his assessment of it.

> So the categories, although they have "nothing empirical" in them, can nevertheless be brought to bear upon intuitions; for even if the naked categories cannot be applied to intuitions, at least their schemas can be so applied because they contain the empirical element of temporality.
> This solves nothing. If one is wondering how the concept C can be applied to the class of Bs, it is no solution to say that the naked concept C does not apply to the Bs but that the specially adapted concept CB does apply to them. No difficulty about calling cats "carnivores" could be overcome by calling them "feline carnivores" instead. Calling something a feline carnivore is just calling it a carnivore and a cat; and saying of something that the concept of conditionality-in-time applies to it is just saying that the concept of conditionality applies to it and that it is temporal. The incoherence of Kant's problem about category-application is matched by the vacuity of its supposed solution.[31]

Everything has gone astray in Bennett's account. He refers to "the empirical element of temporality"; but in the very passage (quoted earlier) in which Kant introduces the notion of a third thing, Kant says, "This mediating representation must be pure, that is, void of all empirical content" (A 138 = B 177). The points about B's and C's and carnivores and cats are not interesting in their own right, but they are interesting as symptoms of where Bennett goes wrong. He tries unsuccessfully to recast the problem as a problem about words. He then takes the proposed solution to suggest that problems about the application of one word can be solved by adding another to it. There is nothing in Kant's text to warrant this reconstruction of the problem and solution. Finally, when Bennett finds the problem incoherent and the solution vacuous, he does not for a moment question his interpretation. But he ought to. Whatever problems there may be about calling cats carnivores cannot possibly be complex enough to shed light on the general foundations of experience.

Wolff thinks "the solution is a sheer *non sequitur*."[32] The reasons he gives again show a failure to appreciate the complexity of the question Kant poses.

> If A is identical with B in respect R, and B is identical with C in respect R′, then what sense does it make to say that B mediates between A and C? Either appearances can be subsumed under the categories without the aid of schemata, or else they cannot be subsumed at all. Bachelors and spinsters are both unmarried; spinsters and mothers are both women; but it does not follow that bachelors are mothers. As Kemp Smith points out, Kant undoubtedly has a quite different sort of subsumption in mind here, namely that whereby the minor term of a syllogism is brought under the major term. In a syllogism in Barbara, for example, the major term A is related to a middle B, by the fact that All A are B. Similarly, the middle and minor bear the relation All B are C. A is then subsumed under C in the conclusion, All A are C. But here a partial identity does exist between A and C. The middle term serves to demonstrate this identity, not make up for the lack of it.[33]

Wolff thinks that a dilemma confronts the notion of mediation, which works if there are partial identities and fails if there are not. Like Bennett on calling cats carnivores, Wolff is correct on his points of elementary logic; but that is as far as correctness goes. How is the syllogistic subsumption that Kant "undoubtedly" has in mind actually supposed to work? Wolff must, if he thinks his points are objections, take Kant to be saying, for example, "All causality is temporal. All temporality is connected with sensibility. Therefore, all causality is connected with sensibility." That is the best I can do to fit the little model in Wolff's criticism to anything that Kant might think is true.[34]

Kant might also think it pretty trivial. The doctrine of the mediation of the categories by temporal transcendental schemata has a longer title than text if it reduces to Wolff's reading of it.

Wilkerson says, "The Schematism serves no useful purpose and can in my opinion be ignored without loss. But Kant clearly thinks that it is extremely important, and for that reason alone we should attempt to understand it."[35] Wilkerson's attempt is then made as a survey of what other critics have to say about the Schematism. Not surprisingly, his attempt to understand the Schematism just bears out his opinion that it can be ignored without loss. As Wolff turns to Kemp Smith, and Bennett to Warnock, so Wilkerson turns to Walsh, Wolff, and Bennett. One of the problems with secondary literature is that it can take on a life of its own, quite independent of the original text, and self-reinforcing as each critic reiterates the findings of other critics.

17. Transcendental Schemata

The Metaphysical Deduction introduces the categories without fully giving the reasons for their introduction. The Schematism introduces the connection of the categories with time without fully explaining the reasons for the connection. Neither insufficiency should concern us at once because neither spells the end of the matter. If we need more reasons, we should look for them later. Then if they are not forthcoming, we have a legitimate complaint. However, as we go along, we should take note of what we are given.

The Schematism sets a problem and outlines its solution. The problem is the application of the categories to the things given in sense. There can be no more legitimate or serious problem for a general theory that maintains the importance of a priori capacities for experience. If there are such capacities, how do they find employment in respect of intuitions and appearances? This question ought to be foremost in the reader's mind almost from the beginning of the *Critique*. With that question in mind, no one should look for a problem about applying *the words* for the categories, nor for some simple syllogistic proof *that* the categories are connected with sensibility. Even if such a proof were provided, it would be singularly uninformative. What the reader should demand to know is *how* the categories are connected with the things given in sense; and he should demand that the connection be explained for the categories themselves, not for their names. In making this demand, the reader should look for two things corresponding to the two conditions on transcendental exposition. First, the forthcoming explanation should work—it should be *a* way to explain experience. Second, it should be the best available explanation— *the* way to explain it.

With some relief, the reader should discover that the Analytic of Principles begins in the Schematism with Kant's recognition of the problem. One then finds that certain concepts (those having to do with spatial form) are not as problematic, and not even problematic in the same way as the categories since they admit of *partial* explanation, at least, in terms of rules for the production of images. Some account in terms of the matching of conceptual images to sensory images can be given for them. Kant explicitly denies that the image-account can be extended to cover the categories.

A modest bit of reflection reveals that, however much the image-account can be developed and extended, there will be aspects of concept-application, and many concepts other than the categories, that cannot be accounted for by its devices. This is as it should be. If the categories really are a priori capacities that make experience possible, and if experience is—as it surely must be—the source of many of our concepts, then, in the absence of an account of the role of the categories, much else should remain unexplained.[36] If, without any explanation of the categories, all other concepts and their applications could be explained, it would more than begin to look as though the categories were just idle extras. It would be proof that the categories do not have the indispensability that Kant claims for them. Fortunately for Kant, this is not the case; and, when critics think that they *object* to Kant when they point out that the categories are not the only concepts which cannot be applied to things just on the basis of how they look, they instead just confess their own failure to reflect.[37]

A confusion may arise from the contention that many concepts must have their origin in experience. We must not confuse an experiential origin with an empirical one. For Kant, the empirical consists only in what we require our senses to supply. Experience does include sensory inputs; but, if there are a priori conditions for the possibility of experience, then experience also includes elements contributed by our capacities to have experience. Thus, for example, the concept of being very warm obviously has a origin partly in sensations of warmth; but, in its qualitative aspect— the modifier *very*—it originates from our capacities to rank sensations according to their degrees of intensity. We will see in the discussion of the Anticipations why Kant thinks that the capacity for qualitative comparisons of sensations can be explained only in terms of the category of limitation. For now we need only note that, while he does think most concepts have their origin in experience, he does not think they are wholly empirical in their origin. In the introduction to the second edition, he says,

> But though all our knowledge begins with experience, it does not follow that it all arises out of experience. For it may well be that even our empirical knowledge is made up of what we receive through impressions and of what our own faculty of knowledge (sensible impressions serving merely as the occasion) supplies from itself. If our faculty of knowledge makes any such addition, it may be that we are not in a position to distinguish it from the raw material, until with long practise of attention we have become skilled in separating it (B 1–2).

It may be just a slip, but Bennett's reference to "the empirical element of temporality" is nonetheless a serious mistake.[38] Time is anything but an empirical element for Kant because we do not receive it through impressions. If we did, it would be part of the problem of the Schematism, rather than part of the solution. If time were empirical, we would have to explain the lucky circumstance of our being given in our sensations the most comprehensive ordering feature of experience. In fact, time belongs to the additions our faculty of knowledge makes to experience. Because time is not empirical, it may serve to schematize the categories. Nothing empirical could provide the connection which is presumed to be a precondition of the empirical.

Time has something else going for it: it is involved in every aspect of experience at every level. If, as it seems not unreasonable to hope, Kant is able to explain the interconnections of all the various features of time, he will have at least a partial explanation of the connections of one faculty with another, and of one level with another.

Kant's method combines the metaphysical with the transcendental, the analytic with the explanatory. His description of the need for the mediating representation to be in one respect intellectual and in another sensible is an expression of the requirements of his method. Of course it is more than that; he adopts the method because of the nature of the problem it must solve. In its most general terms the problem is to account for knowledge arising from two sources: the capacity for conceptualization, and the capacity for receiving sensory impressions.[39] The two-aspect method addresses a two-aspect problem; and time lends itself to both aspects of the method, and it is involved in both aspects of the problem. Time can be analyzed because it has a variety of features of just the sort that Austin commends, "the distinctions men have found worth drawing, and the connections they have found worth marking, in the lifetime of many generations."[40] These distinctions and connections also (though not in Austin's eyes) have the virtue of plainness. For example, it seems uncontentious to say, "Time has only one dimension; different times are not simultaneous but successive" (A 31 = B 47), or to say, "Different times are but parts of one and the same time" (A 31–32 = B 47). There are some things we could say about time that are contentious enough to require support and constraint from transcendental argument. For example—and leaving aside technical claims that arise only within Kant's account—we could say, "Space and time are *quanta continua,* because no part of them can be given save as enclosed between limits (points or instants), and therefore only in such fashion that this part is itself again a space or time" (A 169 = B 211). This claim is clear enough to admit of analysis; we know just what it means and involves, but we can think of counterclaims that are equally clear and analyzable. We therefore require an explanation that determines and constrains the analysis. There are many matters having to do with time that require a combination of metaphysical analysis and transcendental explanation.

In respect of the applicability of Kant's methods, the problems of time are very like the problems of the categories. The categories also admit of analysis that requires constraint by explanation. While the categories are, as high-level concepts, paradigmatically intellectual, they also are, as putative conditions for the possibility of experience, involved with things of the senses. There are suggestive parallels between the apparent pervasiveness of time throughout experience and the fundamentality claimed for the categories as its conditions.

There is yet more that connects the categories with time. The analysis of some temporal notions leads directly to some of the categories, and vice versa. For example, the notion of duration involves the category of substance fairly directly; and, just as times are but parts of one and the same time, substances (material bodies or types of stuff) are but parts of one substance (matter). For an example of the converse, consider how inevitably an analysis of causation leads to the temporal notion of succession. Kant thinks there are more than a few such interconnections. At the end of the Schematism, he sets out temporal notions associated with each category, and categories associated with each temporal notion.

Wolff wonders about the associations, and he raises some questions about them. Since it will prove instructive to consider the source of Wolff's doubts, I will quote the entire paragraph in which the questions occur.

> In commenting upon the Metaphysical Deduction, I had occasion to note the *ad hoc* character of the tables of Judgments and Categories. There seemed no justification for some of the items in the Table of Judgments other than to prepare the way for the categories, and even the latter appeared in several instances to serve the interests of systematic neatness more than the demands of logic. This sense of arbitrariness is increased by the doctrine of Schematism. How is it that there are just the right number of transcendental determinations of time? Could the understanding contain a category which failed to find its mode of time? Would a transcendental determination of time, as it were, coerce the understanding into producing a corresponding category? The whole business smacks of that pre-established harmony which Kant elsewhere rejects as the very denial of philosophical explanation.[41]

Wolff intends his questions rhetorically as expressions of his doubts about the whole business, but his questions admit of replies on Kant's behalf. I will first give what I take to be the Kantian answers, and then address the doubts.

Each of the questions can be taken in two ways: either as a question about Kant's system, or as a question about the nature of time and cognition. I will take them in the first way first.

Wolff asks how it is that there is just the right number of transcendental determinations of time. Taken in the first way, the question asks how, and why, Kant has as many features of time as he has categories to associate them with. The answer is that he regards as categories only those conditions for the possibility of experience whose explanation involves time.

This answer extends to the second question as well: "Could the under-standing contain a category which failed to find its mode of time?" The answer is no, for two reasons. There are indeed a priori capacities that fail to find temporal modes—those involving space and the schemata of images are obvious examples—but Kant does not use 'category' as a term for every a priori cognitive capacity, only for those that involve time. The second reason for answering no is in anticipation of the system of prin-ciples. He argues for the principles according to the two aspects of his method, and he requires the close pairing of categories and temporal notions for each aspect. In part the pairing sets up the possibility of analyzing both time and the categories. In part it gives him a way of arguing for the categories, by arguing that without the a priori capacities represented by each of the categories there could be no explanation for each corresponding temporal aspect of experience. With each category there is an explanation of its corresponding temporal notion, and that explanation goes beyond the temporal. For example, the category of lim-itation explains the continuity of time, but it also explains our capacity to make qualitative comparisons of sensations in respect of their intensity. Now, it is because the categorial explanations of time explain so much else besides—sensing, perceiving, empirical thought, the objective/sub-jective distinction, and more—that Kant calls them categories. 'Category' is not, as the first reason by itself might suggest, just *arbitrarily* restricted to those a priori capacities which happen to have temporal counterparts. It is restricted to them because they explain experience in all its funda-mentals.

The second way of taking Wolff's questions amounts to asking why there are there are as many temporal as categorial features of experience. Why, in short, do the categorial capacities prove also to be the deter-minants of time, and vice versa? That is, why are the principles by which experience is *temporally* structured also the principles that govern, and make possible, sensing, perceiving, thinking, differentiating the subjective from the objective, and so on? This may seem remarkable; but think how much more remarkable it would be if we were equipped with two *inde-pendent* sets of a priori principles: one set to handle all the temporal aspects of experience, the other to constitute and regulate the processes of cognition. The two sets of principles would, because of their indepen-dence of each other, require a preestablished harmony between, say, the perception of a change and the temporal ordering of its constituent parts; for, if the harmony—the coordination between the temporal and the rest—were not preestablished, but rather the result of our capacity to effect it, then we would be right back to Kant, with a single set of fundamental capacities responsible both for the temporal structuring of mental acts and objects and for cognition's processes and products.

Leibnizian monads contain within themselves representations of the entire universe. These representations, as phenomena, are organized in space and time; but, according to the monadic ontology, neither the monads nor their representations are really spatiotemporal. The containment of the entire world within the microcosm of each monad is logical and atemporal. If we could analyze fully the concept of any monad, the analysis would unfold the entire complex representation at once. Such analysis of a complete concept of an individual is available only to God, and to us only to the extent of our limited powers of reason. For the most part, our knowledge is not by reason, nor of that which is strictly logical and out of space and time. Instead our knowledge is by perception of phenomena. Since there are no causal interactions among monads, the connection between the representations within each monad and the things to be represented throughout the universe must be preestablished at Creation. For Leibniz there can be no acquisition of information as one goes along.[42]

I do not find in Kant's frequent critical objections to Leibniz's doctrines any indication that he rejects them "as the very denial of philosophical explanation"; he takes Leibniz seriously and discusses him patiently, but he does think that Leibniz gives the wrong explanations, and preestablished harmony is one of the things he objects to.[43]

Wolff's third question is, "Would a transcendental determination of time, as it were, coerce the understanding into producing a corresponding category?" If this were intended as a genuine question, I would take it to be asking whether there would have to be a category (i.e., a principle fundamental to experience) for every transcendental determination of time (i.e., for every a priori principle governing a feature of temporality). In other words, could there be a temporal principle that was just a temporal principle? Or must every temporal principle determine more than just time? I suppose that, subject to the condition that *in general* temporal determinations are coordinated with the rest of experience by principles fundamental to both, there could be a temporal determination that is just that and nothing more. It is a somewhat idle conjecture.

The important point is that the categories are in fact revealed throughout the system of principles to be both temporal principles and also the principles of experience itself.

Wolff intends his questions as expressions of his doubts. Having already answered them as questions, I will now take them in the context he provides to see what is left to doubt. He finds the tables of the Metaphysical Deduction ad hoc in character, and then his sense of the arbitrariness of Kant's enterprise is increased by finding the one-for-one pairing of categories and temporal notions in the Schematism. The answers just given explain why this pairing is not artificial and arbitrary, since without it the temporality of experience would be governed by principles independent of the principles governing the rest of experience. Such independence is incompatible with the ways time is central to, and inseparable from, consciousness and all its processes, on the one hand, and the enduring objects and transitory events in the world, on the other. To this answer, we can add a reminder of the point made in section 16 about the reduction of arbitrariness by the combination of things which, while arbitrary in isolation, cease to be so when taken together. It is not just as Wolff suspects that there is "no justification for some of the items in the Table of Judgments other than to prepare the way for the categories." There would not be any *sufficient* justification for the inclusion of *any* form of judgment that failed to prepare the way for a category. The mere inspection of judgments to find their form could yield any number of forms. Not that it is useless to look to the forms of judgments for clues to the discovery of categories, but just that it helps to know what one is looking for. In fact, we cannot even make sense of some of the entries until we get much farther on in the *Critique*.[44] Maybe it is unfair to take the narrative sequence in Wolff's paragraph to suggest that Wolff neglects the fact that Kant must himself have gone back and forth from one part of his system to another as it was developing in his mind.[45] Each part of the *Critique* is fairly obviously designed to support the other parts.[46]

What doubts remain? One might have doubts about the whole notion of principles, thinking that experience is just not orderly and regular enough to be the topic matter of a proper theory. One might think that experience can be dealt with by a theory, but doubt that Kant's theory is right, or even of the right sort. To show that there can be a theory of experience, and so settle the first doubt, one need only show how Kant's theory works. To address the second doubt—which neither can nor should be settled—one must consider whether the theory has merits and whether alternative theories have more.

Even if we grant that Kant adopts a method appropriate to his topic matter, that he picks as his categories concepts that have temporal counterparts, that his architectonic ordering of the categories is with an eye to planning the system of principles, that his explanations of temporal determination are intended also to explain the basic processes and objects of experience—grant it all and the question will remain: Is it all an elaborate exercise for nothing, or does it actually reveal the structure of experience? The serious questions are about the adequacy of a very complex and difficult theory. They cannot be answered in advance of knowing in detail how the system works.

One final point about the Schematism. Kant uses the same word for both the image-producing rules and the categorial rules of time-determination. This ought never to have caused confusion because he is explicit that the latter do not involve images. Also he uses the adjective *transcendental* only for the latter. One might nonetheless wonder why he calls both sorts of rules *schemata*.

In engineering, a schematic diagram is a plan that lays out only essential components and their connection, without specifying the installation in detail. For example, the instrumentation schema for a heavy machine shows only the major components and the points at which they connect on one end to the parts of the machine to be monitored and, on the other end, to the control panel. It is left to the machinist on the site to find suitable routes for the pressure lines and electrical wires between the specified endpoints. Routing is left unspecified because it is too complex to do in advance, because it must accommodate all the minor bits and pieces in the way, and because it does not affect function anyway.

Image-producing schemata are likewise inspecific. Just as the instrumentation schema does not show the length of wire needed to connect the temperature-gauge to a thermocouple, the concept of a triangle does not specify the length of sides. In general, concepts that are applied by virtue of figure or shape require only that objects brought under them conform to a few essential specifications, leaving inessential details to vary freely.

The transcendental schemata do not generate images, but they do lay out for us the basic temporal patterns of experience. What we will have to work with are sensations, and many of the details are left up to us; but our a priori capacities for experience give us a layout showing its basic components and connections. As sensations occur, they are first grouped and sorted by the temporal patterning of the schematized categories of quantity and quality. The schematized categories of relation then lay down temporal patterns to which objects and events must conform if they are to be represented by the grouped and sorted sensations. (I leave the modal categories for later.) All Kant concerns himself with in the construction of his system is the basic—and basically temporal—layout of experience. He is able to show that there is enough structure in the temporal aspects alone to account for its main features and functions. Just as we may think of spatial forms as objects lacking only matter to make them into physical things, we may think of the temporal forms of the categories as lacking only sensation as content to be transformed (on site, and with only as much ingenuity as we can reasonably be expected to acquire with practice) into states of empirical consciousness, objects perceived, and things thought about.

The architectonic is not a rigid blueprint of experience; it is a schematic diagram.

18. Outline of the system

The stages of constructive argument are set out in detail in the chapters that follow. Here is an outline of what is to come:

Stage One: Sensory Apprehension
> Sensations are taken up into consciousness according to rules that combine and compare them. Combination groups together successive sensations in unified segments. Comparison groups together sensations of like qualities.
>
> *Categories:* Of Quantity and Quality
>
> *Temporal aspects:* Combination pairs with part/whole relation of times/time itself
> Comparison pairs with infinite divisibility
>
> *Text:* Axioms and Anticipations (chapter four)

Stage Two: Perception
> The intuitions that result from the twofold structuring of sensations in apprehension are taken to represent appearances. Appearances are first considered as objects and their properties (First Analogy); then as events and their causes (Second Analogy); finally, as distinct from intuitions, that is, as objective entities (Third Analogy).
>
> *Categories:* Of Relation
>
> *Temporal aspects:* Objective modes of time distinguished from, but based on, subjective
> Duration, succession, simultaneity
>
> *Text:* The Analogies (chapters five, six, and seven)

Stage Three: Empirical Thought
> Phenomena are constructed from appearances by corrections and extensions of perceptual information, and rules are laid down for the empirical employments of reason.
>
> *Categories:* Of Modality
>
> *Temporal aspect:* Empirical thought restricted by (and to) temporal structuring of intuitions and appearances—not by merely logical constraints of consistency
>
> *Text:* Postulates (chapter eight)

(Note: Many other general features of the construction are left to be discussed along with the detailed presentation of the system. For example, the contrast between constitutive and regulative principles, which could be marked as a line between the first stage and the second and third stages, is sufficiently complex to be given separate discussion. Moreover, though the division between subjectivity and objectivity could likewise be represented by a line drawn after the first stage; the distinction is really an ongoing concern throughout all of the second and third stage. The

addition here of such matters would defeat the purpose of the outline—
to present in barest outline what is yet to come. The outline is only a key.
The value of Kant's system lies both in the overview it affords of experience, and in the way he works out the details.)

4   Axioms and Anticipations

Introduction

The form/content distinction is sufficient to account for the division of
the construction of the first stage of experience into two parts. In the
Aesthetic, Kant contends that space and time are forms of intuition; we
have already considered what can—and what cannot—be done with the
spatial form of intuition. In the Axioms, Kant shows what can be done
with the temporal form, which is just the serial relation that results from
sensations occurring one after another. What Kant shows is that the seriality of sensation results in its part/whole structuring by the categories
of quantity. In the Anticipations, the discussion turns to sensation itself.
Because the a priori can be defined as the exclusion of the empirical, it
is impossible to say much about sensation in advance of having it; but
Kant discovers that the relation of sensation as content to time as its form
depends on acts of apprehension that can be investigated a priori. The
actual content of our senses can be known only empirically, as it is given
to us; but we can say a priori that in order for sensation to be given to
us, we must respond to the things that affect our senses. It is our capacity
for response—the possibility of having any sensations at all—that Kant
investigates. The features that acts of apprehension must have for sensation to be possible confer structure a priori on all sensations in accordance with the categories of quality. Our responses to the effects of things
on us can vary in strength; and this links together, as qualitatively similar,
all sensations that belong to acts of apprehension that differ only in the
degree of intensity in our response. Just as the seriality of time connects
with the form of intuition, its infinite divisibility connects with the content
of intuition (sensation).

My *exposition* of the twofold structuring of intuition departs from Kant's
in two ways. First, I bring together the discussions that Kant separates
into the Axioms and Anticipations to try to show more clearly than he
does how the principles of extensive magnitude (quantity) and intensive
magnitude (quality) are interdependent. Second, I roughly sort the two
aspects of his method of argument—the metaphysical or analytic and the
transcendental or explanatory—into separate sections. Most of the terms
and their analyses are presented in section 19. Then sections 20 and 21

present the transcendental arguments that tie the terms together in the explanation of the conditions for the possibility of empirical intuition. My sorting is only rough, but I think that even a partial separation of the aspects is an improvement—in respect of intelligibility—over Kant's technique of bringing in bits of analysis whenever they are needed in the explanation. These expository departures from Kant do not effect any substantive change in his system.

19. Extensive and Intensive Magnitude

The principle of the Axioms is that all intuitions are extensive magnitudes, and the principle of the Anticipations is that they are also intensive magnitudes. Kant defines these terms in the following passages:

> I entitle a magnitude extensive when the representation of the parts makes possible, and therefore necessarily precedes, the representation of the whole (A 162 = B 203).

> A magnitude which is apprehended only as a unity, and in which all multiplicity can be represented only through approximation to negation = 0, I entitle an intensive magnitude (A 168 = B 210).

As magnitudes, both extensive and intensive magnitudes have to do with size or amount, but they are different sorts of amount. An extensive magnitude is an amount made up by the composition or aggregation of parts. Thus, one may have more or less gold by having more or fewer pieces of it; to measure the amount of gold by determining the quantity of pieces would be to measure it as an extensive magnitude. Equally, the calculation of the volume of gold, by reckoning the size of the pieces, would also be a measure of extensive magnitude. The calculation would determine how many pieces, each the size of one unit of volume, are equivalent in amount to the pile of gold coins. Because gold can be more or less pure, we would be interested also in a different sort of measure of the amount. If there is only a trace of gold in the metal of the coins, we may have little gold despite having many pieces. A calculation of the proportion of gold in the metal would be a measure of intensive magnitude. Knowing that gold is heavier than most metals, we might heft a coin. Knowing that it is softer, we might bite a coin to feel how much give it has. Whatever their (dubious) value as assay techniques, heft and give are worth their weight in gold as contrasts to the counting and measuring that determine extensive magnitude. Although we might repeat the tests for purity on various samples, the determination of intensive magnitude is not reached by addition of parts to parts until the whole total is obtained; rather intensive magnitude is an amount arrived at, as it were, all at once.

Gold shows the two sorts of magnitude, though markedly different, are not exclusive of one another.

Since the principles of extensive and intensive magnitude are applied to intuitions, we would do well to consider other examples involving sensation. There are two ways one could suffer more pain: on the one hand, corresponding to extensive magnitude, the pains one feels could occur more frequently, or last longer, or be more widespread throughout one's body; or, on the other hand, corresponding to intensive magnitude, the pains—however often, however long-lasting, however widespread—could be more severe, sharper, more intense. Our sensations of the blue of the sky would grow less if we spent less time looking up or if, as it clouded over, a smaller proportion of the visual field was filled with blue. These would be decreases in extensive magnitude. The other way our sensations would grow less is if the blue of the sky faded. To figure out the extensive magnitude of pains, colors or other sensations, we would go from parts to whole, arriving at the amount only after having considered *how many* (joints ache, moments are pain-filled, or regions of the sky are blue). There is no such part-to-whole process leading to the amount as an intensive magnitude; we do not add up a lot of lesser pains to arrive at a severe one.[1]

In the definition of intensive magnitude, however, Kant does recognize that intensive magnitudes do have a complexity or multiplicity, even though it is one that can be apprehended only as a unity. Kant says the multiplicity "can be represented only through approximation to negation = 0." What he means could not have been shown clearly with the gold examples; for we could as well say that purity can be represented, not as how far we are from having no trace of gold at all in the metal of the coins, but as how close we are to having nothing but gold. The sensation examples show what he means. We have no notions of complete pain or complete blue, nor are our sensations intensively less for being mixed.[2] There *may be* an upper limit to the pain that can be felt—after which we become insensible, or whatever—but there clearly *is* a lower limit: feeling no pain. We would have problems representing the degree of intensity of our pains as a percentage of maximal pain, but we can represent it instead in terms of how far we are from being pain-free. Likewise, the intensity of blue can be represented in terms of how much fading there would have to be before the color disappeared. We can directly sense that something is not at all painful or blue or salty, but there is an asymmetry here. There is no way of directly sensing that the upper limit (if there is one) has been reached. From feelings alone we cannot rule out possible increase in intensive magnitude. This is not the case with the lower limit. We can represent the multiplicity of an intensive magnitude right down to nothing, to the point at which the sensation just fades away, or up from the point at which it first begins to be felt. The degree of sensation is thus a measure of how much it would be reduced before it ceased to be felt.

As the examples suggest, extensive magnitudes are closely related to the forms of intuition. Our pains are more extensive as more times or places are filled with pain. The spatial dimensions of a sensory modality, together with the dimension of time, supply a number of locations at which sensations may occur. The extensive magnitude of a sensation depends directly on the number of locations at which it occurs. Thus we have more or fewer sensations of blue depending on how much of our visual field is filled with that color, and for how long. Intensive pairs with content of intuition, because it does not turn on how many sensory locations are occupied. What matters is how strong the sensations are—how much, not how many.

If one grants that space and time are, as Kant claims in the Aesthetic, forms of intuition, it follows directly that intuitions are extensive magnitudes because they can be part/whole structured just as are the places and times that contain them. I will not presuppose acceptance of the doctrines of the Aesthetic, so I will offer a proof of the principle of extensive magnitude in sections 20 and 21.

Here I will clear up a confusion of Wolff's. He finds a contradiction between the definition of extensive magnitude and a passage in the Aesthetic. The definition says that a magnitude is extensive "when the representation of the parts makes possible, and therefore necessarily precedes, the representation of the whole." The passage that Wolff quotes from the Aesthetic reads as follows:

> Space is not a discursive or, as we say, general concept of relations of things in general, but a pure intuition. For, in the first place, we can represent to ourselves only one space; and if we speak of diverse spaces, we mean thereby only parts of one and the same unique space. Secondly, these parts cannot precede the one all-embracing space, as being as it were, constituents out of which it can be composed; on the contrary, they can be thought only as *in* it. Space is essentially one; the manifold in it, and therefore the general concept of spaces, depends solely on [the introduction of] limitations (A 24–25 = B 39).[3]

In the definition the representation of the parts precedes the representation of the whole; but this is hardly "something of a shock to the reader who has mastered the Aesthetic."[4] In the passage from the Aesthetic, Kant is talking about space itself in relation to space*s*. In the definition he is talking about extensive magnitudes. There is no contradiction. Spaces (and times) are indeed extensive magnitudes; but space itself (or time itself) is not an extensive magnitude. We routinely ask about lengths of times in which something or other has occurred, but we do not ask how long time itself is.[5] There is no contradiction, but there are two different aspects to the representation of a space or a time. First, it must be marked off within space itself or time itself; and, second, its magnitude is determined by the number of its parts.

Consider the first and last sentences of the passage Wolff quotes from the Aesthetic. The first says that space is not a general concept; but the last sentence refers to the general concept of spaces. We would think there is a contradiction here: if we did not take account of the distinction between space itself and *a* space or space*s*. As a whole of which all spaces are parts, space itself shares logical features with mass terms like *water, coal,* and *iron;* but, by contrast, *a* space or space*s* functions as a count noun for which we could substitute *region(s) of space* much as we use *body of water, lump of coal,* and *piece of iron.* The same points apply to time itself and times.

The categories of quantity supply this part of the logical structure of time. The categories are Unity, Plurality, and Totality, whose corresponding judgment-forms are Universal, Particular, and Singular, respectively. The universal is the form in which we would put a judgment with a mass term subject. Thus "Iron rusts" becomes "For all x, if x is iron, x rusts," and *piece of* in ordinary discourse supplies us with the x we need to get a noun that takes plural forms. Particular judgments express plurality and diversity. For example, "Some pieces of iron contain traces of cobalt" *suggests*[6] both that there are numerous pieces and that some do, while some do not, contain traces of cobalt. Finally, the singular judgment, for example, "This piece of iron is bent," works in syllogisms like a universal judgment even though it stands in contrast to possible judgments about other pieces; for just as we would not ordinarily say "This piece of iron rusts" in place of the general truth "Iron rusts," that this piece is bent implies *informally*[7] that other pieces are straight. Judgments of a universal form suggest the category of unity because they are all-embracing (like space or time itself). Particular judgments suggest plurality (space*s*, time*s*). Finally, singular judgments combine the features of universal and particular in a third form (this space, that time). Kant says, "It may be observed that the third category in each class always arises from the combination of the second category with the first" (B 110). The category of totality does not return us to the all-embracing unity of the universal; rather it sets up analogous unities, among diverse particulars.

A time is analogous to time itself in respect of being a whole made up of parts; but it is a *totality* because the representation of *its* parts—*un*like the parts of time itself—makes possible and necessarily precedes the representation of the whole.[8]

The categories of quantity provide the following analysis of time. Time itself is given as a whole and as an all-embracing unity. This is then broken up into times—different segments—by the introduction of limits or points marking boundaries between one time and another. The time between any two limits is represented within time itself, into which the limits were introduced to mark it off; but to represent the time as an extensive magnitude we must think of the constituent times (the subintervals) that make it up (as the totality of its parts). Every time is both a part of time itself and a whole made up of parts.

We can also analyze intuition in the way we have analyzed time. In place of time itself put the entirety of what is given to us in sense. This is the manifold of intuition. It is an ongoing series of sensations. Particularity (this, that, and the other intuition) is introduced by marking off different segments of the series of sensations. Each segment is itself a whole, a sensory unit; a complex, among other and diverse complexes; and a totality, the sum of its parts.

The categories of quality provide an additional analysis of time and intuition. They are Reality, Negation, and Limitation; and they are taken from the judgment-forms Affirmative, Negative, and Infinite. Bearing in mind the intended application of these categories to the content of intuition we can use the following examples.[9] For affirmative judgment, "It hurts." For the negative, "It does not hurt." But we are not restricted to a choice between simply affirming or else outrightly denying the presence or absence of pain. We can affirm *and* deny if we qualify, "It does not hurt much," "The pain is easing off," etc.; from which it follows that it does hurt a bit, but only a bit, and not nearly so much as it would if we were to say, without qualification, that it hurts. Of course, we could also say that it hurts very much or is most severe; but these still warrant inclusion as intermediate between affirmation and negation, even though they express more pain than is expressed by unqualified assertion. It is not that the pain they express is intermediate, but that qualified judgments are intermediate between outright assertion and outright denial. It may well be that we let simple affirmation express some commonly experienced point on intensity scales, and that we then use qualifiers to mark things out of the ordinary, whether above or below the common point; but it is the affirmation/negation contrast that sets up the scales of intensity expressed in infinite judgments—*infinite* because of the indefinitely many gradations that are possible in qualification (especially those involving relations such as less than, half as much as, more than, etc.).

The categories of quality can be connected with time if we think of changes in the intensity of sensations occurring gradually. Suppose we were to mark a time as the time during which we felt a pain. The endpoints of the time would be the moments of the onset and cessation of pain. If there were only the categories of reality and negation, the pain would just be unqualifiedly present or unqualifiedly absent. If there were no qualitative variations in the intensity of pain from its onset to its cessation, every subinterval of the time in pain would have exactly the same content as every other subinterval. Nothing then in the whole time spent in pain could serve to represent its parts; but, if we were to suppose that from its onset the pain grows *gradually* worse and then fades *gradually* away until it ceases, we could see how every moment during the period of time in pain could—despite the common sensory content (of pain sensations)—be nonetheless represented as distinct from every other: by virtue of the different *degrees* of pain.

This sort of analysis of time and intuition is *possible,* though the assumption that all sensations begin and end gradually is unacceptably ad hoc. That assumption will, in sections 20 and 21, be replaced by a more plausible one. For now, there is a different point to be made. The part/whole structuring by the categories of times, and of the intuitions of which they are the forms, requires that every time be an extensive magnitude whose representation requires, and presupposes, the representation of the parts that make it up. If we are to be able to represent the constituent parts of a time as diverse, we must do so in terms of their different contents. One way of securing a diversity of content sufficient to represent times that are wholes made up of times that are wholes made up of times, and so on, would be by the assumption that the content admits of the infinite diversity of gradual change. The point, then, is that the structuring of time and intuition by the categories of quantity *can* be bound up—as to a necessary condition—with the categorial structuring of sensory content by the categories of quality. The definitions of extensive and intensive magnitude, the forms of judgments and their corresponding categories, and the applications of the categorial structures to time and to intuition need not be regarded as so many isolated and separate points. They *can* instead be fitted together as interconnected parts of a unified way of looking at things.

Nothing in the mere analysis of a set of notions, however, forces us to adopt them as the correct terms in which to view things. Nor is analysis by itself constrained to take one course rather than another. Both to show that the analyzed notions, or ones very like them, alone enable us to explain something and to bind them together nonarbitrarily, we need argument.

20. Representation of Determinate Times

The text that Kant puts in the proof section of the Axioms contains the definition of extensive magnitude and the claim that apprehension (that is, the taking up of sensation into empirical consciousness) depends on "that synthesis of the manifold whereby the representations of a determinate space and time are generated'' (B 202). The rest of the text in the section is an effort to explain how the fact that intuitions are extensive magnitudes makes possible the application of mathematics to nature. Kant really relies on the Aesthetic to prove the principle of extensive magnitude by establishing that space and time are the forms of intuition. If the forms of intuition admit of part/whole structuring (if, that is, time itself and space itself contain all times and spaces as parts, and if those parts are themselves in turn wholes made up of parts that are again times and spaces), then intuitions, in respect of their form, also admit of part/whole structuring. Kant seems to take all this as established sufficiently in the Aesthetic to free him to go on to its implications for the applications of mathematics to nature. Not having dealt with the Aesthetic, and being more interested in the basic theory of experience than in the offshoot theory of mathematics, I will not discuss the text of the Axioms.

There is something interesting, though, in the remark just quoted. One (not presently interesting) aspect of it is simply a reminder of the doctrines of the Aesthetic. This is the implicit claim that empirical intuition is not just sensing, but apprehending sensations at locations within a spatiotemporal manifold. The interesting bit is the advance on the doctrines of the Aesthetic. Kant talks about the synthesis whereby the representations of a *determinate* space and time are generated. In the Aesthetic (as in the theory of spatial forms), we are dealing with *pure* intuition. Pure intuitions lack (sensations as) empirical content; as a result, they also lack determinateness. If one imagines (has a pure intuition of) a certain shape, or sequence, or spatiotemporal pattern, there is indeterminacy in what is imagined or intuited. Since space and time are homogeneous manifolds, any such imagined or intuited form could be located anywhere throughout the space-time manifold.[10] For example, to visualize a square is simply to consider a certain sort of shape; it is not to think of four *specific* points in space joined by straight lines. The square could be marked by any four points at right-angles to one another—anywhere in space. Only in empirical intuition is determinateness possible. We do not, for example, just sense a square patch of red. We sense it in a determinate place at a determinate time. Which is not to say its spatiotemporal location is *objective;* at this stage we are still dealing only with intuition. But even in intuition, provided it is empirical intuition, locations are, though merely *subjective,* nonetheless (partially) determinate. The red patch must be at some particular location in our visual field, and the sensations must occur at some particular moment of time, even if the moment is defined only subjectively in terms of the occurrence of other sensations. What is interesting in the mention of *determinate* space and time is that attention is finally being given to the differences that arise only when we move from the pure and formal to the empirical.

The inadequacies of the text in the Axioms (its failure to provide a self-contained argument for the principle of extensive magnitude) are not worrisome because, in the proof section of the Anticipations, in the course of proving that (and, more importantly, why) intuitions are intensive magnitudes, Kant argues well and at length for both principles. He shows the interconnection of the two types of magnitude; and, in proving the principle of the Anticipations, he proves again the principle of the Axioms—at least he supplies whatever might be thought to be lacking in the arguments of the Aesthetic. The combined argument for both principles depends on showing how they alone make possible the determinate representation of time as the form in which all intuitions are given in sensibility.

We can represent the serial character of time by a schema such as t_1, t_2, t_3, . . . , t_n. This schema does not represent three *specific* times and their successors. The symbols represent any succession of moments; or, to put it another way, what they represent is not the moments themselves, but the series of moments. Because time is a homogeneous manifold, it has the same formal properties throughout; so no pure schema (by itself) can represent particular or determinate times in contrast to other times. In order to represent times in a determinate way, there must be differences in their contents that serve to differentiate them. There must be variety among the contents of different times (that is, in what occurs at those times) in order for it to be possible to represent a time, not only as it serially relates to other times, but also as a unique location. Therefore, in addition to the first schema representing the seriality of time, there must be a second schema that represents times as locations when such-and-such occurs: as the t when ———. This schema is also formal and pure—an abstract representation of a time as a container or location. It too is insufficient (by itself) to represent a particular or determinate time, since any time can be thought of in this way.[11] (We shall see what happens when the two schemata are combined.)

There is nothing that makes the first schema, taken by itself, a schema of *temporal* succession. The feature it represents is not common only to any succession of moments, it is common also to any succession whatsoever. For example, the series of numbers is also represented by the schema t_1, t_2, t_3, . . . , t_n, where t is read as *the number*. There is nothing in the pure schema itself that precludes such a reading; alternatively, there is nothing in the schema that supplies the sense of what is meant by a reading of t as *the time*. The operative bit of the schema is not the letter at all, but the open-ended numerical succession.[12] Likewise, the second schema is by itself incomplete; for it only represents location/content, and this is not unique to times and their content. Consider, as other examples fitting the second schema, spaces and their content; variables and their values; open sentences and arguments. We do narrow things down when we put the two schemata together, for we then have a series of locations.

For the representation of determinate times, both schemata are necessary (though insufficient). Since the second schema involves the notion of location/content, care must be taken to make this a distinction. That is, there must be difference between location and content—between the *t* and *what is at t*—because, if locations are not distinct from their contents, we are back to simple seriality, without the addition of the location feature that sets the time-series apart from series in general. There must be variety or multiplicity and diversity in what occurs in time; otherwise reference to its content would not distinguish one time from another. Suppose, however, that there was just variety, that every sensation differed from every other. In that case, the distinction between a location and its content would collapse. Whatever designated a location would serve to designate its content, and vice versa, since locations and their contents would be uniquely paired one to one. So, as well as variety among the contents, there must also be similarities or repetitions, such that a content could occur at several different locations. Their difference could still be expressed, despite their common content, by reference to other times to which they are in serial relation. (E.g., "No, not the *x*-filled time after the *a*-filled time—the one after the *b*-filled time.") With some variety in content *and* some repetition, both schemata find employment. And, since the first applications of these schemata are to the series of subjective times, and to sensations as their content, it is a welcome finding that the content must exhibit both variety and repetition.

In advance of the construction of an objective realm in which alternative courses of sensory experience can be envisaged, one cannot impose on times the parallel conclusion, and describe them as locations in which different contents can occur. That is, although one sensation, or set of sensations, can occur at different locations, we cannot describe how one location can contain different (sets of) sensations *until* we can describe a realm in which different persons can have different series of sensory experience that can be temporally coordinated with one another.[13] Despite the impossibility, at this stage, of representing alternative courses of experience, locations are nonetheless independent of their content in virtue of their pure relation as forms, to time itself.

The relation of times to time itself was mentioned in the last section, in reply to Wolff's contention that the definition of extensive magnitude contradicts the doctrine in the Aesthetic that holds the representation of space or time itself to be prior to the representation of a space or a time. Kant maintains that we begin with an undifferentiated whole (the homogeneous pure manifold of space or time itself), and that we then mark out bits of them as space*s* or time*s;* but he also maintains that, as extensive magnitudes, the representation of the parts of a space or a time makes possible, and necessarily precedes, the representation of the whole (definition of extensive magnitude). Our interest in the two aspects of representing a time can now be increased by adding the qualification *determinate*. The problem is not an abstract problem of dividing an imaginary time-line into segments that represent times (in a general or indeterminate fashion). It is a problem rather of explaining how, in experience, we form the series of determinate (though subjective) times in which our sensations occur as content, and of how we maintain the two (temporal form and sensory content) as distinct though related to each other.

Consider the following passage from the proof section of the Anticipations.

> Space and time are *quanta continua,* because no part of them can be given save as enclosed between limits (points or instants), and therefore only in such fashion that this part is itself again a space or a time. Space therefore consists solely of spaces, time solely of times. Points and instants are only limits, that is, mere positions which limit space and time. But positions always presuppose the intuitions which they limit or are intended to limit; and out of mere positions, viewed as constituents capable of being given prior to space or time, neither space nor time can be constructed (A 169–70 = B 211).

I will begin by arguing against any attempt to construct time empirically—that is, from constituents given prior to it. Suppose we were to attempt to construct an interval of time empirically by constructing it merely from the order in which sensations occur.[14] Suppose, that is, that we try to work only from the content of intuition and regard the forms of intuition as a posteriori. Then we must construct time from sensation. Let *A, B, C,* etc., be sensations. The time when *A* occurs cannot be a temporal interval unless it is a whole made up of parts (subintervals), and it cannot be represented as an interval unless there is some way of representing its parts. It may at first seem that there is a way to do this—by having other sensations accompany *A*. Thus, for example, if, while *A* is occurring, first *B* occurs and then *C*. The time when *A* occurs can then be represented as having two parts: the time when *B* occurs, and the time when *C* occurs. However, the tactic of using *B* and *C* to represent the times that are parts of the time when *A* occurs just stalls the inevitable failure. The tactic fails to confer extent on the time when *A* occurs unless the times of *B*'s and *C*'s occurrence are themselves wholes made up of parts. They too must be extensive magnitudes if they are in combination to confer extent on the time of *A*'s occurrence. But even repeating the tactic indefinitely one never arrives at times that are more than momentary—just unextended instants. For several reasons this is unacceptable.

In the first place, durationless points are not locations *in which* anything can occur. Suppose that we had started with intervals, but bit by bit reduced them to extensionless points. Suppose, for instance, that we had started with a pain that lasted for a spell, then replaced this with a pain that lasted just a few moments, then a pain that lasted just a moment, and, finally, replaced even this by a pain that lasted no time at all (that all our pains should be such). The sensation that occupies no interval of time is never felt.[15]

Another reason to be unhappy about any construction that fails to provide more than momentary times has to do with the nature of the third in each trio of categories. The third arises from the combination of the second with the first, but it adds something of its own. The failed construction deprives us of the additions that would be made by the third categories of quantity and quality. Consider the deprivation of the extent effected by totality—first in connection with time, and then in connection with intuition. Totality brings together a plurality into a unity. With respect to times, a number of subintervals are considered to be parts of a whole—subsegments of a segment of the time-line. But we give all this up if we go to extensionless points. The seriousness of the loss is more apparent in respect of intuition. With no temporal extent (supposing them still to occur despite the previous reason), sensations become temporally structureless. They have no beginning, no middle, no end, and therefore, no overlap. One is never still going on while another begins. Never does one last long enough to undergo change in degree of intensity, because none last any time at all. We might, of course, think that several could occur at the very same instant, or that several in succession might differ just a bit from one to the next—an ersatz change, though not the real thing because we do not have a sensation varying in intensity in ways that might be explained. The best we could have with extensionless sensations would be inexplicable strings of successive sensations differing in quality from one to the next. We would not have intuitions because they require form in addition to content; but in saying that sensations have no extent, we deny them form. It is the absence of form that makes the ersatz quality-change from one sensation to the next inexplicable.

We do not lose just the third category of quantity, we lose the third category of quality as well.[16] We may be able to retain the first and second with extensionless sensations, for a sensation suddenly occurs, and just as suddenly vanishes—and this instantaneous alternation of presence with absence might be taken as some reflection of the affirmative/negative or reality/negation distinctions; but times without extent have no continuity, and the sensations that occur *at such times*[17] never exhibit, and never can exhibit, the sort of gradualness possible in times that have extension. If we could explain how sensations might—perhaps not always, but at least on occasion—begin and end gradually, we would thereby explain how our sensory experience affords us direct acquaintance with quality-kinds. Pains that did not simply click on and off, but that gradually worsened or gradually eased, would be continuously connected one with another despite their differences in degree of intensity. Consider what happens if they do come and go with absolute suddenness. They then differ discontinuously from each moment to the next; and they must differ instant by instant because, without extent, they cannot *stay* the same; indeed they cannot stay at all. But differing as they do, that is, discontinuously, there is no explaining their connection together within a single quality-kind.

One might think to explain the connection of different atomic (Gk *a*-not, *temnō*-cut) sensations, as Hume tries to;[18] but their lack of form, and consequent indivisibility, makes any such attempt unsatisfactory in two respects: first, it must be a connection imposed from without, because there are no features *within* (sensory) *simples* to support the connection; second, if the imposition is either by virtue of the mind's tendency to slur together small differences or by its capacity to effect the connection, we are, one way or the other, giving up the strictly a posteriori account by bringing into the explanation some (backhanded) recognition of the mind's own contribution to experience. If we must anyway recognize the part played by the mind, we should admit to doing it—and do it properly. One should not fool oneself into thinking that a professedly empirical account, which nonetheless does make covert ad hoc assumptions about the mind's capacities (or its incapacities), is still somehow more tough-minded and rigorous than any account of experience that *admits* to having truck with the a priori.[19]

What is good and right in the attempt to be strictly empirical need not be given up. Sensation does play a large and vital part in experience, but there is no need to promote its part by the professed rejection of the part played by the mind itself. Questions about the *determinate* representation of times give the empirical or sensory aspect its due by drawing attention to the fact that only their contents differentiate one time from another; but we must wonder also what the mind brings to experience—for, without its response to the action of objects on the senses, there would be no sensations. Because inert objects have no sensations, we must be able to ask how the mind acts in sensory apprehension. There must be meaningful questions—not just about the operations of the sense organs—but about how the inputs from the senses are taken up and understood. Sensations presuppose acts of apprehension and capacities for response. We cannot assume that the acts and the capacities of the mind are mere catalysts, and that sensation alone provides the stuff of knowledge. Or if we assume this to give it a try, we should judge critically the results of the attempt: seeing how far it can be maintained; how well it works; and whether conditions for the possibility of sensory experience must be regarded as being, in part, constitutive of knowledge.

21. Acts of Apprehension

Hume contends that all our ideas are just faint copies of more lively impressions first given in the senses.[20] Having made the claim he then briefly considers what he calls a contrary phenomenon. He sets up a counterexample to his thesis of the origin of ideas by describing someone who, in the course of experience, has seen all shades of blue but one. He then asks whether this person will be able to notice that he lacks that idea, and also whether he will be able to supply himself with the missing idea without having to get it from his senses. Hume admits that almost everyone will grant both points. First, by arranging his ideas of blue in order, the person will be able to notice the discontinuity of the scale at the point where the idea is missing. Second, his imagination could supply the shade of blue that would have to be added at that point to make the scale continuous. Hume does not address this hypothetical exception except to remark that it is *so singular and unimportant* that it does not warrant the modification of his doctrine that all ideas have their origin in the senses.

Consider someone who lacks two ideas of blue, or three, or more. He seems as well-placed as the person in the example to make up his deficiencies with a little imagination—with no more imagination, and no other capacities than Hume supposes he has. Hume claims, just a page before his discussion of the missing shade of blue, that the mind has the capacity to augment or diminish the materials given in sense. He evidently does not appreciate the consequences of this claim for his doctrine of the origin of ideas.

Given both the capacity to arrange the ideas in order and to augment or diminish them, the person need not experience more than *two* ideas of blue in order to supply himself with all the rest. He can imagine another blue halfway between the first two, then ones halfway between those, and so on. He can extrapolate to shades as much greater in intensive magnitude as the greater of the two given ones is than the lesser, and, again, so on. From the capacities that Hume casually supposes us to have, we could generate whole spectra of qualities from a few examples and the relations of comparison that obtain between them.

One should wonder where Hume goes wrong—in making the claims about our capacities, or in failing to take account of just how contrary the phenomenon is. I think he goes wrong both ways. We are straining at gnats if, in the empirical construction of experience, we worry about some matters like induction and causal connection, while capacities to augment and diminish ideas, to associate and combine them, to order and arrange them have all been tossed into the pot without first having been inspected. But we do have these capacities, and so must give up Hume's doctrine of the origin of ideas.

Hume's doctrine must go because the capacities involved in qualitative comparisons of sensations cannot be denied. Not only are they evident in experience, but without them we could not make any use of sensory impressions. If sensations did not admit of the comparisons in virtue of their intensive magnitudes, each sensation would either differ completely from any other or else be identical with it. In which case, even the slightest change in the effect of an object on our senses would produce different sensations in us, and these could not, in the absence of the capacities for qualitative comparison, be related to each other as minor variants of a common kind. However, if sensations do admit of difference in degree only, and if we have the capacities to compare them in respect of intensive magnitude, we can overcome slight changes in the effects of objects on our senses by regarding any sensation as practically equivalent to its near neighbors on a sensory continuum. Thus, for example, a thing can have a normal range of color, rather than a set of discrete, different, and internally unrelated colors. One might think to avoid the admission of such capacities by positing *incapacities* instead. To overcome the problem of slight changes in the effects of objects, one might think to describe us as built with fairly loose tolerances such that we just do not pick up on the minor variations. This would work to explain the perception of objects; but it would render inexplicable our perception of gradual changes in events such as fading, softening, etc.[21]

Just as we can combine intuitions in respect of their form by reference to the continua of shape described in the theory of spatial forms, we can also combine them in respect of their content by reference to continua of degree. What must now be explained is how the latter combination is possible.

It is implausible and unnecessary to suppose that sensations at all times admit of the gradual sort of change that would occur if we watched butter soften or heard a dynamic variation in music. Sensations may on occasion change gradually in this way. Perhaps it is arguable that they must on occasion change in this way to acquaint us directly and perspicuously with the variation to which they are susceptible; but the thesis to be argued is that, in *all* appearances, the sensations of them have a degree of intensity—whether they show it by the gradual change of their sensory qualities or not. What must be argued against, then, is that sensations are either just present or else just absent—that is, that their occurrence is governed only by the first two categories of quality, without the third governing their occurrence as well. When sensory qualities of objects change gradually, it is unproblematic to represent the passage of time; but it is no less important—if much more problematic—to represent, as an interval of time, the time during which a sensation of fairly constant intensity occurs. Suppose my pain stays constant for a time. How am I conscious of this fact, when there is no moment-by-moment change (in intensity—we have seen that the accompaniment of other sensations will not do) to register the passage of time?

Since, by hypothesis, the answer cannot be found in the accusatives of apprehension—for we are supposing the sensations *not* to be changing gradually—the answer must lie in apprehension itself. If consciousness of the moments of pain cannot be traced to changes in the pain sensation because the pain stays constant, then the temporal consciousness must be traced to consciousness itself, rather than to its object. In sensation we have two things: the effect of an object on us, or an effect of a cause within our bodies; and our response to that effect. If, because of its constancy, the former cannot supply determinate representation of time, the latter must.

Explanatory arguments that work by excluding alternatives are satisfactory only if there is assurance that what is left at the end of the eliminations does explain the matter in hand. We have ruled out empirical construction by argument. We have set aside gradual change within every sensation as an implausible assumption. We are left with the acts of apprehension themselves as the only possible explanation of our consciousness of the passage of time. But we need assurance. In part, Kant supplies this in the details of his proof. In part, it is supplied by virtue of the fact that the explanation of the temporal matters also explains our capacity to compare sensations. We can be more content that we have the explanation of one matter if the same explanation will cover another matter as well; for in that case we can wield Occam's razor in our defense, since the rejection of the one unifying explanation would require that two explanations be found to take its place.

Extensive magnitudes are apprehended *as multiplicities*. We are aware that there are pains in many places; and we go from parts to whole in reckoning the extent of our pain. And when we represent to ourselves how much of the sky is blue, we do so on the basis of how many patches of blue we see. By contrast, intensive magnitudes are apprehended *as unities*. We do not add up a lot of mild pains to get a severe one, nor go from many faint blues to a rich blue.

Because the representation of extensive magnitude goes from part to whole it takes time; and the time it takes has the seriality (first this, then this, then this, . . .) for which the categories of quantity are responsible through the schema of number. In contrast to the apprehension of an extensive magnitude, the apprehension of an intensive magnitude can be described as momentary or instantaneous. Kant says this in the first sentence of a paragraph beginning on A 167 = B 209: "Apprehension by means merely of sensation occupies only an instant (if, that is, I do not take into account the succession of many sensations)."[22] Apprehension of *extensive* magnitude is *not* by means merely of sensation since it involves adding together various parts of a whole. Extensive magnitude therefore depends on the spatiotemporal patterns of sensation, and it does not depend merely on sensation itself. In contrast to the apprehension of an extensive magnitude, the apprehension by means merely of sensation can be described as occupying only an instant. This *comparative instantaneousness* should not be confused with the *absolute instantaneousness* of mere points in time (against which earlier arguments were directed on the ground that an instant is not an interval *in which* anything can occur). The contrast is between the succession involved in going from parts to whole (with extensive magnitude) and the arrival at once at intensive magnitude (apprehended only as unity).

In the remainder of the paragraph beginning on A 167 = B 209, Kant makes three distinct points.

First, he associates sensation with the real in appearance, and its absence with negation. The association is intended to set up another offshoot theory like the theory in the Axioms about the application of mathematics. What Kant is setting up for inclusion at the end of the Anticipations is a demonstration of "the great value of our principle" (A 172 = B 213), that is, of the principle of intensive magnitude, despite the fact that it is entirely a priori. This demonstration begins on A 173 = B 215, and it carries on through to the end of the proof of the Anticipations. What Kant means to show is that, by virtue of its admitting of degree, sensation, and the corresponding real, may occupy space in varying amounts—without the variation in amount being reducible, as it is in the Newtonian ontology, to particles per unit of volume. He shows that his principle of intensive magnitude sets up the *possibility* of a plenum theory such as Descartes', though he does not think the principle determines which is right: particles in a void, or space without vacua, but filled everywhere with matter of varying density.[23]

As with the extension of the principle of the Axioms to its role in explaining the application of mathematics, the extension of the principle of the Anticipations to physics takes the discussion beyond the basic theory of experience. I think Kant would have been better understood if he had restricted his discussion to the base theory, leaving its consequences in the offshoots for some later discussion.

The *second* point in the paragraph concerns fundamental matters. Kant says that every sensation "is capable of diminution, so that it can decrease and gradually vanish. Between reality in the appearance and negation there is therefore a continuous connection of many possible intermediate sensations, the difference between any two of which is always smaller than the difference between the given sensation and zero or complete negation" (A 168 = B 210).[24] This is the main point to be proved and explained. In part, the proof and explanation are given on the next page, from which I have already quoted and discussed Kant's remarks about space and time as *quanta continua,* and about instants as mere limits, not times *in which* anything can occur. There is another part to the proof and explanation of the fact that every sensation is capable of diminution, etc. This part is the third point in the paragraph.

Thirdly, Kant says, "the real in appearance has always a magnitude. But since its apprehension by means of mere sensation takes place in an instant and not through successive synthesis of many sensations, and therefore does not proceed from the parts to the whole, the magnitude is not to be met with in the apprehension" (ibid.).[25]

Kemp Smith follows Wille in changing *nicht* to *nur;* and he thus changes the final phrase to read as follows: "the magnitude is to be met with only in the apprehension." This is not just wrong—it misses the main point of the proof. We do not sense the magnitude of a sensation. I feel pain, not *the degree of* pain. I have a sensation of a color, but no sensation of *its degree of* brightness. The pain may be intense or the color bright, and I may be very aware that it is intense or bright; but I do not, in apprehension, meet with measures of pain intensity or of color brightness. It is because intensive magnitude is not to be met with in apprehension that it requires proof and explanation. It is the reason too that the argument for the principle of intensive magnitude requires us to consider the mind's own contribution in the act of apprehension; for, if we did sense degrees of intensity, no account would need to be taken by the mind of its own capacity to respond to the effects of things to varying degrees.

One may in the course of experience learn to judge very accurately the sweetness of a wine, the gauge of sandpaper or emery, the pitch of a musical note, the temperature of a sugar syrup, etc., and so be described as apprehending intensive magnitude; but such capacities for direct awareness of the degrees of some sensory quality are not basic, but derivative. One learns eventually how long to cook the syrup for hard sweets or for fudge without having still to use the candy thermometer; and one may, in time, be able to tell that it has reached 300°F or 235°F—at first indirectly by feeling bits of it that have cooled in water, later by feeling its resistance to stirring, and finally just by a glance at how it is bubbling. But degrees Fahrenheit are not, strictly speaking, met with in apprehension (nor are cycles per second, decibels, parts per million, or any other measures corresponding to degrees of intensity). We have sensations of heat, color, resistance, pain, pressure, saltiness, acridity, and so on. All of these, and some in several ways, admit of degrees of intensity; they thereby allow us to make comparisons. After much experience, we may make such comparisons very easily. But what is basic, and what must be explained, is how we are able in the first place to make the comparisons.

In defense of his alteration of the text (from *nicht* to *nur*), Kemp Smith asks us to compare the paragraph added in B. His translation of that leaves much to be desired because it changes the referents of two key pronouns, as well as the order of the paragraph. Here, with two minor changes,[26] is Max Müller's translation:

> Perception is empirical consciousness, that is, a consciousness in which there is at the same time sensation. Appearances, as objects of perception, are not pure (merely formal) intuitions, like space and time (for space and time can never be perceived by themselves). They contain, therefore, over and above the intuition, the material for some one object in general (through which something existing in space and time is represented); that is, they contain the real of sensation, as a merely subjective representation, which gives us only the consciousness that the subject is affected, and which is referred to some object in general. Now there is a gradual transition possible from empirical to pure consciousness, till the real of it vanishes completely and there remains a merely formal consciousness (a priori) of the manifold in space and time; and, therefore, a synthesis also is possible in the production of the quantity of a sensation, from its beginning, that is, from the pure intuition = 0, onwards to any quantity of it. As sensation by itself is no objective representation, and as in it* the intuition of neither space nor time can be found, it follows that though not an extensive, yet some kind of quantity must belong to it* (and this through the apprehension of it*, in which the empirical consciousness may grow in a certain time from nothing = 0 up to its given amount). That *quantity* must be *intensive,* and corresponding to it, an intensive quantity, i.e. a degree of influence upon the senses, must be attributed to all objects of perception, so far as it contains sensation (B 207–8).

I take each of the pronouns marked with * to refer back to sensation at the beginning of the sentence. Kemp Smith breaks the sentence in two—making intensive magnitude the subject, and predicating empirical consciousness of it. This forces him into the later substitution of *nur* for *nicht*.

The passage as a whole brings to a climax the argument for the principles of extensive and intensive magnitude. It also helps to make intelligible Kant's doctrine of time as the form of inner sense.

The argument for the principles begins with the analysis of temporal concepts. In the analysis times are represented as parts of the whole of time itself, as being in series, and as the locations in which things may occur. These analytic representations are indeterminate because they apply generally and without differentiation to all times. The determinate representation requires that times be individuated—identified and distinguished one from another—by virtue of their differing content; but it is argued that with nothing but difference the form/content distinction would collapse since the representation of any content would also uniquely specify the time of that content's occurrence, and vice versa. To preserve the form/content distinction, there must be repetitions in sensory content; and this introduces the notion of qualitative comparisons at the level of sensation. We could, but should not, with Hume, just posit the capacity to find resemblances among sensations; for, if we do, then the similarity relation is just imposed on sensations without any features within them warranting the imposition. If we think how a gradual change in the intensity of a sensation reveals continuous connection, and then consider how the differences in degree afford differentiation in the content of intuition from any moment to the next—requisite for the determinate representation of times as intervals *within which* sensation occurs—then we can take it that there can be perspicuous evidence of the mind's capacity to respond more or less strongly to the effects of objects on it. It is not necessary to suppose that in every case the onset and diminution of a sensation are gradual; but it is essential to recognize that every sensation occurs only because there is a corresponding capacity for response to the cause of the sensation, and that this capacity is exercised in the case of every sensation as an act of apprehension. When the object of apprehension is a sensation of fairly constant intensity, there is nothing in it to mark the passage of time; nor can the passage of time be marked by accompanying sensations, for that leads to an infinite regress. There is, however, the possibility that the mind somehow monitors its own actions; and that it is because it goes on responding, and knows that it does, that it is conscious of the nonmomentary character of the time in which a sensation of constant intensity occurs.

Sensations are either constant or not. If not, then the times in which they occur are sufficiently represented as intervals by their content's continuous variation in degree. If, on the other hand, they are constant, the mind must be supposed to be in some way conscious of the passage of time through its consciousness of its own act of apprehension, for it can then find no difference from one moment to the next in what it senses. Suppose the first alternative occurs—a gradual sensation is given in sensory awareness. Then we have a basis for knowing that sensations and the empirical consciousness by which they are accompanied are susceptible of difference in respect of their degrees. Suppose the second alternative; then the nonmomentary character of the time of the occurrence of any sensation—a fortiori of the occurrence of a constant sensation—again ensures that the act of apprehension be somehow recognized by the mind. Whether by direct acquaintance with the variability of the strengths of its responses, or by inference from the nonmomentary character of the times of the occurrence of its objects, the mind reveals its own temporality.

In the long passage just quoted, Kant talks of the *possibility* of a gradual transition from empirical to pure consciousness, and vice versa. It is not that we actually experience every sensation through its onset by degrees and its gradual diminution—just that we could have. We could not be so constructed that causes acting on our senses, as it were, flipped a switch and we just had a sensation or ceased having it. They rather start our motor, and it runs for as long as it may. The onset or cessation may *seem* both sudden and imposed from without; but reflection on the requirements of the *determinate* representation of times *as intervals* should persuade us that we do, whether we realize it or not, build into our consciousness—even that consciousness which is based on constant or invariant sensations—some temporal structuring that derives from the acts of apprehension, and not from their objects.

What sort of thing must the mind take account of in its own operations in the acts of apprehension? Minimally, it must know the amount of its arousal in response to sensory stimulus. As a simple sensation a mild pain is as unlike a severe pain as it is unlike a color; but of course we do apprehend the connection. The connection could be perspicuously represented by a mild pain that grows continuously until it is severe, or by a severe one that eases until it is mild; or it might be that even with the sudden onset of a severe pain the mind still recognizes its kinship with, and departure from only in degree, a mild pain that *could have* come on gradually, and that the basis for the recognition is the mind's cognizance of the identity of the acts by which it suffers pains whether mild or severe.

If the mind does somehow account for its own action in response to the effects of objects on its senses, the relation of its a priori forms, conceptual or intuitive, to their concrete embodiment in experience is not the utter separation in kind that one finds in Cartesian dualism. The twain can meet gradually as the first flicker of response to the effects of objects acting on our senses begins to be felt in sensibility, and on up as the response grows stronger. Or from the full flush of sensory arousal down through the diminution of response to the sorts of pure forms we consider in geometrical or other reflection.

There is a link between the empirical and the pure that binds all conscious states together. Kant says,

Whatever the origin of our representations, whether they are due to the influence of outer things, or are produced through inner causes, whether they arise a priori, or being appearances have an empirical origin, they must all, as modifications of the mind, belong to inner sense. All our knowledge is thus finally subject to time, the formal condition of inner sense. In it they must be ordered, connected, and brought into relation. This is a general observation which, throughout what follows, must be borne in mind as quite fundamental (A 98–99).

He makes that comment to introduce a section of A Deduction entitled "The Synthesis of Apprehension in Intuition." He also says, elsewhere, "Time is nothing but the form of inner sense" (A 33 = B 49); and, "inner sense, the essence of all representation" (A 177 = B 220).

I do not propose to offer here any attempt at a full account of Kant's doctrine of inner sense. My reason for mentioning it at all is that I think it must be brought in with the mind's recognition of its own acts of consciousness, especially when that recognition provides the basis for whatever aspects of temporal structuring cannot be supposed to be grounded in the objects of empirical awareness, but which must, instead, be supposed to be grounded in the mind's recognition of the temporality of its own acts.

In the paragraph added in B, Kant says, appearances "contain the real of sensation, as a merely subjective representation, which gives us only the consciousness that the subject is affected, and which is referred to some object in general." Then, a bit farther on he says, "Sensation by itself is no objective representation. . . ." The subjective/objective distinction is not yet established at this stage of the construction, but there is consciousness that the subject (one's own mind) is affected. This consciousness comes about because the mind cannot attend only to its sensory ideas, but must take account also of its own capacity for response. The mind recognizes that it is being affected, and responding to the effect— though it can refer the effect only to some object in a general (= indeterminate) way. The mind knows that something is happening to it, that it is being acted on by an (unspecified) object, that it is responding to the effect, and that its response has a certain measure of strength.

Notions like consciousness, awareness, and knowledge are not suited to drawing sharp lines between what belongs or does not belong to cognition. In saying that the mind must be aware of its own acts, and that it must know something of them, I am not even trying to isolate candidate answers that we would readily give to the question, "What are you thinking about?" I am not interested in what we may, or may not, come up with when we are prompted to introspect.[27]

There are ways of using the terms that do lend themselves to greater definition in the scope of application. This is most easily illustrated in experiments. We could wonder, for instance, whether a certain factor plays a part it cognition, and construct an experiment to find out. For example, we might wonder whether the apparent direction of the sources of incoming sounds plays a part in the ability to walk in a straight line when blindfolded (or blind).[28] I could conjecture how experiments might be designed to test this, but that is not the point. The point is rather that, should the experiments show that we use sounds much as airplanes use radio signals to steer by, we could say things like the following: "We know how to maintain a straight course when walking blindfolded because we know how we are oriented with respect to sound sources, and we know how to correct continuously for the changes in orientation that occur as we move along." I have not the slightest idea whether it is true that we do use sounds to steer by, but that is just the point. If I do steer by sound, I know all the things that the report of the experiment attributes to me as cognitive capacities, whether I know that I know them or not.

Some of the things we know (perhaps without knowing that we know them) can be determined nonexperimentally. This is Kant's project: to determine a priori some of the essential constituents, mechanisms, abilities, and capacities that function as conditions for the possibility of experience. His claim that sensation gives us only consciousness that the subject is affected must be understood to be using *consciousness* in a report of what has been ascertained by analysis and argument—not in a report of introspective findings. Introspection may come up with nothing but sensations, memories, and certain ideas, but we have no reason to suppose that everything in thought—or all that is central to cognition—is accessible to introspection.

We must not think of inner sense as comprising only what we perceive in ourselves in the sort of self-perception that Berkeley means when he says that, "Everyone is the best judge of what he perceives, and what not."[29] If we were so to restrict the content and nature of inner sense, we should be hard pressed indeed to find in it enough to justify saying that time is nothing but the form of inner sense. Of course, even in introspection we find that our thoughts follow one another, and that many of them have temporal aspects; but we will no more find the root and source of temporality by merely turning our gaze inward than we will by directing it through our senses to the world around us. Time is not given as part of the empirical input to the mind, whether the input originates within our bodies or without. Inner sense cannot be restricted to introspection or to the overt consciousness that accompanies sensing, though it includes them. It includes *also,* and with relevance to the origins of time, *especially,* the self's monitoring of itself that is discoverable only experimentally, or by such arguments as Kant's.

22. Kant's Characterization of Sensing and Intuition

We could say much more than Kant does about the sensorily given and the giving of it if we turned to psychology. Extensive magnitude invites reference to Gestalt psychology, and intensive magnitude at once suggests Weber's (or Fechner's) Law.[30] We could say more, too, if, with Hume, we helped ourselves to a posteriori observations concerning our capacities to modify and connect our ideas. It is not sheer cussedness, or the sort of fun we have in a sack race, that commends Kant's method of investigation, which works hard for a modest result. In part, he wants to determine how much, and what, of our cognition is essential to it. Psychological or philosophical characterizations that are observationally based find only what we *in fact* do—not what we *necessarily* do. In part, this concentration on essentials reveals things that would be hidden among more details. I will let these parts stand without discussion, but there is another part I will discuss. The given and the giving of it do not occur in isolation from the rest of experience. They are not preconceptual data unaffected by what use the mind makes of them. Whether we introspect or observe in others, what we see when we look at sensing and sensations are things shaped by their participation in experience. To find what the given and giving contribute of themselves to experience, one must somehow strip them of whatever aspects they have because of their associations with the rest of experience. This is what Kant's method of investigation is designed to do; and, if his findings are somewhat less rich than those of rival methods of investigation, they are also more accurate in their characterization of sensing and intuition.

Kant discovers only two features of intuitions. They have extensive and intensive magnitude. Possession of the first feature means that sensations can be part/whole grouped according to the categories of quantity. Possession of the second means that they can be compared one with another as sensations of the same kind because, despite their differences in degree, they are products of responses of the same kinds, which differ only in strength. By the first, we can take a segment of different sensations in succession as parts of a totality, as we do when we break the string of speech sounds into chunks corresponding to units of meaning. We, as it were, introduce brackets around bits that represent words, larger bits representing phrases, and still larger bits representing sentences. By the second feature of the given, we recognize speech sounds as the same (allomorphs) whether they are spoken by voices of higher or lower pitch, at more or less volume, or otherwise variant in intensive magnitude. Kant refers to the combinations by grouping or by qualitative comparison as "the synthesis of the *homogeneous* in everything which can be *mathematically* treated. This synthesis can be divided into that of *aggregation* and that of *coalition,* the former applying to *extensive* and the latter to *intensive* quantities'' (B 201n).

Two points about the quote. First, *mathematical* pairs with *constitutive,* in contrast to *dynamical* which pairs with *regulative.* Those contrasts are the topic of the next section. For now, think of mathematical treatment as pertaining to the properties of the number line, which admits of bracketing (division into segments which are themselves lines that can be further divided into lines that . . .) and consequently admits of infinite division (corresponding both to the flow of time and to gradual changes in the intensity of sensation). The dynamical or regulative principles are those of the Analogies. They govern perception and the representation of objects and events, in which causal (= dynamical) considerations play a major part. The second point about the quote has to do with the word *homogeneous.* The contrast here is obviously to *heterogeneous.* When very disparate things are joined together—as, for example, when sensory states are joined to the objects and events they represent—the combination is of things heterogeneous (as the continuation of B 201n says). The principles of magnitude are of the combination of homogeneous things because (a) sensations are joined to sensations, and (b) even though, in the grouping of merely adjacent sensations by the principle of extensive magnitude, very *different* sensations may be combined with one another, still the possibility of their combination rests, not with them, but with their temporal locations. It is the homogeneity of time that permits grouping of what occurs in time. For example, the eight different sounds in the spoken word *adultery* are, as sounds, heterogeneous; but *time* is homogeneous, and *its* homogeneity allows the introduction of brackets anywhere within it—hence, just before, and just after, those eight sounds.

Such bracketing is one of the two ways in which sensations can be combined to form the content of an intuition. The other way involves the sort of qualitative comparison by which all *a*-sounds—in all the words in which they occur, and by all the speakers who utter them—are recognized as tokens of the same type. Together, *grouping* and *comparison* exhaust the features of structure that Kant finds in intuition.

One might think to find more by introspection but there is an important reason to stay with Kant's method of investigation. When we reflect on the content of subjective awareness, we turn our attention to one aspect of experience. We isolate part of a whole, but the part we isolate is already imbued with qualities of the whole to which it belongs. It is as though we were to try to listen to the sounds of our mother tongue as mere sounds, as the sounds an uncomprehending foreigner would hear. We can never put aside all the patterning that comes from familiarity with, and understanding of, the whole to which the sounds customarily belong. Nor would we be any closer to the *raw* (= unprocessed) given if in reflection we discovered sensations that were not parts of familiar patterns of representation. The given, so far as we are concerned with it in the theory of experience, must belong to experience as a whole; and, if we happened to become aware of something in sensation that did not conform to a pattern of representation, it would not be an input prior to its conceptualization; rather, it would be something that did not enter into experience at all.

Suppose, for example, we were to reflect on our auditory experiences during a car ride. We could attend to the sensations of the identifiable traffic noises of the motor, the tires, the wind, the other cars, and so forth. All of these sensations are described in terms of what they represent, and they are all conceived as the effects of certain objective causes. Suppose we detect certain other auditory sensations that are unidentifiable, and that cannot be assigned causes. These would be sounds that were not conceptualized; but they would not be the preconceptual basis of meaningful auditory experience; they would be *extraneous* to experience. For a description of sensation to be a part of an account of experience that does not presuppose what it is meant to explain, it must eschew what we discover introspectively—since that, in general,[31] is either already part of experience and colored by it, or else it plays no part at all. This leaves only the starkly formal descriptions of structure to which Kant restricts himself.

I do have a hypothesis to explain what can and what cannot be discovered introspectively. For the most part we are attentive to the world around us, and inattentive to our subjective states of awareness. The mind gets its information by means of, and through, its sensory states and its monitoring of its own acts; but what we need to be conscious of are the things that confront us in the world. For the most part, representation mechanisms of the mind work automatically or spontaneously, and reliably, to provide the information we need. For the sorts of information that go hand in glove with action, for instance, maintaining balance, running over rough ground, catching a ball, etc., we rely on the devices of depth perception that Berkeley denies we have because he cannot find them on introspection. But if from a glimpse of a portion of its arc, we had to work out *consciously* the trajectory of the ball, the speed of run required to intersect with it, and the timing of our jump, we would be too slow to accomplish the end. With the rest of the animal kingdom, we share most of our spatial skills as blind (= introspectively inaccessible) capacities. If we stumble when running, other mechanisms take over automatically—to regain our balance, or to ease the fall. Mistakes or inadequacies in the information that serves action lead only to failures of the action; and there would, in general, be no utility to access to the sensory elements or processes that led to the misinformation. Where there is utility in having introspective access is only where there remains something to be corrected. With us, unlike the rest of the animal kingdom, information is not largely restricted to the service of action, at least not of immediate action. We store information and base general knowledge on it. Here the passage of time does not leave failures, mistakes, and inadequacies behind. We must have corrective mechanisms for setting right any errors. Combined with the ability to reason, introspection allows an alternative to, and hence a check on, the spontaneous—and sometimes inaccurate—representation of the objective world. According to this hypothesis, we should have introspective access to the sensory base of the beliefs that we maintain. And if nature does nothing in vain, that should be the extent of what we can be conscious of in ourselves.

The hypothesis seems to be borne out by the inaccessibility of the mechanisms of depth or distance perception. The distance of an object is not part of the abiding information we have about it because its distance is relative to us, and so constantly changing as we and it move about. Of course, we do keep track of the locations of things, and from that can work out their distance; but systems of location are the sorts of things we *can* review on reflection—the imaginary map of the walk described in chapter two.

Not only is introspection inadequate to reveal all the components of cognition, and to reveal them independent of their usual experiential associations, it belongs—at least according to my hypothesis—with reason to a deliberative procedure for reviewing and correcting perceptual information. The Cartesian epistemological tradition (the two-element model) mistakenly construes perception as involving two main aspects: consciousness of a subjective or sensory state, and inference to an objective correlate (a physical thing or event). Why this mistake is made can be explained with the hypothesis. When we slowly and deliberatively work out what is represented in sense, it is by immediate awareness of the subjective and by inference from it. Now, it is natural enough—though a mistake—to suppose that perception in general has whatever features we observe it to have whenever we are conscious of it. When we stop and ask ourselves, "What is that?" or "Can that really be such-and-so?", we are conscious of our sensations and of the inferential constructions that can be put on them. It is easy to miss the fact that, though the two aspects are present whenever we stop to think, they are there *because* we stop to think. It is easy to assume they are there all the time, and just brought occasionally to our attention.

Perhaps the strongest point in favor of Kant's method of investigation is that it avoids that mistake. That it is a mistake can be shown by the impossibility of inference from sensory states to objects when there is not the support of collateral information that must have been noninferentially obtained. We can have some success when we stop to think because we have a wealth of fact to work with. We know generally what the world is like, and generally how it correlates with our sensory states of consciousness. Though that general knowledge stands in need of the odd correction, the corrections themselves are possible only because they can be conducted within the body of reliable information. The whole body of information cannot be the product of inference from sensory states— for all the reasons urged earlier against the two-element model, and especially because sensory states lack truth-value.

One of Kant's conditions on transcendental exposition is that it provide the only explanation. The failures of the two-element model leave the way open to Kant to provide, if not the only explanation, the better account of cognition. The other condition is that the explanans be sufficient. What must be shown now is that the characterization Kant gives of sensing and intuition is rich enough to explain our knowledge.

If we had started with introspection or observation of the given, we would have the problem of explaining the five senses—their ranges of operation and their interconnections. Why have we only five? Why these five? We could have had a sense of magnetic field, and hearing could have extended to infra- or ultrasound. No doubt there are good evolutionary reasons for our capacities and our limitations; but evolved capacities, though preserved because of the advantages they confer, are initiated by chance. We cannot start with what we are—or, rather, with that small portion of what we are that is introspectively accessible (or the somewhat larger portion that is observable)—and treat that as the *sine qua non* of knowledge. The mere fact that it is indubitable in some sense (i.e., that it is that portion of our conscious content unaffected by Cartesian and Humean skeptical arguments, so long as it is maintained only as subjective[32]) does not entail that it is either necessary or sufficient for knowledge. Different content, from different senses, might serve as well. More than can be found by introspection may be required.

One of the virtues of Kant's approach is that it ignores (or never discovers, never turns on the fact that) we do have five senses. Intuition is characterized just in terms of certain structural features that pertain to any sensations, however they may be given.

23. The Manifolds of Intuition and Appearance

The whole of whatever is given in sense—by whatever senses we possess—makes up the manifold of intuition. Everything that intuition represents makes up the manifold of appearance.

The term *manifold* reflects the fact that Kant's treatment of the sensorily given in its relation to what it represents proceeds from ill-defined generality to greater definition. That is, the relationship is not established part for part between sensory elements and things and events in the world. Rather, with echoes of Quine (and very significant departures from him) the objective contents of our beliefs meet collectively with the sensorily given, *en bloc*. In a sense, this is just a restatement of Kant's claim that "Our knowledge springs from two fundamental sources of the mind . . ." (A 50 = B 74). Our capacity for receiving sensory impressions combines with our capacity for conceptualization; and the products or objects of the one capacity relate to the products and objects of the other; intuitions relate to appearances.

Apprehension itself confers a certain amount of structure on intuition, but the structuring of intuition by apprehension is in certain respects indeterminate.[33] One way of looking at the minimal characterization of the structure of intuition invites the doubt that merely the principles of extensive and intensive magnitude can lay a sufficient basis for the representation of objects. They provide only for certain groupings and comparisons of sensations. There is another way of looking at the fact that apprehension does not wholly determine the character of the given. Consider that what remains indeterminate remains to be determined, and that it may be determined by its relation to what it represents.

By the principle of extensive magnitude, adjacent parts of the manifold of intuition can be grouped as totalities, as pluralities considered as units (a bunch of different sensations regarded/apprehended as a block or Gestalt). Because the space-time manifold is homogeneous, the bracketing of it into parts is indeterminate. We can make the cuts anywhere. We can treat the sensations of a moment as a unit; but because the moment can be of any length, the division of the flow of sensation into unitary segments (= intuitions) is not determined. The indeterminacy is, however, reduced by the other principle of sensory apprehension. Adjacent sensations of like quality invite collection because they admit also of comparison. It is therefore not utterly arbitrary to group together a certain block of sensations if, for instance, they are all of the same color, and are in contrast to neighboring (background) sensations of another color. However, because there are two principles, there may be choices between the two ways of combining sensations. For example, we may pick out the bittern in the clump of swamp grass despite its protective coloration by enforcing the principle of extensive magnitude against the principle of intensive magnitude—by ignoring the blend of color to discern the shape. Likewise, we may spot the deer behind the bush despite the fact that its outline is hidden from us, because we apprehend together the flecks of its color as combined despite being separated and scattered throughout an ill-defined portion of the visual field. Whether the principles support one another or conflict, they do not fully determine the structure of intuition.

Nor do the principles of extensive and intensive magnitude suffice to determine all aspects of the temporality of experience. They go some way toward characterizing the part/whole structure of time, and toward the securing of content that is needed for the determinate representation of time; but they do nothing to establish duration, order, and simultaneity. *Nothing* may be too strong a word; but *not enough* is too weak. There are anticipations of duration, order, and simultaneity in the temporal structuring of intuition, but they are far short of the full notions of objective temporal relation. The intervals of times as wholes made up of parts are only on occasion determinately represented by their content, unless we (implausibly) suppose that sensations are constantly undergoing gradual changes in intensity. For the rest, we are left reliant on an inner clock— the consciousness of our own continuing act of apprehension—for knowledge of the nonmomentary character of the times in which constant sensations occur. The consciousness is implicit (established by argument), not direct (not clearly accessible to introspection); but even if it were direct, it provides no measure of duration, and no representation of that which endures *in relation to* that which is transitory. With gradually changing sensation, the transitory is well represented; and with constant sensation, that which endures is represented. But both are not represented together. Likewise, the mere succession of subjective times only suggests the proper ordering of times. First this, then that, then that, and so on— the *and next* relation of succession—could as well take us in circles as in a straight line. We do not apprehend the relation of times remote from one another. Again, their presence together in apprehension is a sort of simultaneity that is apprehended in respect of sensations; but, that it is not the full relation of simultaneity can be shown in conjunction with the indeterminacy of order. Subjective succession, as the mere *and next* relation of one sensation after another, can loop back on itself in such a way that we do not know if we are having the same sensations over again or if we are having new, but qualitatively identical, ones. Think of going back to the same object from time to time as you survey a scene. With respect to apprehension it is indifferent whether we say the qualitatively identical sensations are *new* or *re*occurrences. But the representation of times is by their content. If these are new sensations (though identical with earlier ones), they occur at different times; but if they are mere reoccurrences they are at the same time. In short, the principles of apprehension leave aspects of time undetermined.

In Kant's system, grouping and qualitative comparison provide the only ways of combining sensations; but the problem is not that they give us too little to go on, but too much. They afford more possibilities of combination than we can take up. They do not constrain us to make certain combinations rather than others. By making cuts in other places, by taking wider or narrower ranges of differences in degree to be mere variants of the same quality, we can apprehend sensations in any combinations whatsoever, and still operate only according to the principles of extensive and intensive magnitude. Since all thought must relate to intuition,[34] the indeterminacy of apprehension is a problem. Depending on the combinations we make, there are any of an infinite set of possible intuitions to which thought might be related.

Kant's terminology is an indication of how the problem is solved within his system. The fact that thought is to be grounded in intuition, which can be structured only by the principles of magnitude, prompts Kant to call those principles *constitutive*. But the alternatives open to apprehension require that other principles enforce a selection from among all the possible intuitions that result from all the different possibilities of combining sensations in apprehension. These other principles, because they constrain apprehension by determining which combinations are actually made, are the *regulative* principles.

The constitutive principles arise from the categories of quantity and quality. The regulative arise from relation and modality.

The categories of relation create the structure of the manifold of appearance. They do so by outlining the temporal features that the objects and events of perception must exhibit. Only if the things we perceive have these features do they satisfy two conditions: first, of being representable by intuitions, which requires also that they be distinct from them; and, second, of providing an objective time in which the subjective time of apprehension is more fully determined. More fully—but still not entirely. Perception does acquaint us with a realm of physical objects and events within which our acts of apprehension take place, and, by reference to which, the subjective time of apprehension and inner consciousness is given an objective time. The correlation of subjective time to objective time introduces duration to correspond to the intervals of time as an extensive magnitude; necessary succession in accordance with causal laws, to correspond to (and make more determinate) the merely serial ordering of the *and next* relation found in apprehension; simultaneity of enduring objects, to correspond to (without being restricted to) merely being sensed at the same time. The things we perceive belong to the manifold of appearance, which has a temporal structure that is more detailed and complete than the temporal structure to be found in the manifold of intuition; but, because the two manifolds are connected both as sign to signified (intuitions represent appearances) and as cause to effect (appearances cause sensations), the inner clock of consciousness can be adjusted and regulated to correlate with the outer clock of appearance. However, even perception is insufficient to provide the complete determination of time, and additional regulation is required (and supplied by the principles that arise from the categories of modality).

The first set of regulative principles is to be found in the Analogies of Experience (and my chapters five, six, and seven); the second set, in the Postulates of Empirical Thought (and chapter eight).

Kant's principles always have the double function of temporal determination and experiential rule. The former, as just sketched above, is often—because more abstract—more difficult to grasp. It is probably easier at first to follow Kant's system through in terms of the latter, the experiential rules.

We can feel the constitutive rules at work in cases where apprehension is not automatic. Suppose we look at what we initially take to be a random collection of dots. These could be joined up in any number of ways. Suddenly we discern a pattern. It fairly leaps from the page—and often thereafter we are unable to look at the dots without at once seeing the pattern. This is a good example both of the indeterminacy of apprehension (when we cast our eye back and forth over the dots, trying different connections) and of the grouping that is effected according to the principle of extensive magnitude. Such cases have another dimension to them. When the pattern suddenly emerges, it is not just *one* of the many ways of joining up the dots; it is *the* pattern of something. One of the many possible combinations is—can be taken as being—a representation. We see, in the field of dots, a chair, the number seven, a duck, or whatever. Perception thus joins with apprehension, and regulates apprehension. There are not just dots anymore, but dots and the duck they represent. The dots are no longer just joined in a possible combination. One combination becomes *the* combination because it serves up the duck. Where did the duck come from? Kant's answer is that it comes from the mind's capacity for the production of concepts; and, in this case, we might think of our concepts as the schemata of images.

We need another example of the indeterminacy that remains even when perception is added to apprehension. For this, we could use the vase-and-two-faces drawing or the duck-rabbit. With these there remains a choice in how to apprehend because there is a choice of what to perceive. Looked at with one aspect as figure and the other as ground, we see two faces; but by reversing figure and ground, we see a vase. Likewise, the little line drawing accommodates both the representation of a duck (if the projecting curve is taken as a beak) and the representation of a rabbit (if it is taken as ears). We can feel apprehension shift back and forth between the alternatives. If the drawings are a bit off, no such shifts occur. The representation of each alternate object of perception must be equal to the other. If not, we will no more get an alternation between vase and two unrecognizable blobs or rabbit and nothing than we can go back to seeing the initially random field of dots as still random. What this shows is that the possibility of representational significance, where present and unique, enforces a particular apprehension against all other possible combinations.

As adults we do not often encounter perspicuous cases of the indeterminacy of perception. This is because our general conception of the world is well-established and already determinative of our perception. We often see children misclassify things for which there is a basis in apprehension both for the aberrant classification and for our standard one. We have long since learned enough general information to preclude the possibility of perceiving (except momentarily, and under the influence of a child's observation to that effect) the neighbor's dog as a bear. However, even as adults, we encounter occasional ambiguities of perception—particularly in language—that do require resolution by empirical thought. When we first move in, the tones of the neighbors' voices are perceived by us as angry *or* playful. In time, with collateral information about them, we come to perceive them as *at it again* (meaning by that the one thing or the other that we have general reasons to believe goes on next door).

Apprehension involves the combination of sensation. Perception involves matching intuition with the concept of some objective correlate. Empirical thought involves connecting up all our perceptual information in a unified whole. Each successive stage has its rules: apprehension has the rules of grouping and comparison; the rules of perception are rules for forming concepts of things and events; the rules of empirical thought sort out what is actual, possible, and necessary. Each stage (except the last) provides alternatives for the one above, or determinateness for the one below (except the first). There are all sorts of combinations of sensation possible in apprehension, which thereby makes available to perception a variety of forms, any one of which can be linked to a conceptual pattern. Once there is a link found to a conceptual pattern, apprehension is restricted to the combination that supports it unless alternate combinations are equally suitable as representations. If there are alternatives of perception, empirical thought is then offered a choice of information about what is going on in the world; it is then up to it to decide, on the basis of its rules for putting all our information together, which, of the possible objects of perception, is in fact the one present.

The two sources of our knowledge meet then in two ways. From the sensory end, we have the constitutive inputs that are rich in alternatives. From the conceptual end, we have regulative controls that elect among the alternatives. But there is no sharp division such as we find in the two-element model between input and control. There is nothing like the plethora of logically possible worlds just waiting for sensory experience to say which is actual. Rather, understanding is at work the whole time—increasing stage by stage the determinacy of the input, as it incorporates stage by stage the input into conceptual structures of greater objectivity. The avoidance of the two-element dichotomies is a considerable gain in that it affords explanations of conceptual growth and change that are otherwise not possible. As our repertoires of recognitional concepts grow and become more discriminating among things sensed, and more enhanced by auxiliary modes of sensing (microscopes, and all other sorts of experimental device), we apprehend more, and more discerningly. As empirical thought has more knowledge to incorporate, and more to draw on, it more tightly controls what we perceive.

Quine objects to the dichotomy of analytic and synthetic, and to the reduction of belief to the sensorily given, but his objections are not the rejections they should be. He retains the dichotomy as one between total science and experience, and replaces *reduction* with *germaneness* as a relation between the two.[35] Experiences germane to the truth of a statement are those which, if different, would incline us to revise its truth-value. Likewise, the truth of certain statements inclines us to expect certain experiences. Quine softens the edges, and he stresses the indeterminacy of total science by the experiences we have, but he retains the opposition and contrast of the one to the other. He argues the indeterminacy by contending that any statement can be held come what may, or given up despite the occurrence of germane experience. Empiricism, even without the dogmas, retains both the dichotomies and the reductionism; the old empiricism fails not because it tries to draw the lines too sharp, but because it draws them in the wrong places, and draws too few of them.

The manifold of appearance does stand to the manifold of intuition in ways that include some features of the loose association that Quine describes between total science and experience; but remoteness from the sensory periphery is a feeble metaphor that is no replacement for Kant's conception of phenomena as the products of empirical thought. The difference between appearances and phenomena is not just of distance or degree. Appearances are tied to intuitions as things signified are related to their signs; and the tie is both one-to-one and general: one-to-one in the correlation of apprehension to perception; general in the determination of perception by empirical thought. The considerations that are involved in the unification of all our perceptual knowledge do, collectively, require the adoption and rejection of various perceptual concepts. We believe in neural dysfunctions and give up the ghosts; but the belief that this patient has a particular disorder is not just loosely associated with what we perceive in our examination of him, nor do our experiments in neurology just *incline* us more to talk about nerves than demons and ghosts. Rather, the advances in thought *force* advances in perception, and whatever patterns of apprehension are consistent with the old concepts are displaced by the new. We do not have two elements that are tied together in a rough and redoable bundle, but three elements with fairly precise interrelations.

Two more matters of terminology require explanation. Kant calls the principles of perception *analogies;* and he pairs the contrast between constitutive and regulative principles with the *mathematical/dynamical* distinction.

It is common in modern philosophy to regard perception as posing problems of justification. It is asked how we are justified in thinking that there are objects that correspond to our sensory states. The argument from analogy attempts to establish the existence and nature of other minds on the presumption that they stand to the behavior of others as our own minds stand to our behavior. With the general concern for justification and the argument from analogy both in mind, one might think that Kant's principles of perception are intended as an attempt to establish some sort of analogical extension from what is evident to what is not—from how things seem to be to how they are. However, that reading would neglect Kant's doctrine of two sources of knowledge.

All the terms in Kant's analogies are equally accessible, though in different ways. Sensibility supplies the material of experience. Understanding supplies its conceptual form. As in the Schematism, the problem is one of bringing about the relation between the two, not of going from the one to the other. Perception involves both the sensory material and the concepts of objective things; the rules for perception effect and sustain the balance between the two. Analogical relation is maintained between the two manifolds as the two sets of structures are constituted and regulated in enough ways to conceptualize all intuitions and give content to all (empirical) thought. Kant says, "*Understanding* is, to use general terms, *the faculty of knowledge.* This knowledge consists in the determinate relation of given representations to an object; and an *object* is that in the concept of which the manifold of a given intuition is *united*" (B 137). The manifold of intuition is related to the manifold of appearance as representation to represented; but the relation also goes the other way as regulation to regulated. We do not first have a structured given and then infer something objective from it, but a coordination of both structures together that is ongoing. Concepts must accommodate sensory input, and sensory input must be apprehended in acts that are made determinate by concepts of objects.

Part of Kant's reason for calling the principles of quantity and quality *mathematical* (as opposed to the *dynamical* principles of relation and modality) has to do with their introduction of the numerical features of magnitude, and with the causal considerations introduced by the principles of relation (and utilized by the principles of modality, since causal considerations are paramount in empirical thought in determining what is possible or necessary). As well, Kant frequently associates the mathematical/dynamical distinction with a distinction between intuition and existence.[36] The usual contrast to intuition is of concept, so the less usual contrast to existence needs explanation.

It is one thing for us to possess a representation of an object; another to know that it exists. Intuition gives us representations, and so supplies us with a *subjective* basis for knowledge. Kant does not raise the epistemological question by asking how this subjective basis is sufficient evidence that there exists an object corresponding to it. The subjective basis is clearly insufficient. What Kant does is supply an *objective* basis for knowledge. Instead of regarding the subjective basis as *inadequate,* and calling for the justification of knowledge based on it, Kant regards it as *indeterminate.* Alternatives of apprehension supply possible representations of various possible objects, and intuition alone is insufficient to determine which objects (among all that could be represented) do exist. As we shall see throughout the Analogies, we know objects by their works, by what they do. Of course, what they do must show up in intuition. The effects must be evident, but the causes must exist to have those effects. For Kant, the mark of existence is causal efficacy.

One must at once wonder how having representations of things as causes is in any way an improvement over having the subjective basis in intuition for representing objects of any sort. Why, in short, are we not still stuck with intuitions that *could* be regarded as having objective correlates? How does the representation of causes introduce an objective consideration? The long answer takes up the next three chapters. The short answer is that we do not just have (subjective) evidence of causal effects *in* intuition, we have them *as* intuition. Recall that the comparability of sensations requires that the mind take account of the strength of its responses, that it know (in some sense) that it is being acted upon. This knowledge is indeterminate, perhaps—and, perhaps, inaccessible to introspection. However, common sense tells us that there is indeed a two way connection: we know there is a dog there because we see and hear it; and we see and hear it because it is there. Without the sensory states (in the absence of the subjective basis for knowledge), no objects could be represented. Without any objects acting on us (in the absence of the objective basis), no sensory states would occur. The dynamical principles portray perception not as merely coming to know about a world out there, but as also coming to know that we are out there in the world, and very much part of it. Not just mind and nature, but minds in nature.

5

Substance and Attribute

Introduction

For Descartes, matter is essentially spatial. Material bodies occupy space; they are extended things. Having characterized intuitions as extensive, Kant must adopt a different criterion for matter. He regards matter as essentially permanent. It is that which endures throughout time as the stuff out of which all physical things are made, and to which they all in time return. Descartes and Kant have a common objective: to find an essential feature in terms of which our knowledge of material existence can be explained. The First Analogy is Kant's account of our knowledge of the external world.

Through the category of substance and attribute, Kant analyzes the general relationship of things to their properties. His analysis supports the division of properties into those that are changing and transitory, and those that are responsible for changes—the dispositional and abiding. On its own, that is, within the proof of the First Analogy, this analysis and its explanatory argument remain somewhat obscure in purpose and insufficient; but the other two Analogies build on the results of the First. The Second develops the distinction between changing and dispositional properties in its account of our perception of events and our acquisition of knowledge of the causal powers of things. The Third shows how our knowledge of causal powers acquaints us with the effects of objects on us, and how it enables us also to differentiate their actions from our own. The subjective/objective distinction begun in the First Analogy is brought nearly to completion in the Third, though it remains to the Postulates to provide some final details.

The Analogies collectively indicate that our perception is of substances as stuffs—types of matter—more basically than it is a perception of substances as particulars or individual objects. Our relation to the world is not first and foremost to its separate objects, that are somehow later gathered into kinds according to their material composition, with empirical generalizations then made about various matters from observations of the particulars. We relate first and fundamentally to various sorts of matter (e.g., to milk, water, wood, soap, skin, hair, cloth, metal, etc.), learning their properties of both sorts, and in time discovering more material kinds, more of the events in which they display both the changes of which they are capable and the capacities for those changes. Particularity and individuation are finally based upon the extensive causal knowledge required to represent the objective spatiotemporal framework in which identification and differentiation are possible.

Kant never solves the problem of induction because he never has it as his problem. His problem is to explain our knowledge of the world. He shows that our knowledge does not advance from particular to general via induction (nor have proponents of induction ever shown how it could work). His explanation throughout the Analogies goes from an initially indeterminate generality to increasing specificity and detail. The developmental progression within the account is an accurate reflection of the actual growth of our knowledge as an ongoing refinement of information, not an accumulation of separate pieces of data from which inductive projections are supposedly made. While anti-inductivist, Kant's position is far from Popper's in that the ongoing refinements are not to ideas that are mere conjectures. For Kant, we start with very general concepts essential to experience.

24. Kant's Departure from Descartes

Descartes argues that extension in space is the essence of material bodies, or (as he also calls them) corporeal substances. Descartes argues that colors, textures, resistance or solidity, rigidity or hardness, and all other sensible qualities of corporeal substances inhere in something that fills spaces. Any other quality may be seen, or supposed, to vary, and yet the object itself will remain. Only extension is essential. Without its occupancy of space there can be no material body, but there is nothing other than extension such that it need be present. Descartes concludes that material bodies are essentially extended, that matter itself is (identical with) extension, and that matter is that in which all other qualities inhere.[1]

From his identification of matter with extension, Descartes draws conclusions in his science against the possibility of vacua and the existence of atoms.[2] In his epistemology, which he takes to be equivalent to a methodology of scientific thought, Descartes employs the identification of matter with extension to connect the clarity and distinctness of geometrical thought to knowledge of the natural order. For example, in the Sixth Meditation, Descartes acknowledges possibilities of all sorts of empirical error; but he insists that all that is clearly and distinctly conceived in geometry pertains to extension and thereby to external reality, since extension is the essence of matter, and matter is the real in the external. Thus, in his doctrine and method, Descartes relies on the identification of matter with extension; and he promotes geometry as the fundamental science of nature.

Descartes also relies on other identifications: of the clarity and distinctness of conceptions with their truth; and of the truth of what is conceived with the existence of the object of the conception.[3]

What is right in Descartes' argument is that extension is indeed essential to *corporeal objects*. What is wrong is to think it essential to them *qua corporeal or material*. It is essential to them only *as objects*. Descartes considers particular objects such as the piece of wax in the Second Meditation, or the stone in *Principles* II, xi. He reflects on the variability of all their sensible qualities, and he finds that only extension is irremovable. He then draws his conclusion by generalizing too restrictively—not, as he should, to all objects, but just to material objects or bodies. His error consists in the mistaken supposition that the conclusion that extension is essential pertains to the *material* character of the examples, where matter is taken to be the stuff of nature, distinct from, and external to, thought. But the conclusions would be the same for *any* objects, including the ones met only in dreams: imagination, hallucination, mirages, apparitions, miracles, and so on. We can no more *imagine* a nonspatial stone than find one.

The things that do exist in nature are a subset of all possible objects. There are many things that could exist that happen not to; but they are just as spatially describable in their characteristics of extension as any of the objects that do exist. We can calculate the height, the floor area, and any other property of spatial extension as surely for a building just at the planning stage as for one already built. There is some distinctive condition that real buildings alone satisfy; but it cannot be spatial since we are able to carry out plans to the last spatial detail. One might think that being actually *present* in space is distinctive of objects that do exist, as opposed to those that are merely possible or fantastical. This is quite right, but useless. Apparitions are present in space too—though not *actually* present—and so it is the actuality of presence that counts, and not just whatever sort of presence is common even to nonexistent or unreal objects. But what is it to be actually present except to be present and to be real?

Space is very important to the representation of objects even if it provides no criterion of the real or of existence. Indeed, all our intuitions of objects, whether pure or empirical, have space as their form; and spatial concepts of objects do provide—through the schemata that are rules for the production of images[4]—ways of uniting intuitions in respect of their spatial form. Moreover, we cannot represent the sensible qualities of objects unless we employ spatial concepts. The combination of qualities in an object requires that the qualities be represented as being in a certain common region or extension. If qualities are not considered as found in a common region, then any combination of them is conceived merely as a conjunction of universals. By uniting intuitions on the basis of their spatial forms, spatial concepts also unite the sensory contents of the intuitions, and so unite qualities—not just as conjuncts in a logical combination, but as joint determinations of, and in, the object. As well, space plays its part in the perception or visualization of objects by supplying the variety of orientation or perspective. However, the importance of space obtains equally, and by any of the above considerations, for objects of all sorts: for material objects, imaginary objects, shadows, geometrical forms—the lot.

The concept of an object must be grounded in the concept of substance (= matter) if it is to yield the concept of a physical thing. Otherwise the system of spatial forms remains pure and does not give rise to appearances. Otherwise objects remain mere objects of thought. Only by adding substantiality does the understanding fashion for itself concepts of objects that are not just reducible to the intuitions that represent them. But the addition must be analyzed, explained, and proved.

Kant offers two versions of the principle to be proved:

> All appearances contain the permanent (substance) as the object itself, and the transitory as its mere determination, that is, as a way in which the object exists (A 182).

> In all change of appearance substance is permanent. Its quantum in nature is neither increased nor diminished (B 224).

Some commentators suggest the revision is intended to create a closer relationship between the Analogies and the fundamental laws of Newtonian mechanics. They take the reference to the quantum of substance to echo the conservation law.[5] Like the claim that Kant is committed to Euclidean geometry, the claim that he is committed to Newtonian mechanics should be advanced, if at all, with some caution—not with the assurance that "Everyone knows Kant thought that. . . ," with no texts given in support. In this case one of the texts to be reflected upon occurs just prior to the Analogies, and it gives us three pages of argument showing that the Newtonian account of differences in density is not the only one possible. Kant says that his alternative (Cartesian) account of difference in density "has the merit at least of freeing the understanding, so that it is at liberty to think this difference in some other manner, should it be found that some other hypothesis is required for the explanation of the natural appearances" (A 174 = B 215–16). I think Kant shows commendable caution in *not* thinking that the metaphysics of experience extends automatically to physics.[6] I will have more to say about the quantum of substance later on in my discussion of the proof.[7]

I regard Kant's principle-and-proof format as being somewhat misleading *in so far as it suggests* that his project is to show that certain claims are true. That substance is permanent is, Kant himself says, tautological.[8] What is not trivial and obvious is the role that the category of substance and attribute has in experience. I take both versions of the principle, everything Kant says in the proof, and the general plan of the architectonic to be aspects of an attempted explanation, not steps in a deductive argument. Even in Hempel's nomological-deductive model of explanation, argument-structure is only one of a number of features of a good explanation.[9] In short, Kant is not so much *proving that* as *showing how*.

The category of substance and attribute is relational. The first version of the principle brings this out in the two paired contrasts: of the permanent and the transitory; and of the object itself and its determinations. The relational aspect is only implicit in the revised version. The emphasis goes on substance to the neglect of attributes; but the contention that, in change of appearance, substance is unchanging carries a hint of the relational contrasts.

Kant is in agreement with Descartes in the analysis of the category. Both belong to the tradition that regards the subject-predicate relation in judgment as an indicator of the substance-attribute relation. Both regard substance (= matter) as the basic stuff of the world, that in which properties, qualities, or attributes inhere, that which contains the causal forces and principles of nature, and so on. They differ only in their identification of the essential character of substance or matter.

Kant begins the proof in both editions by remarking that "All appearances are in time" (A 182 = B 224). In B, he continues by saying, "in which as substratum (as permanent form of inner intuition) the *coexistent* as well as the successive can alone be represented" (B 224).[10] The point of emphasizing *coexistent* can be taken as being directed against Leibniz, who tries to distinguish between space and time as the orders of coexistence and succession, respectively.[11] Kant's point in reply is the observation that *coexistence*—whether it involves spatiality or not—is a temporal relation.

The point behind Kant's point is that spatial ordering depends on temporal ordering, and that the two sorts of order are not exclusive of one another. Things must be present to our senses at the same time if we are directly to apprehend their spatial relation to each other. If things are not present at the same time, then there must be some way in which we work out their spatial relation by connecting up successive experiences. One way or the other, the spatial involves a dependence on the temporal. This cuts against Descartes as well as Leibniz; for, even if space were essential to the material world and its objects, space alone would not be the essence of material reality, but space and time together.

In the next bit of the proof, Kant says,

> Time, then, in which all change of appearances must be thought, re-
> mains and does not change; because it is that in which the successive
> or coexistent can be represented only as its determinations. Well, time
> itself cannot be perceived. So there must, in the objects of perception,
> that is, in the appearances, be a substratum to be met with, which time
> represents in a general way, and in which all changes or coexistence
> can be perceived through relation to it (B 224–25).[12]

Since time is not, as Leibniz thinks, limited to succession, everything in
appearance must be related to time.

Kant here begins the parallel between the temporal structure and the
empirical content of the manifold of appearance that repeats the pattern
of argument in the Axioms and Anticipations in respect of the manifold
of intuition. There, the representation of times had two aspects: the general features revealed by analysis and expressed in the schemata of seriality and containment; and the determinate features that come from the
content. The same two aspects are to be found here—now not in respect
of the subjective times of apprehension and intuition, but in respect of
the objective times of perception and appearance.

Again (in accordance with the doctrine of the Aesthetic),[13] *time itself*
must be represented first, and all time*s* and their contents must be represented in it. The initial representation of time itself is merely general
and indeterminate, but it is not useless, even though determinate representation is only by reference to things in time. In order to serve as an
empirical determinant of times—a point from which we can date things—
an appearance (such as an event) must be regarded as actually taking
place. Within the manifold of appearances, empirical objects and events
do serve as the benchmarks for placing and dating things in the spatiotemporal framework of the world. To qualify as suitable reference points,
appearances chosen for the role of markers of objective locations must,
no doubt, satisfy pragmatic criteria such as centrality, stability, regularity,
accessibility, and so on; but first of all they must satisfy the much more
basic condition of being objects in the world. They must be in the manifold
of appearance. They must exist. The determinate representations that are
possible with physical objects and events therefore depend on the prior
representation that establishes them—and all other things located by reference to them—as physical.

Having remarked that time cannot be perceived, Kant concludes that
the objects in the world must include a substratum that can be met with,
and that is represented in a general way by time itself. This substratum
will, as the argument unfolds, turn out to be substance or matter. Time
itself represents it in a general way as the permanent, as that which exists

always. It also represents it as the whole of which all things physical are parts, just as time itself is the whole of which all times are parts. How this substratum is met with is only partly revealed in the First Analogy (and that partial revelation will be discussed in sections to follow); Kant indicates that there will be more later when he says that change or co-existence can be perceived through relation to the substratum. The perception of change is the topic of the Second Analogy, and that of coexistence is the topic of the Third. The task in the First is to lay the groundwork for the other two by establishing permanence as the criterion of material reality.

Before I continue with Kant's adoption of permanence as the criterion, I will venture a concluding remark about where Descartes goes wrong, and why he chooses space as the essence of material existence. There are some obvious reasons such as the paradigmatic clarity and distinctness of geometry that would understandably prompt Descartes to turn to the spatial in his pursuit of certainty. There is also, I think, a reason tied in with his method of doubt and the *cogito*. Every*thing* that he thinks can be doubted—except the thinking itself. From his method and approach, Descartes develops, as fundamental to his system, the contrast between thought and its objects, or between thinking of and thought of, or mind and matter. In respect of his basic dualism, space is indeed of the essence. Space is essential to that which is thought, and not to the thinking of it. Any *thing* that is thought is automatically accorded spatiality or extension. The mind that thinks it is, by contrast, unextended, and so possessed of that unity and indestructibility by removal of parts that Descartes is eager to ensure as doctrines of the soul.[14]

For Kant, the cut comes in a different place. While extension may set objects apart from thought, it also sets mind apart from nature, and locks us into a skeptical or dogmatic idealism that Kant finds intolerable.[15] So for Kant the subjective/objective distinction cuts, not between the mind and its objects, but between some of its objects and others. All objects are spatial, and none are more spatial than others; but not all endure, persist, and belong to the external world. Extension is useless to differentiate *among* objects those that do exist. Moreover, mind belongs among things that exist in the world. Therefore, the subjective/objective distinction cannot be allowed to be collapsed into the mind/matter and internal/external distinctions where they have the effect of separating us from the rest of nature. What I said in this chapter's introduction about the First Analogy being Kant's solution to the problem of the existence of the external world I will now qualify by saying that we belong in that world. For Kant, the issue is how we determine which of the objects we think of are real. To address this issue, he abandons the criterion of extension for physical objects because it includes objects of all sorts.

25. General Remarks on the Representation of Substance

As the form of inner sense, time relates all intuitions to each other. That most general relation among intuitions is the basis for the most general relation among appearances. To belong in the manifold of intuition, the given must belong to inner sense—we must be conscious of the sensation produced in us, or, in the case of pure intuition, we must be conscious of the form we produce in ourselves by imagination.[16] To exist, to belong in the world, to be in the manifold of appearance, an object—whatever its figure, extent, or other qualities—must stand in relation to other objects as its representation in intuition stands to other intuitions that represent other objects. Several arguments for this follow.

First, no matter how far we specify the properties of an object, no matter how lengthy our descriptions of it, we do not thereby ensure its existence. So the condition that an object satisfies when it is a *material* object is something general, not a property in addition to other properties.[17]

Second, if by this general condition, material objects are not brought into universal relation to one another, the world does not constitute a whole that is subject to the criteria of empirical thought. Instead, any object in any part of the manifold of appearance could be quite unrelated to any other object in that or any other part; and, in that case, no science of nature would be possible, since empirical thought could not expect consistency and coherence among appearances, nor conformity to laws of nature.[18]

Third, the general condition of any object that makes it a material object, and that brings about its universal relation to other material objects, must have some basis of representation in intuition. Otherwise, consistency among objects in the world, conformity of objects to law, and existence apart from being perceived—all the real results of the condition—are just arbitrary fictions of empirical thought (as all the unrepentant empiricists are quite ready to believe[19]).

Fourth, the basis for the representation of matter cannot be found in the *content* of intuition, so it must be found in its *form.* The reason for this is as follows.

In the *Essay,* Locke says,

> The idea of *solidity* we receive by our touch: and it arises in the resistance which we find in body to the entrance of any other body into the place it possesses, till it has left it. There is no idea which we receive more constantly from sensation than solidity. . . . This, of all other, seems the idea most intimately connected with, and essential to body; so as nowhere else to be found or imagined, but only in matter. . . . This is the idea which belongs to body, whereby we conceive it to fill space.[20]

Locke here assigns the representation of matter to the sensation of resistance; but that sensation, like any other, is a content of consciousness. It remains to be explained why a feeling within us (of resistance) is taken to represent a feature of objects (their occupancy of space). Moreover, one may *imagine* encountering resistance, or *dream* that one is pressed or struck or weighted down. Besides, there are many material objects that offer us no sensations of resistance at all. The obvious examples are those too distant to be touched or too small to arouse sensation when touched—stars and smoke.

The proper objection to Locke is the general one. The content of the manifold of intuition is aroused as feeling or sensation in the subject. Any effect within us is distinct from what it may represent in whatever object, if any, arouses it. The duality of representation and represented cannot arise from the sign itself.

Time provides what we require for the representation of material objects since it pertains both to consciousness and its objects. Time also avoids the objections, and meets the considerations, advanced in each of the four arguments. It is wholly general: every intuition and every appearance is in time. Through their connection in time, all appearances are in universal interrelation. The demands of empirical thought are thereby met (provided temporality can be shown to carry with it other interrelations, especially causal ones): that the objects of empirical thought form a consistent system, subject to natural law, and independent of the particular thoughts and experiences of any individual. Yet the whole of reality, though independent of subjective particulars, has a general connection to the manifold of intuition, by virtue of the temporality common to both manifolds (provided that too can be established). The general connections both within and between the two manifolds distinguish objects of experience from the objects of dreams and imagination.

The problem raised against Locke is to account for how the duality of representation arises. This problem is part of the problem of the representation of substance. The representation of objects is a lesser problem. An object is simply that which in its concept unites intuitions. As a mere unifier, an object is not required to be distinct from what it unifies.

Modern logic represents an object by a proper name or a bound variable linking together a collection of predicates. In one sense, such objects are dispensable; they can be replaced, without loss or residue, by the sets of predicates they collect. The idea of such replacement is to be found first in Locke's musings on the unknowability of substance (= that in which qualities inhere). In the analysis of an object, we encounter only its properties, never the thing itself that has the properties, the *that which*. Any effort to describe the thing that has the properties only generates more properties.[21] However, as a mere collection of properties, an object raises a dilemma that the representation of substance (= matter) is required to resolve. *Either* the properties so collected are sensory states, and then the object is nothing distinct from the consciousness of it; *or* the properties are not sensory states, and then the object is distinct from consciousness of it. With the first alternative, there are problems of differentiating one object from another—sorting into the real or existent and the illusory. All objects alike are given in sense; and if being is being perceived, only ad hoc features like the *vivacity* of some sensations in contrast to others,[22] or some arbitrary postulate such as the uniformity of nature, can rule out some objects as unreal. With the second alternative (= empirical realism), objects are distinct from consciousness of them so the problem is to say how we are entitled to regard sensory states as representations of properties. Kant has the latter problem; the empiricists have the former. The dilemma is genuine because predicate logics do schematize a basic feature of objects and their properties. Objects are collectors of properties or qualities—the question is whether they are, or are not, reducible to their qualities, and whether the qualities are identical to sensory states.[23]

The representation of matter would provide, in conjunction with the representation by predicate logic, the other part of what is needed for the representation of corporeal objects. The empirical realist opposes the empirical idealist by denying the reductions and by saying that to be is to be material or substantial, but to make the opposition effective, he must also say what it is to be material. That is, the empirical realist must explain the relation that appearances have to the substratum in addition to the relation they have to us in sense; for, if they have only the relation to us, idealism provides the correct account of them—not for nothing do Berkeley and Hume argue against matter as the substratum of empirical reality.

The difficulties of realism are compounded by the need not only to explain the grounding of reality in matter, but to explain how we know it. The difficulty is that, if one posits a sensory basis for the knowledge of matter, one invites the very reductionism that realists must prevent; but if one says there is no sensory basis, one must either deny knowledge or find another basis for it. Kant finds a rational or theological basis unacceptable, but he also finds both idealism and skepticism unacceptable. This seems to rule out every possibility, but since Kant thinks he has found the answer, we must overlook something if we regard rationalism and empiricism as exhausting the possible bases of knowledge.

To find Kant's answer to the problems of representing the material substratum, we need to go back to the fact that he describes the principles governing appearances as *regulative*. There is a basis for knowledge of matter in the rules we must employ to make any sense of anything given in sense.

I will explain how this works by dealing briefly and dogmatically (i.e., without argument) with a parallel problem: our basis for the knowledge of other minds. All of our determinate knowledge of another's thought must relate, directly or indirectly, to what is evident—to his words, gestures, expressions, actions. We know that he thinks this rather than that because he says so, or acts as though he believes it, or nods as in agreement when someone else says it, and so on. For knowing just what it is that he thinks—that is, for determinate representation of his thought— we need the sort of evidence that only his behavior can provide. We have no direct rational acquaintance with what he thinks, and our only acquaintance is by means of sensory evidence; but we nonetheless think of him as having a mind that is not just reducible, first to his behavior, then ultimately to *our* sensory states. Our attribution of mind to him is without content additional to the evidence (which is why behaviorism can seem reasonable), but from the fact that the attribution of mind is without content it does not follow that it is gratuitous. His behavior means nothing unless we take it as a partial determinate representation of that of which we have general conception. In thinking of him as having a mind, we think nothing specific; but we do think that the things he does are things *he* does—not just *movements* of his body, but *actions*. And through the general conception of mind, we think lots more besides—that his actions reveal his decisions, intentions, preferences, values, beliefs, etc., and that they form a fairly coherent and interrelated package. No knowledge comes merely from the presupposition that he is a creature with a mind; but, equally, no knowledge of him comes except on that presupposition, for it is only by construing the evidence as evidence of thought, feeling, attitude, etc., that we arrive at any determinate knowledge. Utterances, gestures, expressions, and the rest of what is evident in sense, do not enforce knowledge; they are mere noises and visible movements. They take on meaning only when they are presupposed to have meaning, only when we construe them as expressive, indicative, significant.

Neither behavior nor the sensation it arouses in us is unambiguous, perspicuous, naturally segmented into tidy units. There is all sorts of extraneous sound and movement that must be filtered out; and even what remains is open to selective emphasis and various combinations and divisions. Behavior is constitutive of our knowledge of other minds, but the apprehension of behavior must be regulated in some way if it is to yield any knowledge at all. The general conception of mind as active, purposeful, and internally integrated provides, by itself, no knowledge of other minds; but knowledge does arise from the combination of the general conception with the input from the senses. When apprehension of behavior is regulated by the demand that it reveal desires, choices, beliefs, etc., then our general conceptions of mind are given determinate content, and our sensory evidence takes on meaning.

The *bare* presupposition of the presence of mind brings nothing to the interpretation of behavior. The regulative basis of interpretation consists in what we think is implicit in having a mind. We attribute to minds in general such things as unity and consistency, goal-directedness, responsiveness to the environment, and self-consciousness. These attributes of mind constrain us in what, on the basis of the evidence, we can suppose another to be saying, doing, or thinking; but they are *enabling constraints*. They do not hinder us in the acquisition of knowledge; they make it possible by directing interpretation, ruling out wrong guesses, enforcing one construction against others. With the freedom to construe the evidence *as we pleased,* there would be no right and wrong constructions; and with no right and wrong, no knowledge. But having to make sense of it in certain ways, we are able, because we are constrained to do so, to take the evidence in one way rather than any other—and thereby know what is going on. Even though very general, the constraints are genuine.

Similarly, nothing is gained by simply supposing that there is a substantial or material substratum to appearances. For the supposition to be useful, it must be extended by its implications. There are various qualities that we attribute to substance. It is that which is subject without being a predicate of anything else. It is the substratum of reality. It is that which acts. It is that in which attributes inhere. Finally, it is permanent. Kant chooses the last feature as the basis for the initial application of the category to appearance. The choice is not of a particular *description* to be given to substance, but of a respect in virtue of which perception can constrain apprehension. By contrast, the logical feature of substance, that it collect predicates without being a predicate itself, is unconstraining— since it is satisfied equally by all objects, whether material or not.

It is neither a matter of only proving that there is substance nor of describing it in one way rather than another. What is at issue is how the category functions in experience. More precisely, with respect to the place of the First Analogy within Kant's architectonic, the issue is how the category can be shown to be essential to the perception of appearances, how it functions to regulate sensory apprehension, how it sets up the possibility of the other principles required to account for perception. If these things are shown, it will be proved a fortiori that there is substance underlying appearance. If the proof requires, most of all, one characterization of substance rather than another, that character will be shown to be the most essential feature of substance; but the primary aims are not *proving that* or *describing as*—but *showing how*.

A clue to why permanence is the ground of the application of the category can be found by a comparison of permanence to the most central characterization of mind that functions as a presupposition of our knowledge of other minds. Among other things, we presuppose the relevance of another's behavior and thought to immediate circumstances. If the introduction of a certain object (say a rabbit) to his sensory field is followed by a certain utterance he makes, we take the utterance as a verbal *response to* the object introduced. We also presuppose consistency. We look for sameness of responses to circumstances that are the same. Neither relevance or responsiveness nor consistency are *absolutely* presupposed, only by and large. The subject of our linguistic anthropology may not notice the rabbit. He may not care to talk about it. He may mention it first time, think that enough has been said about it, and go on to talk of different things on subsequent occasions of rabbit-presentation—perhaps venturing criticisms of our methods of research. Still, by and large, we must look for and find enough relevance to immediate circumstances in his responses, and enough consistency of response, to have any reason to continue crediting him with a mind. So both conditions are *both necessary and defeasible*.

To find an analogue of what permanence is supposed to be to appearance, we must look for an *indefeasibly necessary* presupposition of mind. I think that the unity of mind is absolutely presupposed. We can accept that there are occasional inconsistencies in behavior or thought (lapses) and a certain independence of immediate circumstances, but we cannot accept a lack of unity in the mind. It must be of a piece. The behavior must express thoughts, purposes, and feelings. And all the things expressed must cohere together in whole. Otherwise we have no evidence. For example, suppose we observe a certain motion of his body, and presume that he has a mind, and yet can find no way that the motion would serve his purposes or tie in with the rest of what he does. We do not then say that he acted thus, we say that he stumbled, or just moved, was bumped. A person may say one thing and do others, have beliefs but not act on them, have goals to which none of his actions could lead, and so on; but there comes a point where we deny the presence of mind, or posit several. We cannot find enough coherence to warrant continued efforts to regard the evident as evidence of a mind; or else we can find coherence only if we posit several minds in a split personality. Of course, we may not *find* ways of linking each sensory presentation of him to every other; but we must presuppose that there is some link to the whole for each and every part or think that that which lacks a link is no part of his action or thought.

The indefeasible condition of unity operates at two levels of generality: with respect to the whole of what is manifest, and with respect to each bit we can apprehend. Unless *en bloc* what is evident can be treated as the representation of a integrated whole, we deny the presence of mind altogether. Unless particulars can be fitted to the whole, we deny them significance. For example, suppose the sounds emitted cannot be thought to have enough coherence in their internal patterns, enough relation to things in the environment, enough consistency in the thoughts they would express if taken as expressive of thought. We then regard the noisemaker as being not a user of language—as merely babbling, out of touch with reality, or as not knowing what he says. Suppose there is generally enough of the above to regard him as a speaker of language. We may still regard some of his noises as just noises, or as insincere (= unmeant assertions), or as ill-considered blurts, or whatever.[24] To regard collectively what is evident as evidence, we must satisfy the presupposition of the unity of mind; and, once we start satisfying this presupposition by finding constructions of the evident that make it meaningful, or evidential *of,* we set up a context into which further evidence must fit. Of course, enough misfits may force us to save the phenomena (in Duhem's sense, not Kant's) by entirely reappraising the context initially set up—for instance, after so many he's-got-to-be-having-us-ons, we realize that, by God, he means it. It is necessary to presuppose unity because no item given in sense is, on its own, constrained in its apprehension or determinate in its meaning. The reason that unity is indefeasible is that it provides the second half of what we must have to have evidence. There must be something given in sense and apprehended; that is the first (and constitutive) half of what it is to have evidence: the having of it. But the second half of having evidence (the regulative) is that the given indicate something: that it be evidence. With no presupposed unity—among its signs, between the signs and what they signify, and among the things signified—there is no knowledge whatever of the mind.[25]

Behaviorism does not deliver everything the evidence entitles us to have; it destroys the evidential character of the evident (or would if it were rigorous) by stressing the givenness of having it to the point of excluding the possibility of it meaning anything. This is a clue to the role that Kant assigns to permanence in the perception of appearances. Empiricism is just the behaviorism of appearances in general. Which is to say, behaviorism is just the restrictive application of empiricist reductionism to the special case of mind. Of course we must *have* evidence of the appearances we perceive, but the evidence must *be evidence.* The reductivist accounts attend entirely to the former to the neglect of the latter.

The primacy of the unity of mind is a clue to the permanence of substance for several reasons.

First of all, unity and permanence are related notions. One of the easiest ways to accommodate inconsistency—that is, to maintain that thoughts belong to one mind even though they are in logical opposition—is to have the mind think these thoughts at different times. In assigning these thoughts to different times, we regard them as being episodic rather than dispositional. We think the person once thought this, then changed his mind and thought that; but to have a reason to think this we must have both evidence for each occasion and a general conception of what he thinks that makes the switch intelligible. Suppose we have only the occasional indications, but that everything we know about his mind makes the switch improbable. Then we do not think that he first thought this and then thought that; instead we think either that he never meant the one or that he never meant the other. He could not have because, by hypothesis, he could never shift from thinking the one thing to thinking the other. What this shows is that even the allocation of different states to different times is subject to a consistency criterion overall. Change is possible, and with change, the accommodation diachronically of things that would, taken synchronically, be incompatible; even change cannot accommodate everything, but only those alterations that preserve unity at a deeper level while allowing a surface diversity. Permanence is the deeper-level unity which obtains throughout surface-level change.

Just as behaviorism is a restricted case of empiricist reduction, the presupposition that there is substance in appearance is a general case of which presupposition of mind is an instance. The evidential character of the given is taken in the instance of mind from the supposition of unity, and in general it is taken from the supposition that, as Kant says,

> Coming to be and ceasing to be are not alterations of that which comes to be or ceases to be. Alteration is a way of existing which follows upon another way of existing in the same object. All that alters itself *persists,* and only its *state changes.* Since this change thus concerns only the determinations, which can cease to be or begin to be, we can say, using what may seem a somewhat paradoxical expression, that only the permanent (substance) is altered, and that the transitory suffers no alteration but only a *change,* inasmuch as certain determinations cease to be and others begin to be (A 187 = B 230–31).[26]

As I oppose the presupposition of mind to behaviorism, Kant puts the presupposition of permanence throughout change in opposition to the empiricist doctrine that objects are the mere sums of their (changing) states. He contends that they are more than that—that they are that which persists through change. This adds no content to the description of them, but the treatment of them as things that endure does constrain us in what we may suppose them to be liable to do. Thus the evident change may, for instance, be in shape (say from being straight to being bent) and, just as we might consider the mind of another capable of transition from a passionate commitment to something to disillusioned rejection of it, we consider the object capable of transition from one shape to another. That is, we consider it flexible. This is not just a fancy way of saying that at t_1 it is observed to have one shape and at t_2 another, because the attribution of a dispositional property to it is a way of accommodating change at the surface-level while preserving an underlying constancy. In short, to combine the two different (evident) properties in one object, we must create two levels within the object: its transitory states and its capacities to go from one state to another.

Moreover, something of our general strategy of understanding change is revealed by the way we distinguish between what someone *is thinking* (on a particular occasion) and what he *thinks* (in general). The given—utterance, gesture, or whatever—is taken to represent the particular or episodic, which is in turn taken to represent the general and dispositional. By thus distinguishing between the evident character and the latent character of the mind—by taking the sensorily given to represent the former, and then by repeating the representation relation between the two characters—we (a) create a ground for treating the given *as evidence* (of the way in which that which abides manifests itself), and (b) preserve the fundamental unity of that which abides—setting both limits on, and reasons for, the changes of transitory properties to which it is liable. Whatever we credit to it as a capacity for change is assigned to its permanent character—hence *could* show up in its other changes of evident characteristics, and, more importantly, *must* show up whenever the appropriate situations call for it. For example, suppose we combine the evident cheer and evident gloom in one person—apprehending the sensorily given on one occasion as an indication of high spirits and on another as an indication of low—by saying that the person is susceptible to swings in mood. If we think of the person as given to mood changes, we have a ground for regarding what seems evident as being actually evidence of how he feels; but we also take on a commitment to regard him as having that sort of nature (all the time). If subsequent evidence were not to bear out the attribution to him of variability in mood, we would have to rethink what we had thought we had evidence of. For instance, if everything else points to him being tiresomely, but indefatigably, cheerful, then, though on one occasion he *seemed* evidently morose, we have *no* evidence of this. Instead, we must take the signs of low spirits, not in their usual signification as evidence of being down, but as a pretense of the sort to which an obnoxiously happy person is liable; we say he is just playing at being unhappy.

The division between evident and dispositional characters of an object sets up the possibility of construing the evident as evidence, and it regulates the ways in which the evident is construed. It does so by creating a context of permanent properties to which transitory properties can be related.

A basic consideration in the representation of material objects is the diversity of their changing states. Unless a ground is provided for our doing so, we cannot consider an object that is x to be identical with an object that is not-x. The qualitative difference is a *prima facie* reason to think that there are two distinct objects. The change is not to be explained away by the mere addition of a temporal determinant to the incompatible predicates to create x at t_1 and not-x at t_2. First, being at t_1 and being at t_2 are not determinable differences given in sense. Second, if they were, they would not cancel the other difference; they would compound it. That is, if time were a determination inhering in things as a property,[27] there would be two grounds for considering the objects to be numerically distinct.

In order to reconcile the diversity of x and not-x with the identity of the object supposed to be both x and not-x, we do need to employ a temporal difference to admit the possibility of the thing's change of properties. But the temporality cannot be that which is given in apprehension; it must be that which is in the object. Suppose you at one time see an object that is x and at some other time see an object that is not-x. The differences in the times of your apprehension do not entitle you to suppose that it is one and the same object just apprehended as x at t_1 and apprehended as not-x at t_2. You must have reason to suppose that the object would undergo alteration; otherwise, it is simpler to suppose that the change from t_1 to t_2 is only in the content of your senses, and that it comes about because you look first at one thing and then at another. To suppose that it is the same thing on both occasions you must add to the change in sensory content an additional and corresponding change in the properties of the object. It is, of course, possible to do this; but it is not possible to do it on the basis of the sensorily given alone, since that will be the same if we view two different objects or one changing one. We need to know at what times things have one state or another, not at what times we apprehend them as being in one state or another.

26. Why a Kantian Account Must Be Given

Kant thinks that the permanence of substance is required for the representation of objective time. He says, "Only through the permanent does existence in different parts of the time-series acquire a magnitude which can be entitled duration" (A 183 = B 226). Duration is essential to change; for, unless an object persists throughout the times of its various states, we just have a diversity *of* objects, not diversity *in* an (enduring) object. What is not obvious is why permanence is required.

One might wonder why some set of relatively permanent, stable, and regular things would not be sufficient as points of reference for a system of spatial and temporal locations. Of course, for the measurement of the passage of time it would be necessary to have some series of regular happenings, and for the series to be unbroken. Walker amplifies these ideas in the following two paragraphs:

Whichever way one takes it the argument of the First Analogy is quite remarkably unpersuasive. The main argument in A says that something permanent is required in order to determine objective time-relations; in B an argument is added which is similar except that it appears to say the permanent is needed in order to have any time-relations at all, objective or not. So far as any grounds are offered for this remarkable allegation, they consist in the thought that unless something were permanent time could not be measured, to which there are two obvious replies. One is that to measure time all we require is regularity, not permanence; a regular series of flashes would do as well as a clock. The other is that experience of temporal order would be quite possible even if we could not measure time; we could still relate events as contemporary or successive.

He does also say that if there were only relatively permanent things we could not have a single unitary time-order. But (leaving aside the question whether we need such a thing) for that we do not even require that the same regularities should continue. If we have been used to measuring time by the sun, and the sun stops rising and setting, we shall need some new regularity to measure time by; but provided that the two have worked side by side for a period we shall be able to carry the old measurements over. And even if there is no overlap—even if, at an instant, the entire world of physical objects with all its regularities changes completely—this does not destroy the unity of the temporal ordering of events, for this is sufficiently established by the general agreement of observers.[28]

Each of Walker's objections misses the point; and each counterproposal he makes begs the question. Consider the second paragraph first. He stipulates that instead of permanence to establish the time-order, either overlapping regularities or the general agreement of observers would suffice to order events. It is true that they would suffice, but the point is to account for our acquaintance with regularities. Walker misses the point because he mislocates the level of Kant's concerns. Of course, if our experience includes experiences of things that are regular, or if there could be common observation by several observers even in a world without some series of overlapping regularities, then we could establish temporal order.

There is an old joke about an engineer and an economist cast away on an island with tinned food but no opener. The engineer says, "Let's build a fire and heat them until they explode." The economist says, "Let's suppose we have an opener." Walker supposes we experience the regularities or general agreement sufficient to establish an objective temporal ordering. He might as well suppose that we have wristwatches or can phone for the time.

It is the whole notion of regularity that is at issue. Regularity obtains within the objective order. Once one can account for our knowedge of a world wherein some events take place at fixed intervals, the account can readily be extended to the selection of devices to measure time.[29] Likewise, with a community of observers able to reach agreement on their observations, it is relatively unproblematic to explain how their agreement might extend to the ordering of events.

Kant takes up the matter of objective time-determination not at the level on which it is no longer problematic, but where it still is a problem. There may be sensations that occur at seemingly regular intervals in portions of our sensory input; but one cannot expect a priori that they will be sufficiently regular and thoroughgoing to ensure a subjective measure (of sorts) of the passage of time, and a posteriori reflection reveals nothing sufficient to establish temporal order. Until we relate our inner experiences to a world of things, "apprehension is only a placing together of the manifold of empirical intuition; and we can find in it no representation of any necessity which determines the appearances thus combined to have connected existence in space and time" (B 219). I have quoted that before, and repeat it here to stress that Kant is concerned to explain how we come to have experience of the connected existence of things.

In the first paragraph, Walker makes rather too much of temporal *measurement*. The setting up of clocks and calendars is an empirical concern that is not essential to experience. There could be people with experience—with a full-fledged system of thought—who had not yet advanced to chronometry. The magnitude of time (which it is Kant's concern to establish in the First Analogy) is distinct from the measure of the magnitude of time (which is not his immediate concern, though the possibility of measuring it does require that it first be established; and, in establishing it, Kant sets out those features—especially causal regularity—on which the possibility of measurement rests). Again, Walker misses the point and begs the question. Once we know that things do endure throughout the changes of their states, we can then ask questions about the extent of their durations, compare their rates of change, etc.; but, first, we must know that they do endure. If one plunges straight into the questions of measurement, one misses Kant's primary concern: to show that, and how, we have knowledge of things of the sort that can be measured in respect of how long they last or how often they occur. To assume that we know the sun and its rising and setting is to pass over what Kant thinks needs explanation. The project of the Analogies is to account for our experience of material objects and their changes of state. If one is happy to take for granted the results of the account, and to begin with the presumption that we have experiences of objective regularities and that we enjoy interpersonal agreement, then one does not need to take notice of Kant's project. But Walker cannot convert his own preparedness to take things for granted into an objection to Kant's efforts to explain.

One final point about Walker's remark that permanence is not required, only regularity. He says, "a regular series of flashes would do as well as a clock," meaning (one hopes) not that it would do as well as a clock would do, but that, as a clock, a regular series of flashes would do as well as the permanent. Apart from the misplaced emphasis on measurement (misplaced because the permanent does not provide a clock, but only the dispositional characteristics that account for the regularities of change by which time can be measured), there is another objection to be made to the remark. That a series of flashes would do as well is beside the point since we lack such a series of flashes. The castaways would not need to open the tins were there a restaurant on the island. I have already remarked that we have neither a priori ground for expecting, nor a posteriori observation of, the sorts of seeming regularity in sensation that would provide a representation of time. All through his book, Walker helps himself to the convenient fictions of empiricist methodology by which one may dispute the necessity of anything by freely inventing an alternative to it. There is less under heaven than is dreamed of in empiricist methodology. Unless philosophy is to be regarded as simply a game of unbridled imagination, it must restrict itself to what can be shown to be necessary as part of an overall account. Why stop at flashes? Why presume that they are regular? Why not suppose that the BBC broadcasts the time to us continuously as part of what is given to us in sense?

Walker's method of argument is puzzling. The absence of any development of, or argument for, the counter proposal—that a series of flashes could do as well—suggests that he intends the objection as an instance of Hume's test for conceptual necessity: Hume takes the necessary to be that which cannot be consistently denied, so one may dispute any purported necessity by merely stating consistently some rival possibility. The test is fair enough, perhaps, for elementary necessities like p or not-p whose denial yields a contradiction straight off; and fair enough too for obvious contingencies whose denials are obviously contingent. For more complex necessities, more than the bald and unsupported assertion of an alternative seems required. Since Kant does not think that his principles are mere tautologies, the test seems rather to bear out what he thinks than to object to it. The necessity of the principles is not to be understood as being a merely self-contained and verbal matter. Instead, the necessity of representing the permanence of substance in appearance is a matter that ties in with the whole theory of experience. To object to that sort of necessity, one would need not a rival remark, but a rival account. Walker scorns the "quite remarkably unpersuasive argument"; but, given what he thinks is adequate as an objection to it, he seems unsure whether to construe what Kant says as a purported analyticity or as an explanation.

The First Analogy is argued in the context created by the Axioms and Anticipations. They create the necessity of the regulative principles of the Analogies by revealing the indeterminacy of apprehension. The regularities to which Walker appeals are not available to Kant at the outset. All that he may avail himself of are the features of magnitude and temporality established in the earlier sections on intuition. These alone must make it possible to represent substance and attribute in appearance.

Kemp Smith, in his *Commentary,* finds a contradiction between two things Kant says in the proof of the First Analogy. Kant says,

> all change and coexistence are only so many ways (modes of time) in which the permanent exists. And simultaneity and succession being the only relations in time, it follows that only in the permanent are relations of time possible (A 182–83 = B 226).

Just a few lines later Kant says,

> change does not affect time itself, but only appearances in time. (Coexistence is not a mode of time itself; for none of the parts of time coexists; they are all in succession to one another.) (A 183 = B 226).

Kemp Smith says that these two passages involve "assertions directly contradictory of one another. The one asserts change and simultaneity to be modes of time; the other denies this."[30]

Of course, there is no contradiction; but there is a need to take account of the differences between time itself and the things in time. These differences are an important aspect of Kant's discussion throughout the Analogies. He is concerned both with the nature of the things that we experience and with the nature of the temporal framework within which our experiences and their objects occur. Kant repeatedly plays the one off against the other. One moment does not differ from another, except in virtue of its content, so various sensations must be present at some moments and absent at others. The categories of reality and negation find their application in the awareness that we must have of what is, or is not, given in sense. But the continuity of time, and the extensive magnitude of a time in which a sensation can occur, require that the category of limitation find application too. With the category of limitation comes awareness of the acts of apprehension by which we respond to the effects of objects on us in the production of sensation. This awareness of our own action carries with it awareness of the nonmomentary character of times, and the possibility of qualitative comparison.

However, the Axioms and Anticipations are not complete in themselves. They threaten to collapse without the additional support of principles structuring a second level of experience. Kant says, "Only through the permanent does existence in different parts of the time-series acquire a magnitude which can be entitled duration. For in bare succession existence is always vanishing and recommencing, and never has the least magnitude" (A 183 = B 226). One might think that the problem alluded to in the second sentence has been met by the category of limitation and the accompanying awareness of the times in which sensations occur as intervals. The reference to vanishing and recommencing alludes to just the sort of moment-by-moment change provided by reality and negation without the addition of limitation. But that addition is not enough on its own to establish duration. We must indeed be conscious of our own acts of apprehension—conscious, not just that we feel this and no more feel that, but that we *continue* to feel this (with the constant content supplying no differentiation of the succession of moments implicit in the notion of continuation). However, the awareness of the nonmomentary is not (yet or quite) the knowledge of duration. An inner clock such as we must be supposed to possess records only that time is passing, not how much time is passing. In subjective temporality there is only partial representation of extensive magnitude.

One might wonder why awareness of the passage of time is not sufficient for experience. That is, one might wonder why knowledge of duration is essential to experience. In part, the response to that speculation takes us into the consequences of adding duration and substance to what we already have; for, once they are added, it becomes possible to explain our knowledge of causality, and with causal knowledge much else can be explained. In the passages just quoted Kant refers to this part of the justification of adding enduring substances, when he says that only in the permanent are change, succession, and coexistence possible. So part of the reason for enriching our subjective awareness of time's passage by transforming it to knowledge of duration rests with the possibilities that the transformation gives rise to. If we add substance and its dispositional properties, we can get causality; then with substance and causality, we can get a subjective/objective distinction; and, with all that, we have a basis for the ampliative and corrective functions of empirical thought: with knowledge of causal laws we can make inferences to things we have not directly observed; and, knowing the effects of objects on us, we can correct misperceptions when the effects of one object on us have been mistaken for the similar effects of another object. The First Analogy is justified in part because it is foundational for the other Analogies, and for the Postulates.

Kant also justifies the First Analogy by appeal to common belief. He says, "I find that in all ages, not only philosophers, but even the common understanding, have recognized this permanence as the substratum of all change of appearances, and always assume it to be indubitable" (A 184 = B 227). He goes on to describe some philosopher's calculation of the weight of smoke by subtraction of the weight of the ashes from the weight of the unburnt wood. He also cites the propositions that nothing arises from nothing and that nothing reverts to nothing as instances of the standard presupposition in philosophy of the permanence of substance. Common belief satisfies Austin's advice that we look to what many have thought over long periods of time. What the common understanding has recognized in all ages is deserving of our serious regard. As well (though Austin does not think so) what philosophers have thought also deserves regard.[31]

Kant is not content either to leave it to subsequent developments of his system or to appeal to common and philosophical belief in it to prove his principle in the First Analogy. He says,

> Throughout all changes in the world *substance* remains and only the *accidents* change. But I nowhere find even the attempt at a proof of this obviously synthetic proposition. Indeed, it is very seldom placed, where it truly belongs, at the head of those laws of nature which are pure and completely a priori. Certainly the proposition, that substance is permanent, is tautological. For this permanence is our sole ground for applying the category of substance to appearance; and we ought first to have proved that in all appearances there is something permanent, and that the transitory is nothing but determination of its existence. But such a proof cannot be developed dogmatically, that is, from concepts, since it concerns a synthetic a priori proposition. Yet as it never occurred to anyone that such propositions are valid only in relation to possible experience, and can therefore be proved only through a deduction of the possibility of experience, we need not be surprised that though the above principle is always postulated as lying at the basis of experience (for in empirical knowledge the need of it is *felt*), it has never itself been proved (A 184–85 = B 227–28).

Kant distinguishes his principle from the sort of proposition that is conceptually necessary because its denial is self-contradictory. The principle is that *in nature,* and *in all change of appearances,* substance is permanent. These qualifications added to the tautology produce a nontrivial claim that requires proof—among other things that there is something permanent in appearance. No such proof can be by logical analysis alone. It must be by transcendental argument.

We make things much harder for ourselves if we describe the proof without regard for Kant's transcendental idealism. He is not trying to show that the category of substance applies to the world as it is in itself, but only to the world as we experience it, as it appears to us. This allows us to look for a proof that rests on the requirements of cognition. To appear to us, objects must be given in sense; but to be regarded as real, objects must be material. These necessities arise as conditions for the possibility of experience in the following way: if, without the employment of the category of substance and attribute, nothing can appear and there can be no experience (= knowledge which *determines* an object through perceptions[32]), but if employment of the category is an essential part of a set of conditions sufficient for experience, then it is necessary that appearances have the features that allow the application of the category.

The point of the last paragraph can be made in another way. Kant's overall objective in the *Critique* is to show that our knowledge is limited to things as they appear to us. Both in support of, and because of, this limitation, certain features (such as their permanence) of the things that we know can be, and can only be, proved to obtain if one takes account of our coming to know them. The proof of each principle may draw on features of objects that are contributed by the mind. This makes the proofs easier to provide. But if the proofs would be impossibly difficult without reference to the a priori contributions of the mind, then the theory that works by taking account of the mind is the only theory that works at all, and the general thesis of transcendental idealism is supported.

To find the proof of the principle, we must look first to how reference to the conditions for experience helps to establish it, and then consider why that reference is essential.

Without the selectivity imposed by the representation-relation, apprehension is undetermined. Sensations may be combined or compared in indefinitely many ways. The intuitions that result from arbitrary combination or comparison cannot be considered sufficient as objects of knowledge because they have no necessary connections among themselves. By reference to them, no inferences can (as Hume so ably proves) be drawn concerning the future, the past, or the otherwise unobserved. Only objects *with* necessary connections sustain inferences. Not even Hume can consider the immediate objects of apprehension adequate to experience. He invents expectations and fictions to transform what is actually given into what we commonly believe.

Hume shows the need for an account of objective belief, but he does not supply it. The mechanisms of belief formation that he proposes are too productive. Each person has a myriad of sensations, and all lend themselves to the production of all sorts of expectation through the variety of their chance repetitions and connections. One need not deny that habit plays some part in our lives; but one need only regard the variety and difference in habit—and contrast its person-to-person variability with the interpersonal agreement on matters of fact—to realize that Hume has the wrong mechanism. Even within the individual, the reconciliation of beliefs, the correction of errors, the revision of opinion, are all indicative of something quite different from behavior reinforced by operant conditioning.[33]

As one might object to Descartes that the problem is not so much with the representation of objects as with the restriction to objects that are material, to Hume one might object that the problem is more with the restriction of belief than with the mere production of it. Which is not to say that he is right about the production of it, but that his misidentification of the production mechanism results from his misconstruing the objective as basically something *more than* is given in sense (an extra step that is illegitimate, but taken anyway).

Our beliefs do go beyond what is sensorily given, but Kant sees that, more important than the extension, there is a restriction involved. In fact, a whole family of restrictions. We do not recognize something as real by adding predicates to its description,[34] but by having to regard it as real. The need for some representation of reality arises from the lack of order and connection in intuitions in themselves. To be the content of a mind, intuitions need order and content—if not in themselves, then in virtue of what they represent. Without the connection they can derive from their representation of an orderly world, sensations would be a random jumble of noises and feelings, utterly meaningless. What objects we represent, and how we represent them, must also be constrained if the representation of reality is to accomplish its end of unifying intuition as a meaningful whole. To achieve the reduction of its sensory diversity, the combinations possible by the principles of the Axioms and Anticipations must be applied to the manifold of intuition. It would do no good to have each sensation represent a different object, for that would just reduplicate the sensory diversity on another level. But the combinations cannot be arbitrary— not if we hope, by reference to what they represent, to find connections binding one sensory experience with another. If combination takes in changing properties, unity must still be preserved in the object; and we are forced to regard the object as that which is changeable in certain ways. All these constraints on what we may, and must, regard as real are *enabling constraints*. *Must* also implies *can*. Kant concerns himself with regulative principles, limiting conditions, and constraints, but his resolution of these concerns does reveal the mechanisms that produce knowledge.

Hume's account is comparable to an effort to discover the laws of logic by considering the ways one idea may lead to another. By contrast, Kant's account is comparable to considering the restrictions that are necessary to avoid invalidity. The rules of logic preserve truth. The rules of experience preserve empirical content. There is as much need to eliminate what is not signified in sense as there is to guard against what does not follow from premises; and one understands legitimate representation or inference by understanding the constraints under which it operates.

27. The Quantum of Substance and the Unity of Time

In the statement of the principle of the First Analogy in B, Kant uses the Latin word *quantum* as though it were German (*das Quantum*). Earlier—in the Axioms—he uses it as Latin in a parenthetical contrast to *quantitas* to differentiate between two senses of the German word *Grösse* (magnitude): "These are the axioms which, strictly, relate only to magnitudes (*quanta*) as such. As regards magnitude (*quantitas*), that is, the answer to the question: 'How big is the thing?' " (A 163 = B 204).[35] The *quantum/quantitas* distinction is between the measurable and the measure (like the *verum/veritas* distinction between the thing that is true and the truth-value of the true).

The distinction is important because it indicates what it is that Kant means to prove. I chide Walker for being too concerned about measurement, and he is. When we are ready to raise questions such as, "How long has this been here?" or "How old is that?", we are ready to employ empirical devices to determine a feature of things that we presuppose they have—namely, duration. Of course, the utilization of empirical measuring devices also presupposes our acquaintance with, and knowledge of, material objects and their processes. Kant does not want *to presuppose* either that things endure (that we can ask how long or how old) or that we know objects that behave with enough regularity to measure time. In short, he is not interested in *quantitas*.

His primary concern is to explain our knowledge by perception of objects, but he couples this with a concern to prove that the objects we perceive endure. The combination of concerns is reasonable since an account of our knowledge of objects that did not explain our knowledge of them *as things that endure* would be woefully inadequate. More than that. Kant thinks it impossible to provide an account that leaves out duration because it is in virtue of being things that persist that things are known to us (as real objects, and not merely things thought).

In the quote just given from the Axioms, Kant says they relate to *quantum*. Here he is again concerned with *quantum*. This is not a repetition, nor is he retracting the principle of extensive magnitude when he now says that "only through the permanent does existence in different parts of the time-series acquire a magnitude which can be entitled duration" (A 183 = B 226). Sensory apprehension does confer magnitude on sensations, but the magnitude is not measurable. We are subjectively aware of the passage of time; but we are not, at the level of sensory apprehension, acquainted with time as something that can be marked out in uniform lengths. That is why Kant refers to existence *in different parts* of the time-series. One may be subjectively aware of time's passage either by the succession of many sensations or just by the consciousness that one must have of one's own ongoing response to a constant sensation; but neither awareness, though it carries with it the extensive magnitude *of one time,* relates the magnitude *of one time to another.* In subjective time, each part has a magnitude; but there is not a magnitude that each part has—which is not to say that there is no common measure of each part, that is, no length common to them all (though that is true). Rather it is to say that there is nothing all parts of the manifold of intuition have in common by virtue of which their extent could be measured. It is not as though intuitions vary one to the next as wallets each containing some amount of a common currency; it is instead as though we have wallets each with its own currency. We know the times of subjective awareness as intervals, but we lack a standard of comparison. One intuition occurs in the time in which a group of sounds are heard; another in the whole time in which we feel thirst; a third in the apprehension of a movement; and so on.

Chapter four explains the indeterminacies of apprehension implicit in the principles of magnitude: sensations can be grouped or compared or both; they can be grouped in one way or another, compared in this respect or that. There is now an additional indeterminacy in respect of temporal extent. Subjective times have no quantity that can be entitled duration. However, relation to objects that endure, that are stable or orderly in their changes, would confer a derivative duration and order on subjective times by connecting them to the times of the occurrence of regular things (in ways to be described in detail throughout the next chapter).

There is empirical corroboration of the fact that we do make reference to things in the world to determine the passage of time; but the empirical is not the origin of the relations of inner experience to outer—between intuition and appearance, subjective time and objective time. The empirical supplies only the content of the first term of the relation.

The analytic a priori—that is, the connections of concepts—exhibits many of the structural features of time intuition and appearance as having a common form (e.g., part/whole relations) or as having interrelated forms (e.g., continuity and limitation); but, as Kant says in the long passage quoted a few pages back, "a proof cannot be developed dogmatically, that is, from concepts, since it concerns a synthetic a priori proposition. . . . such propositions are valid only in relation to possible experience, and can therefore be proved only through a deduction of the possibility of experience'' (A 184–85 = B 227–28). One cannot prove that the relations of our experience hold for any creature that has sensation. All that is required for sensation is some sensory apparatus; we could call anything from an automatic door to a phototropic plant to an elephant a sensing device. What one can prove is that a sensing creature with a capacity for self-consciousness and for knowledge must relate its sensory input to objects according to certain rules. More specifically, one can prove that the principle of the permanence of substance is among the rules required.

This may be rather less than a transcendental realist would want proved; for he would want it shown that the permanence obtains in respect of things as they are in themselves, not just in respect of appearances. But it is more than the empirical idealist thinks provable. Both ought to be satisfied with the transcendental idealism and empirical realism that Kant proposes. The limitation to appearances (the transcendental idealism) shares the empirical idealist's objection to objects that are purported by transcendental realists to be both real and beyond all possibility of experience. Yet it does not reduce objects to mere collections of ideas. Instead, the objects of experience are more than collected sensations but more by virtue of a restriction on the apprehension of the given—not by virtue of a dogmatic principle such as 'God is no deceiver' or the principle of sufficient reason. There is nothing proposed for which we will lack evidence in experience; and, hence, nothing to draw the principal reproach of the empirical idealist against claims of knowledge that cannot be backed by evidence. What is proposed is that there is more to experience than sensory input, and more to evidence than the having of it. Experience includes the principles that transform sensory input to knowledge, and what we have must conform to those principles to be evidence. The realist wants a world out there—not just some surrogate supplied by a specious projection or combination of what, properly understood, exists only in our minds. He can have it if he will admit the near tautology that it is a world *known to us* only as it appears to us. This does not require him to deny that the world may have an unknowable nature as it is in itself, only to restrict knowledge of objects to knowable objects. Provided that as it appears to us the world must be stable, orderly, objective, and irreducible, there is no positive reason to want knowledge of more than appears to us. Kant gives each side what it wants: to the empirical idealist, evidence; to the transcendental realist, objectivity. He just denies them what they wrongly think they need if they are to have what they want. They do not need reduction to the given or dogmatic principles.

Recognition that objects are known to us only as they appear to us, together with discovery of the conditions they must meet in order to appear to us, leads directly to empirical realism. That is, transcendental idealism proves everything that exists in nature is material in the sense that carries with it permanence, stability, objective spatiotemporality, causal regularity, uniformity, etc.

First of all, permanence. Kant says,

> We have only to deal with appearances in the field of experience; and the unity of experience would never be possible if we were willing to allow that new things (in respect of their substance) could come into existence. For we should then lose that which alone can represent the unity of time, namely, the identity of the substratum, wherein alone all change has thoroughgoing unity. This permanence is, however, simply the way in which we represent to ourselves the existence of things (in appearance) (A 186 = B 229).[36]

The passage raises two questions: why the unity of experience is necessary, and why we cannot allow that things new in respect of their substance could come into existence.

The first is answered almost definitionally by reflection on what Kant means by experience. Experience is not whatever may be given in sense, whatever we may feel, dream or imagine, what we may wish for or decide; no, it is just our knowledge of objects by means of perception (with whatever essentially accompanies that knowledge). Experience in the ordinary and all-inclusive sense lacks unity; one entertains inconsistent ideas, and the mind wanders. Knowledge, however, is the subset of thought that is consistent (for on the discovery of inconsistency we suspend belief), coherent, objective (for on proof of subjectivity one must relegate knowledge-claims to expressions of opinion), tied to sensory experience (for without the tie there is no evidential backing). These criteria of knowledge are all aspects of unity; and experience, as Kant defines it, has all these aspects. They are particular ways in which it has unity. It is not that we look at experience and find that it has these features. In advance of the features all that there is to look at is the diverse content of sensibility and whatever thought might cross a mind that did not employ the criteria. Rather, we produce the subset of our thought by regulating admission to experience (in Kant's narrow, technical sense) in accordance with the various aspects of unity. The claim is not that every sensing creature does this, nor even every person; the claim is rather that to have knowledge is to be able to distinguish between what one merely thinks *of* and what one may think (*that*) by using rules that restrict judgment and assertion. In short, knowers are sorters of mental content into two piles: the merely thought of, and the representation that it must be possible for the 'I think' to accompany[37]—that is, assertable mental content. Those who don't sort, don't know. But the sortings are not once done and over with; we continually move things back and forth as later evidence undermines earlier knowledge-claims, and guesses prove correct, and we discover and resolve conflicting beliefs, and so on. Its unity is not something we discover about our experience. Unity is the result of the conditions that we employ to create experience.

The second question is why we cannot allow that things new in substance could come into existence. Kant gives the answer when he asserts that we would lose the unity of time; but to understand the answer we must understand why it is the one he gives.

To maintain the unity of well-established experience, we must do all the proper things: put controls on experiments, try replication in other labs, worry about consistency, see if rival hypotheses would work as well. All fine and good, for experience that *is* underway; but what Kant wants to explain is how it *gets* underway. By showing that the principles of sensory apprehension are indeterminate he shows that knowledge cannot arise from only a sensory origin. The variability of apprehension and the variety of thought and imagination require the imposition of constraints on what may be represented as real. The first constraint he places is the substantiality of the real. To represent something as existing in the world is to represent it as material.

What is it to represent it as material? It is to represent the diversity combined in the object as grounded in the object—as the properties it has. If these change, the object persists; and its alterations are changes of states for which it, in virtue of its dispositional characteristics, is responsible. That is, the material character is the ground for uniting different properties in a single object. To express the point in terms of a rule, we could say that one may combine various properties in an object provided one can consider the object to be such that it can go from the one state to the other and remain in existence throughout the alteration.

Notice that Kant does not preclude the possibility of *new things* (obviously not). What he rules out is the possibility of things *new in respect of their substance*. Which is to say, our entitlement to regard changing states as inhering in an object that endures is a constraint on combination that makes possible the accommodation of surface diversity so long as underlying continuity is preserved. If the substratum could also change, there would be no constraint. I covered the point earlier in the discussion of our evidence of mind. We can take the sensory indications of various moods as evidence that the person feels what is indicated only if we have an objective ground for construing the evident as evidence. The appropriate ground in that case would be that the person has the sort of personality that has those sorts of moods. The ground in general (that is, for all material objects) is that whatever would be taken to be a sensory representation of them must represent that which can be united within them by virtue of the sort of object they are. *Now suppose* that an object could change sorts, that is, be new in respect of its substance. Then it could undergo any change whatsoever in its evident characteristics. If one set of dispositional characteristics cannot accommodate the change, one is freed, by the supposition, from having to think that some one of the following is true: what seemed to be evidence for the earlier state cannot have been; what seems to be evidence for the later state must not be; or, we are dealing with a different object. The supposition that sub-stance itself can change lets anything happen.

When anything goes, everything goes. We lose the constraint on the representation of appearance that would be supplied by the principle of the permanence of substance. This does not leave us free to represent anything we please. We are left unable to represent anything at all because we can regard no combinations as determined in sense by virtue of, and by reference to, the sort of object they would represent if taken as rep-resentations. Except on the principle of permanence, objects do not have natures restricting their changes to those they are capable of. Any com-bination in sense is as good as another, and the mind is left with random patterns of sensation.

When Kant points out that novelty at the level of substance would destroy the identity of the substratum "wherein all change has through-going unity," he says, "we should then lose that which alone can represent the unity of time." He develops that thought in the concluding paragraphs of the proof of the First Analogy. In the second and third paragraphs from the end of the section, he considers both sides of the question of what would happen if substance is (is not) permanent.

First, *with* the permanence of substance, we *can* maintain constancy while accommodating two sorts of change: "from one state to another, and from not-being to being" (A 188 = B 231). When change is from one state of an object to another, the relevant material considerations are those pertaining to the sort of stuff comprised in the object. When change involves the beginning of a new object (birth, manufacture, etc.), the change is accounted for in terms of that which exists before the new object comes along. Either sort of change involves a moment-to-moment diversity in what is evident; and, with substance, there is a connection between the different things evident at different moments. If the sensa-tions of one moment are taken to represent a certain state, and those of some other moment are taken to represent some other state, the two states may nonetheless (that is, despite their differences) be related to each other as various determinations of the same object; the sensations may be related to each other as the contents of different perceptions of the same thing; and the times of the two sensory experiences may be related to each other by virtue of their related content. The details of these relations are yet to be given; but the possibility of giving them depends on the fundamental relation of properties to an underlying substratum—either the matter in the object, or the matter from which the object is composed.

We have now to consider the other side. There are two texts, one in each paragraph. Here is the first.

> If we assume that something absolutely begins to be, we must have a point of time in which it was not. But to what are we to attach this point, if not to that which already exists? For a preceding empty time is not an object of perception. But if we connect the coming to be with things which previously existed, and which persist in existence up to the moment of .this coming to be, this latter must be simply a determination of what is permanent in that which precedes it. Similarly also with ceasing to be . . ." (A 188 = B 231).

I read the "If we assume" at the beginning of the passage as saying "Suppose we try to represent an absolute coming to be," and the rest of the passage as explaining why this fails. To be a thing that has just started to exist, it must be represented as a thing that did not exist a little while ago. But how are we to represent that? That is, what sensory evidence could we possibly have for its not having existed a moment ago? Our not having seen it will not do.[38] Our not having evidence of it earlier may be because there is no evidence to have, but it may as easily be because we happened not to see it before, though it did exist. The point is, we have to attach evidence to the not-having-previously-existed component of the representation of it as new. We can do this only by having evidence that something previously existing produced it; but that connects it into the permanent that precedes it. The same argument applies to ceasing to be.[39] Now here is the second text:

> Substances (in appearance) are the substrata of all determinations of time. If some of these substances could come into being and others cease to be, the one condition of the empirical unity of time would be removed. The appearances would then relate to two different times, and existence would flow in two parallel streams—which is absurd. There is *only one* time in which all different times must be located, not as coexistent, but as in succession to one another (A 188–89 = B 232–33).[40]

The first of the two texts argues against any coming to be or ceasing to be that is absolute (and not relative to the productive or destructive actions of other things). The second text argues against diversity at the level of the substratum. Kant's own example of the fire's reduction of wood to ash and smoke shows that he well recognizes transitions from one substance to another; but such changes of substances must themselves be grounded in more fundamental substances, until finally we get to matter.

Kant could extend his previous objection; but he has a second objection to make—one somehow involving (the impossibility of) *two* parallel streams of time.

Here is a counterproposal that fits the meager description Kant gives. Suppose that among the substances of the world there are some that do not arise out of, or revert back to, a single common substratum of reality (= matter). Many consider our minds to be just such substances. There is then within the world that which happens and is grounded ultimately in matter, and that which happens and is not so grounded. In ways long made familiar by discussions of the mind/body problem, transitions from thought to action or from physical to mental, on the supposition that mind and matter are fundamentally different, are broken off at some point. The result is Leibnizian parallelism of the two clocks. They can keep time together by mutual influence, by continual adjustments, or by being crafted and set so perfectly at the beginning that their preestablished harmony is maintained. Leibniz, of course, opts for the third way of explaining the relation of mind to body.[41]

Given the brevity of his description of the counterproposal, Kant must have Leibniz in mind. At least I can think of nothing else so familiar that so few words would suffice to allude to it. There is a second reason to think so in the reply Kant gives to the notion of two independent orders of reality with their appearances related to two different times. Kant says, "There is only *one time* in which all different times must be located, not as coexistent, but as in succession to one another" (loc. cit.). This is a rather neat reply to Leibniz, who holds that coexistence is the order, not of time, but of space.[42] Leibniz recognizes that the problem of mind/body coordination is essentially *temporal;* but he fails to recognize that his solution in terms of preestablished harmony and the two-clock model runs counter to his own doctrine of the coexistent as *spatial*.[43]

Kant opts for the first solution to the problem: mutual influence. Minds are not substances independent of the rest of the material order—not minds as we know them, as they appear to us. Kant's account of the causal interaction is a main part of the Third Analogy (and my chapter seven). The unity of time is all-inclusive—within subjective and objective time and between them. It must be. There is no unity of subjective time except by virtue of its relation to objective time. Kant may be a bit quick in dismissing the Leibnizian proposal as absurd, but he is right to dismiss it. There is no clock on the inside. Subjective time has no magnitude that may be entitled duration, no necessary succession of well-ordered moments. The fiction of a mental order that mirrors exactly a physical order of the body with thoughts, feelings, and decisions clicking away in exact correspondence to the goings-on of the objects of thought, the effects of things on the body, and the actions of the body—all without interaction but just by initial design—this fiction is just that: a fiction; or, as Kant's word for absurd (*ungereimt*) has it: bad poetry.

6   Cause and Effect

Introduction

Kant's theory starts with what is given in sense. It develops by adding constraints that must be put on sensory apprehension if the given is to represent reality. He argues in the Second, as in the other Analogies, that we must regard what is given in sense as representing that which is necessarily connected in appearance.

Hume's doubts concerning causality presuppose the perception of events, and question only the projection of observed regularities to the unobserved. Kant questions the presupposition by asking how it is that we are entitled to take the succession of our inner states of consciousness as having objective import—that is, as representations of what is going on in the world. It is not that we see events and think that the regularities to which they so far conform will be continued in the future, with the only, or basic, question being whether we are entitled to think this. There is no perception of events *at all* until there is an objective ground to regard what is given in sense as representing what happens in nature. The causal principle supplies this ground by making it a requirement that such diversity as would be represented by the given is in conformity with the regularity that would be observed if the diversity were real. That is, to be evidence of an event—of an objective occurrence, something really happening—sensory states must be taken to be representations of changes in the world; and this requires that only certain of the successions in apprehension be regarded as having objective import. Where Hume thinks we perceive local regularities from which we make dubious projections, Kant thinks that we can perceive as regular only that which is in accord with universal causal laws. On discovery that what we take to be the perception of an event is not in conformity with universal causal law, we must discount the purported perception as mere seeming (*Schein*) and not a genuine appearance (*Erscheinung*) at all. We could not have the difficulty that Hume envisages: hitherto observed regularities sometimes ceasing to be observed. We cannot count *as observations* the thoughts that this or that *was or is* happening unless what is thought of as a happening can be thought of as grounded both in sense *and in nature*. The former does not suffice as an adequate ground for objective representation.

154

The First Analogy finds application in the Second. The successive states that can be represented as stages of an event are those that are the changing determinations of material objects, whose dispositional characteristics are both revealed in, and responsible for, any alterations objects undergo.

28. Order-Indifference and Order-Dependence

Kant again, as in the First Analogy, revises his statement of the principle. In A, he says,

> Everything that happens, that is, begins to be, presupposes something upon which it follows in accordance with a rule (A 189).

In B, he says,

> All alterations take place in conformity with the law of the connection of cause and effect (B 232).

The first version emphasizes the relation of the Second Analogy to the First, by repeating the point that the representation of something as beginning to be requires the representation of it as having not existed previously. This, as discussed at the end of the last chapter, involves representing it as produced by things existing earlier, since its non-occurrence (empty time) is not perceivable. The first version is vague about the rule. The second version drops the reference back to the First Analogy,[1] but makes it explicit that causal laws govern all alterations. Each version covers an important aspect of the Second Analogy.

In the second of two paragraphs added to the beginning of the proof in B, Kant summarizes his argument: "I perceive that appearances follow one another, that is, that there is a state of things the opposite of which existed in a former state. Thus I am really connecting two perceptions in time" (B 233).[2] When there is perception of a change there is perception of what did not exist earlier; for if it did exist, there has been no change. The perception of an event is the perception of something happening or changing. As such, it essentially involves the combination of opposites. For example, if we see the sky darken, we see it light and we see it dark *and* we connect the two. It would not be enough just to see a light sky and then see a dark one, for this might be due to a difference of a numerical rather than a qualitative sort (i.e., two skies). Of course, we know that there is just one; but we know this because we know it changes in ways that accommodate the variety. Kant's concern is to explain how we know that it changes, and hence how it is that we perceive events. There is no event perceived when we see a straight stick and a bent one; and, given the opposition of the two (of straight to bent), there is reason to regard the difference as numerical unless we can *combine* what is given at one

moment with its opposite given at another moment *in the same object*—
as its changing determinations, that is, as alterations of that which persists.
Without such combination there is simply the perception, in quick succession, of a straight stick and a bent one—a diversity of objects instead of
diversity in an object.

In the remainder of the paragraph, Kant explains that the combination
is not given in perception. He says, "The *objective relation* of appearances
that follow upon one another is not to be determined through mere perception" (B 234). We do perceive, as the first sentence says, "that appearances follow one another"; but we do not see *the connections* between
the two appearances.[3] What is given is first one state and then another,
but we must supply the connection between them.

> In order that this relation be known as determined, the relation between
> the two states must be so thought that it is thereby determined as
> necessary which of them be placed before, and which after, and that
> they cannot be placed in the reverse relation. But the concept which
> carries with it a necessity of synthetic unity can only be a pure concept
> that lies in the understanding, not in perception; and in this case it is
> the concept of the *relation of cause and effect,* the former of which
> determines the latter in time, as its consequence—not as in a sequence
> that may occur solely in the imagination (or that may not be perceived
> at all). Experience itself—in other words, empirical knowledge of
> appearances—is thus possible only in so far as we subject the succession
> of appearances, and therefore all alteration, to the law of causality;
> and, as likewise follows, the appearances, as objects of experience, are
> themselves possible only in conformity with the law (B 234).

The main argument of the Second Analogy is sketched in this paragraph—
from the need to represent the connection of appearances in order to
regard the succession of appearances as combined in an object, to the
role of the category in supplying the necessity of the connection.

Kant begins to unpack the proof with an example that contrasts the
perception of static diversity with the perception of the diversity of change.
The former is supplied by the example of a house; the latter by a ship
moving downstream.

In both the perception of a house (any static object) and the perception
of a ship's motion (any event), there is a succession of apprehension. We
notice one feature after another of the house, one position after another
of the ship. Yet only in the latter case is there a succession in the object
that corresponds to the succession in the apprehension of it. The problem
presented by the contrast between the two cases is to account for how
we sometimes know to take the subjective succession as representing a
corresponding objective succession, when we know at other times to
discount the subjective succession as having no correlated succession in

the object. The problem can be expressed as being relatively greater in either of the two cases. That is, we can accept as unproblematic the attaching of significance in the ship case, and then wonder how it is that we know to refrain from attaching significance in the house case; or we can wonder how we are ever entitled—as we are in the ship case—to regard the subjective succession as significant (as having a direct objective correlate) when the house case shows that this is not always so.

Both versions of the problem are legitimate, and Kant addresses both. Since his general procedure is to begin with apprehension and then to investigate the restrictions that let us regard the given as representing reality, Kant first (in the Second Analogy) concerns himself with how we can ever regard the succession in apprehension as an apprehension of succession. Having solved this problem in the Second Analogy, Kant turns, in the Third, to the problem of the perception of coexistence (static situations). That is, he first provides an explanation of how we attach significance to the subjective succession in any case; and he then explains what we do in other cases. He orders the problems in this way because he needs events even for the perceptions of coexistence, since he shows that they too involve events: the activities of the perceiver. But of that, more in the next chapter. Our present concern is with the perception of events, that is, with the conditions under which we can regard the changes in our sensory states as representations of changes in the world.

Since the subjective temporal features of both sorts of perception are the same, Kant argues that the difference must be found in the objects. His explanation of the difference is that "it is impossible that in the apprehension of this appearance the ship should first be perceived lower down in the stream and afterwards higher up. . . . In the previous example of a house my perceptions could begin with the apprehension of the roof and end with the basement, or could begin from below and end above" (A 192 = B 237–38).

The explanation immediately raises the question of how we know that perceptions in the house case are order-indifferent, but that those in the ship case are order-dependent. What is actually given in sensory experience has a particular order of occurrence (whatever it may be). We, in fact, see the roof first, then the basement; and we see the ship here first, then there. How do we know that we *could have* seen the basement first, then the roof; but not the ship there first, then here? We have no direct experience of alternative content. Recall the finding in chapter four of the asymmetry between times and their contents: the same content can occur in different times, but the same time cannot (be shown to) have different contents until there are different persons to have different sensations.[4]

One (unsatisfactory) answer is to suggest that longer segments of experience could exhibit the order-indifference of the perceptions of the house. If we continue to look at the house we may have both sequences: first roof, then basement; and first basement, then roof. This would seem to show that the sensory representations of the house are order-indifferent. However, this will not answer the difficulty in general since it depends on our having repeat performances of all perceptions of static objects. Moreover, even if we did always experience static objects twice over and in different order, this would still not suffice to differentiate the static from the changing. Stand there long enough and the ship may return upstream; so experience may contain the reverse sequence even in the case of events.

My description of the difficulties raised by the examples follows Bennett's account. He points out that whatever we experience has, perforce, the particular order in which it happens to occur—so the basic problem is to attach sense to the could-have-been-otherwise in respect of the order of the perception of unchanging things; or to the could-not-have-been, of events.[5]

When we have several perceptions of a static object, such as a house, the order in which these perceptions are combined does not make any difference to the composite representation that is formed. A jigsaw puzzle presents the same picture no matter which pieces are fitted in which order. The order of assembly does not affect the outcome. Like the solution of a jigsaw puzzle, the synthesis (= combination) of the manifold (= complex) of intuition in the representation of a static object is order-indifferent. If we were to describe the house, it would not matter if we first described the roof, then the basement, or vice versa.

With events, the situation is quite different. The order of the parts is an essential feature of the complex. It matters whether the ship is first at A and then at B, or first at B and then at A; in the one case it is moving one way, in the other, the opposite. Nor can we omit order from the complex and just represent ship-at-A and ship-at-B, for that is compatible with there being two ships. Which shows that to represent an event we must also represent the opposition to an earlier (or later) state. Thus, to differentiate the event from the static situation of two ships moored at the two spots, we represent the event of its motion as follows: *first* ship-at-A-and-not-at-B, *then* ship-at-B-and-not-at-A. Though neither order nor opposition plays a part in the representation of a static complex, both are essential to the representation of an event.

The difference then between the house case and the ship case is not to be found in apprehension, but in the concepts in which the manifold of intuition is united.

It is true that the ship can sail upstream as well as down; but that does not remove the order-dependence of the concept of its downstream motion. It means only that the concept of its upstream motion is also an event-concept, and also order-dependent. The concept of either motion (up or down) has the order of its parts as an essential feature, and as a feature that sets either concept apart from the order-indifferent concepts of static objects, in which the variety contained in the concept can be put in any order without change of the concept. The possibility of upstream as well as downstream motion enforces, rather than collapses, the distinction between the two sorts of concept.[6]

Because the ship could have gone upstream instead of down, we must still figure out what Kant means when he says, "It is impossible that in the apprehension of this appearance the ship should first be perceived lower down in the stream and afterwards higher up" (A 192–B 237). It is easy to read this as wrong, but it is scarcely harder to read it as making a correct observation. To make sense of it we need to distinguish between synthesis in imagination and synthesis in apprehension, and between order-indifference and reversability. We can *imagine* various motions of the ship, and form a variety of concepts that differ only in the order of their parts. For instance, we can imagine the motion from A to B to C or the reverse motion from C to B to A. There are other more complex motions as well, for example, from A to B then from C to B; but these involve discontinuities (the ship must disappear at B to reappear at C for the movement back to B) and can therefore be ruled out as concepts of *possible* motions, since they violate the permanence of substance (as well, they violate the conditions of the theory of spatial forms). But there are indeed two motions that are possible (at least two), so we cannot appeal to any conceptual considerations to tell us which motion is taking place. Kant does not say that it is impossible *tout court* to see the ship lower down first and later on up; he says it is impossible *in the apprehension of this appearance*. The imagination can provide us with the concepts of both motions; as concepts there is nothing to choose between them (though either is conceptually favored over any concept of discontinuous motion). When what is given in sense is apprehended (= united as an intuition), one of the concepts *will* be favored over the other. The order in one of the concepts will conform to the order in which the appearance is apprehended; the order in the other concept will run counter to it.

Suppose I took photographs of a ship and showed them to you. If you could assemble these as representations of different parts of a whole *without* taking account of order, you could regard them as showing different details of an unchanging thing. However, if a picture shows a ship at A but none at B or C; another shows nothing at A, ship at B, nothing at C; etc., then you *cannot* now regard the whole as an order-indifferent complex because, without order, there is inconsistency from one picture to the next (ship at A, no ship at A). If you are to regard them as partial representations of a whole, you must employ an event-concept. You, however, will not know which event-concept (up or down) to use. You will be able to arrange them in order of continuous change of place; but when you have them in a row, you will not be able to tell which end of the row is the start and which the finish. You can use your imagination to put them in their proper order (just as you can use imagination to find the solution to a static jigsaw puzzle); but the imagination does not determine in which direction the order is to be taken. Obviously not; for, if it did, only one motion would be possible, and there would be no need to rely on the order of apprehension as a part of the representation of reality. (In apprehension, our situation is not as it would be with a pile of pictures. We do not have a bunch of intuitions, and then go home to sort them out. We make sense of the given as it is given, not afterwards. Imagination supplies both order-indifferent and order-dependent concepts. The opposition of one bit of the given to another requires that we use the latter—*some* event-concept. The order in which the given occurs tells us *which* event-concept to use.)

By the remark that follows it,[7] Kant indicates that the following passage is concerned only with serial successions in appearance.

> All empirical knowledge involves the synthesis of the manifold by the imagination. This synthesis is always successive, that is, the representations in it are always sequent upon one another. In the imagination this sequence is not in any way determined in its order, as to what must precede and what must follow, and the series of sequent representations can indifferently be taken either in backward or in forward order. But if this synthesis is a synthesis of apprehension of the manifold of a given appearance, the order is determined in the object, or, to speak more correctly, is an order of successive synthesis that determines an object (A 201 = B 246).

In the imagination the order is not determined *as to what must precede and what must follow*—which is not to say that it is not determined *at all* in imagination. What is explicitly said to be undetermined in imagination is whether the series is to be taken in backward or in forward order. The concepts of events, as fashioned in imagination, are not order-indifferent, though they are reversible. As we can imagine an upstream motion, we can imagine a downstream one. The differentiation of the two is not to be found in imagination—either an upstream or a downstream motion contains the same sequence of states. The concepts agree even in the internal ordering of their parts—the same sensory states, given simultaneously, would fit both if they fit either.[8] All that differentiates between the two is the order in which the sensory states are given, as we actually apprehend the appearance. The order in one concept (say the concept of downstream motion) conforms to the order of apprehension, while the other (the concept of upstream motion), has the same internal order, yet begins in a different place. Both concepts fit equally the sensory states themselves. The difference comes only in the order in which sensory states occur. If they occur one way, we see a downstream motion; if they occur in another way, we see an upstream motion. Thus, it is more correct to say that the order of synthesis determines the object (= determines which motion it is that is taking place) even though the (concept of the) object determines that *some* event is taking place, because order figures in the concept of either motion. The concepts of events supply order; apprehension supplies direction.

The order-indifference/order-dependence distinction applies to concepts, distinguishing, even at the level of imagination, the concepts of events from the concepts of static objects. The reversibility/irreversibility distinction arises only when order is significant, that is, only with respect to events. One event is different from another that has the same order but a different direction; and we perceive the difference in virtue of the order in which the constituent states are taken up in apprehension.

29. Two Senses of Causality

The concepts of events combine opposing states. If there were no regulations upon the formation of event-concepts, then any change whatsoever could be imagined. We could apply a concept of an event to any succession of sensory states. For example, we could regard the sensation of x followed by the sensation of y as a perception of a change from x to y, and do this for any pair of sensations in succession. However, in order to regard the sensing of x and the sensing of y as the subjective components of the perception of a change actually taking place in the world, we must think that there is a ground for regarding the x-*to*-y change as taking place not just in the manifold of intuition.

The problem of events is the same as the earlier problem of objects. As mere sequences of states, events are like objects that are mere collections of properties. To be real, an object must be material. Events are subject to the same condition. As changes they involve successions of states; but as changes in the world, their successive states must be objectively connected. Kant's contention throughout the Second Analogy is that "I render my subjective synthesis of apprehension objective only by reference to a rule in accordance with which the appearances in their succession, that is, as they happen, are determined by the preceding state" (A 195 = B 240).

The category is not of cause alone. It is the relational category of causality and dependence, or cause and effect. The relation is not just of one state to another, with the antecedent the cause, and the consequent the effect. In fact, for Kant, the cause is not primarily the state that precedes the other state. Instead the cause is the reason that the two states are connected. The effect is not primarily just the later of the two states, but both states together—that is, the event. In one sense of *cause,* A is the cause of B, and B the effect of A; but in the other, and primary, sense, the cause is the reason that A is followed by B, and the effect is the A-to-B succession. I will explain in a moment why I call the latter sense of causality the primary one.

One (Humean) way of posing the problem of causal connection is in terms of an example such as a ball's breaking a window. We take A (the impact of the ball) to be the cause of B (the shattering of the glass). What contributes to the intractability of this version of the problem is the utter difference between A and B. No thought of A leads, by any relation of ideas, to the thought of B. One must wonder how—if not just by repeated presentation together in sense—we could ever come to connect such dissimilar things. And one must wonder how—if connection has been established only by repetition in sense—we can legitimately project the connection to unobserved A's and B's.[9]

There is a more primitive and more tractable version of the problem. Though the A-to-B transition in the example is an event under causal law, it is neither a primitive event nor an example of what is essential in an event. The example sets up two fairly self-contained happenings, and then poses problems about the connection between them. The first happening is that the ball goes from unimpeded flight to impact; and the second is that the window goes from intact to shattered. What is essential to change is the transition from not-B to B. That is, to represent something as happening we must represent the opposition between an earlier state and a later one. A primitive event is, for example, the ball's coming to rest, or the window breaking. Windows break other than by being struck by balls; balls hit things other than windows; and balls sometimes hit windows without breaking them. The example of A's causing B involves so many extraneous factors it is not surprising that we can find no connection between the idea of A and the idea of B. If we thought about it, we would realize that not even experience affords repeated instances of the two (at least not in the days of tempered glass). When a ball does break a window, there is a causal connection; but we must set such complex events aside until we have made some sense of the simple cases.

Though B and not-B are opposing states, they are not utterly different. When the ball's free flight is impeded, one motion ceases and another begins. There is a change of direction and velocity, but there are continuities: the one motion begins where the other leaves off (i.e., at the same point); the ball looks much the same before and after impact; and angle of incidence probably approximates the angle of refraction, etc. Likewise, there are similarities (usually) between the intact window and the shattered one. Like the ship here and the ship there, or the straight and bent sticks, these cases require us to combine opposing states as parts of a whole; but the change is usually in only a few features, and against a background of constancy.

We have made some progress over the earlier example in which we somehow had to get the idea of glass-shattering out of the very different idea of ball-striking. To think that something is happening in these simpler cases, we need only be able to represent a coming to be or a ceasing to be of a state (usually among other and unchanging states) of that which persists while altering. To be able to represent this, we must think of the object in terms of the relevant dispositions for change: of the ship as mobile; the stick, flexible; the ball, resilient; the glass, brittle and breakable. These attributions of capacities to objects are not wild leaps from what is evident, nor are they trivial. If we are to see the fragments on the floor as what is left of the window (that is, perceive that the window has been broken) we must, among other things, think of the window as having been made of a breakable substance (to be able to undergo the change from intact to shattered). But it is no idle rewording to say that it has that capacity. In the first place it allows us to combine opposing states in the same object; and, in the second place, it gives us the wherewithal to handle the complex cases. The admission of dispositions in objects provides a basis for their causal interaction.[10]

Although the earlier example belongs properly to the next Analogy, a few words on it may be in order here. We see balls bounce and glass break, and to preserve the continuity and permanence of the object, we attribute to substances a variety of dispositions. These dispositions are then available to us to connect the action of one thing with the action of another. We think of the ball as impacting upon anything in its way, and the window as breaking when struck. The connection is not made between the two at the level of surface appearance, where there is utter difference, but at the level of substance, where there is close correspondence. We do not directly connect ball-striking to window-shattering. It is not because it is a ball that it breaks the window, and it is not because it is a window that it shatters. We have no general rules that make *that* connection—no rule holds between balls and windows. Hume's problem is intractable because he seeks a surface-to-surface connection that does not exist. The connection obtains just below the surface: between the ability of one thing to impart a blow, and the inability of another to withstand it. Causal interactions take place between substances with a capacity for x-ing and substances with a capacity to be x-ed. Such interactions fall under the third category of relation, and they belong to the next chapter. The Second Analogy (this one) is concerned to establish the relation of all happenings to causal grounds.

In any case such examples as those discussed above are in advance of this stage of the development of the system. They involve specific forces and liabilities to be affected, and so presuppose the possibilities of experience through which we could learn about such things. Kant is here still concerned with the conditions that make learning experiences possible. I have yet to give an account of the conditions he sets out here; and I refer to the examples only to forestall Humean objections, and to relocate the discussion of the Second Analogy away from the usual (and premature) emphasis on complex events and causal interactions.

Kant repeatedly indicates that his topic is not the complex causal interaction between A and B, but with the simple change from B to not-B, or vice versa, and with the relation of simple change to rules that involve substance. The ship's movement is a simple change of position. The paragraphs added in B both begin with reference to the succession of states in opposition to one another. Later, in both versions of the proof, Kant says, "When something happens, the mere coming to be, apart from all question of what it is that has come to be, is already in itself a matter for enquiry" (A 206 = B 251). Kant does employ two-object examples in the Second Analogy to deal with special cases of causes simultaneous with their effects, but he generally (even in these cases) considers the very simplest sorts of happening.

This may be an appropriate place to mention something that often figures in recent work on the Second Analogy. In modern physics there are certain events that are, in principle, indeterministic. As Kant's account of space is often pitted against non-Euclidean geometries, his principle of causality is questioned in the light of modern physics. No one would think to challenge Kant in this way if the distinction were recognized between appearances and phenomena. The Second Analogy is not concerned at all with the deepest levels of the analysis of matter. It is concerned only with issues that are incomparably more primitive—such issues as our entitlement to regard some successions in apprehension as apprehensions of succession. The three Analogies together carry us no further than to the barest outline of the conditions under which we perceive appearances. The indeterminacies of modern physics are not among appearances at all; they are phenomena we know only through empirical thought of a very high order. We must not suppose that the findings of advanced scientific research will necessarily conform directly and simply to the features that things must have as objects of possible perceptions. We would not expect an account of the basic features of language to anticipate the features of Shakespeare's language, or Donne's, or Joyce's.

There is another reason to set physics aside. It delves into the reasons for change—the actual mechanisms of dispositions and forces. Kant explicitly disavows any attempt to give a philosophical account of the mechanisms of change. He says,

How anything can be altered, and how it should be possible that upon one state in a given moment an opposite state may follow in the next moment—of this we have not, a priori, the least conception. For that we require knowledge of actual forces, which can only be given empirically, as, for instance, of the moving forces, or what amounts to the same thing, of certain successive appearances, as motions, which indicate such forces. But apart from all question of what the content of the alteration, that is, what the state which is altered, may be, the form of every alteration, the condition under which, as a coming to be of another state, it can alone take place, and so the succession of the states themselves (the happening), can still be considered a priori according to the law of causality and the conditions of time (A 206–7 = B 252).

The last lines are a pertinent reminder of the project as it is outlined in the Schematism. The first lines a warning against taking the project as a (half-baked) attempt to do physics in an armchair. Kant may in other places (such as the Axioms) be guilty of wandering from the basic theory of experience into offshoot *theories of* mathematics or science—but not here, and nowhere does *he* wander from the basic theory *to physics itself* (as do critics who bring considerations of microindeterminacy into what ought to be a discussion of cognition).[11]

With that said, let us return to what can "be considered a priori according to the law of causality and the conditions of time."

30. From Action to Force to Substance (contra Leibniz)

This section is an exegesis of two important paragraphs (A 204–6 = B 249–51). Kant here gives his clearest statement of the purpose and accomplishment of the Second Analogy. He begins by saying,

Causality leads to the concept of action, this in turn to the concept of force, and thereby to the concept of substance.

He then sets aside detailed exposition as belonging elsewhere—since it is analytic and clarificatory, and his enterprise is the extension of synthetic knowledge a priori.[12] He says,

But I must not leave unconsidered the empirical criterion of a substance, in so far as substance appears to manifest itself not through permanence of appearance, but more adequately and easily through action.

This completes the first paragraph. It is merely an introduction to the next, in which he outlines the connections between substance and causality.

> Wherever there is action—and therefore activity and force—there is also substance, and it is in substance alone that this fruitful source of appearances must be sought. This is, so far, well said; but when we seek to explain what is to be understood by substance, and in so doing are careful to avoid the fallacy of reasoning in a circle, the discovery of an answer is no easy task. How are we to conclude directly from the action to the *permanence* of that which acts? . . . Action signifies the relation of the subject of causality to its effect. Since, now, every effect consists in that which happens, and therefore in the transitory, which signifies time in its character of succession, its ultimate subject, as the substratum of everything that changes, is the *permanent,* that is, substance. For according to the principle of causality actions are always the first ground of all change of appearances, and cannot therefore be found in a subject which itself changes, because in that case other actions and another subject would be required to determine this change.

Up to the ellipsis[13] Kant presents the problem. After it, his answer.

We can see what the problem is if we take the question in conjunction with the preceding warning against circularity. The question asks how we are to conclude from the action that the agent is permanent. Just before he poses that question, Kant warns against circularity in the explanation of what is to be understood by substance. To understand either the warning or the question, we must tie the two together; and we must relate both to Leibniz because the passage makes sense only as a contrast to some other system that has a problem Kant does not have, and Leibniz's system does have the problem.

Hacking begins a lovely paper on Leibniz with the following sentence: "I am concerned with a notion of substance captured by Leibniz's repeated assertions that individual substances are *no mere aggregates,* but are *active principles of unity.*"[14] The aggregation of qualities or attributes is a view of substance most easily associated with Berkeley; Hacking shows that it can be attributed to Descartes and Leibniz too, but that Leibniz qualifies it by making activity the basic reason for considering certain things, and not others, to be individual substances. Hacking says, "Leibniz and perhaps even Descartes had the idea of substance being a bundle of qualities, just as much as Berkeley. The important question is the reverse. Which bundles are substances?"[15] This is a perfectly Kantian question. Apprehension affords possibilities of alternative combination; the issue is which objects are real. The answer that Hacking records from Leibniz is as follows: "Only those bundles that are active, in the sense of having laws of their own."[16] In Kant's words, "This is, so far, well said"; and the reason that Hacking gives for the Leibnizian answer to the question, "Which bundles are substances?", is completely Kantian: "There is a tendency in much analytic philosophy to conceive *things* as given, and then to speculate on what laws they enter into. On the contrary, things are in the first instance recognized by regularities."[17]

Now we can understand Kant's warning against the fallacy of reasoning in a circle. We do need activity to determine which aggregates or bundles of attributes or properties are individual substances; but we require substances for the possibility of action. With no substances there is nothing that endures while altering, and there is mere change in apprehension without corresponding change in appearance. To unite one state that is the opposite of another in the same object, we must be able to attribute to that which persists the capacity to alter from the one state to the other. Without the object and its capacity to alter, nothing connects the one state to the other. With no connection, there is no change. With no change, there is no action. At most, there is mere diversity—at one moment a sensation of one sort; at the next, a different sensation. Action thus presupposes change, and change in turn presupposes that which changes (= the permanent, substance), and if substances presuppose action, we come full circle. In other words, we try to pull ourselves up by our bootstraps if we try to explain what is to be understood by substance by *immediate* reference to action.

Kant says, in the first of the two paragraphs under analysis in this section, that substance *manifests itself more adequately and easily* through action, and he also says that he must not leave unconsidered the *empirical criterion* of a substance. Both phrases hint at a way of avoiding the circle while preserving the important truth of the Leibniz-Hacking account of individual substance. What we must do is regard their account as an explanation of how, in experience, we determine which aggregates are mere aggregates, and which are substances. Kant is quite willing to accept their account (so far, well said); but he sees the need to give more than their account because action presupposes change, which in turn presupposes the constancy or permanence of substance. So he starts with a general and a priori criterion of substance as the permanent, and then allows action to be the determinate representation of substance. The division between general and determinate (and between a priori and empirical) removes the circularity.

The real is that which is represented generally by what (ever) is given in sense. The representation of this object or that depends on our sensory content (whether we represent the world as containing, for instance, hot things depends on our having sensations of heat); but the representation of anything as an object in the world cannot depend on its specific characteristics or our particular sensory states—these are contingencies that arise in experience, not the very conditions of its possibility. Objects, to be real, must satisfy some general condition of materiality. As Kant presents this condition in the First Analogy, it is the requirement that to be real is to be in part/whole relation to the manifold of appearance just as the sensory state that represents it is in part/whole relation to the manifold of intuition. In other words, the general condition on being a material object is that the object stand to reality as its representation stands to inner sense. At a less exalted level, this boils down to the requirement that the things we represent as real be things whose existence is confirmed by, or at least not counter to, everything we sense. We do not regard as real *anything* that has *some* basis in subjectivity, but only that which is a well-integrated part of all that is representable by the subjective. If we could bit for bit represent things as real only requiring some subjective basis for doing so, we could populate the world with, inter alia, dream objects, illusions, imaginings—worse still, given the indeterminacies of apprehension, we could not determine, because of alternatively possible combinations of qualities, which objects as mere aggregates to represent. The first requirement on representation of the real is the general requirement that the real relate *as a manifold* to the manifold of intuition.

Because Kant sees the need for a general pairing of the two manifolds, as a precondition of the item for item pairing of elements in the one manifold (intuitions) with the elements in the other (appearances), he is able to avoid circularity when he explains what is to be understood by the concept of substance. When Kant first introduces the concept of substance (in the First Analogy), he makes no prior or concurrent mention of action. He says that time represents the substratum in a general way. He then goes on to say that change and coexistence must be perceived in relation to the permanent.[18] He now, in the Second Analogy, first gives a general explanation of change in terms of substance, preserving still the priority of substance; he then points out that substance is revealed more adequately and easily (hence, more determinately) by virtue of what it does and the changes it undergoes.

As in the explanation of the transcendental object $= x$,[19] the explanation here first sets up the object *as to be known,* giving only a general characterization of it (as having a permanent nature in relation to its changing states); the relation between the material nature of the object and its states is then described, also in general terms (matter supplies grounds or reasons for the changes). We acquire empirical knowledge of things and events by making the data of the senses conform to the general characterizations. Sensory input makes the general representation determinate. The general representation supplies, as it were, a use to which the given may be put: it can be regarded as representing things and events provided it is taken up and structured (= apprehended and conceptualized) in accordance with the regulative principles of the Analogies. We have no specific knowledge of things until we actually have experience of them; but we cannot regard inner states of consciousness as experiences (of outer things) unless we can regard what they represent—if they are taken to represent anything at all—as a possible appearance.

The suspicion of circularity arises in the following way: in the philosophical account, change and action presuppose that which acts as permanent; in the actual course of experience, change and action reveal the presence of substance. There is no circle if we keep the distinction between the philosophical account of experience and experience itself.

Within experience itself, there is something *remotely* akin to circularity, but it is a welcome relation. There is a mutual and ongoing buildup of our knowledge of things and our knowledge of events. The more events we observe, the more we learn about the forces, actions, dispositions, and changes pertaining to various sorts of matter. The more we know about matter, the more we know about the events in the world, because (to take just one instance) we are able to employ our knowledge of material characteristics (dispositions and the like) in inferences to unobserved events (think of Carbon-14 dating of events which occurred millennia ago, etc.) The relation between the two sorts of knowledge is one of mutual support—not a circle, but a feedback loop. Knowledge of their actions leads us to knowledge of substances, but the flow of information is not all in the one direction.

The Leibnizian view of substance is not complete with the restriction to aggregates that are active. The result of the restriction may be to include things that are active only for a time. A composite object, while it is intact, behaves as a unit; but if it disintegrates or decomposes, the unity of action ceases. As Hacking's discussion continues, we learn that, just as there is a question about which aggregates are substances (to which the answer is: those that are active principles of unity), there is a further question about which active principles of unity are substances (to which the answer is: only those that are permanent). Since material bodies are composite, they cannot, for Leibniz, be true substances. They come into being, for a time act as a unity, and then cease to be. Material bodies also undergo complete transformations (in manufacture, fire, and in simple divisions— like being sawed in half), which are sufficient to remove their unity of action. Only that which is utterly simple (= noncomposite) and completely isolated from constructive and destructive processes can, for Leibniz, be a true substance.[20] To preserve the unity as absolute and permanent, the activity of that which is truly an individual substance can be only something that does not involve change, transition, causal interaction and the like; and this leaves representation as the only activity (if one can call it that) that takes place at the level of individual substances in Leibniz's system. All that monads *do* is represent themselves and other substances. It is all they can do without risk of destructive change.[21]

Kant's question has an easy and noncircular answer in his own system. "How are we to conclude directly from the action to the *permanence* of that which acts?" Easy. *Before* action and change were introduced, permanence was brought in as the general condition of representing anything as real. So we know from the outset that appearances *contain* that which is permanent (even if *they* are transitory); and we know this because to be real they must be parts of the world-whole, and because their changing states—to be changes—must be combined in a common object that persists throughout the change. In concluding that that which acts is permanent, we are merely making explicit what is presupposed by action: any coming to be or ceasing to be, whether of a state or of an object itself, involves a transition from B to not-B, or vice versa, and to represent this change we require the permanent as "its ultimate subject, as the substratum of all that changes."

Leibniz's way will not work. If the aggregation involves opposing states (i.e., changes), we already presuppose duration with mere bundles of qualities. If the bundles of qualities do not combine opposing states, we cannot select out those aggregates which are active—because there is no activity, since nothing is changing. If one tries to bring in permanence as the *third* condition of being an individual substance—that is, *after* the condition that individuals combine qualities and that they be active principles of unity—the explanation of what is to be understood by substance is circular. To get activity and combination we must have already presupposed permanence.

Leibniz goes wrong at the very start. He tries to make the purely formal principle of noncontradiction the first principle of reality, antecedent even to creation and the principle of sufficient reason. One cannot start with sets of *atemporally compatible* qualities and ever get to changing objects just by successively restricting which sets of qualities are to be considered real. Even if the principle of sufficient reason is taken as reasonable, and taken to entail the principles of harmony, identity of indiscernibles, maximum diversity with a minimum of fuss, etc., the problem is that the initial set of possible objects comprises things that lack the diversity that one finds with things that act and change. Logic, with its timeless view of things, does not provide a rich enough base for the operation of restrictions. No matter how we tinker and fix, we cannot get out more at the end than was made available at the beginning.

In the section of the paragraph I omitted, Kant says, "According to the usual procedure, which deals with concepts in purely analytic fashion, this question would be completely insoluble." I think that *usual* must allude to the Wolffian-Leibnizian way.

Kant goes on to say that the question, "presents no such difficulty from the standpoint which we have been formulating." That standpoint involves starting with the complex spatiotemporality of sensibility and the rich diversity of sensations. The first restrictions limit apprehension to groupings and comparisons, but these are sufficiently indeterminate to permit further restrictions that still leave us with everything we could want.

Leibniz's way leads inevitably to isolated substances engaging only in the "activity" of eternal and unchanging representation. Kant's way leads to progressive ordering and unification of the diversity given in sense: sensations are combined in intuitions; intuitions in the properties they represent in objects; properties in the objects to which they belong; objects in the types of matter of which they are composed; and types of matter in matter itself. Instead of an ultimate fragmentation of reality, we get the unity of a natural order. And the activities that are possible for objects in Kant's system are genuine actions. Their changes are real. They can even arise and perish. And space and time do not disappear in the last analysis.

Kant follows Leibniz in so far as he develops his system by means of successive restrictions, not the empiricist method of development by addition; but he starts with what is given in sense, not logic. If the Second Analogy is Kant's reply to Hume, it is also his reply to Leibniz.[22]

31. The Temporal Aspects of the Argument

In this section I will begin with some general remarks and reminders. I will then cite and discuss passages that deal with the temporal aspects of the argument of the Second Analogy.

Event-perception involves the perception of something as happening or changing. Whatever may be the specific states that change, any change essentially involves the combination of opposing states. There is a recognition that a state now obtaining did not obtain earlier. We cannot differentiate in purely subjective terms between having just begun to notice something that has existed previously and noticing something that has just begun. In either case, there is a succession in apprehension; hence, the two cases are subjectively equivalent. There are three possibilities created by the succession of opposing states in the moment-by-moment change of intuition. We may be perceiving first one object, then another. We may be perceiving an event. Or we may not be perceiving anything at all. That is, there may be numerical difference, qualitative difference, or merely some modification of inner sense that has no significance. I will consider each in turn, beginning with the third, to show what is accomplished by the perception of an event. But first, some general remarks.

According to the Axioms of Intuition, we can parcel out the alphabet of sensations by grouping them. Because of the homogeneity and linearity of time—the form of inner sense—we can combine sensations in the following way:

(ab)(cdef)(g)(hij)(kl). . . .

Though we can group freely in a variety of ways, there is also a possibility of combination by comparison; and that may make some groupings more natural than others. The Anticipations show that the string of sensations can contain elements of the same kinds. There could be the following sort of sequence:

abcdeabfbghiabjklabcdegf. . . .

The repetition of *ab* may incline us to group them together, whatever we may do with the rest of the string:

(ab)cde(ab)fbghi(ab)jkl(ab)cdefg. . . .

Although there may be more determinacy when the principles of extensive and intensive magnitude are taken together than when either is employed on its own, even when governed by both principles, the apprehension of one combination rather than another is arbitrary. We could bracket (abcde) instead.

Kant addresses the problem of the indeterminacy of apprehension in the introduction to the Analogies. The regulative principles of the Analogies are intended to supply the necessity and determinacy that are lacking in mere intuition.

The third possibility set out above is that the given be not taken to represent anything at all. If this obtains, there will at most be the chance connections of association among ideas that are not regarded as having objective correlates. Imagine yourself listening at length to recordings of speech in a strange language. I think it would be generous to suppose that you could ever come up with a classification of all the basic types of sound (knowing that this is another token of the same type, not a token of a very similar, but distinct, type). Suppose, though, that you could. You might still have problems of grouping strings such as the following:

hewillratify . . .

Is it (he)(will)(ratify) . . . ? or (he)(will)(rat)(if)(I) . . . ? Even supposing that such problems could be overcome in a sophisticated analysis of very large segments of speech sounds, the whole exercise remains pointless if none of it means anything. Not only does the notion that ideas might be associable in and of themselves rest on generous assumptions about our capacity for analysis, and on optimism about the susceptibility of the given to analysis (What would happen if the tapes included noises and samples of bad speech?), but the association of mere ideas, with no thought to what they could represent, is an empty and idle exercise.

Kant does not dismiss the given as a source of knowledge; but he does add to it a source within the mind itself. The understanding supplies concepts of things that the given could be taken to represent. To follow the progress of Kant's argument, we must begin with the completely general (= indeterminate) object that is represented in sense. We then ask how anything that could be represented (as existing) would stand to whatever is given in sense. This sets up a demand for some balance between the *independence* and *connection* of the signs and what they signify. If the balance tips too much towards independence, the signs lose their relation to what they are intended to signify. Too much the other way, and reductionism results (and we are back to mere ideas whose collection accomplishes nothing). Kant finds the balance between independence and connection in the analogical relation between two manifolds. On the one hand are sensations; on the other, things that exist. These are too distant to be directly connected, but the conceptual structuring of each can be connected to the conceptual structuring of the other. The structuring of sensation produces the manifold of intuition, and concepts of objects structure a manifold of things as they appear to us. The connection is then made between one sort of conceptualization and another: ways of apprehending the given are regulated by the possibilities of conceiving of objects that would correspond to one or another combination of sensations, and concepts of objects are weighed against what is given in sense.

In advance of experience one cannot determine what will be given in sense or what exists in the world. If one turns to experience to find out, all one can discover is what is *in fact* the content of sense and the world, not what is essential to the two to bring about our experience.

Kant leaves aside the actual content of experience to consider only what sort of conceptual structuring must be employed to bring about, and maintain, the analogical balance. Each manifold contains its own elements (intuitions and appearances) within a general system of relations and formal features (in subjective and objective time, respectively). Whatever else may be involved in the conceptual structuring of intuition and appearance, the temporal features of each must be determined and interconnected.

Without supposing that *every* item in sense must signify something objective, we can reject the possibility of a mind that does no more than collect ideas. We could build a machine that could sense, and then sort its sensations into complexes according to some principle of association; but it would not be a cognitive device, and it would be less useful than an egg-grading machine, since it would deal only in its own inner states.

We may also reject the possibility of a world without change, without, of course, rejecting the possibility of some unchanging things in the world. As a museum of static objects, a world would not have temporal features requiring that perceptions of it take one form rather than another. Moreover, the perceptions themselves of such a world could not take place as acts within the world perceived because, by hypothesis, the world has nothing changing within it.

If the indeterminacy of apprehension requires that states of consciousness represent objects that are not reducible to the sensory states that represent them, and the objects cannot all be static, there must be perception of change. Since the representation of change requires not just the representation of the several states of an event, but also of their objective succession, there must, in some cases, be a ground for taking the seriality of sensation as having correlated to it a succession in the object. Since the First Analogy already establishes the real as standing to the given in virtue of the part/whole structuring applicable to both manifolds, the successive states of an object can be treated as temporal parts of that which persists. That is, as subjective time itself represents the substratum in a general way, the real can be taken to be the whole of whatever is represented by what, taken in its entirety, is given in sense. Likewise, particular real things are parts of the whole of what is real, and they are represented by the parts of what is given. Successive states are parts of the parts of the substratum. That is, they are parts or (temporal) stages of particular objects. In each case of something changing—whether it is the beginning or the ceasing to be of a particular material object, or the start or end of one of its states or stages—there must, in that which persists, be the basis for the representation of an underlying continuity and a cause of the change. The continuity is required to permit the combination of opposing states in a common object. The cause is required to provide a ground for the combination.

We must be able to represent changes as objective successions; and this requires that they be distinct from things that we have merely begun to notice, though they have been present all along (or from that which we have ceased to notice though it nonetheless continues to exist).

Kant says, "Understanding is required for all experience and for its possibility. Its primary contribution does not consist in making the representation of objects distinct, but in making representation of an object possible in a general way. This it does by carrying the time-order over into the appearances and their existence" (A 199 = B 244–45).[23]

Leibniz thinks that the role of the understanding is to make distinct the confused sensory representation of objects.[24] Kant disagrees. Understanding makes it possible to represent objects at all. Objects are not hidden within sense experience, needing only to be sorted out by the intellect. They stand in contrast to what is sensed. By determining the forms that objects must take, and the relation that must obtain between sensible intuition and objects, the understanding makes it possible to have perceptions of objects. Kant says that the understanding carries the time-order over (from the manifold of intuition) into the appearances and their existence. He is here concerned with the cases in which we do regard the order of apprehension as representing something objective. As in the ship example, the order in which the stages are represented (that is, the order of the apprehension of those stages) is transferred to the stages themselves. Without this transference there can be no perception of the ship's motion; and given the equivalence of content of the concepts of upstream and downstream motion, no amount of intellectual effort after the fact (assuming order of apprehension was ignored) could later determine which motion had taken place. If sensory experience was a preintellectual confusion, it could not be made distinct. However, if the understanding enters into sensory experience from the outset, perception is not opposed to thought as the confused to the distinct.[25]

The contention that the understanding carries the (subjective) time-order over into appearances must be examined in relation to the earlier contention that "we must derive the *subjective succession* of apprehension from the *objective succession* of appearances" (A 193 = B 238). One aspect of time is carried from subjective to objective; one aspect goes from objective to subjective. To avoid circularity or self-contradiction, we must find the difference between the two aspects; for otherwise we would have the same thing moving in opposed directions. In other words, we must find a difference between time-order and succession.

Immediately following the claim just quoted, Kant says,

> Otherwise the order of apprehension is entirely undetermined, and does not distinguish one appearance from another. Since the subjective succession by itself is altogether arbitrary, it does not prove anything as to the manner in which the manifold is connected in the object. The objective succession will therefore consist in that order of the manifold of appearance according to which, *in conformity with a rule,* the apprehension of that which happens follows upon the apprehension of that which precedes. Thus only can I be justified in asserting, not merely of my apprehension, but of appearance itself, that a succession is to be met with in it. This is only another way of saying that I cannot arrange the apprehension otherwise than in this very succession" (A 193 = B 238).

We are not looking for the meanings of two technical terms, but just for what it is that is transferred the one way or the other.[26] As both the passage and the house and ship cases indicate, there is an order to any apprehensions; and the first of the two contentions is that this order can be transferred to the object. The second contention places a condition on the first. We can carry the order of apprehension over into the appearances, but only if the order of apprehension (= the subjective succession) can be derived from the order of appearance (= the objective succession). Because sensations occur one after another, they always have *some order* (or other). The question is whether any significance attaches to the order. Is it the order in which they merely happened to occur? Is it the order in which they had to occur? That matter is not resolved in apprehension: "the subjective succession *by itself* is altogether arbitrary" (my italics). What determines the matter is the appearance. The arrangement in apprehension is more than mere happenstance when the concept in which the manifold of a given intuition is united is an order-dependent concept, that is, the concept of an event. When the concept is order-indifferent, the order of apprehension cannot be carried over into appearance and regarded as significant.

The required difference is as follows. What is transferred from subjective to objective time is a certain arrangement or order. What is transferred in the reverse direction is something that determines that arrangement as nonarbitrary.

What sort of something can do this? For a start, we need the something to be a concept of an event, because its order-dependence dictates a certain arrangement. However, if we could arbitrarily produce and employ event-concepts, subject to no constraint or restriction, the order of apprehension would remain undetermined. Any event-concept capable of fitting the given would indeed involve an order-dependence among the elements it combined, and the order would have to be the same as the order found in apprehension; but, in the absence of restrictions, "concepts" could be fashioned freely to fit anything and everything. The "concepts" would be brackets arbitrarily grouping segments of successive sensation, and arbitrarily taking their order as significant; but true concepts do more than this. They provide a reason to represent one thing rather than another. In order that the appearance may be more than something freely associated with what is given in sense, there must, in the concept of the appearance, be a connection to the manifold of appearance that entitles us to regard the particular appearance as a part of what exists.[27]

Legitimate concepts of experience have two aspects. On the one hand they combine elements that are found together in sense. On the other hand, they tie in with other concepts to structure a whole system of formal and material relations. For example, the concept of a house (by means of some schema for generating images) finds application to sensations that can be apprehended according to any of the variety of patterns contained in the schema of a house. But, to perceive a house, it is not sufficient to have the concept and its schema, together with sensations that could be apprehended in that way. We must be able to regard the house, if represented, as real. For that we require that it have connection to appearances in general, that is, that it be a member of the manifold of appearance. In addition to the variety of images generated by the schema, there is in the concept of a house—because the concept is order-indifferent—the concept of a thing that is permanent. So we cannot represent a house as existing just on the basis of some fragment of sensation that could be apprehended as a representation of a house; we will want additional sensory evidence that the object endures. This could be supplied, perhaps, by repeated perceptions over time; but, in fact, the evidence is usually supplied by the context of surrounding objects. Further consideration of the perception of static objects would be somewhat in advance of the present stage of Kant's unfolding system. We must return to considering the perception of events; but their concepts must also have the two aspects: on the one hand, tying into sensory experience; and on the other, connecting with other concepts to bring about the unity of the manifold of appearance.

Instead of permanence, which is found in all concepts of material objects, all concepts of events contain the concept of objective succession.

Various segments of experience, apprehended in various ways, provide a basis for representing a variety of changes. Which change, if any, gets represented depends on which satisfies the requirement of being an objective succession. In the last passage quoted, Kant claims that our entitlement to assert that the succession is not merely in the apprehension consists in its conformity with a rule. The A-version of the principle of the Second Analogy says, "Everything that happens, that is, begins to be, presupposes something upon which it follows according to a rule" (A 189). The rule need be nothing more than the thought that the succession is necessary, that there is some (unspecified) reason that the transition takes place. Even without knowing precisely what the cause is, the thought that there is a cause sufficiently constrains the representation of change.

Suppose that we regard a certain sequence in sensation as (the content of) a perception of a change; but that to do this we must think there is a reason in the nature of things that makes the transition occur. In an isolated instance, having to think this does not constrain us in any way; but the representation of reality cannot be treated as a collection of isolated instances. The connections of representation between the two manifolds must obtain generally. The question is whether we can think that there is *in general* a reason for the change. We are not constrained by the isolated case, but by the implicit generality of reasons (or of rules). If there is some reason (whatever it may be) that *B* follows *A,* then whenever *A* occurs, *B* will follow. In a first instance, we may think there is a reason; but if later cases provide *A* without *B,* we must regard ourselves as having been mistaken.

Kant makes the point that the reason or cause need not be known specifically toward the end of the following passage, which sums up the main argument.

> Immediately I perceive or assume that in this succession there is a relation to the preceding state, from which the representation follows in conformity with a rule, something is represented as an event, as something that happens; that is to say, I recognize an object to which I must ascribe a certain determinate position in time—a position which, in view of the preceding state, cannot be otherwise assigned. When, therefore, I perceive that something happens, this representation has first of all as its content, that something precedes, because only by reference to what precedes does the appearance acquire its time-relation, namely, that of existing after a preceding time in which it itself was not. But it can acquire this determinate position in this relation of time only in so far as something is presupposed in the preceding state upon which it follows invariably, that is, in accordance with a rule. From this there results a two-fold consequence. In the first place, I cannot reverse the series, placing that which happens prior to that upon which it follows. And secondly, if the state which precedes is posited, this determinate event follows inevitably and necessarily. The situation, then, is this: there is an order in our representations in which the present, so far as it has come to be, refers to some preceding state as a correlate of the event which is given; and though this correlate is indeed indeterminate, it none the less stands in a determining relation to the event that is its consequence, connecting the event in necessary relation with itself in the time-series (A 198–99 = B 243–44).[28]

Midway through the passage, Kant again indicates his concern with events as transitions that essentially involve a coming to be (or ceasing to be) in the phrase "existing after a preceding time in which it itself was not." I will consider another aspect of this in the next section.

32. The Metaphysical Aspects of the Argument

As a purely logical notion, the second category of relation is the notion of entailment, implication, or ground and consequent. As with the earlier categories, the logical component of the category of causality and dependence does not apply directly to sense, but only mediately, by means of its temporal schema: succession subject to a rule,[29] that is, objective succession. Objective succession in time has the same formal features as implication, but it also corresponds directly to a feature of sensibility (= the order of apprehension).

One property of implication-relations is their formal equivalence to a disjunction in which the first disjunct is the negation of the antecedent, and the second disjunct is the consequent. Thus, *If p, then q* is logically equivalent to *Not p, or q*. This property plays an important part in Kant's account of causality and events.

A cause is either the reason for a certain event or the antecedent (= earlier state) in an event. When the reason is presupposed—that is, when we assume that the laws of nature are operating normally, that things are behaving in accordance with their dispositions—we cite only the initial conditions in the explanation of a thing. Why did the window break? Because the ball hit it. The capacities of balls to impart force and the incapacities of glass to withstand it, are left unspecified; but they are the reason (= cause) that the ball breaks the window, and when we tacitly assume the existence of such reasons we content ourselves with citing the antecedent of the window's breaking, which is its being struck by the ball. Few of us know the reason in any detail; all we usually know is the mere existence of a reason (one thing's capacity *to x,* and another's *to be x-ed*). This much is implied by what we do say when we cite some initial condition as cause, so there is no point in adding explicitly the completely general (= indeterminate) premise: "and the one thing is an *x-er,* the other an *x-ee*"—unless, of course, we do have special information about the nature of the dispositions involved.

Hume's mistake is to think that unless we have such information all we have is the observation of first the one thing, then the other. Kant draws attention to a fundamental presupposition of any such observation: there must be a change that takes place. To have any observation of something happening, we must relate it to "a preceding time in which it itself was not." An event is essentially a coming to be or a ceasing to be—a transition from not-*B* to *B*, or vice versa. The reason or ground of the event may be indeterminate, and even the antecedent may be unknown (that is, we know not *what* it was, but only *that* it was), but both the reason and the antecedent are essentially involved in the perception of an event. Why they are essential is evident from the property of implication mentioned above.

When a transition is from *A* to *B*, we think that *If A, then B*. Kant maintains that there is a more primitive thought involved: of a transition from not-*B* to *B*—and, hence, of *If not-B, then B;* but this, by virtue of the property, is equivalent to *Not-not-B, or B,* which is equivalent to *B or B,* which, in turn, is equivalent to *B*. On the principle that, when we

have grounds to represent something, we have grounds to represent anything logically equivalent to it, any grounds for representing *B* at all would
be grounds for representing *B's coming to be*—that is, they *would be if*
any *A-to-B* succession can be properly represented by *If A, then B*.

Suppose Hume were right to regard us as observing merely *A-to-B*
successions, without any proper thought of an underlying reason for the
succession. If we observe a succession at all, we observe that something
that did not previously exist now does. That is, we observe a succession
from not-*B* to *B*—and we do not need *A* at all because, given that successions are properly represented by conditionals, we have the conditional
If not-B, then B, from which *B* follows directly, without need of any
reference to *A*. Therefore, Hume cannot be right about any creature
capable of having knowledge of anything—not even its immediate objects
of perception—because his principles give rise to Post-inconsistency, that
is, they allow the derivation of individual existence claims for which no
reasons need be given.[30]

To retain even the sense of cause as antecedent, we must either abandon
the representation of succession in terms of the form *If . . . , then . . . ,*
or else we must put some restriction on the representation even of a
simple coming to be. If we allow that we just, *sine causa,* see that *B*
happens, we open the floodgates. We not only do not require *A* as the
cause of *B;* but we can take what we please to be the cause of *B*, since,
given *B*, anything whatsoever entails it. Therefore, if we want to show
how and why *If . . . , then . . .* constructions do find proper application
in experience, we must put restrictions on the representation of even a
simple coming to be. Which is *to say,* we must show how the category
of causality and dependence finds application in experience; it is also *to
explain* why Kant's account of the application-conditions concentrates on
not-B-to-B transitions, and why it then argues that there must be rules
governing their representation, and, finally, why the rules must be universal. If one allowed *some* simply-seeings, all the other principles of
perception would become worthless in the face of possible "Well I was
there, and I saw . . .". If there is *any* case in which that is *sufficient* for
knowledge, nothing stands. Someone can always find some subjective
basis for representing anything, and if a subjective basis is sufficient for
knowledge, contradiction is possible; and it becomes meaningless to talk
of knowledge at all.

To back up a bit, consider the alternative to universal reasons required
for any representation. The alternative is to disallow the representation
of succession in terms of implication. That is *either* to suppose that no
implications hold among the things that we know, *or* to suppose that
succession is not central to the involvement of implication in experience.
However, *the former* destroys the possibility of knowledge. Where there

are no implications, there can be no rules and no restriction on what is thought—hence, no difference between merely thinking of something (or seeming to perceive) and thinking that such-and-such (or actually perceiving). *The latter,* by contrast, is not so easily dispensed with. I suppose it remains possible, however unlikely, to find some wholly different way of accounting for how the body of knowledge comes to be structured by implication-relations, but it is worth noting that the best efforts throughout the history of philosophy, including Hume's, have assumed a connection between succession, causality, and implication. Since we have on hand an account that succeeds in making the connections, without opening the floodgates, it seems pointless to worry in the abstract about a wholly different way of finding application of the category (and implication-relations) to the things we know.[31]

The purely logical component of the cause-effect relation is the relation of implication or entailment. Analysis of it shows that, if applied to successions, it must not be allowed to hold without restrictions. This is just to say that we need some reason to think that one thing succeeds another. A mere antecedent is not enough. There must also be a reason that the later thing follows the earlier. We can even do without the specification of the antecedent—leave it simply that *something* has caused the window to break—but we cannot dispense with the causal ground itself. We must, if we think that something has happened, think that there are things with the capacities to make it happen. The reason for these necessities is provision against the inconsistencies that would result if things could be represented (as beginning to be or ceasing to be, but the issue is actually general with respect to any representation whatsoever) without resort to some reason—even an unspecified one—in addition to the subjective basis for the representation. It does not matter that we do not know the hidden qualities of balls and of glass, or even that we do not know that it was a ball that did it; what matters is that we think that every alteration takes place in conformity with the law of the connection of cause and effect.[32] If we are not prepared or able to think this, we cannot legitimately—however much it seems so (subjectively)[33]—think that anything has happened. If we think that some things can be without there being reasons for them, we have no objection to make to any assertion of the form *that p,* which is to say, we cannot object to anything. In particular, if we allow that changes can be observed without reasons for the changes having to be thought, then we take assertions about events to rest only on immediate perception. The report that *B* happens rests on on the immediate datum of sense—namely, a sensation taken to represent *B*—without reference essentially required to reasons or to a broader base of intuition.

Hume's atomist treatment of perception leads to the problem of induction; Kant's holism avoids it.

To set up the problem, Hume maintains that the senses are the origin of all legitimate empirical thought. Present input and memories of past inputs are held to be sufficient to determine thoughts concerning things directly observed. Hume notes, however, that our thoughts are not scrupulously restricted to immediate observation. They carry implications concerning the unobserved. The problem of induction questions the legitimacy of any such implication.

There are two initial responses possible: accept the account of observation, and accept the problem as legitimate; or dispute the account. Kant does the latter by showing that it is not a certain want of strictness on our part that leads us to thoughts more general than the immediate data of the senses. We do see things happen; but such perception is not reducible to sense data because it includes the representation of a coming to be or a ceasing to be. One way or the other, it rests not just on what we do sense, but on what we do not. However, merely failing to observe *B* before or afterwards is insufficient to show that *B* did not occur then, and we need an assurance, that we can never get directly from sense data, that the absence of any earlier (later) perception is due to the nonoccurrence of *B*. We can get the requisite assurance if we relate *B*'s occurrence to the occurrence of other things. This means that we never (can) just see *B* happen. We must also regard the happening as a change in that which persists and has the capacities to undergo such changes of its transitory properties. If we know that *B* happens, we know the capacities of the things involved in the event, and, hence, the changes to which they are liable. Our present perceptions inevitably have consequences.

To have a problem of induction, present experience must be held to have an incorrigibility to which upcoming experience is put in contrast. Otherwise, there is an alternative to questioning our thought concerning the general relations of things. It is, in the abstract, possible to regard the empirical connections of ideas as inherently open to question, and the simple ideas themselves as certain whenever they are sensorily based. This abstract possibility is essential to the problem of induction: we take the present and past ideas for which we have a sensory basis as being certain; we note our tendency to generalize and project; we point out the fact that these projections involve ideas that are not yet attested to in sense; we then ask how generalizations based only on some instances can make provision for others. The alternative is to hold the simple ideas themselves to be open to question, and we then make sensory data conform to general belief. But then the problem cannot arise. For example, we hold certain beliefs about the rate of the combustion of gunpowder. Yet,

> Who would not laugh at mee, if I should say,
> I saw a flaske of *powder burne a day?*

Donne is right; the proper response would be ridicule, not consternation at the falsification of a general belief.

It is *possible* to regard sense data as simple and incorrigible and utterly unrestricted in occurrence—such that any datum could next be given, no matter what data have preceded. It is also possible to regard them as having some content or import that makes certain connections of them admissible and others not. Though either is possible on its own, the two possibilities are not compatible; yet both are required for the problem of induction. The second is essential to preclude wholly arbitrary combination that could tolerate anything whatsoever. The first is essential to provide the potential disconfirming instances that (purportedly) make any projection from present experience inherently uncertain. The two are not compatible. The second view of sense data entails that there are restrictions on their occurrence, whether we know them or not. Those that have already been given have certain features that enjoin certain alternatives of combination, and preclude others. No subsequent sense datum can enjoin what has been previously precluded. All that remains open is a further narrowing of the alternatives already enjoined.

Of course, we can (and we should) question whether we have correctly understood our sensory input to date, and whether we are on the right track; but we should equally question whether, on the basis of what has gone before, a particular subsequent experience is possible. Hume wants to contend that anything is possible; and that *will* really disconcert us *if* we let ourselves be forced into wondering *only* about the general beliefs that reflect our current understanding. But he can cry havoc in this way only if we allow that future experience is utterly open in its possibilities. We have the option of denying this, and of demanding that he show the potentially disconfirming experience to be possible. If he tries to argue that anything is possible, we can retort that this can be only if ideas carry no implications concerning other ideas; in which case, any combination of them is acceptable, for if there are implications, known or not, then with certain ideas already given, certain others are (already) impossible. We may be mistaken in a general belief, or he may be mistaken in thinking that an exception to it is possible.

The latter is intrinsically more probable if all one has to go on is how things seem on a particular occasion. General beliefs are usually framed in relation to many occasions. One can increase the probability of an exception until it is greater than the probability of that to which it is an exception, in which case we should abandon the belief. One may do this by showing that the exception has a better fit with experience in general than the belief it opposes. If the probability of the exception is lower than the probability of the general belief, it is always more reasonable to reject the exception.

Once we start weighing what is given in sense against what we think, and vice versa, the problem ceases to be all on the side of thought. Hume does not show that our thought is inherently dubious in so far as it extends beyond what we have immediately experienced. Accommodation is two-sided. What is thought must fit with what is given in sense; but what is given in sense must, to be taken seriously, fit what can be thought. What is actually shown by Hume's attempt to treat the matter one-sidedly—trying to derive thought from simple ideas of sense—is that any such account of experience is bound to fail; it simply will not provide a coherent account of such obvious matters as our success in prediction, our rejection of certain seemings as illusory, our ability to perceive that something has begun or ceased, our knowledge of the dispositional characteristics of substances, and so on. To plead that all these are to be given up is more than a bit like saying, "The suit is just fine, it's your body that's the wrong size." If ever *reductio ad absurdum* has an application in philosophy, it is to the doctrine of the sensory origin of all ideas. What more does one want than the problem of induction to show that something has gone wrong in the assumptions of a system?

33. "Kant's Reply to Hume"—and the Actual Problem

In deference to the tradition of treating the Second Analogy as Kant's reply to Hume, I have gone on at some length about the problem of induction. I have done so without footnotes to Kant. This was unavoidable since he does not discuss the problem with any sign of taking it seriously. All he says on the matter is contained in the following passage:

> The accepted view is that only through the perception and comparison of events repeatedly following in a uniform manner upon preceding appearances are we enabled to discover a rule according to which certain events always follow upon certain appearances, and that this is the way in which we are first led to construct for ourselves the concept of cause. Now the concept, if thus formed, would be merely empirical, and the rule which it supplies, that everything which happens has a cause, would be as contingent as the experience upon which it is based. Since the universality and necessity of the rule would not be grounded a priori, but only on induction, they would be merely fictitious and without genuinely universal validity. It is with these, as with other pure a priori representations—for instance, space and time. We can extract clear concepts of them from experience, only because we have put

them into experience, and because experience is thus itself brought about only by their means" (A 195–96 = B 240–41).

"Kant's Reply to Hume" is an *idée fixe* of interpretations of the Second Analogy. It is not an altogether bad idea, but its fixity is objectionable.

To contrast one thing to another it is essential to be able to characterize each independently. One must be able to say, "*X* has these features, *Y* has those; and between these and those there are the following differences: . . .". If one tries instead to say, "*X* has these features, so *Y*— which is meant as an objection to *X*—must have the following features: . . .", two unacceptable risks are taken. First, the opposition is assumed rather than shown. Second, the assumption *dictates* the contrasting properties of *Y*, rather than letting them be sought prior to any consideration of what contrasts they may form to the properties of *X*.

What happens if we get it in our heads that the Second Analogy is Kant's reply to Hume's skeptical doubts concerning causality and induction? Well, to begin with, we accept the doubts that Hume raises as legitimate. This requires us also to accept the assumptions that he makes in order to raise the doubts. We then read Kant within the framework of those assumptions, looking for some way out of the skeptical conclusions—that is, looking for a solution to the problem.

In the abstract, a procedure of this sort *might not* be worthless. If it happens that *Y* is accepting the same problems as legitimate and making the same assumptions that *X* makes, then we will not come to grief if we wonder only how *Y* arrives at a different conclusion. The question is what assurance we have that this happy chance obtains in respect of the Second Analogy (with Hume = *X*, and Kant = *Y*). Well, Kant does somewhere say that recollection of Hume wakened him from his dogmatic slumbers.[34] Moreover, *we* think Hume's problems are among the most crucial in philosophy, so Kant must think so to. At least we should assume he does, to give him the benefit of the doubt.

It is not clear that Hume's doubts are taken by Kant as we take them; and it is mere prejudice to think that Kant is to be taken seriously only in so far as he resembles us.

Kant is not a contemporary analytic philosopher sharing our problems on our terms. Within his lifetime, Prussia was just recovering from war and plague, and moving from northern obscurity and isolation onto the mainstage of European affairs.[35] Because of this, there are certain oddities in Kant's work—for instance, his preoccupation with the *vis viva* controversy long after it had been set aside in the rest of Europe.[36] But, because the sorts of development that took two centuries to unfold in France and England were compressed into his lifetime, Kant brings a unique perspective to the radical changes of the modern period. He works his way from a rather antiquated seventeenth century thought into the most advanced thought of the eighteenth century.

To imagine what he accommodated in his intellectual development is virtually equivalent to imagining some French intellectual, contemporary at the beginning of his life with Arnauld and Port Royal and at the end (almost) with Comte. *We* can casually scan the timeless problems of philosophy, with no thought to their historical development; but, as one of the developers, Kant enjoyed no such luxury. He had to work out the strengths and shortcomings of earlier positions to arrive at later ones.

It makes more sense to see Kant as deeply indebted to Hume than as in opposition to him, and to be replying to Leibniz rather than to Hume. What Kant owes to Hume is the recognition of the inherent inadequacy of the usual (= Leibnizian), analytic, and reflective approach to philosophical questions. Kant did not retrench himself in dogma; Hume wakened him *from* it (dug him out). In the Dissertation Kant says,

> The use of things intellectual is pre-eminently two-fold. The first is *elentic,* whereby they are of value negatively, namely when they keep things conceived sensitively away from noumena, and although they do not advance science by the breadth of a fingernail, yet they keep it safe from the contagion of errors. The second is *dogmatic* and in accordance with it the general principles of the pure intellect, such as are displayed in ontology or in rational psychology, issue into some exemplar only to be conceived by the pure intellect and which is a common measure for all other things in so far as they are realities.[37]

I quote the passage primarily to illustrate Kant's pre-Humean slumber. Consider his association of *science* with the dogmatic uses of things intellectual, and his dissociation of science from evidence given in the senses. The dissociation is not entire—which is to say, Kant does not owe all to Hume. Consider the following two passages:

> Now although phenomena are properly appearances of things and are not ideas, nor do they express the internal and absolute quality of objects, none the less cognition is most veridical.[38]

> *And so there is a science of things sensual,* although, as they are phenomena, there is not given a real intellection of them but only a logical intellection.[39]

Two points about these passages. First, there is a grudging recognition of the possibility of serious intellectual interest in the objects of the senses, though the highest and most proper interest is reserved for noumena. Second, the real/logical distinction presupposes (in its first term) that the intellect can supply its own objects.[40] The presupposition is thoroughly Leibnizian (also Cartesian); but there is a pre-Humean recognition that—

at least in ordering and sorting them—the intellect can concern itself with phenomena. We can suppose that Kant's physics and his reflections in the *Enquiry* of 1763 on mathematical method are already seeds of discontent with a purely rationalistic approach. But, in the Dissertation, Kant thinks he has found a resolution of conflicts between the proper rational sciences of psychology and ontology, on the one hand, and the "science" (such as it is) of things sensual.

The resolution depends on two things: treating the deepest and most serious concerns as purely intellectual; and, regarding observation as being worthy of intellectual regard to the extent that it can be sorted out by reflection in accordance with the principle of contradiction.[41]

Hume overturns this early resolution of classical metaphysics with observational science. Attention usually focuses on Hume's devastating criticisms of the *real uses of reason*—its supposed capacity to supply itself with objects; but, to understand Kant, we should not ignore the (implicit, and partly unwitting) challenge to the *logical uses of reason*. Contemporary philosophy too easily helps itself to the supposition that all the analytic capacities are available to the individual in advance of experience or action (which is why Leibniz and Hobbes enjoy such favorable regard). We tend to wonder only how, given a certain sensory input, or certain desires and preferences, the rational man (capable of the most elaborate ratiocination) would work out what to believe or do. Thus, we see Hume as dispensing with such transcendent entities as causality, substance, duty, God, etc., leaving us with certain inputs of sensation or of feeling and desire, *and with unlimited capacities of reason in its logical (= analytic) aspect*. Thus, Carnap or Goodman can employ anything analytic or logical to construct beliefs from a sensory base; and decision-theory can assume the availability and applicability of rational strategies.[42]

Kant begins the Analytic of Principles with a discussion of formal *versus* transcendental logic (cf. A 130 = B 169 and ff.). Then the problem of the Schematism specifically questions the application of concepts to what is given in sense. Of course, Kant thinks that the application is possible, but difficult. His recognition of the difficulty may be what recollection of Hume awakened, for Hume shows more clearly than anyone how little can be inferred from sensory data.

I think that the Analytic of Principles makes more sense as Kant's reply to Leibniz, and as a reply prompted by considerations that originate with Hume. Let me sum up my reasons. Kant works his way from an initially Leibnizian position, through a compromise position with respect to pure intellect and observation (in the Dissertation), to a final rejection of Leibniz in the *Critique of Pure Reason*. (There is no *Critique of Skeptical Naturalism*—Kant never held a Humean position.) The overall structure of the Principles points to Leibniz—from the initial setting-aside of formal logic,[43] to the concluding Amphiboly. Many passages throughout make sense only if taken as objections to Leibniz: both the beginning and end of the First Analogy; the paragraphs about action and permanence that I discuss in section 30; the whole chapter on the Leibnizian division between phenomena and noumena (which Hume would approve for its repudiation of the quote from the Dissertation about the elentic and dogmatic uses of things intellectual); remarks about various principles of classical rationalism; and, of course, the Amphiboly. Only the passage quoted at the beginning of this section seems to be directed *against* Hume. Moreover, a Humean realization that connection is not given in sensory apprehension is central to the whole course of Kant's argument—from the initial problem of how reason can be applied to that which lacks truth-value, to the characterization of intellectual activity as the successive imposition of order on an indeterminate manifold.

7 Activity and Passivity

Introduction

The Third Analogy completes Kant's account of perception (i.e., of our knowledge of appearances). Like the other Analogies, the Third shows the application of a relational category in experience. The category is dynamical community: the reciprocity or interaction of active and passive things. The schema is the temporal relation of coexistence. With the Third Analogy, Kant completes his account of the three modes of objective time, adding coexistence to permanence and succession.

The preceding Analogies leave unfinished business. Much of it has to do with space. Throughout the Principles, Kant minimizes space to give priority to time. Here he makes up for, and explains, the previous neglect of spatial considerations by reintroducing space, and by showing that knowledge of objective spatiality depends on the prior introduction of objective temporality. I granted in the anti-Cartesian arguments of chapter five that space is essential to the representation of objects, complaining only about the identification of materiality with spatiality. Space may—though this has not been much discussed—be directly involved in the perception of events. This will be the case when the event in question is one like bending or bulging that involves the comparison of states that differ only spatially, and dispositions like flexibility and elasticity. The most significant aspects of spatiality in respect of appearances remain to be discussed. An account must still be given of the relation in empirical space of one object or event to another.

Having a certain shape—and being a *res extensa*—is essential to all objects, material or otherwise. However, being *at* a certain location, or *in* a certain relation to other things in space, has not yet been shown to have objective or empirical significance.[1] When we think of an object, we do not just think of a certain logical conjunction of properties; we think of a shaped extension through which, and in which, the properties combined in the object are either manifest or dispositionally present; but it remains to be shown that location with respect to other things is equally a feature of appearances and not just a feature of our apprehension of them. We already know from the house example in the Second Analogy that a form of intuition may, in some cases, carry no representational significance for the object of the intuition. The temporal succession among the perceptions of the house does not represent a corresponding succession in the house itself. Since it is not generally true that features of apprehension are features also of appearances, it must be shown what ground we have for regarding the apprehended positions of things as having any objective significance.

There are other aspects to what remains to be done in the Third Analogy. The First accounts for the representation of material objects, and the Second accounts for the perception of simple events, but no account has yet been given of the representation or perception of situations among objects, or of complex events—ones involving a number of interacting substances. We do perceive situations among objects, ongoing processes, changes that change, and other sorts of complexes in the manifold of appearance; but it still must be explained how—and why it is necessary that—we do.

A third piece of unfinished business is the distinction and relation between the subjective and objective. The option of regarding some states of consciousness as lacking objective import (and others as having it) anticipates the subjective/objective distinction. The distinction must be defined in more detail, and then the relation between the two explained; for no theory of experience can be complete without an account of the general relationship between them.

In summary, what must still be explained is the knowledge we have of the universal system of locations and spatial relations: the layout of the world in empirical space; of situations involving a number of objects interacting; and, of the full subjective/objective distinction.

34. Pretextual Expectations

This section reviews the unfinished business mentioned above with reference only to the entry under the third category of relation in the Table of Categories: Of Community (reciprocity between agent and patient). With the categories of the First and Second Analogy, it was necessary to begin by countering certain misleading expectations that might naturally arise in respect of such familiar topics as substance and cause. Here there is the opposite problem, and it seems to me necessary to generate some expectations by relating the unfamiliar category to what remains to be done.

Consider how Kant's choice of the term *community* might be taken to indicate the nature of the discussion. Consider also how activity and passivity might figure in the account.

Distinct objects have their own intrinsic spatiality; but they are also intuited to have an *ex*trinsic spatiality, that is, a relation to one another in space. The intuition we have of the relation of objects to each other is a subjective ground for regarding them as being actually so related. If there were no objective ground also binding them to one another in the same relations, we would have no more reason than in the house example for regarding the intuited relation as transposable to appearance. So there must be some relation among objects themselves that entitles us to transpose the form of outer sense, to regard it as having empirical significance. This relation cannot rest on a perception of position in objective space; it is not as though we can somehow read off the coordinates of empirical space at the same time as we perceive the objects. Like time, space itself is not perceived. Nor can the intuited relations be carried over unchanged into appearances. Spectators on one bank see the ship move left to right; those on the other bank see it move right to left. What we need is an objective ground that will enable us to transfer the spatial relations among intuitions to appearances, and to alter them so that they become independent of perspective.

In the house example there is a succession *in* perception, but no perception *of* succession; but why, we might ask, is there a succession in perception? The answer lies in what we do when we perceive a static object—in how, for example, we move our eyes. By contrast, what we do seems irrelevant to the succession both *in* and *of* the perception of an event. The dispositional ground determines the order in the event, and the event itself determines the order in perceptions of it. In the contrast between the two examples, we already have something of a contrast between activity and passivity: we act to produce order in the one case; and we are acted upon in the production of order in the other case. There is also an obvious association of this active/passive contrast with the subjective/objective distinction, though we should expect other manifestations of activity and passivity and a more general distinction between subjectivity and objectivity. But suppose that we can develop the contrasts and associations to provide an objective ground entitling us to carry the form of outer intuition (that is, the spatial aspects of apprehension) over into appearances. We would then not only have an explanation of our knowledge of the situation of things in an objective and universal system of spatial relations; we would also have some account of how we act in the world as perceivers, and of how the world acts on us. In short, we would have accomplished two fundamental things: an account of our knowledge of reality as an all-embracing unity and whole, and an account of our place within that whole.

As things stand at the end of the Second Analogy, our knowledge of appearances is fragmentary: material objects unrelated to each other except by virtue of their character of permanence (= the ultimate grounding in the substratum); events being merely simple sequences, not complex processes forming unending chains and extensive networks. Fragmentary appearances are inadequate to provide a correlate rich enough thoroughly to unite and order the manifold of experience. If we stopped at the end of the Second Analogy, experience would, on our account, be no more than a diversity of isolated episodes. Even if we added empirical thought (= reason) to the account at that point, we would be no better off because reason would *find* no inconsistency between one episode and another. For, if appearances are isolated, they cannot conflict. We could *impose* connection and consistency; but we would then have to regard the ordered whole as a mere artifact of reason, not a unity within the appearances themselves.

The unity of apperception requires experience to be of an objective realm in reference to which states of consciousness are united and ordered in a thoroughgoing way, so the realm of objects known must itself be well-ordered and unified; otherwise, against the fragmentary character of what it represented, intuition would itself be fragmentary. We need to find unity in appearance. To this end, appearances—both material objects and events—must be comprehended in a universal and systematic framework of relations. If they can be established objectively, space and time will provide the unity required by the principle of the unity of apperception.[2]

The manifold of appearance extends beyond the individual, even though one's own personal experience is the entire subjective basis for knowledge of appearance. Appearances must tie in with intuitions, without being limited to any one individual's experiences. The principles that secure the analogical relation of the two manifolds must secure knowledge of appearance by grounding representation in intuition, but they must also secure the independence of appearances from the experiences of any one individual.

This suggests the possibility of discovering a relation between intuition and appearance that is not limited to some one specific manifold of intuition. If the principles can secure knowledge without reductionism, it may be possible to employ the principles that structure one's own experience to determine other possible experiences. That is, if the principles do establish appearances as independent—as existing in their own right—there is a possibility that *community* is not just the *realm of the known,* but also a *realm of knowers.* In this connection, reconsider the house example. If the order of apprehension reveals to the perceiver his own action, and at the same time reveals the order of apprehension as merely subjective (= pertaining to the perceiver rather than to the perceived), it equally reveals him to himself as an appearance; for action is an empirical criterion of substance, through which it manifests itself.[3] He learns that his own experiences are events in nature, not by some effort of reflection, but by perceptions that require him to take account of his own action. Just as his actions reveal him to himself as an appearance, he may likewise perceive other selves through their actions.[4]

While not enough can be said at this point to justify the expectation that the Third Analogy will provide a solution to the problem of other minds, it is reasonable *to hope that it will,* because of its original accounts of self-knowledge and of the subjective/objective distinction. And if we may not expect a solution, we may at least demand one: holding this, or any other, theory of experience to be seriously inadequate if it fails to explain our experience of others. It is obvious a posteriori that much of our knowledge does rely on the experiences of others; so we should at the very least be able to show that we know others, and are able to judge independently the credibility of their testimony (but that requires the capacity to determine what they experience *without* being told).

In summary, we can expect the Third Analogy to tackle a wide range of metaphysical problems. It should provide objective grounds for location and relation in empirical space. It should explain the perception of complex situations and events, at least showing that the complexity is sufficient to permit the introduction of reason as empirical thought. It should complete the theory of objective time, showing how the category of community finds application by means of its schema—coexistence. It should locate consciousness with the empirical order, and establish the general interrelation between subjectivity and objectivity.

35. The Main Argument of the Third Analogy

In the Third Analogy, Kant again revises his statement of the principle.

> All substances, so far as they coexist, stand in thoroughgoing community, that is, in mutual interaction (A 211).

> All substances, in so far as they can be perceived to coexist in space, are in thoroughgoing reciprocity (B 256).

This revision makes two important additions: first, the principle is limited to *perceived* coexistence; and, second, the coexistence is described as being *in space.* By his other corrections to the proof section, Kant does not change what he does in the argument; but the changes in the principle make his intentions much clearer. As in the other Analogies, Kant is here putting forward a principle of perception.

In keeping with his general procedure throughout the Principles, Kant's deepest concern is with time, even in the Third Analogy where the topic is space.[5] Space does unify the manifold of appearance; but it is neither space as we merely imagine it (see theory of spatial forms) nor spatial relations as apprehended that unifies appearance. If space pertained to objects only as we imagine or apprehend them, it would be merely an ideal or subjective condition of appearances. To be properly empirical, space must be grounded in some condition of the objects themselves. This condition of objectivity is (as in the other Analogies) essentially temporal. Just as the first two take substance and causality as their topics but are nonetheless basically temporal, the topic of the Third may be space, but the principle is a rule for the determination of a temporal relation.

The argument to come will show in detail that one cannot start with coexistence (as an assumed or perceived feature of appearances) and then afterwards find causal laws (= dynamical connections) interrelating all appearances as parts of a unified realm of nature. Rather, one must first show the dynamical connections, and use these as the ground for establishing spatiotemporal interconnection. As Kant says,

> The unity of the world-whole, in which all appearances have to be connected, is evidently a mere consequence of the tacitly assumed principle of the community of all substances which are coexistent. For if they were isolated, they would not as parts constitute a whole. And if their connection (the reciprocal action of the manifold) were not already necessary because of their coexistence, we could not argue from this latter, which is a merely ideal relation, to the former, which is a real relation. We [will show] in the proper context that community is really the ground of the possibility of an empirical knowledge of coexistence, and that the inference, rightly regarded, is simply from this empirical knowledge to community as its condition (note to A 218 = B 265).

We will see that the community to which Kant refers is the interaction of things at the level of their dispositions to act and be acted on. The coexistence is first of all temporal—simply being present at the same time— but the argument is that the dynamic interaction necessary to establish the coexistence of appearances also establishes their spatial relations.

Things apprehended at the same time are apprehended (usually) in some spatial relation to each other. It must be explained why this is so—whether it is a feature just of the way we intuit (say, a need to distribute data in several dimensions). If it is a feature of things as they appear to us (and not just of the intuitions that represent them), it must be explained why things have this feature (= how we know a priori that appearances are in space).

This version of the task at hand is prefigured in both of the preceding Analogies: in the First by the considerations governing our entitlement to regard collections of properties as material objects; in the Second by the conditions under which we may regard a succession in apprehension as having a corresponding objective succession in appearance, that is, an event.

No less than the other two Analogies, the Third "rests on the synthetic unity of all appearances as regards their relation in time" (A 177 = B 220). It would not do, however, to take temporal coexistence as an *unexplained* primitive in terms of which to describe existence in space. Just as there must be something other than a succession of perceptions in the experience of an event, there must be something other than merely being intuited at the same time in the experience of objective coexistence. In the former case, a disposition of a substance provides the ground for the experience of an event. Kant uses the same ground in the latter case. When one substance acts on another, their objective coexistence is evident. They are then not just intuited together; their interaction shows that they exist together. Dynamical interaction is the "something other" at the beginning of the following passage. It provides the objective ground of the perception of coexistence.

> There must still be something other than its mere presence through which A determines B's place in time and B determines A's, because only on this condition can substances be empirically represented as *existing at the same time*. Now it is only that which is the cause of another or of its determinations that determines for the other its place in time. Thus each substance must be the cause of certain determinations in the other (since only in respect of its determinations can a substance be an effect), and each must at the same time contain the effects of the causality in the other; that is, they must stand in a dynamical community (immediately or mediately) if their coexistence is to be known in any possible experience" (A 212–13 = B 259).[6]

Though the passage is clear enough we should dwell on it for a moment. It outlines the essential contention of the Third Analogy. We may apprehend various appearances at the same time, whether these are various properties of an object, various objects, the stages of various events, or some mixture of these. They are present together in sense. The question is whether they coexist *merely in sense,* or in the manifold of appearance. Kant's contention is that their coexistence is proved only if they interact.

To think something is not just to have the idea. That is only to think *of* it. To think it is to think *that*.[7] Alternatively, it is to judge that something conceived in the idea exists. Copresence in sense (or the imagination) gives us the idea of things being at the same time; but if we are to make a judgment to this effect, we must have some ground for doing so. I can think of Napoleon while I watch the ballgame, but this does not make him a contemporary of John Mayberry. Judgments of coexistence must be subject to some restriction or regulation. Kant contends that this is supplied by an interaction between the things judged to exist at the same time. How it is supplied remains to be spelled out.

To appreciate Kant's argument, we must keep in mind the material that he develops in the other Analogies. He is not proposing isolated solutions to isolated problems. He purports to present a system of metaphysics, a theory, and a science. The connections within the system are especially important with respect to categories that are the third under any heading in the Table of Categories. He says, "The third category in each case always arises from the combination of the second category with the first" (B 110). In this case we must see how the discussions of substance and causality give rise to the discussion of community.

In the perception of events, a permanent characteristic or dispositional property of a substance provides a ground in the event of any change in its transitory properties. However, there is a problem in this. A cause must *always* be followed by its effect; but, given the *permanence* of substance, it would seem that there *exists at all times* the cause of the succession perceived in any event. The problem, then, is to explain why events are not incessant—why they ever cease, why they have not taken place earlier. There are other ways of expressing the problem: How can a cause of action be present in that which is not acting? If dispositions for change can be latent, what triggers their action? Why do events take place only at certain times?

To these questions there is one ready answer. It is that other dispositions in other substances may be necessary for an event. For example, a stretchable object may stretch only when a force is applied, or only when wet. A solvent may work only when heated to certain temperatures.

There are two things to note about this answer. *First,* it indicates why the move from the Second Analogy on to a third is necessary. In order to perceive events, we must ground succession in the dispositional characteristics of substances; but that proves insufficient as a restriction. We must go on to limit the action of the disposition to certain circumstances (= attach riders to the reason or causal ground: '*x-able* if ———'). If one thing must happen for another to happen, then happenings will take place in complex networks of complementary actions. The alternative is to make dispositions in isolation self-sufficient; but if they are self-sufficient, the events they underlie can never cease. The *second* thing to note about the answer is that it is at best just a temporizing device. Suppose we limit the solvency of a substance to when it is heated, and we do this to account for why there are solvents in which nothing is dissolved (or why a salt begins to dissolve only at a certain time, and not earlier). We merely postpone the difficulty by raising another problem of the same sort. Why does whatever heats the solvent not do so earlier? How is it that the solvent's thermal capacity ever goes unrealized? Because all changes are grounded in the dispositions of things in virtue of their materiality, and so ultimately in matter itself, the problem is why the capacities of matter are ever unexpressed.

A different answer is supplied by common sense. A soluble substance dissolves only when it is *in* a solvent. The thermal agent (= heat source) acts on the solvent only when it is *near* to it. Without denying the interplay among substances that is suggested in the first answer, the second answer returns us to the topic of the Third Analogy. Spatiotemporal presence and absence function as qualifiers on the dispositions that underlie events. Although dispositional characteristics are permanent, and although they are the causes of an event, in order for an event actually to take place it may be necessary for several causes to work together and to be in a certain spatial relation to each other. Thus, along with dispositions, spatial relations emerge as empirically significant. The unqualified existence of an *x-er* and an *x-ee* cannot be sufficient for *x-ing* that is not incessant. Nor can it be sufficient to say that an object is an *x-er* only when it is *y-ed,* for that just raises the problem of why the *y-er* does not always *y* it. There must be a nondispositional cause, or a nondispositional qualification upon a cause.

Together, the two answers provide a satisfactory answer to the problem of the beginning and ending of events. The dispositions of a material object involved in events that begin or end cannot be self-sufficient reasons for the event or they would give rise to it at all times. They must therefore involve the concomitant action of other material objects. To act together the material objects must coexist, but even that cannot be the whole story. If they do not coexist, it can only be because one or the other of them came into existence or went out of it after or before the other. Which is to say, they must be understood in terms of things more fundamental—ultimately in terms of matter itself. But if it is all ultimately grounded in the permanence of substance, there exists at all times the disposition—or the disposition to give rise to an object with the disposition—to bring about the event. Therefore, there must be objective conditions other than the dispositional characteristics of matter that are responsible as necessary conditions for events that begin or end.

In order to be satisfied that the problem is answered, we must resolve two things. We must determine that spatiotemporal coexistence and other relations of position *can* function as conditions on the occurrence and nonoccurrence of events. We must then determine that *only* these conditions, and only when they are taken to obtain in appearance, are conditions of the required sort.[8]

Empiricists such as Hume simply assert the close connection of spatiotemporal juxtaposition and causality. They take action and events to be explicable in terms of conjunctions that are observed in nature. This testimony is not adequate *to prove* that concomitance is tied up with causality; but it is evidence of fairly reliable witnesses to what we do think—so far as that is evident a posteriori. It is evidence that we regard presence and absence—of one object with respect to another—as having empirical significance in respect of the occurrence and the nonoccurrence of events. Moreover, Hume himself challenges us to find anything other than the observed concomitance of certain qualities to account for the causal beliefs we hold.[9]

As already argued,[10] the defect in that challenge is brought out by the house and ship examples. He gives us no principle to decide whether cases of succession in perception are also cases of succession in the things perceived. The fact that is of current interest is that, in addition to the illegitimate appeal to observation of regular succession, he appeals also to observed concomitance. Again he gives no ground that supports the shift from subjective to objective. Our *observations* of certain qualities may be regularly conjoined, but it must be shown that they are observations of objective conjunction. That is, it must be shown that being observed together is not merely the co-occurrence of perceptions, but the perception of co-occurrence.

Despite his failure to appreciate the need for an objective ground to support any judgment of perception, Hume's account of causality is in accordance with the facts—though it is a poor explanation of them. The fact is that we do manage to account for the occurrence or the nonoccurrence of events by taking note of things that are observed together. The conformity of Hume's account to the facts shows that we do attach significance to formal conditions such as being near, or in, or at, or next to. All that Hume leaves unexplained is how and why (it is necessary that) we do.

We know all this from experience. We know that the amount to which something is heated varies with the approach or the withdrawal of the heat source. So we know that approach and withdrawal (= distance apart) are, along with heat, conditions on the occurrence of events such as softening or hardening, melting or solidifying.

What needs to be shown is that we *must* attach such significance to presence and absence, approach and withdrawal, and distance. In part we can be satisfied of this by reflection on the considerations that dismiss appeals to the dispositionals in other substances as only a stalling tactic. We cannot account for the beginnings and endings of events solely by appeal to the dispositions of matter since these are permanent; yet the events caused by them are intermittent. Thus, we cannot say that the entire explanation of an event is to be found in terms of substances and their dispositions; at least, we cannot say this for any event that is not continuous and everlasting.

The fact that the further limitation that is required must account for *beginnings* and *endings* points to the need for a condition that is temporal—or, more generally, formal rather than material. We must account not only for why the object softens or bends or breaks or whatever, but also for why it does so *here* but not *there, now* but not *then*. Because the required limit is in respect of a formal feature of the event, only a formal condition can serve the purpose. In part then, the transference of formal (= spatiotemporal) features to appearances is justified by the fact that they alone are of the sort appropriate to qualify the occurrence of events.

Finally, the transference of spatiotemporal features from apprehension to perception—from intuition to appearance—can be justified by the need to regulate apprehension. In general, the possibility of objective significance constrains the ways in which the given is apprehended. If the objects of perception were not regarded as being formally interrelated in space and time, they would not determine the form taken by experiences of them. At best one would have a system like Leibniz's—objects that are fundamentally not in space and time, and cognition of the objects governed only by logical constraints. Leibniz's deep reasons for excluding space and time in the last analysis of substances have to do with the principles of creation. If space were retained, God could create different worlds just by putting East in the place of West, and vice versa, instead of leaving East east and West west.[11] Since he could possess no reason for the one world rather than the other, there is no significant difference between the worlds—nothing to choose between them. However, there is no particular order that thoughts of a nonspatial, timeless collection of objects must take. We can as well think first of this, then that—or that, then this.

Other considerations will be given later, and these will be developed, but there is a further thing to be noted here—from our point of view, not Kant's. In interpreting the Third Analogy, we must look ahead as well as back. At the beginning of the Postulates Kant indicates that reason in its empirical application does not, strictly, add anything to experience. He abandons the Dissertation's doctrine of the *real use* of reason, that is, its supposed capacity to generate the object of knowledge for itself. All he reserves for reason in the *Critique* is a *logical use,* that is, merely the tidying up and organizing of information that is essentially complete.[12] What this means with respect to the interpretation of the Third Analogy is that we must look for all the essential features of appearance to be established here. In particular, we cannot think that Kant leaves the spatiotemporality of the world to be introduced by reason.

36. Mediate Community

We often think of the causal connections in the world as *serial*. The arguments of the Third Analogy remind us also to think of causal connection as *lateral*. Not only does one event lead to another, which in turn leads to a third, and so on, but one object combines with others to give rise to an event. This is necessarily so; for, if a material object self-sufficiently contained the causes of its changes of state, these changes would take place at once and always, in the presence of a sufficient cause. So there must be other conditions that are sometimes present and sometimes absent, and these conditions must be in other objects. Networks of causal connection are formed by both the chains of events in series and the interplay of substances.

We have so far considered the Third Analogy largely in relation to the Second. This is to consider it in terms of immediate dynamical community. To relate the Third more to the First than to the Second is to turn to the notion of mediate dynamical community.[13]

When substances combine to produce events, or separate to end them, they stand in immediate dynamical community, directly linked one to another by the lateral connections of causality. In events we directly perceive their interactions. But, in order to perceive this interaction, we are required to perceive that objects can be remote from each other and then come together to initiate an event, and that they can be together and then withdraw to terminate an event. We thus presuppose that objects can coexist without being in immediate dynamical community, since they must be causally separated from one another before or after the events in which they are coparticipants. To consider the coexistence of substances that are not directly interacting with each other is to relate the Third Analogy primarily to the First, because it is to consider the perception of static (= unchanging) objects. It is to consider the *mediate dynamical community* of substances, as opposed to the *im*mediate, which obtains where there is interaction and change.

Kant shows that perceivers are the *mediators* of coexistence between static objects that coexist.

> We cannot empirically change our position, and perceive the change, unless matter in all parts of space makes perception of our position possible to us. For only thus by means of their reciprocal influence can the parts of matter establish their simultaneous existence, and thereby, though only mediately, their coexistence, even to the most remote objects. Without community each perception of an appearance in space is broken off from every other, and the chain of empirical representations, that is, experience, would have to begin entirely anew with each object, without the least connection with the preceding representation,

and without standing to it in any relation of time (A 213–14 = B 260–61).

There are several remarks to make about this passage.

First, we must recollect the description of the house example. Just as the perception of the various features of a static object are order-indifferent, the perceptions of various substances that are not interacting are also order-indifferent. Suppose there are various objects, A through E, existing together in space, but not perceptibly influencing one another. Just as one may survey the parts of the house in any order, and yet arrive at the same composite representation, one may likewise encounter the objects in any order. This order-indifference would not obtain if the objects were interacting; for then one object might have to be in a certain state before another would change. A might have to approach B to be heated enough to dissolve C, and so on. With such interactions, the order of perception does matter, as it does in the perception of any causal succession. But we are now considering objects that are not interacting in some such way. Kant asks how we know that they are coexistent, and his answer is as follows:

> We do so when the order in the synthesis of the manifold is a matter of indifference, that is, whether it be from A through B, C, D to E, or reversewise from E to A. For if they were in succession to one another in time, in the order, say, which begins with A and ends in E, it is impossible that we should begin the apprehension in the perception of E and proceed backwards to A, since A belongs to past time and can no longer be an object of apprehension (A 211 = B 258).

This is much the same as the answer to the house example—if one were to ask how we know that the parts of the house coexist.

So far, order-indifferent perceptions have been characterized only negatively, as those in which the resulting composite remains the same, no matter in what order its parts are considered. We can now give a positive account. The order of order-indifferent perceptions does have empirical significance, but not in respect of the object or objects of perception. The significance pertains to the perceiver; it depends on, and reveals, what he does and how he goes about encountering the object(s). Just as interacting substances give empirical significance to the spatial conditions under which they are apprehended (by adding them to material or dispositional conditions as part of the complete reason for an event), so noninteracting substances also give significance to the spatial conditions under which they are apprehended (by interacting with the perceiver).

Suppose that we perceive A, B, C, D, and E only once. There is some order in which our perceptions occur. Maybe we see A first, then B and C together, then D, and finally E. By hypothesis, these objects are fixed and unchanging; but how, in experience, do we know that they *could have been* seen in some other order? (How does coexistence get determined as an empirical relation among *appearances,* and not just remain the sort of relation among apprehensions that obtains in the example between *B* and *C?*) In part we know this because our conception of the whole situation remains the same regardless of the order of its parts; but we also have the distinctive contribution of the Third Analogy. There is, after all, a succession—even if it is just in perception and not in the objects perceived. Our own activity as perceivers accounts for this succession.

Why must perception acquaint us with our activities as perceivers? The most general answer is as follows. If it did not there would be only randomness in the occurrence of all order-indifferent perceptions; but Kant maintains that the manifold of intuition must be taken up, gone through, and connected by the understanding.[14] To whatever extent it remains without order and connection, the sensation and feeling we have is not part of experience.[15] There is experience only where there can be knowledge, and knowledge only where there is determinateness in what must be thought. Where we are free to think without restriction—as in daydreams—there is no determinateness, no knowledge, and no experience. This is no argument for the capacity to realize its own activity on the part of any sentient creature whatever, only for the necessity of self-realization by any creature (such as us) that is capable of experience in the sense Kant means.

Those things that stand in immediate community do so because of their direct interactions, and they provide us with a basis for perception of their coexistence in the events they produce together. Things that are not interacting can be related to each other by means of their several relations to us; but this is possible only if, as Kant says in the passage at the beginning of this section, "matter in all parts of space makes perception of our position possible to us."

To explain how matter makes the perception of our position possible, I will introduce the notion of *relative motion* by making a number of claims about it, and then use the notion to show what matter does. *First,* a relative motion is a contrast to an absolute motion. An absolute motion is a change from one position to another within space itself—whatever else may move or remain. A relative motion is a change of position with respect to other objects. *Second,* any relative motion may be described in a wide variety of ways. Suppose the distance between *A* and *B* lessens. We may say any of the following: *A* moves toward *B; B* moves toward *A; A* and *B* approach each other; *A* recedes slowly, while *B* more rapidly advances; or vice versa. Each description is of the same relative change (= a lessening of the distance). *Third,* we cannot perceive space itself, so absolute motion cannot be perceived. *That,* and *how,* we can perceive relative motion remains to be proved and explained, but we do apprehend relative motions. Things may be given close together in sense at one moment and more distant at another. (The objective significance of this intuited change needs to be accounted for.) *Fourth* (combining the second and third), the intuited motion can always be brought under any of a number of conceived motions. That is, the apprehended lessening of the distance between A and B conforms equally to any of the following concepts: of A's motion toward B; of B's toward A; etc. *Fifth,* neither imagination nor anything given in sense nor geometrical reasoning can determine which of the concepts is the correct one to apply to intuition. *Sixth,* if *nothing* determines which concept is correct, the intuited relations in space must be regarded as lacking objective significance. Which is to say, if it is indifferent whether the motion is assigned to A or to B, motion cannot be regarded as an empirical feature of an appearance. *In sum,* the unperceivability of absolute motion and the spatial equivalences of various conceptions of any relative motion, together point to the need for something nonspatial to determine motion if we are to be able to regard it as real.

Kant says that *matter* makes possible the perception of our position in space, and that we provide the link in mediate community. What he means can now be explained in the context of the claims about relative motion.

A's motion toward B looks the same as B's motion toward A. The two are equivalent in respect of what we apprehend in either case; but they are dynamically inequivalent—the former assigns a change to the positions of A, the latter to B. For the motion to be assigned to one object rather than the other, mobility must be assigned to that object—as a disposition—rather than to the other object. It sounds trivial to say that we can perceive something as moving only if we can think of it as mobile; but it, in fact, makes all the difference. Any motion in intuition is relative. There is the same change within the sensory field whether we move one way and the object remains still, or we remain still and the object moves in the opposite way. Of course, we do see some things move and others remain fixed in one position; but we cannot *just* see this, as a feature *simply given* in sense-experience. Look at the house. At first the roof is in the center of the visual field, the main part and basement lower down. Later they move to the center and the roof to the upper positions in the visual field. This, by the alternatives of relative motion, is the same whether we cast our gaze downward or watch an object rise. There is no difference in intuition between the one and the other, but there must be a difference somewhere; if not, spatiality is an illusion. The difference is in what can do what. Can houses rise (and undergo the many more complex motions by which they would account for the positional variety in intuition)? Or can we shift our gaze? and move about while looking at them? We settle such questions by imputing dispositional capacities consistent, on the one hand, with what is given in sense (= possibilities of apprehension), and, on the other, with what can be thought in the object.

We know from experience that sensations supply us with a subjective basis for representing the motions of our bodies, but even these sensations of motion require an objective basis if they are to be regarded as the contents of representations of actual motion.[16]

We are here concerned only with appearances. The claim is that the perception of their coexistence in space rests on their causal or dynamical interactions with other appearances. Kant shows that in the perception of process and events, we as perceivers are not central to the interconnection of things; but, when things are not interacting with each other, then our perceptual activities become the links causally connecting appearances. Think of watching a game or reading a novel versus taking stock or exploring a new district. With the former, there is so much connection from one to another among the objects that their combination is established without reference to ourselves. When taking stock or exploring, it is, by contrast, essential to proceed methodically—shelf by shelf or area by area. We must (and a fortiori must be able to) keep track of our own motions because they supply the mediate community of appearances.

37. The Metaphysical Exposition of the Category

Kant describes the abstract, logical character of the third category of relation in the passage quoted next, from the Metaphysical Deduction. He also explains the connection between the category and the form of judgment that provides the clue to its discovery.[17] The description is scrupulously abstract; it is supposed to be of the *pure* category, in advance of any application the category may find in experience. Despite the consequent difficulties of reading it, we can find in the passage a formal outline of the relationships between such judgments as those illustrated above by the *alternative* descriptions of any relative motion. (*Disjunction* is the form of judgment paired with community, but it is not disjunction as any pair of judgments with an *or* stuck in.) Kant explains the logic of a judgment such as the following: "*A* is moving toward *B,* or *B* toward *A,* or both toward each other, or. . . ." Disjunctions of this sort have some interesting features. In fact, the best proof of their interest is that they can be generalized as the features central to the subjective/objective distinction; but more of that next section. We are concerned at present with Kant's account of the pure category and its associated form of judgment.

In all disjunctive judgments the sphere (that is, the multiplicity which is contained in any one judgment) is represented as a whole divided into parts (the subordinate concepts), and that since no one of them can be contained under any other, they are thought as co-ordinated with, not subordinated to, each other, and so as determining each other, not in one direction only, as in a series, but reciprocally, as in an aggregate—if one member of the division is posited, all the rest are excluded, and conversely (B 112).

(This is not one of the easier bits of the *Critique,* but it is one of the most important ones.)

Space provides several instances of "the multiplicity which is contained in any one judgment." First consider how we can work out all the descriptions spatially equivalent to one arbitrarily selected description of a relative motion. Say we start with '*A* moves toward *B*'. This has as its content the lessening of their distance apart, but this content is shared equally with '*B* moves toward *A*'—and with the other descriptions already given. Other instances are to be found in the theory of spatial forms. The continuum of related shapes corresponds to what Kant here calls "the sphere" in all disjunctive judgments. Recall the ovals of continuously varying elongation or the cylinders of varying ratios of height to diameter, from rings to tubes. From any member of such a continuum, all the other members of the continuum can be obtained by some imagined modification of a regular sort (e.g., gradual rotation, stretching, flattening, twisting, etc.). Any shape "contains a multiplicity" in the sense that other shapes can be taken from it by some transformation. All the shapes that belong together within a series of transformations are "the subordinate concepts." Whether illustrated by judgments with a common content or by shapes within a continuum, the basic requirement of the sort of disjunction that interests Kant is that any of the disjuncts contains them all.

No member in a set of equivalent descriptions (related shapes) is subordinate to the others. Kant says, "They are thought as co-ordinated with, not subordinated to, each other." The reason that they are thought in this way is that it does not matter which description (shape) we start with; we can as easily get the series of cylinders from rings (by imagining their progressive elongation) as from tubes (gradually squashed). By contrast, consider the one-directional determination of implication among concepts that form a hierarchy of species and genera. If one starts with a mouse, one can work the whole way up, through rodentia, eutheria, mammalia, chordata, vertebrate, to animalia; but if one starts higher in the series (say, subclass eutheria) only the terms above are implied, not the order or species below.

We must now consider *positing* and *exclusion.* Kant says, "If one member of the division is posited, all the rest are excluded, and conversely."

First, take apprehension as an example of positing. We do not at one moment apprehend all the possible apparent shapes of a thing. At any given time, it stands in a certain position. Even though from one angle of observation we may determine the shape of an object (in certain cases— usually we need several perspectives[18]), and even though the shape of the object is identifiable with the entire continuum of apparent shapes it can present to all possible points of view, still, to see it from one point of view at a certain time is to exclude seeing it from any other point of view at that time. *Second,* take assertion as an example of positing. From one description we can work out others, but to assert one is to exclude (assertion of) all the rest that are coordinated with it.

Positing and exclusion are thus not opposites like affirmation and denial or inclusion and exclusion. Rather, they draw on those oppositions while adding to them the notions of implication and codetermination. We should expect this, given that the third in a trio of categories is supposed to be a combination of the second with the first. The second category of relation is, in its purely logical aspect, the notion of implication. The first is co-predication, as when we think of an object as the sum of its properties or determinations.

In symbolic logic, we can easily enough represent disjunction in terms of implication and negation (making separate listing of all three seem redundant).[19] Kant's category of community does involve implication and negation. Implication is involved in the way "the multiplicity is contained in any one judgement," and negation, in the way that exclusion works. Thus, we may from '*A* moves toward *B*' infer the lessening of their separation, which could alternatively be expressed by '*B* moves toward A.' So, in a sense, the one implies the other (not strictly of course—just that we appreciate their equivalence in terms of apprehension). If we know that what we apprehend has empirical significance, we know *that* (using obvious abbreviations) *either A or B;* but this is elementarily equivalent to knowing that *if not A, then B* or *if not B, then A.* The exclusion of one posits the other, and vice versa. We know that if they have got closer together, and one of them has *not* moved, then the other one has. But this is not quite what Kant wants. He is concerned with positing that leads to exclusion—not exclusion that leads to positing.

The complaint that, since disjunction can be defined in terms of implication and negation, Kant's list of categories contains redundancy misses the point. If we start with propositions and set ourselves the task of listing their sorts of possible truth-functional connection, it is true enough that we need not list all three.

Kant, however, starts with certain abstract logical notions, on the one hand, and the material given in sense, on the other. In the Schematism, he sets himself the task of explaining how the former finds application to the latter—propositions are part of the product that arises from the processes he describes. In the analysis of propositional relations and connectives, we find the interdefinability of implication, negation, and disjunction. We find also that exclusion (of one disjunct) leads to positing (of the other). These analytic findings pertain to the pure categories apart from all relation to what is given in sense. We would find the same features if we analyzed our empirical judgments, which shows that we do (somehow) apply the pure categories to sensory input. The problem is to explain the application, and a procedure that starts with propositions cannot provide the answers. What we need is a synthesis of sensory input that results in its conformity to the functions of logical connection.

Elegance—the reduction of primitives to a minimum—has its place among the desiderata of formal systems; but a certain amount of redundancy has its place among the dissiderata of a system of synthetic principles. We have already seen one instance of this in the interplay of our knowledge of events and our knowledge of causes. While either an event-ontology or a substance-ontology might be, in the abstract, sufficient to describe the world, neither one in isolation suffices to constrain the representation of reality. From a complete inventory of the events in the world we might well be able to infer an inventory of its objects and their properties, and vice versa. But we cannot (*pace* Leibniz) start with objects or events and weed out until we are left with what we want. We start with sensory states that admit of two sorts of combination (and of alternatives of combination) in apprehension. We then add the possibility of objective representation as a constraint on apprehension by asking which groupings and comparisons could be significant. It would not be enough to try just to represent objects, or just events, for objects could then be any collection of sensory qualities, events any succession seemingly represented in sense. Instead, we must represent both together: things whose dispositions are evident in the alterations the things undergo, events that are state-changes taking the dispositions of substances as their causes. The Third Analogy shows that even the dual constraint of having to represent both objects and events is not enough to regulate perceptual representation. To the representation of events, we must add the representation of noninteracting substances to account for the beginning and ending of events. To the perception of noninteracting substances, we must add our interactions with them to give empirical significance to their coexistence when it is not evident from their interactions with each other. These additions have substantial overlaps with what precedes; but, for all its inelegance from a formal point of view, such overlap is essential to cognition. It enables us to connect things in a variety of ways, and test each connection against others.

Implication finds application primarily in the perception of events—disjunction, in the resolution of alternatives of either objective representation or apprehension. Alternative representations are those involving a content such as a relative motion that may be distributed in a variety of ways. Alternative apprehensions are exemplified by shape variations. In either sort of case, each disjunct contains the whole sphere to which it belongs, being a particular mode of the whole. An oval is a particular presentation of a round object: when tipped. *A*'s motion toward *B* is a particular lessening of their distance apart. Because disjunctive alternatives arise both in concepts and in intuitions, their resolution is never an isolated matter; that is, it always requires reference to other aspects and parts of experience. From a single image, we cannot determine if it is one shape of object seen from one angle or some other shape of object seen from some other angle (assuming the image could belong to more than one continuum of shapes). To resolve the matter, we need a number of images, which we could get either by shifting the object slightly or by shifting our vantage point. While a single image could belong to any of a number of continua, a series of images is restricted to certain possible transformations of a basic shape. Thus, the indeterminacy among various concepts of shape with respect to a single image is reduced by reference to other images. However, recourse to a broader base in intuition, while resolving the disjunctive alternatives of conceptualization, opens up the disjunctive alternatives of relative motion. The production of variety in sensory images requires either one motion by the object or the converse motion by the perceiver. The resolution of that depends, in turn, on the possibility of assigning dispositions for motion either to the object or the perceiver. Those assignments cannot (as permanent dispositions subject to the conditions of general laws) be made for one case only.

The upshot is that experience involves indeterminacies on every level. The same sensations can be grouped in this way or compared in that, or both grouping and comparison can be involved in a combination in apprehension, and even under one principle there are alternatives. Concepts can likewise unify the same sensory inputs from apprehension, but do so in ways that carry different implications concerning the dispositions of the objects involved. No level of experience is sufficient unto itself, nor is any slice of experience self-contained. It is not enough to find one match-up of apprehension to understanding to empirical thought that works for one occasion. To settle one indeterminacy one way is not just to rule out other ways of settling *it,* but to exclude other ways of settling *other indeterminacies.*

This is not a bad thing. In the first place, it means that experience must be treated as an integral whole. In the second place, though nothing is fixed (in and of itself, but only in reference to the whole of experience), there is so much flexibility at every level we can demand that all reasonable conditions of knowledge be met. Suppose we had to regard empirical inputs as determinate in themselves. Then the demand that thought relate to input could conflict with the demand that thought be consistent. If we must one-sidedly accommodate thought to whatever is given in sense, but also maintain consistency from one thought to another, we must hope that nature will be kind to us in providing only the sorts of input that require no effort on our part in respect of the demand for consistency. Fortunately, such is not the situation in which we find ourselves. Apprehension admits of alternatives, as does conceptualization, as does thought.

38. Subjectivity and Objectivity

The notions of disjunctive equivalence, positing, exclusion, and reciprocal determination can now be employed to describe two parallel relationships: of subjective and objective judgments, and of the manifold of intuition and the manifold of appearance. The basic patterns illustrated in respect of shapes and relative motions are repeated at the most general levels of subjectivity and objectivity.

The subjective (intuition) and the objective (appearance) are related to each other as *disjunctives*. Not as premises to conclusions. Not in one direction only, but as coordinated with one another.

To describe how a person experiences the world is also to describe the world he experiences. Likewise, from a description in objective terms, we can think what it would be like (how it would feel and seem) to be involved in the situation that is described. The coordination is not rigid either way. From the objective description, we can think of disjunctive alternatives of subjective experience within it; and from an account of subjective experiences, we can think of various situations, objective disjunctive alternatives, that would give rise to such experiences. The interrelation here is the same as the one we find in language. Generally, a series of signs represents some cluster of meanings (it is hard to think of speech so precise that meaning is rigidly determined by it, or so vague that it does not represent some set of disjunctively related thoughts). From an account of what someone said (= the meaning he conveyed), we can think of various (disjunctively equivalent) ways he might have said it, that is, different words he might have used. Each sign (intuition or word) is coordinated to the things it might alternatively signify; and it is also coordinated to other signs (different apprehensions of the same sensations). Appearances are similarly coordinated in two ways: with the other appearances that might instead be represented, and with other signs that might instead signify them.

The notions of *positing* and *exclusion* also apply generally to the sub-jective and objective. We have already considered one aspect of this in the resolution of relative motion either in the object or the perceiver. We have alternatives that account for the same thing, so to resolve it one way is to exclude the other resolution. This can be extended to representation in general. We wonder if we are running a temperature or it has become very warm; if the joke is really that funny or we are just in the mood; if we imagined (dreamt) it or it really happened; etc. It may of course be true *both* that we are running a temperature and that it has become very warm, or that we feel chilly *even though* it is very warm; but these possibilities do not show that the disjunctives are not exclusive. Running a temperature when it is also too warm is rather like both *A* and *B* moving toward each other; and feeling chilly when it is actually quite warm is like *A*'s moving away from *B* though *B* moves more rapidly toward *A* to overtake it. The point of these examples is that there is a wide range of subjective and objective alternatives in any episode of experience. The point is not that we set all these alternatives out explicitly and delibera-tively at each moment of experience, then posit one, and thereby exclude the rest. For the most part, we spontaneously represent one thing rather than any other; but that is traceable to the interconnections overall in experience. The positings of a moment before, or the general knowledge we have built up over the course of experience, have already excluded most of the alternatives that would otherwise require to be considered.

The cases where we do have to stop and *think,* to wonder whether things are this way or that, will be dealt with at length in the next chapter; but the possibility of such thought rests on the matters discussed here. Without (deliberative) thought, we apprehend in ways appropriate to the representation of appearances, and we represent those appearances that best conform to our sensations. While the spontaneity of these perceptual processes might seem to argue against there being alternatives, in fact, *because* there are alternatives, there can be spontaneity. The alternatives obtaining throughout experience bridge from one element to another, and make any one element dispensable. Familiar objects are recognizable from virtually any of their sensory qualities—by the time we turn to see the face, we have already recognized the person from the voice that greets us or the sound of the door being opened as only that person opens it. By the time we feel chilly, we have felt ill for some time, and have long since ceased to regard sensations of warmth or cold as having objective significance. These implications would not abundantly overdetermine ex-perience if there were no alternatives both in intuition and in appearance; for then we could not learn to recognize objects from any of a wide variety of sensory representations, or to identify as a continuation some later part of an event seen earlier. A wink is as good as a nod when the context so fully inclines us to expect some such sign that we scarcely need it at all. That we know at once what this wink means does not show that winks are unambiguous, that there are no alternatives. It shows that we already know what is going on, just as we know whose voice to listen for when we hear the door open.

We experience directly a way in which the subjective and objective mutually determine and exclude each other in their disjunctive relationship. This direct experience is in respect of shifts in attention. For the most part, we concentrate on appearances, attending to them and ignoring our inner states. But we can easily shift our attention to our sensations. When we do so, we may easily appreciate how much is available to sensory apprehension, and how little is actually taken up. We may have gone hours unaware of how this or that part of the body feels, but if we make an effort (as in proofreading) to exclude the spontaneity of representation and to attend strictly to the given, we find a great diversity of sensations. When we notice our own sensations, we are distracted from what is taking place around us. Conversely, when we are absorbed in what is going on, we may not be aware of our own inner states. Attention elects either an objective or subjective mode; but, despite the exclusion of the one by the other, the objective and subjective still mutually determine one another.

If we consider what it is that we usually attend to, we recognize that we are seldom very aware of how things seem to us to the exclusion of awareness of how things are. Our preference for appearance over intuition is reasonable since our interests as agents, and as vulnerable participants in the empirical order, require us to attend primarily to what is happening around us. Animals seem only to function in this (unself-conscious) way; yet, *we* do have the capacity at any time to direct our attention inward. There must be some reason that explains why we are able to reflect. Inattention to one's surroundings can easily lead to difficulties, and this makes it puzzling that we have a capacity (for introspective reflection) that involves just such inattention to appearances.

The disjunctive relation of intuition and appearance explains why we (can) reflect. When we recognize that something represented in appearance is amiss or unexpected or inconsistent with other objective representations, we may return from the anomolous appearance to its disjunctive equivalent in intuition—and then proceed back to appearance, but to a different objective representation. We do this sort of thing when a spontaneous linguistic construction fails. Our initial construction does not make sense, and we return to the given to find an alternative (for instance, a homonym or ambiguity). When the spontaneity of understanding leads to some incongruity, we go back from the thing represented to its sign in order to find whether the sign might not signify something else instead.

If, in the spontaneity of perception, the understanding takes the given to represent one thing, and therein errs, it can correct the error only by returning to the given to seek out, and take up, some alternative representation.

Suppose that there were no alternatives on both levels to permit one to go from objective back to subjective and then back again to objective. One would then be at the mercy of immediate understanding. There would be no effective way to countermand the messages of perception. Inconsistencies and incongruities would indicate that some misperception had taken place, but there would be no way to locate the error at its source.

Philosophers have faced this difficulty with the proposal that *objective* belief is really just the largest set of experiences that can be consistently maintained together. In other words, the principle of noncontradiction is supposed to be the criterion determining what is the case, as a mere subset of what seems to be the case. Something like this is to be found in any positivistic or phenomenalist account. Usually there is added some requirement that as much as possible be retained.

The proposal can be argued with some plausibility. As merely subjective states, experiences have maximal certainty because they *are* just as they *are given* to the mind. However, they cannot be retained by the mind if they are left uncollected (= unconceptualized, on the view of concepts as clusters of sensory ideas). Objectivity aids retention by compressing a mass of sensory data into an abbreviating device.[20] For example, numerous observations of the height of the tide against a pier might be summed up in (the mathematical formula for) a simple sine curve, graphing the height of the water over time. There will, of course, be complications if we seek a formula for a line that passes through each of the plotted points. Efforts to reproduce the given in all its particularity and exact detail would trade away the gain to be made if we smooth out the curve. To pick the simplest line with the best fit is to weigh one sort of consideration against another—probably the simpler the line, the worse the fit, and vice versa. So we try to find a compromise that keeps the line simple enough to accomplish both of its tasks: of reducing the complexity of the given to something manageable, and of retaining as much as possible of the original data. There will be points well off the line, but they will be ruled out as errors of observation on the ground that they are inconsistent with the bulk of experience. Of course, we may find other curves to take care of the wild readings (e.g., an offshore/onshore wind curve to go along with our graph of the tides).

The foregoing account has its merits, I think especially as a description of actual applications of mathematics to nature; but I question whether it can be generalized to all conceptualization. Admittedly, concepts do combine the diversity given in sense experience, and enable us to "save

the phenor ⸺ ly retain
consciou⸺ ⸺nent's ex-
perienc⸺ ⸺hildren just
passe⸺ ⸺ne tradeoff of
simp⸺ ⸺ for only as in-
con⸺ ⸺ objectivity against
⸺ ⸺solate the causes of
⸺ ⸺ne offshore wind) that
take⸺ ⸺e a theory on the mere
hope of ⸺ ⸺ope that there will be no
anomalies at ⸺ ⸺et aside some of the basic
data for no other ⸺ fail to fit with what we can
manage to put togethe⸺ ⸺ole.

This raises an academic ⸺ ⸺t how we know that, by opting
for the retention of *as much* as c⸺ ⸺stently be maintained, we thereby
retain the truth and reject error. It m⸺ght be that the epistemological chaff
outweighs the kernal of truth. The proposal invites this sort of objection
because it belatedly recognizes that sense data are not all acceptable. For
epistemological reasons a reduction is attempted to the immediate data
of the senses, with the thought that their immediacy secures whatever
can be traced to them. Then later on, we are forced to recognize that
some of the data may be suspect. So the primitiveness, the givenness,
the immediacy of a datum of sense turns out *not to be a guarantee* of its
empirical truth. But then we admit that some sensory data are not reliable,
and we cannot block the question: "Which ones?" To appeal *then* to the
beliefs based most broadly as the standard against which to judge the
veridicality of any input is to beg the question. If we do not know what
makes an input veridical, we do not know that broadly based beliefs are
based on reliable data.

I describe the problem raised in the preceding paragraph as an academic
problem because it is a bit like asking how we know that the sane are
sane and the crazies crazy rather than vice versa, or how we know that
our waking experiences are basically true and our dreams false. One can
(I think) fairly reply that there is a conventional element in all this: that
sanity is definitionally linked to normal thought, dreaming to nonveridical
states of consciousness, and so on. Sure, we could *say* that delusions are
true, truth a delusion; but this would merely alter the words without
changing the facts.

There is a deeper worry. We need to know not just *what* is wrong, but
also *why* what is wrong is wrong, if we are to modulate and improve our
perceptual skills. That is, if we are to learn how to experience more
accurately and informatively, we need to know more than the consistency

proposal gives us. At best, it tells us which of our thoughts are mistaken, but we need to know what is mistaken for what, wherein the error lies, how we came up with the wrong thing, etc., if we are ever to be able to correct our perceptual practices. The consistency proposal at best tells us which answers are wrong, but it does not properly isolate and explain the error.

The explanation can be provided in terms of our capacity to reconstruct subjective states from their disjunctive equivalents in appearance. As in all determinations, there is a two-sided constraint on the correction of perceptual error. On the objective side, there is the reconciliation of appearances with one another—the consistency of the empirical order. On the subjective side, there is the given, on which all empirical thought must be based. We are justified in the correction of an error when we can *not only* isolate it as inconsistent, *but also* put in its place something that stands equally well-related to the given on which the mistaken perception or thought was based. When we can do that, we then know that the correction is not just an ad hoc preservation of consistency. We know that the substitution is grounded in the given.

Suppose that a two-man crew takes the tide readings—one makes the observations and the other records them. When we come to graph them, we find a '60' that seems utterly wrong. We notice that '16' would be a good fit with the other readings. The similarity in the sound of the two numbers fully justifies the substitution of the one for the other. Of course, not all mistakes may be so easily explained, but the fact that *any* are argues against the view that the objective is merely a simplifying collection of sensory data. Explanations of misperception that point to misapprehension as the cause of the error show that perceptions of appearances are not mere collections of ideas, but representations. There is a vast difference between a tide of sixteen feet and a tide of sixty, and no possibility of confusing the two directly; but the signs are enough alike to account for the confusion.

Language provides easy examples of explicable confusions, and a very perspicuous difference between signs and what they signify; but there are examples in nonlinguistic perception, and Kant's whole theory does much to make evident some of the fundamental differences between intuition and appearance. Any textbook in the psychology of perception provides examples of ways in which context, lighting, color, antecedent belief, subsequent questioning, and a host of other factors can influence perception. To make sense of such examples, we must think of perception as a mapping from subjective to objective, *and* vice versa. We cannot think of it as a process involving one direction only—from subjective simples to objective complexes—because that takes no account of the many ways in which objective factors can shape apprehension.

To conclude the discussion of subjectivity and objectivity, I will deal briefly with two related topics: memory and other minds. These topics are related both to each other and to the subjective/objective distinction.

Any theory of experience must make some provision for the development of knowledge over time. Empiricist theories do this by positing memory as an essential faculty of knowledge. The mind stores up its past experiences. Often, memory is cited as a criterion of personal identity—that is, the self at present is thought to relate back to its earlier stages by virtue of remembering what happened to it in times gone by. Some interesting puzzles about personal identity are posed by asking how we would regard persons whose memories entirely coincided for the time preceding some exotic operation. Within the framework of empiricism, only the present is accorded certainty, and even that is subject to qualification in the cases of inconsistency which we have just considered. Other minds are regarded as being accessible only through an inference that must be justified, and one's own mind at times other than the present is regarded as being like the mind of another—except in so far as memory links it to the mind now.

One of the striking "omissions" in Kant's theory of experience is any significant role of memory in cognition. Memory, which figures so large in Locke and Hume, does not figure at all in the *Critique*.[22]

We do remember things. But it is not clear that the capacity to do so is in any way essential to the development of knowledge. If one supposes that knowledge is the accumulation of sensory ideas, then pretty clearly one will need a storage capacity in which to put past experiences. However, Kant does not suppose this; but he still must make some provision for the development of knowledge. Although it is difficult to make direct contrasts between theories that differ in so many respects, one might say that in Kant's theory the manifold of appearance occupies the same place as memory in empiricist theory.

Appearances are the stable correlates of the flux of sensory input. The buildup of knowledge is not the accumulation of sensory fact upon sensory fact, but the continual addition of details to a structure that obtains a priori. We have, as it were, from the very beginning, a schematic diagram of reality as it must appear to us. As it does appear—in the actual course of experience—we record the specific characteristics of objects, the detailed conditions of events, and the occupants of various locations in empirical space and time, but the general and formal character of the manifold is known to us at the outset.

The manifold of appearance is an active file, rather than an attic crammed with memories. It is under constant revision. Even the past belongs to it as a part of the manifold about which we continue to learn. The past is not fixed and unchangeable, except as a thing-in-itself about which we can know nothing. As an object of knowledge, the past is an appearance open to revision at any time.[23] Of course, the more we posit certain alternatives in appearance the more we exclude all others that are coordinated with them. Parts of the past, along with parts of the present and future and certain general phenomena, are no doubt so fully known that there is only an abstract possibility of coming up with anything new in respect of them (e.g., Bloomsbury), but much of the past is still of absorbing interest.

I think it is useful to distinguish three sorts of memory: vivid reexperience, the production of arbitrary information, and reconstruction. The first two are memory proper, and Kant's theory does not account for them at all. The third can be subsumed in the analogical relation of intuition and appearance. I will consider each of the three in turn.

The most distinctive sort of memory arises within us as a vivid recollection of the past. Memories of this sort can to some extent be summoned at will, but a certain mystery surrounds this power of the mind. We wonder sometimes why a thing so trivial should suddenly confront us after all these years, when other things of much greater importance can no longer be brought back in the same way. We know that they happened, but not in that poignant way in which we again see the face, feel the touch, or hear the voice out of past.

The second sort of memory is the production of arbitrary information such as postal codes or phone numbers. It is arbitrary because there is no logic to it. Numbers and names that are just assigned must be committed to memory. There is no special poignancy to the recollection of a phone number.

Neither sort of memory is essential to experience. The first is somewhat chaotic and very unreliable. The second can be replaced by a small notebook.

The third sort of memory is reconstructive—when we work out where we were in the summer of '64, what year the Dodgers left Brooklyn, or where we might have left the umbrella. Such memories may evoke memories of the first sort, and there may be components of the second sort as well; but what marks off reconstructions as a third type is a possibility of working things out. This possibility rests on the thorough integration of information. Records and general knowledge enable us to work out what happened when and where. We call it memory if we happened to be there at the time, but the reconstruction of the past is not an essentially personal matter.[24]

Memory is a basic faculty of knowledge according to subjectivist or individualistic accounts of experience, in which everything one knows and believes is a product of one's own present and past experience. Such accounts require us to have a capacity for storing and reproducing the past. Otherwise one would never have enough material to produce objective complexes out of sensory simples.

The question is whether storage is an accurate metaphor for the accumulation of knowledge. The alternative is to regard knowledge not as a file in which the past is kept, but as an ongoing project of making the indefinite more definite. To represent anything as empirical we must find a place for it in the manifold of appearance: as an item here or there, a connection between types of things, a distinction to be drawn, etc. We do not talk about remembering the language we use all the time. Because we use it, we know it. I could say I have forgotten most of my Latin, but that is because I put it into storage. We do not, in a similar way, store appearances that are operative in experience. We may, of course, learn things about the Celts that have no bearing at all on what we perceive or think; and of such inert facts it is proper to speak of memory. The point is that they are, like my Latin, stored because they are not in use. There is another point as well. Ideas that are vital to experience exclude some possibilities and point to others; and, as they constrain and guide the empirical advance, they are also reshaped by it. The manifold of appearance, in so far as it bears on experience, is not asymmetrical about the present moment with part past and fixed, part future and uncertain. The whole manifold is subject to constant modifications and realignments, both internal to it and in response to input.

That we bother to make memory claims must be explained in the light of the fact that any competent researcher can come to a more accurate and informative view of an event or situation than is available to a participant on the basis of simply remembering what took place. Whenever we claim to remember, and what we claim to remember, does not so much portray the objective past as ourselves—our values, perspectives, and the influences we think of. When we deny memory of something, we do not deny it happened; we reveal that it is one of the things we no longer carry with us (knowingly).

To about the same extent that we can reconstruct from our knowledge of what was said the words that were used to say it, we can reconstruct what we once saw or heard or felt from knowledge of the objective circumstances in which those subjective states were aroused. However, we are not limited in this capacity to our own past. As much as we can go from knowing what it was like to what it felt like in our own case, we can go from what it was like to what it must have felt like to another person.

Memory is not a special link to one's own past. We often override another's testimony from memory, or let ourselves be talked out of one memory and into another ("No, it wasn't like that at all. You weren't even there because you'd been to the dentist and didn't feel like driving—

so it was *George* that went with the children. Don't you remember?''
Well, maybe now you do—depending more on your capacity for imag-
inative construction and your susceptibility to persuasion than on your
possession of a memory.) Since unsupported memories, however vivid,
may be genuine or mistaken, they cannot count as knowledge unless they
are confirmed by appearances in general. If there is general evidence for
what took place, anyone can determine what must have been experienced
by those involved. Since it is only the objective or reconstructive memory
that yields knowledge, what there is to be known about one's past is in
principle accessible to all. Of course, the facts may be more at *my* disposal
for the reconstruction of *my* past; but that must be weighed against the
poor position I am in to be as objective about myself, and to resist the
force of vivid memories that may well be mistaken.[25]

It is not that there are no differences at all between self and other. It
is that there are no significant differences with respect to knowledge.
What is knowable is in the public domain of the manifold of appearance.

I think that the problem of other minds is not entirely an artifact of
theories that follow the Cartesian and Humean method of beginning with
the first-person singular. One does have access to one's own states of
consciousness in a way that one does not have access to the states of
consciousness in others. The mistake that is theoretically prompted is to
think oneself the best or only *judge* of what is given to oneself in consciousness; and what is mistaken in that is the conflation of privileged
access with judgment. I alone feel my pains, have my sensations, and
think my thoughts; but what does not follow is that I am the best judge
of what I feel, sense, and think. What I alone possess is the sensory base
of my representations; but Kant contends that sensing is not taken up
into consciousness without apprehension, and that apprehension is a selective combination of the given to form a representation of a state of
affairs. Just as I may, in the expectation of perceiving a certain thing,
misapprehend the data given to me in sense (e.g., in the excitement of
deer hunting, construe certain color-regions in my visual field as a deer),
so I may misapprehend any of the subjective states to which I alone have
access, and feel pain (i.e., *think that I am hurt*) when the dentist has done
no more than introduce a cold mirror to my mouth (i.e., produce a sudden
change in my sensory state). Now, it will be I, not the dentist, who feels
the sensations; but he is the better judge of what I actually feel—not pain,
but an abrupt change of sensation, which, given the expectation of pain,
I misapprehend. The very immediacy and spontaneity of apprehension,
together with the representational aspect of apprehension (= its regulation
by the possibilities of producing some intuition with representational significance), combine to give one confidence that whatever is judged to be
so on the basis of immediate sensation is in fact the case. This spontaneous

confidence is, of course, limited to whatever is, or can be judged to be, immediately present; but it is not confined to the subjective; we can (unfortunately) imagine the deerhunter protesting in all sincerity, "I don't know where the school bus came from; I really did see a deer, and that's what I shot at." He makes his mistake, not because he is a Cartesian or Humean, but because of the spontaneity of understanding: whatever is given in sense is apprehended in whatever ways make sense of it.

With matters on which there is better abiding evidence of what actually has taken place (i.e., a bus with a bullet hole), the sincere but misguided protests of those with first-person involvement are easily overridden as mistaken. Conversely, matters without abiding objective import cannot easily be resolved (no causal traces remain to differentiate the dental patient who felt a sudden shock of cold from the patient who felt a twinge of pain). In the absence of evidence to the contrary, we let the first-person account stand (unless we are the dentist, who knows full well he has not hurt the patient, but cannot point to something as incontrovertible as a bullet hole to prove it). There is generally abiding evidence with respect to matters of fact concerning public states of affairs, so we are generally not persuaded to take first-person accounts as being incorrigible; but, because there is seldom such evidence in respect of participants' feelings, we let them have the last word, so long as it does not flagrantly conflict with the ascertainable facts.

Our natural tolerance in respect of first-person accounts of inner matters that leave little evidence should not be taken as consent to the privacy theses of Descartes and Hume. People let my claims about my inner states stand unchallenged because no one has much evidence of what I feel, sense, or think, except in so far as my inner states pertain to matters with externally observable consequences. But, a fortiori, I too can have little evidence on such private and inconsequential matters. Where no one else can be in a place to overrule my account, I am in no place to defend it. Sure, it is what I *seemed to* feel or sense or think, but, in the absence of available determining evidence, no one (me included) can tell whether it is what I *actually* felt or sensed or thought. Should there be available evidence, I lose my special status in the matter. It is then up to anyone to judge what the circumstance is: what sensations it will arouse in one situated as I am, how those sensations may be apprehended, which expectations will predispose me to which apprehensions, what is actually available to be perceived, and hence which of my apprehensions will correctly bring into my consciousness what is in fact given to me in sense, and which will distort what is given.

The disjunctive equivalences of subjective and objective states, on which anyone relies to make sense of what is given to him in sense, serve equally—wherever there is some difference in objective state—to determine the subjective from the objective. For example, if I am ever in a position to know that what I see is a round penny (that perhaps "looks" oval because I view it at an angle), I am equally in a position to know how it "looks" to you (perhaps, round because you are at right angles to it). If we suppose me to be incapable of judging what you are confronted with, we must also suppose me to be incapable of judging what I myself am confronted with; for it is only if I am able to determine the relations between apparent and true shape, between my angle of view and the objective orientation of the object in empirical space, that I will be able to perceive it myself; but, if I am competent to make those determinations, I can know also what is given to you. We can, of course, imagine circumstances in which I would have sensations but lack the capacity to make sense of them (e.g., intoxication); but these are far from being cases of special access to anything interesting. When mental states may be regarded as significant, in oneself or in some other person, then what those states are can be (publicly) determined.

8

The Postulates of
Empirical Thought

39. Empirical Thought

No less than the previous categories, modal concepts have an intellectual aspect that raises the problem of the Schematism. How is it that concepts such as possibility, actuality, and necessity find application in experience? As with the other categories, Kant's answer is that the modal categories find application in experience by giving rise to rules that govern the understanding.

Like the Axioms and Anticipations, and unlike the Analogies, the Postulates establish the relation of the faculty of understanding to another faculty. In their case, the other faculty is sensibility. The other faculty for the Postulates is reason. It is important to bear in mind that even though they are the Postulates *of Empirical Thought* they are first and foremost principles *of the understanding*.[1] The Postulates do not govern reason itself in the way that the logical principles of *modus ponens* and contradiction do. Instead, they connect reasoning to perceiving. We can reason about absolutely anything in propositional form, but the application-problem of the Schematism could be expressed with respect to the Postulates by asking which employments of reason are empirical, and which are mere exercises of abstract thought.

The question of the Postulates thus takes two forms: How do the modal categories apply in experience?, and, How does reason relate to experience? Kant indicates the relation between the two in the following passage.

> The categories of modality have the peculiarity that, in determining an object, they do not in the least enlarge the concept to which they are attached as predicates. They only express the relation of the concept to the capacity for knowledge. Even when the concept of a thing is quite complete, I can still enquire whether this object is merely possible or is also actual, or if actual, whether it is not also necessary. No additional determinations are thereby thought in the object itself; the question is only how the object, together with all its determinations, is related to the understanding and its empirical employment, to empirical judgment, and to reason in its application to experience (A 219 = B 266).[2]

There must always be some other question in addition to the question of how it is that a category finds application; otherwise, we would have no ground to seek the application. So there must be a substantive question such as how it is that sensations are combined, or how it is that we represent the objects of perception, in addition to a technical question concerning the application of a category such as limitation or cause and effect.

The substantive question here concerns thought. Up to this point, the intellectual activity that has most concerned us has been understanding; but at the level of empirical thought, understanding combines with reasoning. Both sorts of intellection are active in so far as the mind constructs a connection between one thing and another, but the activities have a different basis. In the case of reason the connection is implication. The connections of understanding depend on common patterns or similarities of structure or form.

By producing patterns of inference, reason creates structures that can be mapped onto other structures. For example, the concepts of species and genera can be related to the classes and subclasses of things in the world. But there are two points to note about this. *First,* reason never supplies itself with objects corresponding to its inferential structures, because such correspondence is not its concern, and it does not lie within its power to effect it.[3] For instance, from the concept of God as the supreme being, we can infer that He is one, all-powerful, wise, etc. From these, and other subordinate concepts implicit in His supremacy, we may go on to reason that He is no deceiver, that this is the best of all possible worlds, that apart from Him nothing can be or be conceived. Any of these inferences may be questioned or defended from a logical point of view, and further inferences may be drawn; but even if we could satisfy ourselves of the soundness of all the inferences, and no matter how far they were extended, we could still ask whether anything in reality corresponds to the system of theological concepts and propositions. All reason can ever do is elaborate and refine the system of ideas. The *second* thing to note is that the connection of reason to its objects must be at more than one point only, if what is thought is to be known. For instance, the single identification of a straight line with a path of light does not suffice to turn geometry (supposing it to be a system of thought) into a body of empirical truth about optical phenomena. There must be enough connections to ensure, if I may put it so, that it is not merely a coincidence that the rational construct coincides with what actually exists. Neither point is very contentious, but both are worth making explicit. (It is common for thinkers to become so involved in the rational aspect of their endeavor that they neglect to secure its relation to reality—for example, in scholastic theology or contemporary ethics of the decision-theory sort.)

Throughout his system of principles, Kant considers the requirement for determinacy in knowledge. The whole project began with the recognition of the indeterminacy of pure reason.[4] The development within the system—the progression from sensing to apprehension, from apprehension to perception, and now from perception to thought—can be seen as a step-by-step reduction of the virtual randomness that confronts us in sense, but it can also be viewed the other way about—with thought free to fashion what it will, but with only certain thoughts having perceptible objects, and only certain of the possible objects of perception actually perceived. The two views are complementary because the constraints must work both ways to work at all. By supplying sensory content as the determinant of the empirical, the senses—through various stages of connection—cash out the potentiality of the intuitable, perceptible, and thinkable. And, conversely, thought regulates perception as perception regulates apprehension. If it were only the one way or the other, but not both, in, for instance, the relation of perceptions to certain thoughts, there would be no knowledge in the thoughts because it might be possible to relate the perceptions to other thoughts—even ones that are inconsistent with the first ones. Which is just to say that evidence can often be taken in a variety of ways, even to support equally ideas that are mutually inconsistent. We then say that the evidence does not decide the matter, and we do not know. Confirmation requires that the evidence *must* be taken in support of the idea to be confirmed.

I will have more to say about confirmation later in the chapter. The point to be stressed here is *the duality of regulation* (= the ordering of sensory material by the intellect) *and determination* (= constraining the generality of thought and of concepts by giving them content). The *duality of form and content* first appears in intuition as the contrast between the forms of sense and sensation, and it carries right through to empirical thought. Even the term *empirical thought* suggests this—the empirical obviously associated with content, and thought with form. What gets added explicitly to the duality of form and content in the Postulates is the reflexivity of self-consciousness. There are intimations of the mind's consciousness of itself as early as the Anticipations, with qualitative comparisons based on an implicit recognition by the mind of the difference only in the strengths of its responses in the production of sensations that differ only in intensive magnitude. By the Third Analogy, the consciousness has advanced to the level of a recognition of our perceptual activity in the world. Yet, even at the level of perception, self-recognition is spontaneous and automatic in contrast to its later deliberativeness at the level of thought. We do not have to think about our movements to resolve the indeterminacies of relative motions one way rather than the other; but, even though we have not had to figure it out, we do, nonetheless, know that we are moving. Empirical thought does involve figuring out and deliberating, and (to explain what all of this has to do with duality and the form/content distinction) empirical thought involves seeking the application of various ideas, or thinking out what is taking place, or both. It is a deliberative exercise in respect of the ideas and their production— e.g., in the effort to come up with a theory or explanation (to consider it as an advance from the empirical to thought), or to explore the connections among ideas (to consider thought either in advance of, or independently of, any application it may later have in experience). When we actually make the connections that establish thought as empirical, it is not by deliberation. We say that we "see" that the theory works, and we choose a verb reflecting the immediacy and spontaneity of connection when everything falls into place. The content of experience is given a certain rational form, or a rational form is found to apply to things in the world.

To make room, as it were, for reason, we must be able to bring the implicit self-consciousness and self-recognition of apprehension and perception to full consciousness. Sensory content enters into experience only in so far as it is brought under concepts—partly to structure apprehension, and partly to represent appearances. These conceptualizations do not require thought (= reasoning), but they do yield knowledge, even if it is infected with error. Because there is no input that is not spontaneously conceptualized, deliberative conceptualization (= thought) must redo, or at least critically review, what has been done once already at the lower levels of experience. If thought is not essentially critical, reflective, and reconsidering, it cannot be empirical. To be empirical it must have content, and it can take its content only from what has already been conceived. This explains in part why Kant says that these categories do not enlarge the concept, but express the relation of the concept to the capacity for knowledge (see passage quoted earlier).

The definitions themselves explain further the relation of concepts to the faculty of knowledge as expressed by the modal categories; but, before I quote the definitions and discuss them, there is another peculiarity of the Postulates that I want to mention. They are not principles in quite the same sense as the Axioms, Anticipations, and Analogies. There is not the paired-relation to a specific feature of time such as its part/whole structure, its continuity, or one of its three objective modes. The modal categories do have schemata, as we shall see; but the structure of experience is essentially complete with coexistence added to duration and succession. Thought is somewhat optional in experience because there is knowledge at the level of perception, though it is incomplete and mixed with error. It is possible to be knowledgeable without being critical, informed without being thoughtful; and, even if one does think, there is usually some selectivity involved, with certain aspects of experience pondered, and the rest taken at face value. I think it argues for the correctness of Kant's theory that according to it we are not required to reason to know anything at all—this against a theory such as Carnap's that require very complex inferences at every level.[5] Man *can* be a rational animal, but he need not be. The Postulates do not describe a gratuitous activity, but they do describe an activity that is not a *sine qua non* of knowledge.

The analysis of the concept of knowledge is somewhat uncertain.[6] Suppose that someone who asserts *p* has not considered *q,* and suppose that *p* is true, but that the evidence he has does not determine whether *p* or *q.* If we simply ask him the relevant question, he will give the right answer. If we ask him to defend his answer, he may be able to give some reasons (good reasons, even) for it. But if we ask why he does not hold *q* instead, he will, *ex hypothesi,* be at a loss. Now, do we say that he knows *p,* or not? The boundaries of the concept of knowledge are not precise enough to enable us to give an unqualified answer. We ought to say that there are respects in which he does know it, but that his knowledge is in certain ways deficient.

The essential completeness of Kant's account of cognition at the end of the Third Analogy reflects the legitimacy of saying that the person in the hypothetical case does know, even if he has neglected to consider an alternative that, for all he knows, is true instead. The Postulates account for what would need to done by the person to remove all doubt that he knows.

40. The Definitions and Explanations of Modality

1. That which agrees with the formal conditions of experience, that is, with the conditions of intuitions and of concepts, is *possible*.
2. That which is bound up with the material conditions of experience, that is, with sensation, is *actual*.
3. That which in its connection with the actual is determined in accordance with universal conditions of experience, is (that is, exists as) *necessary* (A 218 = B 265–66).

The second definition is entirely in accord with Berkeley's *esse ist percipi* in its insistence on the close connection of actuality with what is given in sense, although, as Kant says in the explanation, the actual is not strictly limited to what is sensed; it also includes whatever follows unproblematically from the things we directly encounter.[7]

The fundamental departure from empiricism is in respect of the first and third definitions. Instead of regarding possibility as being coextensive with conceivability, and, hence, limited only by logical constraints, Kant regards the possible as being much more restricted. With the narrowing of the possible, Kant expands the necessary. In fact, only if the possible is less than the conceivable, is there an empirical sense of necessity at all; for, if the conceivable is all possible, everything empirical is contingent, and everything necessary is nonempirical.

Logical possibility is synonymous with conceivability or describability. The logically possible is that which can be thought or described without contradiction. That we can think something shows only that the components of the thought satisfy the most general condition of thought, that is, that they are consistent. It does not show that there can be an object for the thought. Similarly, that we can consistently put together a description shows only that it falls within the limits of language; it does not show that any thing so described falls within the limits of the world. Kant says, "It is, indeed, a necessary logical condition that a concept of the possible must not contain any contradiction; but this is not by any means sufficient to determine the objective reality of the concept, that is, the possibility of such an object as is thought through the concept" (A 220 = B 268).

To see why consistency is insufficient to determine objective or empirical possibility, we must consider the role of sensation in determining actuality. If "such an object as is thought through the concept" actually exists, then it is something that can be encountered in experience, directly or indirectly.[8] Suppose, however, that an object is such that no experience could ever establish whether it exists, or, if it exists, that it has the properties ascribed to it. Then, provided that the description of it is consistent, it is logically possible, but not possibly actual as an appearance.[9] Which is to say, possible actuality of an appearance (= objective possibility) cannot be the same thing as logical possibility.

The difference between logical and empirical possibility follows directly if it is granted *both* that experience determines what is actual *and* that there are some conditions that things must satisfy in order to be objects of experience. A thing is possible only if it could occur in the manifold of appearance (subject to the qualification in note 8.9). Things can be included in the manifold of appearance only if they are given in sense and the conceptualization of them satisfies the conditions given in the Analogies. We can judge a concept, therefore, not just in terms of its internal consistency, but in terms of what we can apprehend and perceive. It may be, as Hume supposes, that anything whatever could be given in sense; but Kant shows that being given in sense is not to be confused with being perceived. Before perception or observation is possible, the given must in some way be combined in intuitions at the level of apprehension, and then related as a representation to an appearance. Only inputs that satisfy both the constitutive and regulative principles can be regarded as telling us anything about the world. It may well be that we can consistently describe objects or events that would contradict even our deepest empirical beliefs; but no proof, and not even an argument, has been given by Hume or anyone else to show that nature is as free to provide as we are to describe.

Kant does argue that we are by no means as free to say (= affirm, or judge) as we are to imagine. We may be able to imagine things being other than we believe them to be; but the interesting question is whether, if they were as they are imagined to be, we could ever know that they were. If the reply to the question is that whatever we could imagine happening we could observe happening, it is easily defeated. Either observation is being used loosely to describe what we *might* represent, or strictly to describe what we *may* represent. If the former, no exception is *established*. I can imagine a pink elephant; and I might (when drunk or badly hung over) represent (= seem to see) one. This defeats no common belief about the color of elephants, and confirms a few about the effects of alcohol. Am I *entitled* to take what I seem to see as being actually the case? *May* I represent it? If all I have to go on is subjective, I may not; but, if I can find objective grounds for the representation (regard it as a color change that has been produced by some cause), though I may then represent it, I do not represent an exception to common empirical belief. (We may *express* the belief without qualification, "Elephants are grey or brown," without adding "unless painted pink"; but I think that is explicable entirely in terms of an implicit convention to the effect that an operator like 'normally' or 'typically' is to be understood.[10]) In general, since any representation of appearance requires objective grounds, all exceptions must be *within* nature as it appears to us, never *to* nature as it appears to us. If the sun does not rise, we must represent a ceasing to be in accordance with causal forces sufficient to bring that about. The earth must stop turning or the sun must blow up or some large object must block it out. Only if some such thing is possible, is it possible that the sun will not rise. The possibility of it not rising in no way follows from a logical feature of certain imaginings—but only, if at all, from the existence of forces sufficient to bring about the effect.

Kant gives the following example of the difference between logical and objective possibility:

There is no contradiction in the concept of a figure which is enclosed within two straight lines, since the concept of two straight lines and of their coming together contain no negation of a figure. The impossibility arises not from the concept in itself, but in connection with its construction in space, that is, from the conditions of space and of its determination. And since these contain a priori in themselves the form of experience in general, they have objective reality; that is, they apply to possible things" (A 220–21 = B 268).

In the example the possibility or impossibility rests not on the consistency or inconsistency of description, but "in connection with its construction in space," "on conditions of space and its determination." These are difficult phrases to explain because they pertain to nonverbal matters. They are, however, easy enough to illustrate with examples.

One common occasion for thought is when something has been lost. We might, of course, just let perception take its course and wait for the thing to turn up; but, if we decide to look for it, we must *think* where it might be, and direct our perceptions accordingly. Now, to modify Kant's example slightly, we know that it is not possible for two planes to enclose a space. The lost object cannot be between two flat contiguous surfaces. It is impossible for the hammer to be under the book that is lying flat on the table, though it might be possible for a small sheet of paper to be there. The impossibility in the one case and the possibility in the other do arise from a difference in the concepts of the objects, and from the difference in their relation to the concept of the location (under the book that is lying flat on the table); but it is not that there is a contradiction in saying that the hammer is there—it is that the book would not *lie like that* if there were a hammer under it. We are able to see what is possible or not as its location because we are able to visualize. We do not have to move the piano if we can see that the space between it and the wall is too small to permit the lost object to slip behind. Such seeing cannot be merely looking at the gap because, to be relevant to the particular search, it must involve the absent object—some things could slip behind, others are the wrong shape. We must be able to produce the absent object in the imagination. And we must also be able to manipulate what we imagine (would it go if turned?).

We can make a bit more progress with the example by considering a rival account of the same matter. In *The Structure of Science,* Nagel proposes the *definition* of a plane surface as one of any three or more surfaces any two of which "can be fitted smoothly on each other"[11] (one needs more than two surfaces to rule out, say, the fit of concave to convex). The purpose of the proposal need not be discussed here. What is of interest is that he attempts to enforce the two-element model distinction between relations of ideas and matters of fact. It becomes a matter of definition that planes are such surfaces. It will likewise be a matter of stipulation which tests are to be used to determine smoothness of fit.[12] Finally, the selection of a unit length is also a matter of arbitrary definition. Now, once these things are defined, we can go on to see what sorts of empirical truth may be observed.

The choice of a unit length does seem to be a matter of definition, involving the arbitrary selection of some standard; but the definition of a plane, the realization that it must be in terms of three or more surfaces any two of which fit smoothly, the definition of a straight line as the intersection of two planes along a common edge—none of these is arbitrary. If it were, we would not at once see the relations. How does Nagel know that *three* surfaces must be mentioned in the definition? I suggest it is because he is as capable as anyone else of *visualizing* two objects with corresponding departures from flatness that could fit each other but could not both fit a third. *It would not be possible* to have the first curve outwards to fit a certain hollow in the second, and then to fashion a third that fit both the bulge in the first and the hollow in the second. That impossibility is not by definition, "but in connection with its construction in space." How do we know that three are *enough?* Again, by seeing that any hump or hollow will be ruled out by the possibility of the three-way pairing. There is no possibility of introducing a fourth object such that any of the three will fit smoothly as pairs, but some of the three will fit the fourth and some will not. These possibilities and impossibilities governing construction show that the matter is not arbitrary or merely by definition.

Nagel's example is of the construction of objects to a certain pattern. He suggests that, prior to any knowledge of geometry, man can be imagined to be capable of fashioning straight-edges and measuring sticks. My interest in his example is in respect of the tacit assumptions it makes about cognition. Of course, he is interested only in the analysis of geometric thought, not its actual genesis; but he supposes that the description of a primitive situation can show which elements of geometric thought are primary and basic, and logically prior to others that are added in the course of experience. In particular, he wants to show that "expressions like 'point', 'line', and so on [can be] applied to physical configurations that are constructed or identified in accordance with rules specifiable *independently* of the Euclidean axioms."[13] I have no brief to defend the logical priority of Euclidean requirements, nor would any such defense have relevance to a discussion generally about Kant. What is at issue is the relative priority of rationality and understanding. Nagel assumes that at the dawn of intellectual times man *could have* fashioned surfaces and edges in accordance with designs sufficiently specified to ensure that all the products would conform unambiguously to a standard. He further imagines these men to have been *capable* of setting out that standard as a pure stipulation, a matter merely of arbitrary definition. They would then investigate the world with their apparatus to discover its geometrical properties.

The scenario is not unlike imagining men who live without law and society, but who nonetheless possess the intellectual capacities of solicitors.

The capacity to design, and then to fabricate in strict conformity with the design, involves a great many other capacities. It especially involves the ability to see in advance the results of various sorts of action (in the example, the actions would be grinding, hammering, fitting the objects, taking them two at a time, seeing which would need a bit more work done on it, where it would need to be ground down, etc.). One would then have to be able to schedule these activities as parts of a unified project. Finally, *if one were to be able to set out the project as a definition* of a certain sort of artifact, one would have to be able to review the project schedule and know that it would yield a standard product.

One cannot begin *seriously* to imagine a situation in which definition precedes empirical thought—where we ready ourselves, as it were, with all sorts of well-defined terms and careful stipulations, and then advance into the world to view it in relation to the ideas we have fashioned arbitrarily.

The point can be put more generally. In order to stipulate the meaning of a term, we must be able to consider what we do, think what it is that we propose to mean by it, know how we will judge uses of the term as correct or incorrect, know that the procedures for testing are sufficient and consistent. In short, we must know a great many things about the term, the world and ourselves before we can have any success in definition. Even at that we are unlikely ever to be able to specify things so fully that there is no room for ambiguity. Even with adequate specificity in the definition, there are still questions of its application, like Wittgenstein's, "Does the sign-post leave no doubt open about the way I have to go?"[14]

The two-element model of the mind portrays the possible as rationally determined and as logically prior to the empirical. Kant's postulate takes issue with both aspects: the possible is not in contrast to the empirical, nor is it determinable in advance of all knowledge of the world. Rather, it is only by having some appreciation of our activities and capacities—and of the related features of things—that we are able to determine what is possible. For instance, we suddenly realize that we could produce surfaces that would meet the definition *but fail to be flat,* if they were corrugated with ridges the same size as the grooves. They would still all fit smoothly; they would maintain their fit even when moved back and forth (in the direction of the corrugation); they could even retain their fit in other rectilinear motions (if the corrugations were crosshatched). We may easily come to discover ways of doing things that seemed impossible, find loopholes that need to be plugged, and possibilities that never occurred to us before; but Kant does not (like the empiricist) try to define the *im*possible (as the self-contradictory or inconsistent) leaving the rest to be possible *unless shown not to be.* (Consider how the empiricist's imagine-a-world-wherein method of argument puts the onus on the objector to show that the description is in some way inconsistent.)[15] Kant defines the possible. The determination of possibility requires knowledge—knowledge of how something can be done, how it could come about, or how it could be perceived.

I think that common sense and history support Kant's ordering of things. Our experience is nothing like the result of our having been placed in the world with all the skills of analysis, and all the powers of rational thought, necessary to determine what sorts of relations obtain among ideas. We learn bit by bit what is possible by reflection on our doings and on the things that we encounter. A study, such as Kant's, of what is essential to cognition and to appearances, does determine a priori the common characteristic of the possible—that it is "that which agrees with the formal conditions of experience"—and it tells us what (some of) those conditions are; but it must be left up to empirical thought to discover particular possibilities. All that Kant tells us is how such discoveries are possible—viz. by the relation of the concept to our capacity for knowledge, not by mere inspection of the concept to see if it is self-consistent. When we look to history, we see it as a record of discoveries that things that were once thought impossible can in fact occur. (They were not originally thought contradictory and later found not to be.) The progress of experience is not the narrowing down of initially broad possibilities (as the two-element model suggests). Rather, the reverse—as experience progresses, more and more becomes possible. The growth of possibility does occur within the constraints that obtain a priori in respect of experience; but those constraints are broad enough to hold anything we can find in history.

41. The Schemata of the Modal Categories

Because the Postulates are not principles in the same sense as the rules associated with the other categories, and because the temporal notions assigned to the modal categories in the Schematism are not later incorporated in the explanation of the Postulates, there is ground for some suspicion that Kant here (if nowhere else) is simply indulging a penchant for systematic neatness.

Here are the associations to time as set out in the Schematism:

> The schema of possibility is the agreement of the synthesis of different representations with the conditions of time in general. Opposites, for instance, cannot exist in the same thing at the same time, but only after one another. The schema is therefore the determination of the representation of a thing at some time or other.

The schema of actuality is existence in some determinate time.
The schema of necessity is existence of an object at all times
(A 144 = B 183–84).

I think any suspicion of contrivance and artificiality can be laid to rest.
Admittedly, Kant does not draw the schemata of modality into the discussion of the Postulates, and in that discussion there are none of the
sorts of reference to time that abound in the proofs of the preceding
principles; but I think the omissions are a function of the fact that empirical
thought reduplicates the conceptual activity of apprehension and perception. Kant is concerned only with the general relation of empirical thought
to what has preceded; and it is just that he does not bother to explain in
detail how everything at the lower levels of cognition is carried over to
the highest level.

Having already given a full account of the temporal structure of both
manifolds, Kant is content to allude to all that in the phrases: "the conditions of intuitions and of concepts"; "the material conditions of experience"; and, "universal conditions of experience." The conditions
referred to are, of course, the principles.

Suppose that the exposition had proceeded from the higher to the lower,
instead of vice versa. In that case, the explanations of the modal categories
and empirical thought might well have included discussion of time.

To give some content to the supposition, consider an argument that
does in fact go from general objective considerations to items in sensibility.
I have in mind Bennett's ordering argument, which I shall now summarize.

To begin with, the ordering argument says that "recollections *of a
certain kind* are possible only if *each* of them is backed by objective
considerations."[16] As the proof unfolds, we see that the *kind* of recollection whose possibility is to be established is the recollection of the order
of a thing's occurrence in time. How are we to remember what happened
when? The short answer is that we must in general resort to objective
considerations that place the thing in relations of succession and simultaneity to other things. Bennett says, "Because an event's date is not
perceptible it is not recollectable either";[17] and, "The order in which
events occur is no more a perceptible or recollectable feature of them
than are their dates."[18] Bennett notes certain exceptions—for instance,
we might remember one thing while experiencing another, and hence be
able afterwards to recollect directly that the remembered thing (must have)
preceded the experienced thing—but he argues that in general the relations
of things past must draw on objective considerations, not just in a general
and abstract way, but in support of each and every item of the past in
respect of its position in time. He does not bother to make the point, but
one might add that even the exceptions he notes require the support of

objective (especially causal) considerations to connect them up with the entire manifold of the past; for, even if the order of certain pairs of events can be directly recalled, the position of the pair must be determined.

We have, in a way, gone through all this before in the proof of the Second Analogy, which explains how we arrive at knowledge of the objective, causal relations from which the order of occurrence may be derived. However, that argument (of Kant's) took us from what is given in sense to knowledge of causal relations in appearance. The ordering argument (of Bennett's) proceeds in the opposite direction in so far as it presupposes our knowledge of causal relations in appearance, and then asks how this knowledge may be brought to bear to arrange the things we remember. Actually, Bennett's argument is the aspect of Kant's argument that deals with the need for objective considerations to entitle us to regard the succession in apprehension as significant.

The argument that Bennett gives cannot be the whole story, nor can it be entirely correct. It does not explain where we get the causal knowledge to which we refer in establishing the order of recollected items. Moreover, it contends that we do not perceive order; but then, by the contention of the argument, perception cannot supply knowledge of the order in which things occur—apart from the exceptions that Bennett notes. Unless *causally determined order* is perceived, there can be no perceptual basis (= no basis at all if we reject rationalism) for the causal knowledge that is later to be used to order our past experiences. Bennett fails to draw the distinction that is needed to make the argument work: between apprehension (in which connection is not given) and perception (to which the understanding supplies connection in the representation of objective correlates of our intuitions). Despite its faults, the ordering argument does capture an important truth. We must resort to causal considerations to determine the position of things in time (but we must also resort to them to have grounds for objective representation).

There are common situations involving empirical thought that follow closely the description Bennett gives of the reconstruction of the past. Suppose we are confronted by the undeniable fact that something has happened which needs to be explained, but we are given only a bunch of dubious evidence (as in a coroner's inquest, a police investigation, a trial, etc.). To the task of reconstructing the past, we bring whatever causal knowledge we possess, or we seek it from experts such as forensic scientists. Our interest is not in how that sort of knowledge is arrived at, or in how we are entitled to regard it as applicable in this case. We take general knowledge of causes to be universally applicable. Our task is to produce a (probable) chronology of events, and to sort out that which did happen, that which may have, and that which must have. The modal sorting is not separable from establishing the chronology. The impossibility of certain things may follow directly from common knowledge. For example, the ballistics expert tells us the force of impact of a certain caliber of bullet fired by a certain gun at various distances, and medical testimony describes the extent of the injury; from which it follows that the shot cannot have been fired from a certain location because, from there, it would have done more/less damage. However, the possibility or impossibility of other things will turn on opportunity, timing, conjunctions of circumstances, and so on. Our determination of the matter may never be complete, but we are often able to produce a reasonable account of the main events.

The point of referring to such cases is that they illustrate the role of time and the schemata of modality if we begin with empirical thought. Consistency is insufficient as a determinant of either what did go on or what may have gone on. It tells us only that, if we accept his alibi, he could not have done it; but if we accept the report of the eyewitness, he may have. We will be right to seek to establish the movements of all the principals on the night of whatever took place.

Kant does not begin his account with empirical thought, but with sensing and apprehension. If he had begun with empirical thought, he would have needed to say how it involves, not just the sorts of general information supplied by the expert witnesses, but the relation of such information to particular occurrences. He would have had to describe the way in which such relation combines modal and temporal considerations. We may never know just when the accused disposed of the weapon; but we must, if we are to find him guilty, think that there was *some time or other* to dispose of it between the commission of the crime and his arrest, that is, that it was *possible* to dispose of it. Likewise, we must determine that it was possible for him to be on the scene at the time, and so on. But no amount of mere possibilities could convict him. We must also establish some points of what actually happened. If everything stays merely possible, we cannot fix the time of the shooting, and we will not know the relevance of various possible alibis, and so on. Only the combination of some necessities and actual occurrences (and, perhaps, some possibilities) with at least a partial chronology will count as a reconstruction that yields knowledge of the past.

To see the reduplication by empirical thought of perceptual knowledge, consider what we would have perceived had we been witnesses to the events. We would probably have had less of the detailed knowledge that the experts can provide, and rather more knowledge of what actually took place; but the content of the two modes of knowledge (that is, by perception at the time or by the reconstructions of empirical thought afterwards) must be substantially the same. What differs is the way in which we arrive at the knowledge. Empirical thought descends, as it were, from general knowledge to the particular case. Perception ascends from the particular to the general. In the one case, we use common knowledge and seek ways of bringing it to bear in the determination of events. In the other case, our perception of events commits us, according to Kant's proof of the Second Analogy, to (implicit) beliefs of a general sort about the nature and behavior of things. While there will not be complete overlap between the eyewitness's perception of things and the juror's reconstruction, they must basically agree if either of them is to be entitled to regard himself as having knowledge. (I will say more about this in the discussion of confirmation in the next section.)

There are two final points to make in this section. The first concerns Bennett's contention that order is not perceived. The perception of order is not like the perception of dates, that is, equally impossible. Dates are an abstract construction to which we relate events, but order is an empirical expression of the nature of things. We could not first perceive nothing but separate items, and then afterwards arrive at causal laws that would link the items together. If we are ever to know what causes what, we must begin by knowing what precedes what. Recall that event-concepts are order-dependent, that is, that the composite representation varies according to the order in which the components of the complex are taken. Position in the time series is carried over from the subjective to the objective (from intuition to appearance) but the entitlement to carry it over depends on, and is constrained by, the possibility of seeing the sequence in appearance as the effect of a cause necessitating that order. The second point is simply a remark about the reasonableness of Kant's exposition beginning with apprehension and perception and advancing to empirical thought. Proceeding in that way, he is able to follow what must have been the genetic development of knowledge. In the last section, and throughout this book, I have urged the implausibility of regarding experience as the product of any amount of rational capacity assumed in advance, to which sensory data is then supposed to be added. The court and its body of experts (which is rather like the two-element model of the mind), calls witnesses and decides matters; but it presupposes there is truth in some of the testimony, and relevance and applicability in some of the expert opinion. It makes no sense to imagine the court being ever able to find the truth on its own; it needs a world outside itself where people find things out as scientists or as witnesses. The outside world could function (perhaps not as well) without the court, but not vice versa. In so far as the court reflects the mechanisms of empirical thought, it is evident why an account of experience that begins with thought is bound to be unsatisfactory, despite the fact that the determinations of thought are often more cautious and exact than those of perceptual experience.

42. Confirmation, Self-Consciousness, and Duality

This section draws together some of the implications of Kant's theory. It is an application and extension of his ideas rather than a direct commentary. I could not hope to give a full account of the topics in the section heading, nor do I intend to try. I propose only to sketch some of the ways in which the topics are interrelated, and I will begin with the term *duality* since it is not self-explanatory.

Partly because representation is so central to his theory, many of the elements of Kant's system are related to the sign/signified duality. We have already considered sensibility and understanding; content and form; intuition and concept; sensory qualities and dispositions; spatial form and material characteristics; subjective and objective time; and subjectivity and objectivity more generally. With the addition of empirical thought to the system, there are other dualities to be considered, or other aspects of those already discussed.

One of the by-products of duality is reduplication. In sensibility the realm of experience occurs as sensory effect; in appearance it occurs again as object of the effect (and as cause of it too). I have already said that empirical thought reduplicates the conceptualization of perception; and I have also said (in section 41) that empirical thought and perception must have substantially the same content, and differ only in the way in which they arrive at it. These claims will have to be amplified and defended; but, if there is any doubt concerning them, I can now point to undeniable evidence of reduplication in experience that raises much the same problem. The problem—assuming my claims are correct—is why nature should have endowed us with two distinct ways of arriving at the same result. Why do we have two sets of cognitive apparatus: perception and thought? Although I will try to defend the claim that there is this reduplication of cognitive faculties, I can point to a much remarked feature of language that raises a similar question. We can put the entire empirical content of anything we could have to say in either of two modes of discourse: in a *tensed language* that includes token-reflexive expressions like 'now', 'then', 'twenty years ago', 'here', 'to my left', etc.; or in a *tenseless language* that contains no expressions whose reference depends on the context in which they are uttered.[19] There is controversy about whether everything sayable in the one mode can be said in the other;[20] but there is no disputing the fact that *most everything* can be expressed in either fashion. The analogue to the problem about the reduplication of our faculties is just this reduplication in language. Why should there be two ways of saying (most) anything?

I think that Kant's theory extends easily (from the relations established in the Analogies between subjective and objective time) to provide an answer to the question about language. The answer can then be generalized and put in terms of appearances and phenomena. It is then fairly straightforward to explain the reduplication of faculties because appearances belong to perception and phenomena to empirical thought.

Partly to explain the reduplication of tensed and tenseless discourse, and partly to show that the reduplication is not restricted to language, I propose the following device. Suppose we make a map showing the things that exist at various locations. Just as real maps use conventions (the symbols set out in the legend), our imagined map can portray all sorts of information by using various colors and special marks. However, there will be a limit in principle to the information that can be encoded on a single map. We may be able to show the population of a center by the size of dot we use, its ethnic composition by the color of the dot, its resources and industries by symbols, its elevation by contour lines, its relation to other centers by the scalar modeling of the whole map, and so on; but our map will have to choose its moment, representing the things that exist at one time. To overcome the limitations of a static map, we might, like the producers of the recent *Times Atlas of World History* (1978), use arrows to give some sense of the changes produced by migrations, the spread of religion, etc.; but to remove entirely the in-principle limitations of the static map, we can have the map itself change by putting it on film, letting each slide represent things as they exist at a single moment, and projecting any portion of the film to show the moment-by-moment changes corresponding to the differences from one frame to the next. Now only our budget will limit what we can show. We could map each individual at every moment of his life, using a dot to indicate his whereabouts. With cinematic projection the dot would move to show his movements; its color could change to show his changes of mood; accompanying symbols could show his thoughts at any moment; and so on, to the limits of our budget and ingenuity.

Suppose that we initially make the map only for the past; but that, having done so for some time and in much detail, we discover that we, like Laplace's genius, are able to predict the changes that will take place from any frame to the next. We are now in position to show as much as we choose to map—of any segment of time, for any region, to any level of detail.

The point of all this is as follows. The map of the entire region within which one lives out one's life, extended back to before one's birth and on to after one's death, says anything (in principle, and to some arbitrary degree of detail) that there is to be said about one's entire life. One learns it all just by watching the map-film projected. Dots emerge from other dots on the screen, dart about for as much film-time as represents (on average) seventy years, with changes of colors and symbols, then blip out. The point is that one could come to know all that there is to know about oneself (and others) just by watching the cinematic map, but still not know which dot represents him. The paradox is that one could know *everything* and yet not know many things: which one am I? where are we now? and, is any of this true?

The very ordinary sort of map that gets posted in a subway station or shopping center shows where everything (deemed relevant) is located. From it, one can determine where everything is, with respect to everything else. The Boots is just down from the Marks & Spencers, Yonge Street runs north from Front Street to Richmond Hill, etc. But such maps also have an arrow saying "You are here." The need for the arrow is obvious. By studying the map, one can come to know where everything on it is; and yet not have any idea how to find any of it.

There is a paradox from the other side of things as well. We sometimes do not know where we are, but we always do know where we are so long as we are capable of perception. We can see that we are just across the street from a park, that to our left there is a major intersection, beyond it a river valley, to our right and in the distance there is a freeway, in front of us beyond the park there is a lake, and so on. Such knowledge is, in principle, limited so long as we remain in one place; but we could add to it by recalling what was here and there as we walked this way and that. How then can we be lost if we know so much about where we are?

Maps portray everything from a person-neutral point of view. Perception portrays everything with respect to ourselves. The paradoxes do not pick out information that is missing from either point of view. Consider that the person who is lost (make him amnesic with respect to his own identity) may have studied the map-film within which the whole of his own life history is contained (though he will not know that it is). He then knows, or can quickly look up on his portable projector, every fact concerning every person in the region during the period of his lifetime. A fortiori, he knows where *he is* (and what he feels, thinks, does, etc.) during every moment of his life. He also knows that he is just across the street from a park, etc.; feeling lost and confused, etc. In short, he may possess as much information as it is possible to have, and have it in both modes (mapped and perceptual), and still not know who he is, where he is, or what time it is.

All it would take to help him is no more than we do for the tourist who stands puzzling over his street map; we just point out the present location ("You're right here"), and indicate which way the map should be oriented ("North is that way"). To help the person who knows it all, but is still lost and amnesic, we would do the same by telling him which is *his* dot, and which frame maps the present situation of things. The tourist could help himself by finding some street signs, and the other fellow could help himself by finding unique features represented both in the map-film and in perception. For instance, suppose there is only one five-way intersection on the entire map, that only one fire ever occurs near there, and that only one person is nearby when it breaks out; and suppose that he now sees a fire starting in a building at just such an intersection. He then knows straight off who, when, and where he is.

The purpose of setting out this elaborate situation is not to tell odd stories for their own sake, but to describe something very like the situation in which we find ourselves. We perceive things here and there in the vagrant spaces of perception, and we transfer what we perceive to the abiding space of objective location. Perception and vivid memory are largely preoccupied with near and recent things, but empirical thought concerns general features and noteworthy incidents throughout the space/time manifold of appearance. Language marks the two ways in which we know things: by its tenses of verbs, demonstratives, and other context-dependent referring expressions; and by its dates and context-neutral terms. In general, the former are the terms in which things are immediately experienced, the latter are the terms in which they are thought. Language also has ways of coordinating the two in sentences like the "You are here" of fixed maps; for instance, "Today is the 20th," "That tower is just south of King Street," and, "Christmas is on a Friday this year."

We could, in theory, make do with just the perceptual mode; but it would be rather cumbersome to work out the Norman invasion of England in terms of the number of days before the day before yesterday, or years before the year before last, and the calculation would have to be revised every day (year). No one forgets 1066, and it never needs updating. Sentences in the objective mode have the virtue of constant truth-value. If ever true, they are always true. They are thus an ideal form in which to record standing information. By contrast, tensed sentences, and sentences involving token-reflexiveness, vary in truth-value depending on context, who says them, when, and where.

The purpose of the map-film examples is to represent the inadequacy of either mode of representation on its own. Despite a wealth of immediate perceptual information, one is lost unless able to integrate what is perceived into an abiding framework. Of course, we have no maps as rich in information as the one imagined; but even a recent arrival's scanty general knowledge of the layout of a city is soon rich enough to raise the possibility of getting lost (as opposed to being just totally unfamiliar with the city and finding it all strange). The reason for making the map-film complete in its detail is that one might otherwise suppose the problems that may arise with knowledge in the map film mode do so only because we do not know enough. The example shows that even complete knowledge, if possible, would be inadequate if it could not be keyed into present perceptual experience.

It matters to us as agents to know where (and when) we stand in the scheme of things. There is little advantage in knowing one is invited to a certain place for Christmas dinner if one does not also know what day Christmas falls and how to get to the place one is invited to. Well, one presumably has (or can look up) the address (= a context neutral description of the location), and we know that Christmas is December 25th; but that knowledge is useless on its own. We need to know where it is from here, and when it is from now.

Tensed sentences are not subjective in the sense of reporting only inner states of seeming, though they are subjective in the sense of being not independent of the person who utters them. They report on appearances as they appear—as they relate to us here and now. The map-film and tenseless descriptions that correspond to it report on appearances as they relate to each other, without any relation back to the perceiver. When appearances are described in their relations to each other, not as they appear, they may be called *phenomena*—to avoid the awkward description of them as appearances considered not as they appear, but as they interrelate among themselves.

It would be impossible to advance a principle that would neatly sort sentences, descriptions, and concepts into those that are in the appearance mode and those that are in the phenomenal mode. Some sentences are clearly more one way than the other—for instance, "I am feeling ill" versus "Patient Room 203, temperature 101°F, 4 p.m. 06/21/81." The former is not wholly without expression of the relation of the object to other things since illness has certain common characteristics, and the latter has some dependence on context; but the one is much closer to appearance, the other to phenomena. We could never remove entirely the phenomenal aspect because the conception of appearances is subject to constraints that carry general implications. We might be more successful in removing all context-dependence. This is periodically recommended for the production of an ideal language of science.[21]

We can certainly go a long way toward the production of a language of phenomena if we replace all tenses by dates, all personal pronouns by names, demonstratives by descriptions, and so on. We would gain in precision, neutrality with respect to point of view, impersonality, and immunity from the need to revise referential expressions. We could enhance the language if we replaced perceptual terms such as tastes and colors by chemical descriptions and measures of wavelength.

The question is whether a purely phenomenal language (supposing it to be possible) could be adequate for science. I contend not. We might (should) write our reports in such a language, but we could not carry out our observations in it. My contention is *not* that we need distinctively perceptual *terms* such as felt temperatures.[22] My contention is that we must preserve the *formal features of difference* between the two modes of conceptualization—the perceptual and phenomenal. That is, the spaces and times of the two must be distinct.

One of the primary objectives of science is to discover which descriptions of things are true. This determination of truth involves two aspects that must be kept distinct: a rational aspect of coherence and consistency, and an evidential or observational aspect. The rational aspect by itself is insufficient. It provides only conditional truths of the form, '*If* objects are thus-and-so, *then* these general laws obtain'; or, 'If law *L* is true, then, given conditions *C, e* occurs'. We can imagine having an indefinitely large account that reason could assess in terms of the consistency of its descriptions; but, no matter how extensive the account might be, and no matter how coherent and consistent it might be, we could imagine that there might be some rival account possible. We need something more than reason alone can tell us to decide whether an account is true, not just by formal criteria, but in relation to the world. This something more cannot be added to the account itself—as if we were to describe a character in a story having the sorts of experience one would have in a world of the sort the story is about.

However we mark the distinction, we must be able to tell the difference between (a) considering additional details and features of a certain world view, and (b) considering whether that world view is true. The only determination we can make under (a) alone is negative, if some of the details conflict with others. Then, at least, we know that the view is false in so far as it is self-contradictory. But the consistency of additional details does not show that the account of the world is true. At most, it shows that it could be. To show that it is true, that is, to confirm it, we must be able to think of what it says in a different way—not necessarily in other words, or different descriptive terms, but in a way that preserves the distinction between what we think and the evidence we have for thinking it.

The whole point of the phenomenal mode is to free description from contextual dependence and dependence on the person, and this is a desirable end in so far as it makes explicit what is thought, ridding it of all reliance on tacit information. However, it is just such dependence and reliance that must be retained and resorted to in confirmation. We must, in the words of Kant's general remark about the modal categories, be able to "express the relation of the concept to the capacity for knowledge" (A 219 = B 266).

Observations must of course be included *within* any account of the world—"At time *t*, N.N. senses *x*, perceives *y*, and thinks *z*"—for that is as much a factual detail of the world as any other; but the inclusion of such claims within any description of the world no more confirms the total description of the account than a sentence of the form "When he awoke, Frodo felt . . ." confirms the reality of Middle Earth. What is needed is some realization of the form "I am N.N., and I now feel . . ."; and this realization must be weighed against what is thought without being simply added to it. In other words, a complete conceptual scheme—one with provision for confirmation—must have the resources to express, not only a view of the world, but also the self-consciousness that is necessary to establish *a* view as *the* (true) view. The totally impersonal conceptualization of phenomena cannot do this.

Unreflective perceptual knowledge must be possible (one presumes that it is the only sort animals possess); but it has its limitations, principally to the present and immediate. With that limitation, there are others. Unless the perceptual processes were so conservative and so safeguarded that they could never make mistakes, there would be bound to be occasional errors in perception. Conversely, if the processes of perception are to be flexible enough to operate with less than perfect sensory bases (e.g., those arising in poor lighting, at odd angles of presentation, in the presence of obstructions and distractions, etc.) representation must be able to proceed on the basis of partial and variable sensory signs. Given this flexibility, indeterminacy and error are inevitable; but that hardly matters to creatures whose only interests are immediate. If they err on the side of caution, they will survive—sometimes fleeing when the signs of danger are deceptive, but not expending so much wasted energy in needless flight that they ruin their chances for survival. What they cannot do is control their own learning by seeing their mistakes *as mistakes*—taking steps to prevent making them in future. Nor can they act on the basis of general information. They cannot have general knowledge since they have no way of assessing what they represent in perception. There may be implicit generality to animal consciousness in so far as *any* of a range of sensory cues sets off a *type* of behavior in response, but that is more of the generality of vagueness and imprecision than the generality of the universal and abstract.

Perhaps to a very considerable extent our cognitive behavior can be understood as consisting in unreflective perception, without self-consciousness and without thought; but it cannot all be understood in this way, and so far as it can be understood in this way, we must qualify the classification of it as knowledge. What happens when there are mistakes? Is behavior ever directed to circumstances that afford no immediate cues, and which could consequently be known only by inference? Are there cases in which positive reinforcement of certain behavior must have been recognized by the subject as fortuitous because he does not repeat the behavior that just happened to be rewarded? One line of answers to such questions will force us to qualify any attribution of knowledge. The other will allow us to drop the qualifications and claim outright that the subject knows.

Appearances provide information—a great deal of it in fact—but the possession of information only in the mode of appearance is not knowledge full and proper. For that, there must also be standing information, detached from perception, corrected, integrated, deliberately acquired.

Behaviorist and empiricist models of cognition portray the advance of knowledge as just more of the same, more of what is to be found at younger ages or among lower species. The duality of appearance and phenomena provides an alternative model, with the marked advance created by the addition of thought and self-consciousness to perception. The spontaneous representations of perception are a plausible common denominator of all cognition: sufficiently mechanistic to be regarded as innate predispositions to fixed responses to any of a range of sensory inputs, but rich enough to accommodate the development of consciousness. The rival theories are less plausible in one respect or the other: behaviorism does not extend to critical thought, nor empiricism to rudimentary cognition. (The latter needs some defense. If we imagine ourselves starting with awareness of the sensory given and then proceeding in stages to infer material objects, then approximate generalizations governing them, then empirical laws, and finally theories, we do not set out a progression that animals can be thought to share up to a point. The very first stage cannot be attributed to them, though the second can—consciousness of objects, but no consciousness of their inner states that represent the objects.)

There are two ways in which self-consciousness relates thought to perception. *First,* as reflection on apprehension and perception, it supplies thought with the material for the construction of phenomena. The connections implicit in appearance are made explicit, extended, and corrected. This requires access to, and understanding of, both the basis of representation in intuition and the alternatives described in chapter seven. *Second,* when empirical thought has built up a stock of knowledge of phenomena, self-consciousness must continually establish the connection of the self to it. It is not enough to make one isolated discovery of who, when, and where we are on the map-film (that is, in respect of the knowledge of phenomena that it represents). If the wealth of standing information is to have any meaning for us, and be of any use to us, we must *maintain* its relation to our immediate situation at all times.

43. The Refutation of Idealism

In B, Kant adds a refutation of idealism to the discussion of the Postulates. He prefaces the insertion with the following remark: "Idealism raises, however, what is a serious objection to these rules for proving existence mediately; and this is the proper place for its refutation" (B 274). He cites Descartes and Berkeley as proponents of the position he hopes to refute.

The argument itself is given in the form of thesis-and-proof common to the earlier principles. The thesis says, "The mere, but empirically determined, consciousness of my own existence proves the existence of objects in space outside me" (B275). I have made the issue of temporal determination so central to my reading of the principles that I have little to add here in comment on the proof. By and large, Kant himself just goes back to the arguments of the Analogies—without adding anything substantial to them, as he himself admits in the preface to B.[23]

The objection Kant makes to Descartes and Berkeley is that they doubt and deny, respectively, the existence of objects in space, while continuing to affirm their own existence. The counterargument says that to know our own existence as determined in time we must know objects in space. The proof reminds us of the role of permanence in temporal determination; and the second note to the proof refers to the parts played by motion, change, and matter. With all of that having been argued before, in the Analogies, one may well wonder why it should be brought up again, and why inserted at this place—that is, immediately following the Postulate of Actuality.

Kant wrote the *Critique* with opposition to Leibniz foremost in his mind, and he was astonished to find his transcendental idealism taken to be a mere variant on Berkeley. He took pains to distinguish his position from Berkeley's in the B-edition.[24] We need a more specific reason, though, to account for the insertion of the argument at this point.

Kant considers the objection to be raised against "these rules for proving existence mediately." It is not an objection that Kant's own system generates and must deal with, but a very standard worry in philosophy. How do we know that the things we think exist do in fact exist?

Kant begins answering the question at the very start of system, and by the Postulates it has been answered. But he has not, until the Postulates, been able to address the matter directly. Only now does he have an account of empirical thought that lets him attack a false presupposition of the idealist's question. He says, "Idealism assumed that the only immediate experience is inner experience, and that from it we can only *infer* outer things—and this, moreover, only in an untrustworthy manner, as in all cases where we are inferring from given effects to determinate causes" (B 276). Idealism describes us as inferring states of affairs in the world from states of consciousness. Kant's account of perception disputes this, proposing the spontaneity of understanding in place of inference as the basic mechanism in the acquisition of knowledge. Hence the reminders of the arguments of the Analogies.

Once inference is introduced into Kant's system in the Postulates, he must show that empirical thought, when it has been admitted, cannot generate doubts that could sweep away everything he worked to establish in the Analogies. This makes it "the proper place for [idealism's] refutation."

Idealists give content to their doubts by suggesting alternative causes of the inner states that they take to be immediately experienced. How do we know that we do not just dream there is a world? How do we know that some Evil Genius does not put our thoughts in our minds to deceive us? And so on. Kant sets out the assumption behind such questions as the belief that we know the effect and seek the cause. He grants that inference from given effect to determinate cause would be untrustworthy, but he disputes the direction of inference. Halfway through note 1, he says, "In the above proof it has been shown that outer experience is really immediate, and that only by means of it is inner experience—not indeed the consciousness of my own existence, but the determination of it in time—possible" (B 276–77). At the end of the note he says, "Inner experience is itself possible only mediately, and only through outer experience" (B 277).

Kant argues the reversal of the idealist's ordering entirely in terms of *temporal determination*. One might take him to be referring to specific determinations such as knowing one's own age, or general problems of determination such as the reconstruction of one's past; but I think he means something more basic. One's inner experience is determinate; there are definite feelings, particular thoughts, specific images. An idealist who wanted to be difficult could question whether he or anyone has a past to be constructed or an age to be known. What he cannot intelligibly question is the determinateness of his inner states of consciousness *now* because they are what (and all) he purports to know. The very determinateness of conscious states necessary for them to be knowable is sufficient to prove the existence of objects. In the absence of objects in space, there would be no resolution of alternatives. With no perceptions of events, there would be no order and connection imposed on states of consciousness. The inner takes on the definiteness required in an object of knowledge only in relation to the outer.

It is for this reason that we must work back in empirical thought from our knowledge of the world to our knowledge of ourselves, including the knowledge of the sensory states that provide the subjective basis for the representation of the world in the first place.

We can actually test the contentions of idealism by putting ourselves in a situation in which we are deprived of objects represented in sense. One of the easiest ways to do this is to listen to a radio broadcast in a strange language. We do not then merely imagine ourselves suspending all beliefs and having only inner experiences; we are actually forced to do without appearances. But we do not have inner experience by itself. There are just auditory sensations that we are unable even to apprehend.

Notes

As in the text, all references to the *Critique of Pure Reason* in the notes follow the standard A and B convention described on p. 1. All references to Kant's other writings include a roman numeral immediately followed by an arabic numeral to indicate, respectively, the volume number of the Prussian Academy edition of *Kants Werke* and the page number. Thus, V25 refers to *Kants Werke* vol. 5, p. 25. Usually contextual information in the notes will indicate the title of the particular work referred to, and also the translation used, but this information is available in the bibliography as well.

References to other books and articles are by title (or shortened title) and page number, or by author and page number. Full details for these works are given in the bibliography.

Chapter One

1. Things-in-themselves are the objects of moral considerations. Kant defines intelligible character as the character of the thing-in-itself (A 539 = B 567), then at length he associates possibility of freedom of action with intelligible character (to end A 558 = B 586). The *Critique of Practical Reason* says that if we wish to save freedom "no other course remains than to ascribe the existence of a thing so far as it is determinable in time, and accordingly its causality under the law of natural necessity, merely to appearance, and to attribute freedom to the same being as a thing-in-itself" (V95). The next paragraph uses this possibility of attributing freedom to justify moral censure in the face of appeals to the inevitability of wrongdoing. I use Beck's translation of the *Critique of Practical Reason*, and, since he does provide Academy pagination, that is all I need to indicate. For further discussion of things-in-themselves see secs. 8 and 9.

2. *Aufbau* is the standard short title of the great attempt by Carnap to provide an empiricist construction of experience. The empiricist parts of his project have their roots in antiquity, and their main growth in Berkeley and Hume. The constructivist (or constructionist) parts are grafted from logic, physics, and nineteenth century psychology. The immediate precursors of the *Aufbau* are James's *Essays in Radical Empiricism*, neutral monism; Mach's *The Analysis of Sensations*, representing his conversion from Kant to Hume; and Russell's "The Relation of Sense-Data to Physics," logical atomism. After the *Aufbau*, the project is criticized by Goodman in *The Structure of Appearance* and by Quine in "Two Dogmas." My own title is meant to allude to Carnap and Goodman because my interpretation of Kant puts him in direct opposition to Carnap in respect to empiricism, while in agreement with Carnap with respect to construction.

3. Schopenhauer comments on the table of categories in a tone that must reflect a judgment not only on it but on its author. In *The World as Will and Representation,* he says, "These later become the fearful Procrustean bed on to which he violently forces all things in the world and everything that occurs in man, shrinking from no violence and disdaining no sophism in order merely to be able to repeat everywhere the symmetry of that table" (vol. 1, p. 430). In his *Commentary,* Kemp Smith describes the architectonic as something that Kant clings to "with the unreasoning affection which frequently attaches to a favourite hobby" (p. xxii). Along with the stories of Kant's walks being so regular that housewives could set their clocks by him, I think Kant's categories have the status in popular legend of being the products of Prussian rigidity and compulsiveness.

4. See Wolff, p. 35.

5. In the preface to *Kant's Analytic,* Bennett says "I have freely criticized, clarified, interpolated and revised"; and in the very last paragraph of this book—perhaps in anticipation of the comment Strawson makes about Bennett's ordering argument in his review of Bennett—we find this remark: "The passages I have quoted could largely be read in that way; but I should not care to insist that Kant explicitly took this, or any other, view of the matter" (p. 229). See p. 338 of Strawson's review.

6. I do not mean to belittle Paton's achievement in *Kant's Metaphysic of Experience.* My point is that, in contrast to Bennett, Paton does not significantly depart from the text of the *Critique* to try to find his own solutions to the problems.

7. Kemp Smith is most responsible for the reputation the *Critique* has for difficulty. He says, "that Kant flatly contradicts himself in almost every chapter; and that there is hardly a technical term which is not employed by him in a variety of different and conflicting senses. As a writer, he is the least exact of all the great thinkers" (p. xx). As the author of the most influential commentary, Kemp Smith charts the course for most who follow; and it does not help that it is his translation—full of uncalled-for emendations—that first presents Kant to most English readers.

8. As Kant's reply to Hume, the Second Analogy is commonly interpreted within the context of the doubts Hume raises about our knowledge of causal connection. Within that context, it provides—at best—a controversial answer to Hume. I think Kant disputes the assumptions that Hume makes in order to raise his doubts. See sec. 12 and chap. 7.

9. For the patchwork theory see Kemp Smith, pp. xx–xxi.

10. For efforts to depsychologize the *Critique* see almost any treatment of it in this century. See also Findlay's paper, "Kant and Anglo-Saxon Criticism," and note the Transcendental Excisions that he reports or proposes. For the reasons for these efforts, see sec. 12.

11. Further to n. 10, and including the phrase quoted in the text, Strawson says, "the doctrines of transcendental idealism, and the associated picture of the receiving and ordering apparatus of the mind producing Nature as we know it out of the unknowable reality of things as they are in themselves, are undoubtedly the chief obstacles to a sympathetic understanding of the *Critique*" (*Bounds of Sense,* p. 22).

12. In sec. 3 of "Kant's Relation to Berkeley," Turbayne charts eight passages in which Kant argues against idealism.

13. Turbayne assembles passages from Kant to parallel passages from Berkeley that express the main points of Berkeley's idealism. He takes this to show that Kant is a closet Berkelian. Scott-Taggart mentions the "dramatic piece of work by Turbayne, who upsets all our previous views of the relationship of Kant and Berkeley. . . . Turbayne argues to my complete persuasion that (1) Kant could have been acquainted with Berkeley's *Three Dialogues* and *De Motu,* (2) there is a point by point parallelism between Kant's and Berkeley's accounts of the external world, (3) Kant knew that there was, but (4) distinguished his position from that of Berkeley by his theory of the a priori nature of space. Turbayne's argument is a model of clarity throughout, and my only objection to it is a slight tendency

to underestimate the force of (4)'' (pp. 13–14). Turbayne achieves the parallel by substituting 'idea' for 'representation' as the translation of Kant's *Vorstellung*. The verbal similarities are thus forced. Even were they not forced, it is one thing to show that short passages out of context are somewhat similar, and quite another to show that what is meant by the words in context is the same. If Kant had not recognized the superficial similarities, he would not have been at such pains to explain the differences. See secs. 4–7 inclusive.

14. Kemp Smith translates *vermittelst gewisser Merkmale* with 'by way of certain characters'. The word *certain* suggests "unspecified" as in "I have certain things to do before I leave." I prefer my substitution, taking Kant to mean that, if thought does not relate directly to intuition, then its indirect relation must be governed by definite criteria.

15. It is difficult to know whether to take Bennett's attributions of phenomenalism to Kant as seriously intended to reflect his understanding of Kant, or whether it would make more sense to take the attributions as departures from Kant (in the spirit of n. 5). The difficulty arises because of Bennett's attempts to contrive evidence to fit a phenomenalist reading. In *Kant's Analytic,* he uses ellipsis to omit the word *objective* from a passage he cites to show that Kant is a subjectivist, at least in his epistemological method (p. 130). For similar malpractice see the doctored quote on p. 103 of *Kant's Analytic.*

16. Passages Bird uses against Prichard include: A 99–101, IV304, and B 118–20. There is much to admire in Bird's account, but he seems not to appreciate that one can argue against the phenomenalist's empiricist construction without arguing against constructions of other sorts. See p. 3 where he simply identifies construction with phenomenalism. What makes a construction phenomenalist is its reductionism, against which one can well argue without giving up the possibility of nonreductive construction.

17. Since the claim that there is no consistent interpretation is equivalent to the claim that all interpretations will reveal inconsistency, critics who baldly state that the *Critique* is inconsistent (when all they have is their own reading of it) seem to be ignoring an elementary point about confirmation. Similarly, Turbayne's paper just demonstrates that one *can* find—if one ignores Kant's protests—a Berkelian interpretation of some of the things he says. This is far from showing that *any* reasonable interpretation *must* make Kant out to be a Berkelian.

18. Ayer's *The Foundations of Empirical Knowledge* is, I think, the best book-length exposition of linguistic phenomenalism.

19. Wittgenstein's *Blue and Brown Books* and *Investigations* make the case for grounding meaning in use and public convention rather than in mental states.

20. Kant complains that Berkeley degrades bodies to mere seemings in several places. He uses the word *Schein,* which both Beck, in his translation of the *Prolegomena,* and Kemp Smith, in the *Critique,* translate as 'illusion'. Berkeley reduces bodies *zu blossem Schein* (B 71); and Berkeley can have no criteria of truth because, according to him, perceptions have no a priori basis, from which it follows that they must be *nichts als lauter Schein* (IV375). 'Seemings' is not an ordinary word, perhaps, but it seems to me to capture a meaning that is attributable to Berkeley since to be is to be perceived, and so it fits with a complaint that Kant could make without distorting Berkeley in the way Turbayne supposes he does. Things are, for Berkeley, nothing beyond what they seem to be. That is what Kant objects to; and the a priori basis of perception, for Kant, adds to the sensory aspect the permanence of substance and the necessity of causality—making bodies more than mere or sheer seemings, and making possible *objective* criteria of truth. The issue is not about illusions—bent sticks in water, etc. The issue is the nature of the things we encounter—are they just appearance and show, or something more?

21. The first dogma is the sharp split between the analytic and synthetic which yields, respectively, the logical apparatus for the empiricist construction and the material to be

objectified in the various stages of construction. The second dogma, of reductionism, takes us back to bodies being nothing more than composites of sensory ideas.

22. Berkeley, *Essay on Vision,* sec. 143.

23. Ibid., sec. 147.

24. Berkeley, *Principles,* part I, sec. 8.

25. Ibid., sec. 44.

26. The production of a written language is far more complex than my simple examples can suggest. Their purpose is only to show that it is much more complex than Berkeley supposes.

27. For Berkeley's discussion of the two squares, see *Essay on Vision,* secs. 139ff.

28. Evolution should provide some overlaps among the senses to allow for conditions (such as darkness) unfavorable to the operation of one of the senses, and to provide alternatives in the case of injuries, but it would not gratuitously give us five different ways of doing the same thing; and, if the senses are not all monitoring the same information in different ways, they cannot be correlated with one another as Berkeley supposes.

29. My contention that one (= Carnap) might order things in the way indicated in the text is not defeated by the initial generality of the relation Sim. The derived quality classes of sec. 81 do (numerically and procedurally) come before the dividing up of the senses in sec. 85; but the Sim-pairings obtain only among members of each modality. Thus, although the relation is defined for all sensory elements before the application of the relation effects the division into five sensory categories plus the emotions, on the material level one presumably starts with the five plus one sorts of input. This is, in fact, the ordering adopted in part 4, chap. A of the *Aufbau.*

30. The shortest and clearest account I know of the Cartesian and Humean method in its most general and basic terms is Bennett's in "The Simplicity of the Soul," sec. 3, where he defines methodological solipsism. For *analytic* versus *genetic,* see the index to *Kant's Analytic.*

31. Hume's and Descartes' doubts question any advance *from the subjectively given to the objective,* but this is a far cry from raising doubts about the objective *tout court.* One can admit that the immediate content of the senses is quite insufficient to justify inferences to the external world. If the immediate content of the senses were the only possible source of empirical knowledge, we would, as they show, be in deep trouble. This conditional result, in the light of our extensive empirical knowledge, seems to me to prove that first-person states of consciousness are not the only source of empirical knowledge.

32. I am far from competent to judge the technical merits of Bower's work, but if any of his results stand (as surely they must) newborns are not blank slates. My untrained observations of my own children gave evidence of many unlearned cognitive capacities. Besides, any observation of nonhuman young—in which neotony is much less pronounced than in man—would tend to confirm the presence of all sorts of innate capacities. A young bird's first flight, or a mountain goat's first scramble up a rockface, make a joke of the notion that everything is learned through experience.

33. See Berkeley's *Essay on Vision,* secs. 1–41, and weigh his contentions against the first flight of birds.

34. Boring records the genealogy of Gestalt psychology from Kant on p. 249. For Wundt's antimetaphysical propensities also see Boring, p. 332; and on p. 333 we find the very first sketch of the constructivist project that ended with Carnap. Fechner was much more on the Kantian side of things.

35. Kant introduces appearances in the following definition: "The undetermined object of an empirical intuition is entitled appearance" (A 20 = B 34). The Axioms and Anticipations deal with the structure of intuitions that represent appearances; the Analogies describe the aspects of the structure of appearances that are essential if empirical intuitions are to

represent them; and the Postulates introduce phenomena as the determined (= rectified and amplified) objects of empirical intuition.

36. See Phenomena and Noumena, beginning A 235 = B 294.

37. "The *spontaneity* of knowledge should be called the understanding" (A 51 = B 75).

38. "All the manifold given in an intuition is united in a concept of the object" (B 139).

39. The entire Fourth Paralogism in A argues against the view that our knowledge is a result of inference.

40. When Kant outlines the general theoretical notion of an intelligible ground of which "the empirical serves for its sensible sign," he takes man as his example (A 546 = B 574).

41. Kant restricts experience to empirical knowledge. "Experience is an empirical knowledge, that is, a knowledge which determines an object through perception" (B 218).

42. See Bird, pp. 47ff.

43. One measure of the independence of an object of interpretation from the spatio-temporality of the empirical character through which we encounter it is our preparedness to consider the intelligible character's probable responses to counterfactual situations. Everything empirical about a person belongs to a particular culture and time and place. To know the person is to know about such particulars, in addition to the particularities of the individual in question; but to think what the person as he is in himself is really like, we discount many of the particulars (unless we are materialist historians), and consider how the person would have thought and acted in other circumstances. Plato and Aristotle may have kept slaves, but this is not, in their case, the sign of gross immorality it would be today—we are confident that, were they alive today, they would act quite differently (cf. A 556 = B 584).

44. "We have no knowledge whatsoever of the intelligible" (A 360); and "intelligible character can never, indeed, be immediately known, for nothing can be perceived except in so far as it appears. It would have to be *thought* in accordance with the empirical character" (A 540 = B 568). The intelligible character is unknown "save in so far as the empirical serves for its sensible sign" (A 546 = B 574).

45. I am well aware that the sorting out of Kant's terminology—especially the distinction drawn between appearances and phenomena—is weak in textual support. To the extent that I may be guilty of contriving the appearance/phenomena distinction, I plead as my excuse that I can use the distinction to explain more clearly and simply what Kant is doing in the Analogies and Postulates. However, I do stand by the basic sense of the four divisions as an accurate reflection of Kant's thought, if not of his very words. The cautions against using 'noumenon' as a positive term (cf. B 307) must be taken in the context of the theoretical philosophy, and taken as directed against rationalist efforts to bypass the sensible and arrive directly at knowledge. These warnings do not conflict with a different positive sense of 'noumenon' of use in practical philosophy, where the objective is not to extend knowledge, or to arrive at it without recourse to the senses, but to think of the self as agent. My definition of 'noumenon' was with the following passage in mind: "we could defend the supposition of a freely acting cause when applied to a being in the world of sense only in so far as the being was regarded also as noumenon. This defense was made by showing that it was not self-contradictory to regard all its actions as physically conditioned so far as they are appearances, and yet at the same time to regard their causality as physically unconditioned so far as the acting being is regarded as a being of the understanding" (V48).

46. A 109, A 114, and A 250–51 present the notion of the object that precedes and leads to our knowledge. This transcendental object = x is described by Kant as being "not in itself an object of knowledge" (A 251), and I do describe it as an object; but I think there is no inconsistency because I make substantially the same point Kant makes, and he himself revised his way of saying it in the Second Edition.

47. See Kant's resolution of the Antinomies, especially sec. 8, for discussion of the unending empirical advance.

48. For the transcendental/transcendent contrast, see A 11–12 = B 25 and A 296 = B 352.

49. Knowledge has two sources: A 50–51 = B 74–75.

Chapter Two

1. The entries under "Space" in the index to the *Critique* give evidence of how often Kant discusses it throughout the *Critique* and a breakdown of the topics. The changes of example in the second edition may indicate a change of mind on Kant's part.

2. With the exception of mathematics, Kant's special theories are treated by him at book length. His works on ethics, aesthetics, and natural science and religion all show unmistakable signs of the influence of the general theory, but they also show that the transition from the general to the special is not obvious and automatic. Perhaps if Kant had written at length on mathematics, instead of treating it as a side topic in the *Critique,* it would be more evident that the *Critique* is a general account of cognition. See sec. 11 for the risks of overemphasis on the mathematical, and sec. 14 for comments on the one paper of Kant's that deals with mathematical methods.

3. For a general account of Kant's method of argument, see chap. 3.

4. For Kant's reasons for favoring time as the key to the application of the categories (including the categories involved in the representation of appearances), see the discussion of the Schematism in chap. 3.

5. I find the Kantian aspects of Vuillemin's paper very compressed and difficult, but so far as I understand him I think his descriptions of Kant's mathematical opinions are reasonable.

6. For reasons akin to those given in chap. 1, n. 17, when the interpretation of Kant in the light of recent mathematics and physics yields a wholly implausible theory, the interpretation ought to be questioned—*not* because Kant could not have been wrong, but rather because the interpretation is only *one* way of construing what he says; and, when so construed, his remarks are quite without interest. Just as we do not need a reading of Kant that makes him a muddled echo of Berkeley, we do not need him as the proponent of an obviously wrong doctrine of geometry.

7. Hopkins's paper is called "Visual Geometry."

8. Hopkins quotes Einstein (from Barker) on p. 6.

9. Hopkins, p. 3.

10. Critics lax on providing textual support include: Strawson—"He believed without question in the finality of Euclidean geometry" (p. 23; no footnote, no argument); Bennett—no references to support claiming that Kant says, "The outer sense of every human is such as to guarantee that the outer world which he experiences will always conform to the theorems of Euclidean geometry" (p. 15). Cf. Reichenbach's *Space and Time,* sec. 8. Russell gets a tart rebuke from Hintikka in "Kant on Mathematical Method" (p. 119n) for making an unsupported claim about what Kant thought.

11. Vuillemin, pp. 146–47.

12. Ibid., p. 151.

13. See Hintikka's criticisms of Broad's failures to consider the equal applicability of Kant's theory of mathematics to arithmetic and algebra ("Kant on Mathematical Method," pp. 125–26).

14. "Enquiry Concerning the Clarity of the Principles of Natural Theology and Ethics" is in *Kants Werke* II, and in Kerferd and Walford's translation of precritical selections.

15. For my remarks on the role of symbols, see sec. 14. Also see Hintikka, p. 124, and the introduction by Hartman and Schwarz to their translation of the *Logic* (especially pp. xcixff.).

16. Hopkins says, "Kant assumed that geometric proof required construction on a figure" (p. 4). For the reply to Hopkins, see items in n. 15 above.

17. For the modern uses of the terms, see Quinton's "The *A Priori* and the Analytic."

18. See especially chap. 9 of *The Structure of Science*.

19. By the given that is no longer much discussed, I refer to the lengthy treatments of sense-data earlier in this century by Mach, Russell, Moore, Price, etc.

20. In *Logical Foundations of Probability,* Carnap contends that probability is always a relation between sentences. On certain evidence *e* there is a probability *p* that *h;* but we cannot detach *h* from *e* and say that *h* by itself has the probability *p.* Other evidence could give a different probability, and if we detached in both cases we would end up with a contradictory assignment of probabilities. See Carnap, secs. 10A and 42A.

21. See sec. IV, part I of the *Enquiry.*

22. Shoemaker imagines three regions that alternately undergo periods of stasis and change. If the periods vary in length, it might be most reasonable to say that there are times when all three regions are static—frozen in time. Thus, there could be time without change. Anyone who granted the method of argument would have to grant the conclusion. It rather begs the question to take this method of argument for granted when dealing with Kant since he explicitly rejects the notion that everything conceivable is possible (A 219–21 = B 266–68). See chap. 8.

23. "There are certain arguments for scepticism which conform to a familiar, if not often explicitly articulated, pattern or form. These arguments rely, at least for their psychological power, on vivid descriptions of exotic *contrast cases*" (Unger, *Ignorance,* p. 7). After providing a lurid description of an evil scientist who drills holes in people to insert electrodes, Unger mentions "the 'evil demon' argument in Descartes's *Meditations,*" and says, "We may call any argument of this form *the classical argument* for scepticism" (p. 8). He says that no one has ever found serious fault with such arguments (see p. 9). Kant finds fault with the assumption on which they rely, namely, the supposed equivalence of conceivability and empirical possibility (see n. 22 above). To which I add Quine's objections to the first dogma—since the classical form of skeptical argument supposes a separability of meaning from fact such that ordinary connections of meaning are thought to remain intact even in extensively counterfactual situations. The nub of such arguments is whether their lurid stories are consistent, but consistency in ordinary language is not a sufficiently precise notion to be used in proof of conceivability; and, even if conceivability were proved, no reason independent of the two-element model's assumptions is given for taking the limits of what we can say or imagine to be coextensive with the limits of empirical possibility.

24. *Enquiry,* sec. IV, part II.

25. "In experience, however, perceptions come together only in accidental order, so that no necessity determining their connection is or can be revealed in the perceptions themselves. For apprehension is only a placing together of the manifold of empirical intuition; and we can find in it no representation of any necessity which determines the appearances thus combined to have connected existence in space and time" (B 219). I think that this is the common ground between Kant and Hume. They part company in their explanations of connection; Hume traces it to custom or habit, Kant to the principles.

26. Although Popper rejects the inductivist aspects of the two-element model, he does not reject the model outright. He retains the primary division between the formal or logical and the empirical or observational. The substitution of falsification for verification relegates the origin of ideas to extrasystematic psychological sources, that is, to origins not covered by his account. Both the inductivist and Popperian variants of the two-element model begin

theorizing at the point where there already are truth-bearers present to the mind, though inductivists may allude to a Humean (or Skinnerian) prologue. The question I would raise is whether a satisfactory account (I take both Hume's and Skinner's accounts to be, at best, partial and inadequate) of the most basic aspects of cognition would set the stage for continuations different from those of the two-element model.

27. See nn. 22 and 23 above. One particularly objectionable feature of arguments from imaginary cases is that it is left up to those who would dispute their conclusions to point out inconsistencies in the stories told. While the earlier notes dispute the assumptions of this method of argument, even were one to grant those assumptions, there would still be reason to ask that the argument come complete with proof of the consistency of its story. A proof that rests on consistency is no proof at all until the consistency is proved. The difficulties confronting a would-be objector onto whom the onus is placed to find inconsistency in the story by no means show that the story is consistent. Rather they show that consistency/inconsistency is very hard to determine in respect of short stories in ordinary language, but this makes the claimed consistency indeterminate as well.

28. For the doctrine of fictions, see *Treatise* Book I, Part IV, ii.

29. In addition to Penelhum's paper on the doctrine of fictions, see the papers on the closely related topic of identity by Neujahr, Noxon, Patten, and von Leyden. Also see Bennett's *Locke, Berkeley, Hume,* chap. 13.

30. I think Hume worries disproportionately about the principle of individuation to the neglect of a complementary principle of differentiation. If we have a general mechanism for sticking ideas together, we must have another device that prevents them becoming an undifferentiated blob. I supply trial and error as the sort of device in keeping with the experiential mechanisms of habit formation.

31. Pretheoretical expectations are by no means the only standards against which theories should be judged, but they do count for something. A theory of X that forces us to deny all common descriptions of X in favor of radical redescriptions is like the child whose proud parents say, "Look, everybody is out of step but our Johnny." It is important to distinguish—as much as one can—between common observational knowledge of X, which does provide a standard for judgment, and popular theories of X, which may well be overturned. The objection to Humean and skeptical accounts is not that they displace popular theories of knowledge. It is rather that they force rejection of common observations. For example, we observe that careful thought results in better predictions; but Humean and skeptical accounts redescribe the intellectual activity of prediction as a merely subjective expectation produced by habit—leaving no room for thought at all.

32. One passage in which Kant separates the empirical and formal aspects: "Motion of an object in space does not belong to a pure science, and consequently not to geometry. For the fact that something is moveable cannot be known a priori, but only through experience. Motion, however, considered as the describing of a space, is a pure act of the successive synthesis of the manifold in outer intuition in general by means of the productive imagination, and belongs not only to geometry, but even to transcendental philosophy" (B 154n). For examples of pure acts of successive synthesis, see the descriptions of the imagined motions of the penny, the various cylinders, and the gears. For the reasons that the moveability of a thing cannot be known a priori, see chap. 7.

33. See n. 14. Hintikka's paper is an excellent discussion of intuition, mathematical method, and related topics.

34. *Pre-Critical Writings,* p. 6 = II276.

35. Ibid., pp. 9–10 = II278–79.

36. While I do think that we cannot *know* that the inferred explanans is the only one possible, my reasons for thinking this have to do with the in-principle indeterminacy of interpretation. See sec. 8. We can demand that the explanans satisfy conditions of reason-

ableness—that it be well-grounded, nonarbitrary, self-consistent, precise in its claims, and so on. Reasonableness does not exclude alternatives in the way that knowledge does. However, a requirement of reasonableness may, in a sense, ensure uniqueness if the conditions of reasonableness are strong enough that the explanation that satisfies them can never subsequently be dismissed as just wrong. We have advanced far beyond Newton and Darwin, but it would be misleading to say their theories are false, since they do satisfy just such strong conditions of reasonableness, and they have given way only to theories that built upon their genuine advances. See the following note.

37. While Kant's condition (2) calls for uniqueness, one need not take it as a call for the finality of the explanation, because it is phrased in terms of "a given mode of explaining the concept" (*einer gegebenen Erklärungsart dieses Begriffs*). It is *the way* to explain the concept—leaving open the possibility of alternatives *within* the confines of a certain approach. In the preface to the second edition, Kant talks only about having put metaphysics on the path to science; he does not claim to have written the last word. I may be reading a bit more latitude than he intends into the contrast between what he sees as his system's unchangeable aspects and the mode of exposition where he says, "Much still remains to be done" (B xxxviii). But I do not think it wholly Pickwickean to describe advances within an established science as clarifications of the insights that founded the science, rather than as replacements for earlier claims that are now found to be false.

38. For candidate-conditions of reasonableness, see n. 36 above.

39. I think Bennett is right to take the primary meaning of *outer* as "other than oneself" (cf. *Kant's Analytic*, p. 17). Otherwise, if the primary meaning identified being outer with being spatial, the claim that the form of outer sense is space would be flatly trivial.

40. Many of the entries in the bibliography of Neisser's *Cognition and Reality* deal with spatiality in connection with perception and the organization of information. In Neisser there is an account of "the studies of imagined rotations conducted by Shepard, Cooper, and their collaborators" (p. 147). These studies have interesting connections with the quote in n. 32 above, and with my descriptions of Kant's theory of spatial forms.

41. See B 127–29 for Kant's summary of Hume's approach and for his objections to it.

42. *Pre-Critical Writings*, p. 24 = II291. See *Logic*, pp. cx—cxv.

43. I pretty much follow Hintikka in my description of the fusion of particularity and generality in pure intuitions.

44. See Hintikka's "attempted partial reconstruction of the main point of Kant's philosophy of mathematics as applied to modern symbolic logic" (p. 140).

45. Although Quine rejects the analytic/synthetic distinction, and with it the notion that we can separate form from content at the sentential level, he seems to me to retain a consequent of the dogma, namely, the primacy of logical or truth-functional connection. Here is an excerpt from his sec. 6, "Empiricism without the Dogmas," (my italics) "total science is like a field of force whose boundary conditions are experience. A conflict with experience at the periphery occasions readjustments in the interior of the field. *Truth values* have to be redistributed over some of our *statements*" ("Two Dogmas," p. 42). The heavy emphasis on truth, falsity, and on bearers of truth-values persists throughout Quine's redescription of empiricism; but we are not at the boundary between thought and empirical inputs if we are dealing with statements and the like. Logical relations obtain only well within the boundaries, and the primary connections in experience (those truly at the periphery) must be other than logical. See my account of the relation between the manifolds of intuition and appearance in sec. 23.

46. For fine examples of what can be learned from reflections on education, see Whitehead's *The Aims of Education* and Bruner's "The Perfectibility of Intellect."

47. Other authors that add detail to the theory of spatial forms include Whitehead (see n. 46), Hintikka, Hartman, and Schwarz. For those in other disciplines, see Neisser.

Chapter Three

1. For Kant's contentions concerning the path to a science of metaphysics, see the preface to the second edition.

2. I intend nothing controversial by the claim that a science must yield enduring results. The claim is meant to be compatible with Kuhn's or anyone else's views on the growth of scientific knowledge—provided only that they admit that science, unlike philosophy, is not forever starting over at square one. Kant says that if metaphysics is often "compelled to retrace its steps and strike into some new line of approach; or again, if the various participants are unable to agree in any common plan of procedure, then we may rest assured that it is very far from having entered upon the secure path of a science" (B vii).

3. Kant recognizes the probability of faults in his system: "open to objection in this or that respect, while yet the structure of the system, taken in its unity, is not in the least endangered" (B xliv); but then he warns against what will happen if we neglect "the structure of the system, taken in its unity" (= the architectonic). "If we take single passages, torn from their contexts, and compare them with one another, apparent contradictions are not likely to be lacking" (ibid.).

4. See chap. 1, n. 41 for the connection of experience with empirical knowledge.

5. The descriptions of knowledge in terms of its objectivity, unity, and expressibility in judgment figure throughout the Transcendental Deduction. A brief word here on what I now plan as the topic of another book on Kant: the 'I think' of #16 of the Deduction in B is not expressive of mere presence in my consciousness (≠ 'I am thinking of . . .'); rather, it—like Frege's turnstile—signals an assertion or judgment (= 'I think that . . .'). There is no unity to the things that I merely think *of,* nor any objectivity. Unity and objectivity are, however, closely connected with assertion. There is a concern with *my* content of consciousness in the Deduction; but possession is not marked by the mere entertaining of an idea, rather by the willingness to assert it. The Deduction has not been understood because the two-element model has produced a misreading of it that takes its concerns as epistemological, as beginning with all the content of my consciousness (see the first premise in each of Wolff's reconstructions of the argument). The reading then proceeds to say that there is some sort of unity that makes all my ideas mine, that my ideas can have this unity only if they represent things ordered in certain ways by the categories. But the first premise is just false. One's ideas (in the broad sense) have no unity just in virtue of being in one mind; they must, if one ever deliberates, include contradictories; and if one ever reads or dreams, one's ideas must include all sorts of things that do not fit together in a whole. I take the Deduction to argue that, if there is to be a narrower sense of thought (= assertion), one must employ principles of judgment that make the possession of ideas the result of epistemic choice, not the de facto result of just having the idea. So the Deduction does not proceed from a characterization of our ideas such that it follows that we have knowledge. It goes from a characterization of knowledge to our possession of the categories as principles that make that knowledge possible by satisfying the conditions of objectivity and unity. Kant does not and could not prove that whatever one has in one's mind, because it is in *one* mind, must include knowledge of an objective realm structured by the categories. He could not prove this because persons incapable of judgment are possible. He proves, instead, that those who are capable of judgment, those who can distinguish what they think from what they merely think of, those who know things, employ the categories to structure their experience. How they employ them is dealt with in detail in chaps. 4 through 8. What I leave for another work is the general argument connecting objectivity with unity.

6. Piaget's interest in Kant is evident throughout his work. For Piaget's influence on cognitive psychology, see Neisser.

7. Indications of the detail and precision sought in cognitive psychology are evident in paper-titles, e.g., "Selective looking with minimal eye movements"; "A conceptual category effect in visual search: O as letter or as digit."

8. One can make broad and inspecific comparisons between the division of elements in Kant's system, on the one hand, and general physiological divisions on the other. For instance, mathematical thought is controlled by both hemispheres of the brain; but arithmetic, time, inference, and most verbal skills belong to the dominant hemisphere; and the minor hemisphere controls geometry, the initial processing of sensory information, pictorial and pattern sense. However, the conformity between Kant's system and physiological structures does not readily lend itself to any detailed working-out—there is just a general compatibility.

9. Kant's own heading for the section that introduces the table of categories uses the phrase "The clue to the discovery" (A 76 = B 102).

10. Critics who find the Metaphysical Deduction unsatisfactory include Kemp Smith, pp. 192ff.; Bennett, pp. 71–99; Wolff, pp. 59ff. By taking some advance notice of the use to which the categories will be put later in the *Critique,* Grayeff manages to find a more charitable reading (see *Kant's Theoretical Philosophy,* pp. 88–119).

11. Bennett's treatment of Kant in terms of linguistic analysis is evident throughout his work. Bennett's account of analysis as concerned with unobvious analyticities can be found here and there—see pp. 8, 42, 85f.

12. For a bibliography of papers on Moore's paradox of analysis, see Passmore's, *Hundred Years,* chap. 9, n. 12, (p. 560).

13. The example of mathematics is misleading because its notation ensures, in ways that are not possible in philosophy, "that no concept has been neglected and that each single comparison has occurred" (see chap. 2, n. 42). Mathematics and logic do avoid both triviality and the empirical by virtue of connecting together many short and obvious steps (cf. Bennett, p. 14); but what works for them does not work for philosophy, for the reasons Kant details throughout his essay of 1763.

14. Austin, *Philosophical Papers,* p. 130.

15. Ibid., pp. 130–31.

16. For good critical discussion of Austin's methods, see Rorty's introduction to his book, *The Linguistic Turn,* and the papers on Austin in part 3.

17. Austin, p. 131.

18. Somewhere Austin says, "Importance isn't important, truth is." He thinks philosophy should eschew grand theory; but the opposition between theory and truth is false. If one cares about truth, one ought to avoid the self-indulgence to which Austin gives in when he delights in ridicule. Theories can, of course, be wrong; but we ought then to try to find where and how they go wrong, not just wave them away high-table-handedly. Austin's dismissal of theory neglects the contributions it can make to the pursuit of truth. Urmson quotes a note of Austin's: "Shan't learn everything, so why not do something else? Well; not whole even of philosophy but firstly always has *been* philosophy, since Socrates. And some slow successes. Advantages of slowness and cooperation. Be your size. Small men. Foolproof × geniusproof. Anyone with patience can do something. Leads to discoveries and agreement. Is amusing. Part of *personal* motive of my colleagues to avoid interminable bickering or boring points of our predecessors: also remember all brought up on classics: no quarrel with maths etc., just ignorant" (Rorty, p. 236). Theories without detail are empty, details without theory are blind.

19. For Berkeley on the impossibility of a general concept of a triangle, see *Principles,* Introduction, #13.

20. Locke's version of general concepts as blurred images can be found in *Essay* III, iii.7–8.

21. One of Wittgenstein's objections to mental images occurs at *Investigations* I, #56. Cf. *Blue and Brown Books*, pp. 3–5.

22. Cartoonists, in two ways, capture the spatial component of recognition. In editorial cartoons, their stylized emphasis of a feature or two isolates the key to the visual recognition of an individual. In comic strips (especially *Peanuts*), emotions and moods are reduced to their visual essences.

23. The suggestion that family resemblance be redeployed to account for the unity-in-diversity with respect to spatial images might be developed in the following way. There may, for certain fairly diverse classes of things, be no common shape-characteristic that serves as the key to the recognition of all members of the class; but there may, in such cases, be several keys that overlap from member to member throughout the class. This suggestion is distinct from, though analogous to, the original use of family resemblance in application to verbally specified features of games.

24. Bennett sort of credits Kant with the view that concepts are rules or abilities to follow rules. He says, "In crediting Kant with the view that a concept is an ability or skill, I may have flattered him, for his position may be rather that having a concept is being in a mental state which endows one with certain abilities" (p. 54). However, Bennett ties the notion of ability so closely to linguistic ability (see pp. 84f.) that neither alternative gives Kant due credit. The question with respect to Kant is not whether he regards concepts as linguistic abilities or as mental states. Concepts are cognitive abilities, and language is only one of the things we do with our minds. Most of Kant's concern with concepts pertains to the pure concepts of the understanding; and these, throughout the Analytic of Principles, are shown to be rules for the temporal structuring of experience. The pure concepts, or categories, underlie all the fundamental capacities for experience: to apprehend what is given in sense, to perceive, and to reason empirically. The too restrictive identification of concepts with linguistic abilities soon leads to a confusion of the categories with their names (as in Warnock, see n. 29, below. See also the first few pages of sec. 17).

25. I restore the original text. Kemp Smith makes two minor changes.

26. For *Dagegen . . . sondern . . .* , I give 'By contrast . . . on the contrary. . .'. Kemp Smith gives only 'On the other hand'; but there is no earlier 'on the one hand', and he omits *sondern* entirely.

27. I think it as important to recognize the limitations of spatial considerations as it is to recognize their positive contributions to experience. Bennett is quite right to deplore "that preoccupation with the visual which has weakened and narrowed epistemology for centuries" (p. 29); and there may be some justification for his contention that Kant shares the preoccupation. But, on Kant's behalf, it should be noted that spatial forms and images are set aside when Kant gets down to business in the Principles.

28. Wolff, p. 207.

29. Bennett, p. 150. The reference to Warnock is to his "Concepts and Schematism," in which he treats the problem of category-application as a problem about applying words such as *cause* and *necessary*. Bennett says, "This is an ingenious and sympathetic interpretation" (p. 150).

30. Wilkerson, p. 71.

31. Bennett, p. 151.

32. Wolff, p. 207.

33. Wolff, pp. 207–8.

34. The shift in modern philosophy to the linguistic products of thought, and away from thought itself (see sec. 12), results also in the recasting of Kant's concerns as linguistic. Bennett takes problems of word application, and Wolff takes simple syllogisms, as models of Kant's problem. I do not think this trivialization of the problem of the Schematism could occur apart from a general determination to construe every philosophical problem as a problem about language. If the Schematism does have a linguistic analogue to the problem

it poses, it is the very general question of how it is possible for us to use language at all. Since the capacity for language-use in general presupposes, at minimum, the capacity to conceptualize the input of our senses and somehow structure our experience, there is no point whatever in posing the intermediate question about how language is possible—instead of posing the direct question about the conditions for the possibility of experience. Both failure of sufficient generality, and the failure to appreciate that language presupposes experience, count decisively against the attempts to recast the problem of the Schematism as a simple linguistic problem.

35. Wilkerson, p. 94.

36. Bennett seems to take a passage on A 138 = B 177 as indicating that Kant thinks there is a special problem arising only in respect of the categories, and not equally a problem extending to other concepts (cf. p. 148). Whereas I take it that, if the problem of category-application does not extend to empirical concepts in general, then there is no problem at all. Bennett contends "Kant says the problem does not arise for empirical concepts because in their case 'the concepts through which the object is thought in [its] general [aspects] are not so utterly distinct and heterogeneous from those which represent it *in concreto* [that is, in all its detail]'" (p. 148). What Kant actually says is that an account of the categories is required even though no similar account is required *in the other sciences,* because they— unlike metaphysics—represent their objects *in concreto* (recall the 1763 essay). The contrast, then, is between Kant's science of metaphysics and other sciences; and his science must do something that they need not do—it must set out and explain the concepts it uses (the categories) to explain its object (experience)—because metaphysical thought is abstract rather than concrete, and its topic is given rather than constructed. See A 135–36 = B 174– 75. The contrast is to medicine, law, politics, (A 134 = B 173) where examples and actual practice provide the requisite sense of the terms' applications; and, I think, to physics and mathematics where the requisite sense of applicability can be got just from working with the notation. Kant is just explaining why his science must be different. He is not setting the categories apart from all other concepts of experience (except as the highest, and except as distinct from those involving spatial images).

37. Bennett seems to think the failure of the problem to be unique to the categories is an objection (cf. p. 150).

38. See n. 31 above.

39. Cf. A 50–51 = B 74–75.

40. Austin, p. 130.

41. Wolff, pp. 208–9.

42. For the difficulty of accommodating change in Leibniz's doctrine of perception, see Parkinson, p. 180. See also *Monadology,* ##6, 7.

43. Kant objects to preestablished harmony A 274–75 = B 330–31.

44. In particular the categories of limitation and reciprocity make little sense in the Metaphysical Deduction until one looks back from the Anticipations and the Third Analogy, respectively.

45. Wolff does half-recognize the need to understand the *Critique,* not as a story where the order of narration is meant to be carried over into the objects of description, but rather as a more unitary whole (or a less linear one) in which all the parts must be brought together. Cf. pp. 209–10.

46. Kant's descriptions of the organic character of pure reason underscore the need to make sense of the *Critique* as a systematically unified whole. See n. 3 above.

Chapter Four

1. For other examples of the extensive/intensive distinction, see Bennett, pp. 167ff. Bennett's discussion of the distinction is generally clear and good, but he has trouble seeing

the definition of intensive magnitude as saying anything positive. "[Kant says,] 'The reduction of an intensive magnitude, as when the saturation of a red patch lessens, is not the removal of parts but . . .' Now we want something positive, but all Kant offers us is, in effect: '. . . but the magnitude's approximating more closely to negation.' This gets us nowhere. As the red patch becomes less saturated, it approximates to not being there at all; but this is equally true if the patch decreases in size. Analogously, I approximate to not having arthritic pains as my pains become ever milder, or as they diminish extensively by becoming ever briefer and rarer. So the idea of 'approximation to negation' does not mark off intensive from extensive magnitudes" (p. 171). But there is a difference between shrinking and fading: in the place we put the negation. If the patch shrinks to nothing, we say, "There is no patch"; but if it fades, we say, "The patch is not red." We must remember that the application is to intuition, so the patch is not a physical object, but a group of locations in the visual field. Shrinking diminishes the number of locations (it reduces the number of parts). Fading alters the content of the locations. See n. 9 below.

2. *Pure,* as applied to sensations, means being of a single sensory kind—it does not indicate an upper limit of intensity. A pure blue may be of any intensity.

3. The parallel passage for time is to be found on A 31–32 = B 47.

4. Wolff, p. 229.

5. We may, thanks to modern physics, be able to ask meaningfully whether space itself is finite and, if so, how big it is—which would be a question about *its* extensive magnitude. Even so, there would be no contradiction between the Aesthetic and Axioms. The former talks about the representation of a space in space itself, and this stays unchanged in a finite, but still all-embracing, space. The latter talks about the representation of an extensive magnitude. Now, if space itself is finite, then it is an extensive magnitude; *as such* its representation presupposes the representation of its parts—the constituent spaces—even though their representation does presuppose the representation of space itself. But we still do not have the very same thing both presupposing another and being presupposed by it. Rather, we first represent space itself as the unity embracing all spaces, then we represent the regions within space, then we represent space itself as finite. Presuppositions can be mutual when they involve several stages. Otherwise there would be neither chickens nor eggs.

6. I am not saying that *Some* should not be given its usual meaning in logic of *at least one.* I am saying that the informal implication of "Some *A*'s are *B*'s" is both that there are several *A*'s and that not all of them are *B*'s. These implications are not by virtue of the logic of sentences starting with *Some,* but by general conventions that require us to be both accurate and forthcoming in giving information. One should not say less than is warranted— not "Some *A*'s are *B*'s" in place of "All *A*'s are *B*'s"—nor more than is warranted—not "Some are" in place of "This is." See the following note.

7. A continuation of the point in n. 6. I am indebted to Grice for these points and more made in a wonderful paper on conventions governing discourse that circulated widely in the 1960s. I have not seen it in print. One of his other general conventions on informative discourse is "Be orderly—recount things in the order in which they occurred." He uses this rule to explain the mistake in thinking that *and* ever means *and then.* It is not the conjunction, but the rule, that permits the ordering of the conjuncts. With unsurpassable elegance Grice proves the point by asking us to imagine *and* replaced by a period.

8. I think that Grayeff is on the right track in his account of the category of totality (see p. 113). Bennett (who follows Watson in this without acknowledging him) decides that the order in which Kant lists the judgment-forms "is reversed, but this is a slip" (p. 77). So Bennett pairs universal judgments with the category of totality, and singular judgments with unity; and, in support of this reversal, he says, "One remark of Kant's depends on their being taken in that order" (ibid.). The passage he cites is B 110–11, but he does not say

what remark he thinks of. On B 110–11, neither singular nor universal judgments are mentioned. Perhaps the remark he means is the first line of B 111 in Kemp Smith's translation: "Thus *allness* or *totality* is just plurality considered as unity." *Allness* might suggest universal judgments which take *all* as their quantifier, but the suggestion is misleading. When translating the table of categories, Kemp Smith uses *totality* for the third category of quantity; but on B 111 he switches to *allness* to translate the same word in the original—*Allheit*. He is forced to switch because Kant adds *Totalität* in brackets. We do associate *all* with universal judgments, and there is a natural plausibility to Bennett's pairing of unity with singular judgments; but if we are to grasp what Kant means we must not be lead astray by whatever connotations the categorial *names* may have *for us*. Kant is more likely to have Leibniz than Copi in mind. For him universal judgments express unity—as much because of the *gemeine* (= common, general) as because of the *All* (= all) in *Allgemeine* (= universal)— and the singular judgment expresses totality because the individual or one is the sum of its parts. Think about Leibniz's distinction between full and complete concepts (for which see Parkinson, pp. 125ff.). The monad or individual thing that we talk about in singular judgments even has as its principle of identity the complete set of qualities that can be predicated of it. Think again about modern symbolic logic. The universal quantifier includes every object of discourse in its scope, and the predication extends conditionally, and without differentiation, to all things (All *A*'s are *B*'s = Anything whatever, if an *A* is also *B*). The universal judgment expresses unity because it lumps everything together, whereas the particular expresses totality because each judgment adds to what can be said about an individual.

9. Kant's example of infinite judgment contrasts "The soul is nonmortal" with the negative judgment "The soul is not mortal." The example is poor, but the discussion that follows it makes sense. I think that what Kant has in mind in his example (here I fish) is that the negative judgment concentrates on the outright denial of something; but the infinite judgment (though it too denies) directs us to consider what else might be the case, given the denial. Infinite judgments, in effect, take the form "If not such-and-so, what then?" or "Not this, but ———." My example (see n. 4.1) works better. "The patch is not red" (infinite) contrasts with "There is no patch" (negative) because the former does contain a positive or affirmative element: "There is a patch." Kant's discussion fits my example too; for "There is a patch" leaves entirely open what qualities it has when redness diminishes to nothing—and Kant says that it is in this respect such judgments are infinite, because the mere exclusion of one quality (not red) leaves indefinitely many to take its place (as answers to "What then?" or as fillers for the blank in "Not this, but ———"). This makes sense especially in relation to intuition, where a patch is not a physical thing, but a region in a sensory field. If the sensations in certain sensory locations fade away, they are succeeded by others. Kant connects the *infinite* in the title of the third form of judgment with the fact that they leave open what will take the place of what the predicate denies (cf. A 71–73 = B 97–98). This is reasonable enough since the Metaphysical Deduction attends to the analysis of judgment forms. I take *infinite* in connection with the range of degrees, as Kant does in the Anticipations. This is why I move on to "It does not hurt very much" and other examples of infinite judgments in which qualifiers are prominent. The category of limitation draws on both aspects of infinite judgments.

10. The fusion of particularity with generality in pure intuitions (in the absence of empirical determinants) ensures that imagined or intuited patterns could obtain anywhere in space-time. See chap. 2, n. 43, and last paragraph of sec. 13.

11. My use of *schema* is intended to reflect both current use (= a diagrammatic sketch of essential features) and the conditions on schemata that Kant sets out: that they relate on one hand to categories and on the other to sensibility, that they be pure or nonempirical, and that "schemata are nothing but a priori determinations of time in accordance with rules"

(A 145 = B 184). The two schemata, t_1, t_2, t_3, . . . , t_n and the t when ——, are required by the *time-series* and *time-content* (ibid.).

12. "The pure *schema* of magnitude *(quantitatis)*, as a concept of the understanding, is *number*" (A 142 = B 182).

13. The representation of alternative courses of experience requires the principle of the Third Analogy, for which see chap. 7.

14. In denying that space and time can be constructed from constituents given prior to them, Kant may be objecting to empiricists, e.g., Hume, *Treatise,* Book I, Part II. Possibly to Leibniz. For a list of references to his doctrines of space and time as mere orders of appearance, see the footnotes to Parkinson, p. 169.

15. Bennett makes the point that negation can be reached, not only by gradual diminution, but by removal of parts. See the passage quoted in n. 1 above.

16. Early in his discussion of identity, Hume says, "Since then both number and unity are incompatible with the relation of identity, it must lie in something that is neither of them. But to tell the truth, at first sight this seems utterly impossible. Betwixt unity and number there can be no medium; no more than betwixt existence and non-existence" (*Treatise,* Book I, Part IV, ii). Hume goes on to the contradiction he finds between the conditions of identity (invariableness through a supposed variation in time); but I find the passage just quoted interesting because, in denying their possibility, it nonetheless pairs together Kant's third categories of quantity and quality—and recognizes that they would be mediate between their respective first two categories. One wonders if Kant read the passage and questioned the denial of the medium. Hume often puts his doubts in terms of a rhetorical question about a medium. Thus, e.g., "The connexion between these propositions is not intuitive. There is required a medium, which may enable the mind to draw such an inference, if indeed it be drawn by reasoning and argument. What that medium is, I must confess, passes my comprehension; and it is encumbent on those to produce it, who assert that it really exists, and is the origin of all our conclusions concerning matters of fact" (*Enquiry,* sec. IV, part II). When Kant produces it he does so in words that echo Hume's, "Obviously there must be some third thing. . . . This mediating representation must be. . . ." (A 138 = B 177).

17. To support his contention that Carnap's reductionism is in principle incomplete, Quine says there is "no indication, not even the sketchiest, of how a statement of the form 'Quality q is at $x;y;z;t$' could ever be translated into Carnap's initial language of sense data and logic. The connective 'is at' remains an added undefined connective" ("Two Dogmas," p. 40). Quine adds that Carnap abandoned reductionism apparently because of this point. Why is the connective 'is at' so important that failure to define it ends the reductionist enterprise? I do not know what Quine would answer, but he does go on to argue against even attenuated reductionism, and to urge its replacement by a model in which physical object statements face the sensory evidence collectively. If we cannot, in a formal way, introduce the structuring of space and time at the sensory level, I see no choice but to follow Quine in treating the sensory as an undifferentiated mass that presses *en bloc* against our networks of concepts and beliefs. Kant is not attempting reductionism, but he attends far more carefully than Carnap to the relation of times and spaces to their content.

18. Section IV of Book I, Part I of the *Treatise* begins with the words, "As all simple ideas. . . ." Throughout all his discussions of the connection or association of ideas, Hume makes free and frequent reference to what the mind can or cannot do with it ideas—never, apparently, realizing that all concepts of connection, e.g., resemblance difference, similarity, contiguity, etc. are simply imposed on simple ideas without regard for the features of ideas that call for such connections to be made.

19. I think the a priori plays a large, though unacknowledged role in Hume's philosophy. He credits the mind with all sorts of capacities that we may indeed first come to know by noticing ourselves engaging them in experience; but the capacities to know, to notice, to

compare, to remember, to associate ideas, etc. are, and must be, all in advance of experience as conditions for its possibility on Hume's own account.

20. For Hume's discussion of the missing shade of blue, see *Enquiry,* sec. II, 16.

21. For objection to the sort of incapacity Hume invokes to make the doctrine of fictional identity work, see n. 16 above.

22. Kemp Smith reads *vieler* as 'different' instead of 'many', but there is no reason that the successive sensations combined in an extensive magnitude (parts of a whole) should be different.

23. For a short statement of the issue between Descartes and Newton in respect of matter and space, see Dampier, p. 136f.

24. For *ein kontinuierlicher Zusammenhang,* Kemp Smith gives 'a continuity' instead of 'a continuous connection'.

25. In addition to the *nicht* to *nur* substitution noted in the text, Kemp Smith repeats the mistake noted in n. 22 above.

26. The two minor changes in Müller's translation: first, retaining 'appearances' as the translation of *Erscheinungen;* second, replacing his 'to any amount' with my 'up to its given amount' to translate *bis zu ihrem gegebenen Masse.*

27. In his theory of vision, Berkeley attempts to construct our visual knowledge from only those sensory ideas that he finds in himself when he introspects. Sec. 12 of *Vision* reads as follows: "But those lines and angles by means whereof some men pretend to explain the perception of distance, are themselves not at all perceived, nor are they in truth ever thought of by those unskilful in optics. I appeal to anyone's experience whether upon sight of an object he computes its distance by the bigness of the angle made by the meeting of the two optic axes? Or whether he ever thinks of the greater or lesser divergency of the rays, which arrive from any point to his pupil? Everyone is himself the best judge of what he perceives, and what not. In vain shall any man tell me that I perceive certain lines and angles which introduce into my mind the various ideas of distance, so long as I myself am conscious of no such thing." Of course, there is a sense of *perceives* in which I alone can say—or am best placed to say—what I perceive; but it does not follow that cognition draws only on ideas that are accessible to introspection. Sensations in the inner ear play a major role in maintaining balance, but though I may sense that I have lost my balance I do not have introspective access to the inner-ear sensations that are my means of knowing. Similarly, distance perception may turn on many sensory factors that are not open to introspection. Berkeley's principle, in his sec. 10, is false if the first *perceived* entails *find if I introspect.* See Hume's 'correction' in the *Treatise,* p. 636.

28. Although I choose the example because I think the role of sound in maintaining direction is not known (but is an open question), the example is not utterly fanciful since migratory birds in midcontinent use the very low frequency sounds of the surf on either continental shore to steer by. While I would be astonished to find that specific capacity in man, we may make some use of local sounds. Whether we do cannot be settled by introspection. (Having just typed this note, I heard on the radio a coach who works with blind figure-skaters claim they use the echoes in the ice-rink to orient themselves.)

29. Berkeley says this in the passage quoted in n. 27 above.

30. For Gestalt psychology and for Fechner's measurements of sensation, see Boring, chaps. 23 and 14, respectively. For further references, see the notes at the ends of his chapters.

31. I add *in general* to weaken the claim because we can *learn* the cause of an initially puzzling sensation. So we may sometimes be introspectively aware of a sensation that is part of experience, though not yet colored by it. However, the kind of learning required to figure things out depends on knowledge arrived at spontaneously.

32. Descartes maintains the certainty of conscious content by restricting it to its subjective signification. "I see light, I hear noise, I feel heat. But it will be said that these phenomena are false and that I am dreaming. Let it be so; still it is at least quite certain that it seems to me that I see light, that I hear noise and that I feel heat. That cannot be false; properly speaking it is what is in me called feeling" (I, p. 153). Hume says, "For since all actions and sensations of the mind are known to us by consciousness, they must necessarily appear to us in every particular what they are, and be what they appear" (*Treatise,* p. 190). Both treat the subjective as certain, both regard the subjectively certain as immune from all doubt, and both think this immunity an important reason to take the subjective as the basis of all knowledge.

33. Kant says, "Apprehension is only a placing together of the manifold in empirical intuition; and we can find in it no representation of any necessity which determines the appearances thus combined to have connected existence in space and time" (B 219). This must be intended to contrast with the first sentence of the paragraph, which says, "Experience is an empirical knowledge, that is, a knowledge which determines an object through perception"; for, after describing apprehension as indeterminate, Kant repeats the opening remark and then goes on to contend that the determinateness required for knowledge must come about through the relation of objects to time in general.

34. All thought must relate to intuition. See A 19 = B 33 quoted in sec. 3.

35. For Quine's replacement of reduction with germaneness, see "Two Dogmas," p. 43.

36. For Kant's pairing of the mathematical/dynamical distinction with a contrast between intuition and existence, see A 160 = B 199, A 178–79 = B 221–22.

Chapter Five

1. For Descartes' identification of matter with extension, see Fifth Meditation, and *Principles,* Second Part, I.

2. For the argument against empty space, see *Principle* XVI.

3. Descartes connects clarity and distinctness with truth and truth with existence in the sixth paragraph of the Fifth Meditation.

4. For the spatial schemata that represent objects, see sec. 16.

5. Kemp Smith takes the principle of the First Analogy as an attempt to prove the principle of the conservation of matter in his *Commentary,* p. 361f. Cf. Wolff, pp. 249–50.

6. Kant is cautious about the connection between his work in the *Critique* and physics. He thinks that two other works, the *Metaphysical Foundations* and the (posthumous) *Transition* are required to link the metaphysics of experience to physics. Even with the link established, things in the one science need not connect obviously and automatically with things in the other.

7. The quantum of substance is discussed in sec. 27.

8. Kant says, "Certainly the proposition, that substance is permanent, is tautological" (A 184 = B 227). Bennett refers to this when, having just quoted the B-version of the principle, he says, "This puts up for proof the same thing that, three pages later, Kant calls tautological" (p. 183). The principle says that *in all change of appearance* substance is permanent. In every principle there is an analytic or intellectual element, but the proof is to show how that element applies in experience.

9. Explanations of very basic things like the categories and their principles cannot be fitted to the nomological-deductive model because there are no more primitive laws from which they might be deduced. But the spirit of the Hempelian conditions can be satisfied by transcendental arguments, which also oppose ad hoc, redundant, circular, false, and insufficient explanations.

10. My translation differs from Kemp Smith's. He ignores Kant's emphasis (by spacing) on *Zugleichsein*.

11. For Leibniz's distinction between space and time as the orders of coexistence and succession, respectively, see Parkinson, p. 169 and his references in the notes.

12. The original reads, *welches die Zeit überhaupt vorstellt;* and this is ambiguous between "which time represents in a general way" and "which represents time in a general way." I prefer the former; but one might think that the latter is preferable because Kant has just remarked that time is unperceived (and so might be thought in need of something that represents it). But Kant has already urged that objects can be known only by being related in time in general. See B 219 and n. 33, chap. 4. Although unperceived, time is an intuition of the whole in which all times are parts. That notion of time is a general representation of substance in which áll material things are parts. These material things will be required to represent time*s* in a determinate way. The general representation of matter or the material substratum cannot precede the representation of time itself because it is by their relation to time itself that objects are considered material. See sec. 26.

13. On the Aesthetic doctrine of the priority of the representation of time itself, see discussion in sec. 19.

14. Descartes uses the nonspatiality of mind (soul) in contrast to the extension of body to argue for the permanence (immortality) of the former—D.V. See Reply to Objections II, 7. Kant argues against this in the First Paralogism.

15. Kant describes Descartes as an idealist on B 274.

16. By 'conscious of' is meant anything that can be shown to be taken into account by the mind, even that to which we lack introspective access. See n. 27, chap. 4.

17. To make the famous claim that existence is not a predicate in addition to other descriptions of an object, Kant says, "*Being* is obviously not a real predicate; that is, it is not a concept of something which could be added to the concept of a thing, or of certain determinations, as existing in themselves" (A 598 = B 626). "A hundred real thalers do not contain the least coin more than a hundred possible thalers" (A 599 = B 627).

18. Kant would never allow that the world could be just a collection of objects. In one place (A 418 = B 446), he distinguishes between *world* and *nature,* with the latter being the dynamical whole; even the former is not just the items, but the manifold of items as bound up in mathematical relations. (I do not preserve this world/nature distinction in the text.)

19. The uniformity of nature underpins induction; but, following Hume, empiricists are not only committed to induction as the basic mechanism of empirical thought, they are also committed to endorsing the skeptic doubts that Hume directs against any professed knowledge of the uniformity of nature. This leaves the uniformity of nature as an unknowable but essential presupposition of empirical thought. Mill seems a bit oblivious to the problems of knowing the uniformity of nature (in *A System of Logic,* III, iii, I) for which Nagel and Cohen justly take him to task in *An Introduction to Logic and Scientific Method,* pp. 146ff. Russell's postulates of scientific inference, in *Human Knowledge, Its Scope and Limits,* pp. 487ff., are a marked improvement over Mill's vague notion of uniformity, but their epistemic status is as questionable. I think the best the empiricist can do is adopt a pragmatic stance of maintaining that the only possible justification is that without uniformity nothing works—so if anything works, induction does (Salmon's vindication of induction). But that does amount to making the consistency, conformity to law, and uniformity of the objects in nature mere presumptions. See chap. 2, especially secs. 5, 6, and 8, of Salmon's *The Foundations of Scientific Inference.*

20. Locke, Book II, chap. IV (vol. 1, pp. 151–52).

21. Cf. Locke, Book II, xxiii.

22. In the very first paragraph (second sentence) of the *Treatise,* Hume uses their force and liveliness to attempt to distinguish impressions from ideas. Thereafter, since he regards

impressions as indubitable in all respects (cf. n. 32, chap. 4), he thinks that the objectivity of any idea is sufficiently established by showing its origin in a sensory impression.

23. Empirical idealism holds *both* that objects are just collections of properties *and* that properties are just sensory states. Realism, by contrast, denies both reductions. I do not know whether there are, or could be, hybrid positions maintaining just the reduction of objects to their properties or of properties to sensory states, but not both. Locke comes close to holding that the second reduction holds but not the first—that is, he does if one grants that his remarks about the unknown are genuine confessions of ignorance concerning something he does believe in, and not just heavy-handed ironies to dismiss substance altogether. He does regard ideas as both in the mind and in objects, and he may (I think he does) regard the object as more than its properties. Such halfhearted realism will not work because the conflation of properties in objects to (sensory) ideas separates properties from the substance of which they are the properties. However, the doctrine of powers in II, xxi (except for the aspect of will that Schopenhauer picked up on and made into a whole system) puts Locke closer to realism than idealism. Provided that capacities or powers are *not reduced to* the active powers and susceptibilities that we discover in ourselves on reflection, and merely project to objects, they are what an object is in addition to its properties that are sensorily represented. But Locke wavers between just the one reduction: of properties to sensory ideas, and the two-stage reduction that treats objects as no more than their properties.

24. The description of the two levels on which presupposition operates owes much to Strawson's descriptions of the two levels on which accountability is decided. See his fine paper, "Freedom and Resentment."

25. For another example of the role of presupposition in evidence, consider Ventris's decipherment of Linear B. Suppose that when he had had all the clay tablets he had not thought to consider them samples of writing. He might have regarded them as just designs, perhaps magical objects. By presupposing that they were linguistic, he did not *add* to the evidence; but he constrained the ways in which the marks had to be regarded so long as the presupposition could be maintained. The marks had to be ideographic, or phonemic or syllabic, or in some other way representative of meaning. Once he settled that question, still not knowing the language, he was constrained in the possible topics the marks could be taken to represent—only certain types of discourse (e.g., lists and inventories) could be fitted to the pattern of the marks.

26. I add *itself* to the third sentence because Kant uses the reflexive verb *sich verändern*. The addition is fairly minor but its significance is that changes—though in response to external causes—rest with the substance itself and reflect its capacities.

27. Kant contends that time is not a determination or property of things. See A 32–33 = B 49–50.

28. Walker's book *Kant* is in the Routledge & Kegan Paul series, The Arguments of the Philosophers. The quote is from pp. 111–12.

29. There is an interesting history of the measurement of time in Norman Feather's *Mass, Length and Time*, chap. 3.

30. Kemp Smith's *Commentary*, p. 358. Even fairly plain distinctions escape Kemp Smith because his patchwork theory encourages him to find contradictions in the text. The simple point Kant is making is that two things can be simultaneous and distinct; but if a time is simultaneous with another, they are identical.

31. For Austin's endorsement of the common understanding and for his rejection of what philosophers have thought, see sec. 15.

32. The definition of experience is on B 218.

33. For a very funny and brilliant criticism of behaviorism, see Chomsky's, "A Review of B. F. Skinner's *Verbal Behavior*."

34. Representation of the real is not by the addition of predicates; see n. 17 above.

35. The first sentence is Kemp Smith's translation; the second is mine.

36. Several minor changes in translation.

37. The famous passage with the 'I think' introduces sec. #16 of the B Deduction. It is standardly taken as a Cartesian claim about the primacy of self-consciousness. I take it quite differently: as an anticipation of Frege's assertion operator. The 'I think' in the sense in which it is a mark of the unity of thought cannot possibly accompany all that I think *of* (for many obvious reasons, including the fact that I think of *p* and not-*p* when trying to make up my mind, and it would be an odd sense of unity that embraced contradictions; fantasies or dreams are paradigmatically random and at odds with the thoughts of ordinary waking experience, yet both are thought of; etc.) The thoughts that I (or anyone else) think in the sense of thinking *that* have all the sorts of unity listed in the text. The standard interpretation is that Kant starts with the unity of consciousness and then argues that to have that unity our consciousness must be structured by the categories. This seems to me wrong from the start because there is no unity that ideas have just by virtue of being in one('s) mind. I take it that Kant is giving the sort of sorting argument I give in the text: if we are to have knowledge we must distinguish, among the things we think, certain things that can be asserted. The criteria for the sorting are the various aspects of unity set out in the text. Cf. n. 5, chap. 3.

38. Walker replies to Kant's contention that to represent a thing as beginning or ceasing we should have to perceive an empty time by saying, "This is again unconvincing; we should not have to perceive an empty world at all but only a world which did not have that particular thing in it, which is entirely possible and quite commonplace" (p. 112). To perceive a world empty of a certain thing, it would *at least* be necessary to look into every possible location of the thing and fail to find it. Such exhaustive surveys are impossible. Melnick makes the same point on p. 72 of his book on the Analogies (though I have some quarrels with Melnick's book it is excellent on many points).

39. Bennett uses the empiricist's test of conceptual necessity; but, apart from that, I find his treatment of the problems of existence-change well argued (pp. 188ff.).

40. Several minor changes from Kemp Smith's translation.

41. Leibniz's two-clock model of mind/body relation is in the Third Explanation of the New System. See Latta's edition of *The Monadology*, pp. 331ff. Also see Latta's note to p. 46, in which he accuses the Wolffians of giving undue prominence to the model of the two clocks. Latta urges that a different model (of musicians each playing the part of a total work that has been scored for them) is better (p. 47). However, it is doubtful that Kant knew the musician model since it occurs in the *Correspondence with Arnauld*, which was not published until 1846. The familiarity of the two-clock model supports my observation later in the section that Kant is brief because the matter is so well known.

42. See n. 11 above for Leibniz's association of coexistence with space.

43. I think it reasonable to suppose that Kant reread the A-version just before making the changes in B. It is then worth noting that the *coexistent* (as well as the *successive*) is said at the beginning of the B-proof to be temporal—as though Kant wants to signal more strongly that his argument opposes Leibniz. See nn. 10 and 11 above and the text corresponding to them in sec. 24.

Chapter Six

1. In B, Kant moves the reference to the First Analogy to a new introductory paragraph that gives a full summary.

2. Not trusting 'former' to be sufficiently temporal, Kemp Smith translates *Zustand* as 'time'.

3. "No necessity determining their connection is or can be revealed in the perceptions themselves" (B 219).

4. Alternate contents for the same time require different persons with different experiences. See sec. 20.

5. Bennett describes the basic problem of the ship example on pp. 221ff.; but he dismisses Kant's solution as a failure. He thinks that actions of perceivers must be brought into the argument at that stage. However, the order-dependence of event-concepts is sufficient to distinguish them from the order-indifference of the concepts of static objects; actions presuppose events, and cannot be used to explain them; and, despite what one might think from reading *Kant's Analytic*, there is a third Analogy (and it does deal with the actions of perceivers).

6. Bennett (p. 221), Wolff (p. 268), Wilkerson (p. 80), and Walker (p. 101), all take the possible *up*stream motion of the ship (or other more exotic possibilities) to raise difficulties about the necessary order that Kant claims holds among perceptions of its downstream motion. Beck does better; he at least hints at the difference between reversibility and order-dependence, and rightly stresses the importance of the qualification: *in imagination* (in his *Essays on Kant and Hume*, pp. 136ff.). Bird gets it right when he recognizes that the reversal of an event yields another event (p. 155). The reversal of elements in the concept of a static complex makes no difference at all, so the static and the changing are conceptually different: one order-indifferent, the other not; but though some events may differ from others in terms of their different conceptual content, others present special problems that require differentiation in sense (see n. 8 below). Strawson is fairly good on the house/ship difference (pp. 134–36); but he misconstrues the general argument, which he claims involves "a *non sequitur* of numbing grossness" (see pp. 136–37). Beck replies to Strawson's charge (in *Essays*, pp. 147–53).

7. The remark that follows: "The principle of the causal connection among appearances is limited in our formula to their serial succession" (A 202 = B 247).

8. Upstream and downstream motions—or any other event-pair in which the arrangements of constituent parts are temporal mirror images of each other—are temporal analogues of the (spatially) incongruous counterparts to which Kant turns repeatedly in his writings for examples of things that differ in ways not expressible in concepts, but determinably differ only in relation to how they are presented in sense. Such examples are obviously counter to Leibniz's principle of the identity of indiscernibles. This passage is from the Dissertation: "Between solids which are perfectly similar and equal but not congruent, in which genus are the left hand and the right hand . . . there is a diversity which makes it impossible for the boundaries of their extension to coincide although they could be substituted for one another as far as concerns all the things which may be expressed in speech. And so it is clear that in these cases the diversity, I mean the discongruity, can only be noticed by a certain act of pure intuition" (II403). See also II379 and sec. 13 of the *Prolegomena*. (For very brief, but intelligent comment, see Smart in his introduction to *Problems of Space and Time*, pp. 6–7). Just as the spatial counterparts require reference to sensory presentation, upstream and downstream motion differ only in the way they are presented. Hence, among certain events there are no differences in the concepts apart from their relation to apprehension.

9. Hume generally purports that we draw inferences from sensible qualities to usual effects—from the color and taste of bread to its power to nourish, etc. Here is one example from the *Enquiry:* "Adam, though his rational faculties be supposed, at the very first, entirely perfect, could not have inferred from the fluidity and transparency of water that it would suffocate him, or from the light and warmth of fire that it would consume him" (p. 27). Hume's examples mislead. Bread does not nourish *because* it has certain sensory qualities, nor does water suffocate *because* it has others, nor does fire consume *because* it gives off

light and warmth. The inferences are not just impossible for Adam, but for everyone. We may (in odd cases, only) infer from certain sensible qualities that the stuff is bread, water, fire, snow, etc.; and because we know the properties of those things, we might (somewhat perversely) be said to infer the secret powers from the appearance ("Well, it looks like bread, so I guess it might nourish us"); but if it fails to do what things of its apparent type usually do, we deny the *categorization* ("Can't be coal; it doesn't burn"), not the supposed (by Hume, only) *connection* between sensible qualities and usual effects ("Not all coal burns"). We say that though it looks like ———, it cannot be. Sensible qualities are quick devices for type-sorting things; but types that figure in causal connection depend not on their appearance, but their action. See sec. 30.

10. Opium does have a soporific virtue. This is not trivial. To learn which things have which dispositional properties is to acquire the information basic to all empirical thought and practical action. In a world of intricate variety, it is not easy to sort out what does what. Hempel gives a classic account of the scientific method in his description of Semmelweiss's discovery that putrid matter causes puerperal fever (in *Philosophy of Natural Science,* pp. 3ff.). We do not have comparable accounts of the discoveries, by herbalists and medicine men, of the medicinal properties of natural substances, but what they discovered is directly comparable to what Semmelweiss discovered. Neither provides an explanation of the mechanism by which the cause works, but neither is trivial because each provides knowledge essential for intelligent action or precaution. To hold opium's soporific virtue up to ridicule as an empty form of words is to agree with the tobacco lobby that, until the mechanism has been shown, one says nothing in saying that tobacco is a carcinogen.

11. Buchdahl, in *Metaphysics* (chap. 8) and many papers, provides a different, very detailed (and I think very good) way of defusing objections drawn from modern science. He shows that there are quite different sorts of principles (transcendental, metaphysical, and empirical) at issue in Kant's various works, and that there are gaps between one sort of principle and another. See "The Conception of Lawlikeness," and his other works that he refers to in the notes to that paper.

12. Kant says that the analysis he omits is available in text books. He may have in mind things like Wolff's book of metaphysics (on which he lectured).

13. The omitted passage reads as follows: "For that is an essential and quite peculiar characteristic of substance (as phenomenon). But while according to the usual procedure, which deals with concepts in purely analytic fashion, this question would be completely insoluble, it presents no such difficulty from the standpoint which we have been formulating" (A 205 = B 250). Note: Kant's use of *phenomenon* here is one of the few counterexamples I have found to my general thesis that he maintains a distinction between appearances and phenomena. But I am not troubled in this case because of the relation of the passage to Leibniz. The remark is further to the question raised, and so *phenomenon* is addressed to the Leibnizian who is being challenged. Kant, when giving his own answer, immediately reverts back to *appearance* in conformity with my thesis about the distinction.

14. Hacking's paper, "Individual Substance," is in *Leibniz,* ed. Frankfurt, pp. 137–53.

15. Hacking, p. 148.

16. Ibid.

17. Ibid. (cf. n. 9 above).

18. For time representing substance, see n. 12, chap. 5. For the perception of change and coexistence in relation to the substratum, see B 224–25 quoted and discussed in sec. 24.

19. I discuss the transcendental object = x in sec. 9.

20. Hacking discusses short-term active principles of unity that are not true substances on p. 150.

21. Kant says, "Leibniz's monadology has no basis whatsoever save his mode of representing the distinction of inner and outer merely in relation to the understanding. Sub-

stances in general must have some *internal* nature, which is therefore free from all outer relations, and consequently also from composition. The simple is therefore the basis of that which is inner in things-in-themselves. But that which is inner in the state of a substance cannot consist in place, shape, contact, or motion (these determinations being all outer relations), and we can therefore assign to substances no inner state save that through which we ourselves inwardly determine our sense, namely, the *state of the representations*. This, therefore, completed the conception of the monads, which, though they have to serve as the basic material of the whole universe, have no other active power save only that which consists in representations, the efficacy of which is confined, strictly speaking, to themselves" (A 274 = B 330).

22. For "Kant's Reply to Hume," and for reasons to prefer Leibniz to Hume as the foil in the arguments of the Principles, see sec. 33.

23. My 'in a general way' replaces Kemp Smith's 'at all' for *überhaupt*.

24. Leibniz makes *reflection* both the method (logical analysis) and the model of his metaphysics—the model, because the monad is patterned on a soul reflecting on its own inner states of representation. Note the full title of the Amphiboly.

25. To say (*pace* Leibniz) that perception is not related to thought as the confused to the distinct, is not at all to say that perception is error free. Empirical thought does resolve inconsistencies in perceptual information (see chap. 8), but judgments of perception are already fully and properly objective knowledge, seldom needing correction.

26. He cannot be using *time-order* here as a technical term because, in the Schematism, *time-order* is the result of the application of the categories of relation (cf. A 145 = B 184). The time-order he refers to here must be, not the ordered succession of objective time, but merely the order of apprehension.

27. Kant says, "If we enquire what new character *relation to an object* confers upon our representations, what dignity they thereby acquire, we find that it results only in subjecting the representations to a rule, and so in necessitating us to connect them in some one specific manner; and conversely, that only in so far as our representations are necessitated in a certain order as regards their time-relations do they acquire objective meaning" (A 197 = B 242–43).

28. I make several minor changes in Kemp Smith's translation: early in the passage trying to reverse his textual emendations, and removing an ambiguity in the final sentence (his "as its consequence" could be taken with the verb *stands* instead of with *event*).

29. For the schema of cause and effect, see A 144 = B 183.

30. Any system in which individual propositions are derivable is Post-inconsistent, because any substitution rule would permit *P and not-P* for *P*. (After E. L. Post, American logician.)

31. Kant's conditions on transcendental exposition include the requirement that the proffered explanation be the only one possible. I think this is too strong—in fact, unprovable in principle, and opt instead for the best available. See sec. 14.

32. I am quoting the principle of the Second Analogy in B.

33. Beck talks about the "immediate" perception of events in a discussion that starts off right and ends up wrong: "Undoubtedly much of what Kant attributed to the understanding and to the rule-governed operations of imagination is generally well taken care of by the nervous system in its integrative functions. Certainly nature has not left us men, and brutes, dependent upon the knowledge of the First and Second Analogies for our ability to tell the difference between a moving ship and a stationary house. Our nervous system enables us to see the difference between a moving ship and a stationary house 'immediately'. But the trouble is, it does not always enable us, without certain conceptual and methodological precautions and adherence to rules, to do so *correctly*" (*Essays,* p. 139). Much of what Kant attributes to understanding and imagination is indeed taken care of by the nervous

system; but being taken care of by the nervous system is not, as Beck suggests, somehow opposed to being philosophically describable. One supposes it is our nervous system that takes care of "conceptual and methodological precautions and adherence to rules"—unless one can suggest a more likely organ of thought. Beck's mistake is to think that what is physiologically based is somehow off bounds, and that philosophy is concerned only with purely conceptual matters. This forces him into the interpretation of Kant's principles as somehow prescribing procedures that will ensure correctness. But it is as doubtful that we do possess such procedures as it is that we do any thinking that does not involve the nervous system. *Nothing ensures correctness.* What mechanisms we do have for correcting errors that arise in perception belong to empirical thought—hence to the Postulates, not the Analogies. Knowing the First and Second Analogies is no more a requirement of perception than knowing geometry for shooting a good game of snooker; but the Analogies describe what takes place in perception much as geometry describes a bounce off the cushion. The description is not in physiological terms; but if that makes it somehow inappropriate, no philosophical account can be given of any aspect of cognition.

34. Kant's confessed recollection of David Hume is recorded in the *Prolegomena* (IV260). Walker provides a well-researched and well-argued case against the usual view of Hume's importance to Kant. See p. 4f.

35. Within the two decades prior to Kant's birth the plague killed one-third of the inhabitants of the Duchy of Prussia. See Bruford (p. 158) for that and other factors such as war and bad roads and political disunity that contributed to the retardation of developments in the north.

36. Polonoff discusses Kant's late entry into the *vis viva* controversy in the first chapter of *Force, Cosmos, Monads*.

37. II395–96.

38. II397. In this as in other passages from the Dissertation I use Kerferd's translation; but he leaves *species* in Latin untranslated—or translates it as *species* in English. Kant uses *species* in Latin where he would use *Erscheinung* in German. I read *appearance* wherever Kerferd has *species*. (Likewise *appearance* for *specificity* in Dissertation II, #4.)

39. II398.

40. For the real/logical distinction, see Dissertation II, #5.

41. Kant thinks that the logical use of reason is guided by the principle of contradiction. See II393.

42. It is certainly interesting to see what can be got if one assumes unlimited capacities of analysis and assumes their unproblematic applicability to sensations or preferences; but there has been too much of a tendency to forget that these are just arbitrary assumptions. No social arrangement is ipso facto justified by the demonstration that it is the one that rational men would find most acceptable. I think that to complete the justification one would need Kant's sort of proof that reason has practical interests, and I do not (yet) see compelling force to even Kant's efforts to establish a metaphysical basis for practical reason. Spinoza and Freud seem to me nearer to being on the right track in understanding the most basic principles of action.

43. One should also mention the contrast between the highest principles of analytic and synthetic judgments in secs. 1 and 2 of chap. 2 of the Principles. Kant sets synthetic principles in contrast to analytic—himself in contrast to Leibniz.

Chapter Seven

1. On the need to account for location, see n. 17, chap. 4.

2. A universal system of locations automatically provides a relation between any one thing and any other. For a brief discussion of the unity of apperception, see n. 37, chap. 5.

3. Action manifests substance according to A 204f = B 249f; see sec. 30.

4. The self knows itself only as appearance according to B 158.

5. I do not know why Kant neglected the qualifications of the principle in the first edition—maybe to avoid reinforcing the propensities of his Wolffian-Leibnizian readers to identify the coexistent with the spatial, to the neglect of time. In the B-edition he has added to the First Analogy remarks about the temporality of the coexistent, and he may thus feel safe in making spatiality more explicit.

6. Kant uses two words—*Dasein* and *existieren*—where Kemp Smith uses just the one: *exist*. I try to preserve the difference by translating *Dasein* with 'presence'. While I am not sure that it is a distinction Kant always observes, I think he generally distinguishes between a thing's being present and its existence. Things can be present without existing (e.g., pink elephants), and exist without being present (distant objects). The passage turns on this distinction, lost in Kemp Smith's translation. How do we know that things present together (actually) exist together? Not, how does existence determine existence?

7. Hartman and Schwartz compare Kant's identification of thought with judgment to the identification of the straight line with a path of light. As the latter made the science of optics possible, the former made possible a science of metaphysics. See their edition of the *Logic*, p. lxvi. I take their point to be that earlier philosophers took thinking in terms of ideas—the fashioning of the complex out of the simple (Locke) or the reductive analysis of the complex to the simple (Leibniz); but that Kant found an altogether new approach by thinking about conditions for assertion (rather than composition).

8. The two things to be resolved are reflections of the two conditions on transcendental exposition. See sec. 14.

9. Hume's challenge: sec. IV, part II of the *Enquiry*.

10. For argument against our capacity simply to sense that something is happening, see sec. 28.

11. Leibniz uses the argument from the indifference of an East-West reversal to contend that space is not an ultimate feature of things in his Third Paper to Clarke, #5.

12. Kant maintains that the Postulates qualify our knowledge without substantially adding to it in the opening paragraph (A 219 = B 266). For an account of the qualifications see the next chapter, but for now we should recognize how much must be added in the Third Analogy to leave only qualification for the remainder of the system.

13. Mediate community completes the break with Leibniz. For one thing, it reinforces the real interaction of substances by extending causal connections even to static objects. It completes the Copernican revolution in metaphysics. All rationalists had shied away from the sensory because, as a mode of cognition dependent partly on objects and partly on us, it could not provide knowledge of things without some of our influence on them. Kant turns this on its head—saying first that pure reason is empty, and second that our influence on things is essential to knowledge of them. Only by interacting with them is it possible to have experience of them, and knowledge is possible only through experience.

14. Kant says, "The manifold of representations can be given in an intuition which is purely sensible. . . . But the combination *(conjunctio)* of a manifold in general can never come to us through the senses. . . . For it is an act of spontaneity of the faculty of representation; and since this faculty, to distinguish it from sensibility, must be entitled understanding, all combination—be we conscious of it or not, be it a combination of the manifold of intuition, sensible or non-sensible, or of various concepts—is an act of the understanding" (B 129–30).

15. The sentence in the text is just the corollary of many claims in the Transcendental Deduction. I say that *to whatever extent* things lack connection they are not part of experience. Kant repeatedly uses the phrase *in so far as* to contend that connection sets apart those things that possess unity and so belong to experience. Note how often the phrase

occurs in #16 of the B-Deduction—e.g., "only in so far as I *conjoin* one representation with another, and am conscious of the synthesis of them. Only in so far, therefore, as I can unite a manifold of given representations in *one consciousness* . . ." (B 133). That phrase casts very serious doubt on the notion that Kant believes that "All the contents of my consciousness are bound up in a unity" (the first premise in each of Wolff's attempts to reconstruct Kant's arguments). For further doubts, see n. 5, chap. 3, and n. 37, chap. 5.

16. Consider how a pilot must learn to use instruments rather than sensations of motion to determine his horizon. For even commoner examples of the insufficiency of sensations to determine the position or motion of one's body, think of vertigo, drunkenness, dreams of falling, etc. Of course, for the most part, sensations are as reliable on this as on any other matter, but that does not show that the subjective is by itself enough to base knowledge of our own bodies on—just that we have learned what significance to give to our feelings. Consider the process of accommodation to glasses which invert images, the difficulty small children have learning to walk, the practice required to use an artificial limb, the extension of control over the body by training with biofeedback, etc. All of these show that the sensory base is not automatically meaningful; we must learn what it signifies.

17. For remarks on the connection between judgments and categories, see sec. 15.

18. To the claim that shape-determination usually requires several perspectives, I should add "to determine the shape *in the first place*." Once experience makes certain objects very familiar to us, we become very adept at discerning them from very minimal information; and we know what to look *for*, so preperceptual expectation rules out alternatives such as other shapes that could (in theory) also be based on what we apprehend at a glance.

19. The apparent redundancy rests partly on the interdefinability, but also on the assumption that logical equivalences are always accessible. Bennett summarizes Quine's eliminative paraphrasing of singular terms to draw the tentative conclusion that "a concept-exercising language could lack all such expressions" (p. 89). He is tentative only because he is yet to argue against the case Strawson makes for singular terms. He does not continue to question what Quine's paraphrase proves. Is it the case that anyone capable of making judgments of the form 'The *F* is *G*' would also be capable of making judgments of the form 'It is not the case that there are no *F*'s, it is not the case that there are at least two *F*'s, and there are no *F*'s which are not *G*'? Only (I think) if one assumes that logical capacity is never in doubt.

20. Objectivity as abbreviation is discussed at the end of sec. 3.

21. The phrase "save the phenomena" alludes to Duhem's conception of scientific theory as a device for dealing with appearances, rather than an explanation of them.

22. There is not even one entry under *memory* in the index of Kemp Smith's translation.

23. The claim that the past is not over and done with follows Kant's solution to the First Antinomy by means of what Bennett aptly calls "the futurizing move" (*Kant's Dialectic*, p. 123). We know the past only as it appears to us, and it appears to us more and more as time goes on—with the discovery of fossils, the corroboration of new geological theories, etc. As a thing-in-itself, the past—and, for that matter, the present and future—may be rigidly determined for all time; but for us it is the sum of what could be discovered in future, including the discovery that some of our current beliefs about it need modification. Among objects of knowledge, nothing can ever be regarded as absolutely fixed.

24. For more on the reconstruction of one's past, see the discussion of Bennett's ordering argument in sec. 41.

25. Hume regards the vivacity of an idea as a mark of its proximity to the senses. Spinoza knows better. Vivacity is often the mark of the strength of an associated emotion. Boring old truth is seldom more vivid than false hopes and fears.

Chapter Eight

1. The Postulates are principles *of the understanding,* even though they deal with the relation of what we think to what we experience. Because the relation is one of several sorts of *correspondence* (mere compatibility = possibility; tied up with = actual; determined by the conditions of experience = necessary), it is not a matter of *inferring* what to think given what is perceived; it is, instead, a matter of maintaining a semblance of fit between the two. Here, at the upper levels of experience, Quine's observations of slack and indeterminacy between theory and observation are much to the point.

2. I replace Kemp Smith's 'faculty of knowledge' with 'capacity for knowledge' to translate *Erkenntnisvermogen*—in order to reserve 'faculty' for specific capacities, several of which are involved in cognition.

3. If reason could generate unconditional existence-claims, it would be Post-inconsistent. See n. 30, chap. 6.

4. Although they do not occur until the second half of the finished work, the Antinomies started Kant on the project that led to the *Critique* (see Al-Azm, p. 1). (The Antinomies set out problems into which reason inevitably falls, and from which it cannot extricate itself, according to Kant. See A 422 = B 450.)

5. Of course, Kant's theory also requires the innate possession of complex cognitive capacities. However, the skills of matching, fitting, finding resemblance, etc., are much more in evidence at an early age than are the skills of reasoning. Even very small children are able to fit puzzle pieces, take the word for the deed, treat a bent stick as a gun—but just try reasoning with them.

6. The concept of knowledge has an uncertain analysis in large part because it typifies the philosophical concepts that Kant contrasts to mathematical concepts in the 1763 "Enquiry concerning. . . ." See sec. 14.

7. Kant says, "The postulate bearing on the knowledge of things as *actual* does not, indeed, demand immediate *perception* (and, therefore, sensation of which we are conscious) of the object whose existence is to be known. What we do, however, require is the connection of the object with some actual perception, in accordance with the analogies of experience, which define all real connection in an experience in general" (A 225 = B 272).

8. "Directly or indirectly" refers back to the quote from A 19 = B 34 in sec. 3. See n. 14, chap. 1. Up to the end of the Analogies, Kant concerns himself with apprehension and perception, not with thought at all. Now he is concerned with thought in the Postulates; and, as the quote in n. 7, chap. 8, says, the relation to perception may be indirect; but, even so, it requires definite criteria. The quote in n. 7 specifies the required criteria as the Analogies.

9. The qualification "as an appearance" must be added to the restriction of existence. Kant thinks that things-in-themselves also exist; or, at least, he thinks that nonappearances (e.g., God) are possible in a nonempirical sense. Which is not to say that they are merely logical possibilities, but that, like life in an afterworld, they are neither (a) ruled out by what we know, nor (b) intelligible to us in the terms that our experience makes meaningful.

10. It is implicit in Kant's theory of knowledge that all judgments are open to refinement and qualification in the course of further experience, so operators like 'normally' and 'typically' and *ceteris paribus* automatically apply to our judgments. We include them explicitly when the exceptions are already known, but not such as to warrant constant mention in a revised judgment.

11. Nagel, p. 226.

12. Nagel says, "It is also worth noting that in judging whether two surfaces do fit snugly upon one another we may use some optical test, for example, the test that no light shines through when the surfaces are in close fit. Nevertheless, though we may employ such an

optical test, we would *not* be assuming, tacitly or otherwise, that the propagation of light is 'rectilinear,' so that our procedure is not in fact circular. We would simply be employing a type of observable fact as a condition for *saying* that the surfaces fit snugly. It is essential to note, therefore, that thus far the *only* issue of fact at stake when a surface is declared to be a plane is whether the surface satisfies the indicated condition of fitting closely on other surfaces" (ibid.). It is somewhat hard to credit that that passage was written by a very good philosopher a decade after Quine's "Two Dogmas" and Wittgenstein's worries about deciding the precise application of a rule. Suppose we can see that a surface does *fit the definition*, does Nagel really suppose that it is easier to see *that* than to see that it *fits another surface?* We need to shed some light between words and objects too. There is a considerable gap there—which we do get over—but language is not a primitive element to be freely incorporated in explanations of matters that are in fact much more primitive. I would think the evolution of spatial skills, including the ability to see how one shape fits into another, must have preceded the more abstract skills of language. Kant's theory sets out representation-relations at non-self-conscious levels of experience, from which the advance to empirical thought is an intelligible progression. To start with abstract thought, stipulative definition, and all the resources of logic, and only then introduce empirical input, is utterly to mistake the natural progression of things.

13. Nagel, p. 231.

14. *Investigations,* I, #85.

15. On imaginary-case arguments, see nn. 22–23 and 27, chap. 2.

16. *Kant's Analytic,* p. 224.

17. Ibid., p. 225.

18. Ibid., p. 227.

19. The general division between the two modes of discourse follows McTaggart's distinction between the A-series (of tenses) and the B-series (of dates and times specified only by the before-and-after relations that obtain among the things dated, without reference to the present). For references to McTaggart and the subsequent literature, see Gale.

20. The dispute about what can be said or not in either mode is Gale's topic in his chap. 2, "The Static Versus the Dynamic Temporal"—to which he supplies a very complete bibliography, pp. 496–99.

21. From Leibniz on, the idea of an ideal language of science and of rigorous thought has been recommended by many. See Rorty, part 2.

22. Though I have not (yet) read Paul Churchland's recent book, I have twice heard him argue convincingly that we are far more capable than one might suppose of perceptions involving concepts proper to natural science. One of the conclusions to be drawn from his work is that we need not regard qualities such as having a certain mean kinetic energy level as abstract or theoretical or inferred, as opposed to some suppositious immediacy of felt warmth or perceived temperature. I am not disputing this at all. My contention is only that the distinction between immediate experience and thought must be maintained in respect of time and space. Immediate experience must attach a here-and-now to the abiding framework.

23. Kant says, in the preface to B, "The only addition, strictly so called, though one affecting the method of proof only, is the new refutation of psychological *idealism*" (B xxxixn).

24. For Kant's efforts to dissociate his position from Berkeley's, see n. 13, chap. 1.

Bibliography

Kant, Immanuel
  Kants gesammelte Schriften (Prussian Academy, Berlin and Leipzig, 1938–).
  Kants Werke, vols. I–IX of the Prussian Academy edition (de Gruyter, Berlin, 1968).

Translations: (Roman numerals indicate volume numbers in *Werke*)
  Critique of Pure Reason (A occurs in IV, B in III)
    —trans. Norman Kemp Smith (Macmillan, London, 1929).
    —trans. J. M. D. Meiklejohn (Bell and Sons, London, 1917).
    —trans. F. Max Müller (Anchor, New York, 1966).
  II *Kant: Selected Pre-Critical Writings,* trans. G. B. Kerferd and D. E. Walford (Manchester University Press, 1968).
  IX *Logic,* trans. Robert Hartman and Wolfgang Schwarz (Bobbs-Merrill, Indianapolis and New York, 1974).
  IV *Metaphysical Foundations of Natural Science,* trans. James Ellington (Bobbs-Merrill, Indianapolis and New York, 1970).
  IV *Prolegomena,* Beck's revision of Carus trans. (Bobbs-Merrill, Indianapolis and New York, 1950).

Works Cited in Text and Notes

al-Azm, Sadik. *The Origins of Kant's Arguments in the Antinomies* (Clarendon, Oxford, 1972).
Austin, J. L. *Philosophical Papers,* edited by J. O. Urmson and G. J. Warnock (Clarendon, Oxford, 1961).
Ayer, A. J. *The Foundations of Empirical Knowledge* (Macmillan, London, 1940).
Beck, Lewis White. *Essays on Kant and Hume* (Yale University Press, New Haven, 1978).
——— ed. *Kant Studies Today* (Open Court/ LaSalle, Illinois, 1969).
——— ed. *Proceedings of the Third International Kant Congress* (Reidel/ Dordrecht, Holland, 1970).
——— *Studies in the Philosophy of Kant* (Bobbs-Merrill, Indianapolis, New York, and Kansas City, 1965).
Bennett, Jonathan, *Kant's Analytic* (Cambridge University Press, 1966).

———— *Kant's Dialectic* (Cambridge University Press, 1974).

———— *Locke, Berkeley, Hume* (Clarendon, Oxford, 1971).

———— "The Simplicity of the Soul" (*Journal of Philosophy*, 1967).

Berkeley, G. *Philosophical Works* (Dent and Sons, London, 1975).

Bird, Graham. *Kant's Theory of Knowledge* (Routledge & Kegan Paul, London, 1962).

Boring, Edwin G. *A History of Experimental Psychology*, 2d ed. (Appleton-Century Crofts, New York, 1950).

Bower, T. G. R. *Development in Infancy* (Freeman, San Francisco, 1974).

Bruford, W. H. *Germany in the Eighteenth Century* (Cambridge University Press, 1971).

Bruner, Jerome. "The Perfectibility of Intellect," in J. P. Strain, ed., *Modern Philosophies of Education* (Random House, New York, 1971).

Buchdahl, G. *Metaphysics and the Philosophy of Science: Descartes to Kant* (M.I.T. Press, Cambridge, Mass., 1969).

———— "The Conception of Lawlikeness in Kant's Philosophy of Science," in Beck *Proceedings*.

Carnap, Rudolf. *The Logical Foundations of Probability* (University of Chicago Press, Chicago, 1950).

———— *The Logical Structure of the World*, trans. Rolf George (Routledge & Kegan Paul, London, 1967).

Chomsky, Noam. "A Review of B. F. Skinner's *Verbal Behavior*" (*Language*, 1959).

Dampier, W. C. *A History of Science*, 4th ed. (Cambridge University Press, 1948).

Descartes, R. *The Philosophical Works of Descartes*, trans. E. S. Haldane and G. R. T. Ross, 2 vols. (Cambridge University Press, 1970).

Feather, Norman. *Mass, Length and Time* (Edinburgh University Press, 1959).

Findlay, J. N. "Kant and Anglo-Saxon Criticism", in Beck *Proceedings*.

Gale, Richard, ed. *The Philosophy of Time* (Anchor, New York, 1967).

Goodman, Nelson. *The Structure of Appearance*, 2d ed. (Bobbs-Merrill, Indianapolis, New York, and Kansas City, 1966).

Grayeff, Felix. *Kant's Theoretical Philosophy*, trans. David Walford (Manchester University Press, 1970).

Hacking, Ian. "Individual Substance," in Harry Frankfurt, ed., *Leibniz* (Anchor, New York, 1972).

Hempel, Carl. *Aspects of Scientific Explanation* (Free Press, New York, 1966).

———— *Philosophy of Natural Science* (Prentice-Hall, Englewood Cliffs, N.J., 1966).

Hintikka, J. "Kant on Mathematical Method," in Beck, *Kant Studies*.

Hopkins, J. "Visual Geometry" (*Philosophical Review*, 1973).

Hume, D. *Enquiries,* edited Selby-Bigge, 2d ed., (Clarendon, Oxford, 1902).

—— *A Treatise of Human Nature,* edited by Selby-Bigge (Clarendon, Oxford, 1888).

James, William. *Essays in Radical Empiricism* (Longmans Green, New York, 1958).

Kemp Smith, Norman. *A Commentary to Kant's Critique of Pure Reason,* 2d ed. (Macmillan, London, 1923).

Leibniz, G. W. *Leibniz-Clarke Correspondence,* edited by H. G. Alexander (Manchester University Press, 1956).

—— *The Monadology and Other Philosophical Writings,* trans. Robert Latta (Clarendon, Oxford, 1898).

Locke, John. *An Essay Concerning Human Understanding,* 2 vols. (Dover, New York, 1959).

Mach, Ernst. *The Analysis of Sensations* (Dover, New York, 1959).

Melnick, Arthur. *Kant's Analogies of Experience* (University of Chicago Press, Chicago, 1973).

Mill, J. S. *A System of Logic* (Harper and Brothers, New York, 1895).

Nagel, Ernest. *The Structure of Science* (Harcourt, Brace & World, New York, 1961).

—— with Cohen, Morris R. *An Introduction to Logic and Scientific Method,* abridged edition (Routledge & Sons, London, 1939).

Neisser, Ulric. *Cognition and Reality* (Freeman, San Francisco, 1976).

Neujahr, P. "Hume on Identity" (*Hume Studies,* 1978).

Noxon, J. "Senses of Identity in Hume's *Treatise*" (*Dialogue,* 1969).

Parkinson, G. H. R. *Logic and Reality in Leibniz's Metaphysics* (Clarendon, Oxford, 1965).

Passmore, John. *A Hundred Years of Philosophy* (Penguin/ Harmondsworth, Middlesex, England, 1968).

Paton, H. J. *Kant's Metaphysic of Experience,* 2 vols. (Allen & Unwin, London, 1936).

Patten, S. C. "Change, Identity and Hume" (*Dialogue,* 1976).

Penelhum, Terence. "Hume on Personal Identity" (*Philosophical Review,* 1955).

Polonoff, I. *Force, Cosmos, Monads and Other Themes of Kant's Early Thought* (Grundman, Bonn, 1973).

Popper, Karl. *Conjectures and Refutations* (Routledge & Kegan Paul, London, 1963).

—— *The Logic of Scientific Discovery* (Hutchinson, London, 1960).

Prichard, H. A. *Kant's Theory of Knowledge* (Oxford, 1909).

Quine, W. V. O. *From a Logical Point of View,* 2d ed. (Harper & Row, New York, 1963).

—— "Two Dogmas of Empiricism", in *From a Logical Point of View.*

———— *Word and Object* (M.I.T. Press, Cambridge, Mass., 1960).

Quinton, Anthony. "The *A Priori* and the Analytic" (*Proceedings of the Aristotelian Society,* 1963–64).

Reichenbach, Hans. *Space and Time* (Dover, New York, 1957).

Rorty, Richard. *The Linguistic Turn* (University of Chicago Press, Chicago, 1967).

Russell, Bertrand. *Human Knowledge: Its Scope and Limits* (Allen & Unwin, London, 1948).

Salmon, Wesley. *The Foundations of Scientific Inference* (University of Pittsburgh Press, Pittsburgh, 1966).

Schopenhauer, A. *The World as Will and Representation,* trans. E. F. J. Payne, 2 vols. (Dover, New York, 1969).

Scott-Taggart, M. J., "Recent Work on the Philosophy of Kant", in Beck, *Kant Studies.*

Shoemaker, S. "Time Without Change" (*Journal of Philosophy,* 1966).

Skinner, B. F. *Science and Human Behavior* (Macmillan, New York, 1960).

———— *Verbal Behavior* (Appleton-Century Crofts, New York, 1957).

Smart, J. J. C., ed. *Problems of Space and Time* (Macmillan, New York, 1964).

Strawson, P. F. "Bennett on Kant's Analytic" (*Philosophical Review,* 1968).

———— "Freedom and Resentment" (*Proceedings of the British Academy,* 1962).

———— *The Bounds of Sense* (Methuen, London, 1966).

Turbayne, Colin. "Kant's Relation to Berkeley", in Beck, *Kant Studies.*

Unger, Peter. *Ignorance* (Clarendon, Oxford, 1975).

von Leyden, W. "Hume and 'Imperfect Identity' " (*Philosophical Quarterly,* 1957).

Vuillemin, J. "The Kantian Theory of Space in the Light of Groups of Transformations", in Beck, *Kant Studies.*

Walker, Ralph C. *Kant* (Routledge & Kegan Paul, London, 1978).

Warnock, G. J. "Concepts and Schematism" (*Analysis,* 1949).

Whitehead, A. N. *The Aims of Education* (Macmillan, London, 1929).

Wilkerson, T. E. *Kant's Critique of Pure Reason* (Oxford University Press, 1976).

Wittgenstein, L. *Blue and Brown Books* (Blackwell, Oxford, 1958).

———— *Philosophical Investigations,* trans. G. E. M. Anscombe (Blackwell, Oxford, 1963).

Wolff, Robert Paul. *Kant's Theory of Mental Activity* (Harvard University Press, Cambridge, Mass., 1963).

Index